THE RO...N
...O GOTHIC WITHDRAWN

In a wide-ranging series of introductory essays written by some of the leading figures in the field, this essential guide explores the world of Gothic in all its myriad forms from the mid- eighteenth century to the internet age.

The Routledge Companion to Gothic includes discussions on:

- the history of Gothic
- Gothic throughout the English-speaking world, from London and the United States to the postcolonial landscapes of Australia, Canada and the Indian subcontinent
- key themes and concepts including hauntings and the uncanny, Gothic femininities and queer Gothic
- Gothic in the modern world, from youth culture to graphic novels and films.

Covering a vast array of textual examples from the canonical to the contemporary, this book is one of the most comprehensive and up-to-date guides to the diverse and murky world of the Gothic in literature, film and culture.

Catherine Spooner is Senior Lecturer in English at Lancaster University, UK. Her publications include *Fashioning Gothic Bodies* (MUP, 2004) and *Contemporary Gothic* (Reaktion 2006).

Emma McEvoy lectures at the University of Westminster, UK. She has published work on various Romantic and Gothic texts and contributed introduction and notes to the OUP edition of Matthew Lewis' *The Monk* (1995).

Also available from Routledge

Gothic (first edition)
Fred Botting
978–0–415–09219–7

Routledge Companion to Critical Theory
Simon Malpas and Paul Wake
978–0–415–33296–5

Cinema Studies: the Key Concepts (third edition)
Susan Hayward
978–0–415–36782–0

THE ROUTLEDGE COMPANION TO GOTHIC

Edited by
Catherine Spooner and Emma McEvoy

Routledge
Taylor & Francis Group

LONDON AND NEW YORK

First published 2007
by Routledge
2 Park Square, Milton Park, Abingdon, Oxon OX14 4RN

Simultaneously published in the USA and Canada
by Routledge
270 Madison Ave, New York 10016

Routledge is an imprint of the Taylor & Francis Group, an informa business

Typeset in Times New Roman by
Book Now Ltd, London
Printed and bound in Great Britain by
The Cromwell Press Ltd, Trowbridge, Wiltshire

British Library Cataloguing in Publication Data
A catalogue record for this book is available from the British Library

Library of Congress Cataloging in Publication Data
Spooner, Catherine, Ph.D.
Routledge companion to Gothic / Catherine Spooner & Emma McEvoy.
p. cm.
Includes bibliographical references and index.
1. Horror tales, English–History and criticism. 2. Horror tales, American–History and criticism.
3. Gothic revival (Literature)–English-speaking countries. I. McEvoy, Emma. II. Title.

PR830.T3S66 2007
823′.0872909–dc22   2007016568

ISBN10: 0–415–39842–8 (hbk)
ISBN10: 0–415–39843–6 (pbk)
ISBN10: 0–203–93517–9 (ebk)

ISBN13: 978–0–415–39842–8 (hbk)
ISBN13: 978–0–415–39843–5 (pbk)
ISBN13: 978–0–203–93517–0 (ebk)

TO JOHN AND PAT MCEVOY
AND DEREK AND CHRISTINE SPOONER

CONTENTS

CONTENTS

CONTENTS

CONTRIBUTORS

Brian Baker is a Lecturer in the Department of English and Creative Writing at Lancaster University, UK. He has written three books: *Literature and Science: Social Impact and Interaction*, with John H. Cartwright (2005); *Masculinities in Fiction and Film: Representing Men in Popular Genres 1945–2000* (2006); and *Iain Sinclair* (2007).

Fred Botting is a Professor in the Institute for Cultural Research at Lancaster University, UK. He has written on Gothic writing, contemporary fiction, science fiction and cultural theory. His books include *Gothic* (1996), *Sex, Machines and Navels* (1999) and, with Scott Wilson, *The Tarantinian Ethics* (2001) and *Bataille* (2001).

Kamilla Elliott has taught at the University of California, Berkeley and Lancaster University. She is author of *Rethinking the Novel/Film Debate* (2003) and of various essays on literature and film, eighteenth- and nineteenth-century literature and fundamental Christianity. She has also published under the name Kamilla Denman.

Ken Gelder is a Professor of Literary Studies at the University of Melbourne, Australia. His authored books include *Reading the Vampire* (1994), *Uncanny Australia* (with Jane M. Jacobs, 1998), *Popular Fiction: The Logics and Practices of a Literary Field* (2004) and *Subcultures: Cultural Histories and Social Practice* (2007).

Teresa A. Goddu teaches at Vanderbilt University, Nashville, USA where she directs the programme in American Studies. She is author of *Gothic America: Narrative, History, and Nation* (1997). She is currently working on a book on antislavery print culture.

Ellis Hanson is Professor of English at Cornell University, USA. He is the author of *Decadence and Catholicism* (1998) and the editor of *Out Takes: Essays on Queer Theory and Film* (1999).

Richard Haslam is an Associate Professor of English at Saint Joseph's University, Philadelphia, USA. He has previously published articles on Irish Gothic writers James Clarence Mangan, Charles Maturin, Joseph Sheridan Le Fanu and Oscar Wilde.

Benjamin Hervey has taught film studies and English literature at the universities of Oxford and Reading. He now works primarily in the film industry as a screenwriter and film critic/historian. His book on *Night of the Living Dead* is forthcoming in the British Film Institute's Classics series.

Paul Hodkinson is a Lecturer in the Department of Sociology at the University of Surrey, UK, where he is Director of the Sociology, Culture and Media degree. He is the author of *Goth: Identity, Style and Subculture* (2002) and, with Wolfgang Deicke, co-editor of *Youth Cultures: Scenes, Subcultures and Tribes* (2007).

Coral Ann Howells is Professor Emerita of English and Canadian Literature, University of Reading, UK. Her publications include *Margaret Atwood* (1996, 2005) and *Refiguring Identities: Contemporary Canadian Women's Fiction* (2003). She is editor of *The Cambridge Companion to Margaret Atwood* (2006) and co-editor with Eva-Marie Kroller of the forthcoming *Cambridge History of Canadian Literature*.

Kelly Hurley is Associate Professor of English at the University of Colorado, USA. She is the author of *The Gothic Body: Sexuality, Materialism and Degeneration at the Fin de Siècle* (1996), and is currently completing a book on contemporary horror film.

Emma McEvoy teaches at the University of Westminster, UK. She has published work on J. Meade Falkner, G. K. Chesterton, Mary Shelley, Ann Radcliffe and Nick Cave, and contributed the introduction and notes for the Oxford University Press edition of Matthew Lewis's *The Monk* (1995). *Beginning Gothic*, co-written with Catherine Spooner, is forthcoming.

Robert Mighall is the author of *A Geography of Victorian Gothic Fiction* (1999), and the editor of the Penguin Classics editions of Wilde's *The Picture of Dorian Gray* and Stevenson's *The Strange Case of Doctor Jekyll and Mr Hyde*. His *Sunshine: A Love Affair* will be published by John Murray in early 2008.

Alison Milbank lectures in Literature and Theology at the University of Nottingham, UK. She formerly taught at the University of Virginia, where she co-edited a microfilm edition of substantial parts of the Sadleir–Black collection of Gothic novels and chapbooks. Her publications include *Daughters of the House: Modes of the Gothic in Victorian Fiction* (1992), and editions of two Ann Radcliffe novels for Oxford World Classics.

Robert Miles is Professor and Chair of the Department of English at the University of Victoria, Canada. He is a past president of the International Gothic Association, and is author of numerous books and essays on the Gothic, including *Gothic Writing 1750–1820: A Genealogy*, (1993, 2002) and *Ann Radcliffe: The Great Enchantress* (1995).

James Procter is Senior Lecturer in English at Newcastle University, UK. He is the author of *Writing Black Britain 1948–1998* (2000), *Dwelling Places* (2003) and *Stuart Hall* (2004). He is currently principal investigator on a large AHRC-funded project on reception and diaspora (see www.diasporas.ac.uk/large_research_projects.htm).

David Punter is Professor of English at the University of Bristol, UK, where he is also Research Dean of the Faculty of Arts. His most recent publications include *Gothic Pathologies* (1998), *Writing the Passions* (2000), *Postcolonial Imaginings* (2000), and *The Influence of Postmodernism on Contemporary Writing* (2006). He has recently completed a book on the concept of modernity, as well as the new edition of *Metaphor* in the New Critical Idiom series.

Eddie Robson is a freelance writer. He has written widely on film and television, and his books include *Coen Brothers* (2003) and *Film Noir* (2005). He is also the author of numerous short stories, and the *Doctor Who* radio plays *Memory Lane* (2006), *Phobos* (2007), *Human Resources* (2007) and *I. D.* (2007).

Andrew Smith is Professor of English Studies at the University of Glamorgan, UK. His publications include *Gothic Radicalism* (2000), *Victorian Demons* (2004), the *Edinburgh Critical Guide to Gothic Literature* (2007), and eight collections of edited essays. With Professor Ben Fisher he edits two series 'Gothic Literary Studies' and 'Gothic Authors: Critical Revisions' for the University of Wales Press.

Andy W. Smith lectures in the Newport School of Art, Media and Design at the University of Wales, UK. He has recently written critical profiles on Welsh dramatists Ian Rowlands and Ed Thomas for the *Dictionary of Literary Biography* (2005), and contributed book chapters to *Monstrous Adaptations* (2006) and *Theatre of Catastrophe: New Essays on Howard Barker* (2006).

Angela Smith is an Emeritus Professor in the Department of English Studies at the University of Stirling. Her books include *East African Writing in English* (1989), *Katherine Mansfield and Virginia Woolf: A Public of Two* (1999), *Katherine Mansfield: A Literary Life* (2000), and editions of Jean Rhys's *Wide Sargasso Sea* and *Katherine Mansfield: Selected Stories*.

Catherine Spooner is a Senior Lecturer in the Department of English and Creative Writing at Lancaster University, UK. Her publications include *Fashioning Gothic Bodies* (2004), *Contemporary Gothic* (2006) and, with Emma McEvoy, *Beginning Gothic* (forthcoming).

Sue Walsh lectures in the School of English and American Literature at the University of Reading, UK. She is the author of a number of articles and chapters on various aspects of critical theory and children's literature, and is currently writing a book on Kipling's children's literature and its criticism, specifically in relation to postcolonial theory.

Alexandra Warwick is Head of the Department of English and Linguistics, University of Westminster, UK. She has written widely on nineteenth-century literature and culture, and her recent publications include *Oscar Wilde* (2006) and, with Martin Willis, *Jack the Ripper: Media, Culture, History* (2007).

Jason Whittaker is Senior Lecturer in English with Media Studies at University College Falmouth, UK. He has written extensively on new media topics, both as a journalist and in books such as *The Cyberspace Handbook* (2004). His recent publications include *Radical Blake* (with Shirley Dent, 2002) and *Blake, Modernity and Popular Culture* (with Steve Clark, 2007).

Angela Wright is Lecturer in Romantic Literature at the University of Sheffield, UK, and treasurer of the International Gothic Association. She is the author of *Gothic Fiction: A Reader's Guide to Essential Criticism* (2007), and is currently completing *The Import of Terror: Britain, France and the Gothic, 1780–1820*.

ACKNOWLEDGEMENTS

We would particularly like to thank David Avital, Andrea Hartill and Rosie Waters at Taylor and Francis for their enthusiasm and support throughout this project. We would also like to thank all the people with whom we have corresponded about this volume, who are too many to list, but whose professional and intellectual generosity have been exceptional, whether or not they ended up contributing. Colleagues at Lancaster University, and Alex Warwick and Steve Barfield at the University of Westminster, have been invaluable sources of help and advice.

Catherine would especially like to thank Eddie Robson for his encouragement and good humour throughout the editing process. Emma would like to thank John McEvoy, Robert Lee, and Rowan, Finn and May Lee McEvoy for their encouragement, help and support. Whilst working on this project she has been particularly indebted to her mother, Pat McEvoy, and her good friend Joy Bariana for (amongst many other things) their amazing hospitality, generosity and willingness to help at a moment's notice.

1
INTRODUCTION

CATHERINE SPOONER AND EMMA MCEVOY

APPROACHING GOTHIC

What is Gothic? There is no single, straightforward answer to this question. For many years, it was taken for granted that the Gothic novel flourished from the publication of Horace Walpole's *The Castle of Otranto* in 1764 to Charles Maturin's *Melmoth, The Wanderer* in 1820. Gothic novels could be easily identified by their incorporation of dominant tropes such as imperilled heroines, dastardly villains, ineffectual heroes, supernatural events, dilapidated buildings and atmospheric weather. (A helpfully comprehensive list is provided in Eve Kosofsky Sedgwick's *The Coherence of Gothic Conventions*, 1980.) Texts that appeared after this time were considered either as throwbacks to this earlier model (such as Bram Stoker's *Dracula*, 1897) or simply as not being Gothic. As time went on, however, and criticism of the Gothic became more sophisticated, it became evident that not only was this model inadequate to describe texts produced after 1820, from James Hogg's *Private Memoirs and Confessions of a Justified Sinner* (1824) to contemporary TV series *Buffy the Vampire Slayer* (1997–2003), but that there were highly significant Gothic novels, such as William Beckford's Oriental tale *Vathek* (1786), which exceeded these generic presumptions.

Gothic has since been defined according to its emphasis on the returning past (Baldick 1992, Mighall 1999), its dual interest in transgression and decay (McGrath 1997), its commitment to exploring the aesthetics of fear (Punter 1980) and its cross-contamination of reality and fantasy (Jackson 1981). Alternate traditions of 'male' and 'female' (or perhaps more correctly, 'masculine' and 'feminine') Gothic have been identified (Moers 1976, Sedgwick 1985, Ellis 1989), with their focus on the respective psychologies of the villain (who is not necessarily gendered male) and the heroine (or, occasionally, a male hysteric). Most critics now acknowledge that Gothic has continued until the present day, albeit in constantly evolving forms, and is flourishing particularly strongly at the current time.

With this in mind, we have organised this book so as to avoid, as best we can, the old-fashioned list of dominant Gothic tropes. Our organisational principle has been to foreground approaches to Gothic rather than ways of defining it. We have sought to bring together new ways of looking at Gothic, as well as reprising some of the older ways. Our first section, 'Gothic traditions', takes a historical approach to Gothic literature, covering the major periods and movements in which Gothic has flourished, from the eighteenth century to the present day. 'Gothic Locations' explores some of the most significant settings for the Gothic, from America, Scotland and Ireland to the postcolonial landscapes of Australia, Canada, the Indian subcontinent and the Caribbean. By focusing on the geographies influencing the production of Gothic, as well as locations actually depicted in the novels, we have been able to juxtapose multiple anglophone voices, considering those who 'write back' to the Gothic canon as well as many of the most widely read and studied authors. 'Gothic Concepts' offers a range of critical and theoretical tools commonly used to approach Gothic texts, from the uncanny, abject and grotesque to explorations of femininity, masculinity and queer sexuality. It functions both to problematise and to show by example some of the most common critical approaches to the Gothic. Finally, 'Gothic Media' explores some of the ways in which Gothic is dispersed through contemporary non-literary media (one of the most neglected areas of Gothic scholarship).

The volume covers a vast array of texts, including most of the major novels incorporated in the Gothic 'canon', as well as a very diverse selection of less familiar material. Inevitably, some individual favourites will be missing; we hope that the introduction of some exciting new ones will compensate for those. For reasons of space and linguistic consistency, we have regretfully had to omit all non-anglophone material, except in a few contextualising references. We have tried, to a certain degree, to emphasise contemporary texts in a variety of media, as we feel this is an area underserved by existing criticism, and about which there is a substantial student interest. We do not claim comprehensiveness for this volume: it is intended as an introduction. Essays are bite-sized, providing a taster that hopefully will whet readers' appetites to discover more. The experts who have contributed to the book are diverse in their styles and approaches, and do not always agree with one another – we consider this to be part of healthy academic debate. In conclusion, this book aims to provide a useful introduction to the most crucial topics in Gothic studies today, pointing to the diversity of the field and suggesting the great potential for future research.

WORKS CITED

Baldick, Chris (1992) 'Introduction', *The Oxford Book of Gothic Tales*, Oxford: Oxford University Press.

Ellis, Kate Ferguson (1989) *The Contested Castle: The Gothic Novel and the Subversion of Domestic Ideology,* Chicago, IL: University of Illinois Press.

Jackson, Rosemary (1981) *Fantasy: The Literature of Subversion*, London: Methuen.

McGrath, Patrick (1997) 'Transgression and Decay', in Christoph Grunenberg (ed.), *Gothic: Transmutations of Horror in Late-Twentieth-Century Art*, Boston, MA: MIT Press.

Mighall, Robert (1999) *A Geography of Victorian Gothic Fictions: Mapping History's Nightmares*, Oxford: Oxford University Press.

Moers, Ellen (1976) *Literary Women*, New York: Doubleday.

Punter, David (1980) *The Literature of Terror: A History of Gothic Fictions from 1765 to the Present Day*, London: Longman.

Sedgwick, Eve Kosofsky (1985) *Between Men: English Literature and Male Homosocial Desire*, New York: Columbia University Press.

—— (1986) *The Coherence of Gothic Conventions*, rev. 2nd edn, London: Methuen.

Part I
Gothic traditions

2

GOTHIC TRADITIONS

EMMA MCEVOY

In this section we are interested in the chronology of the Gothic, its origins, the contexts in which it originated, and its development from its beginnings to the present day. The discussion of Gothic in terms of chronology yields a number of insights. Most obviously, it foregrounds the development and adaptation of Gothic motifs. Gothic, though it is implicated within numerous other intellectual discourses, is somewhat disturbingly discrete, possessed of a number of recurring motifs, set characters and typical plots, and it is this conventional aspect of the Gothic that has been responsible for much of the critical denigration it has received from the late eighteenth century to the late twentieth. One of the things that the authors in this section are interested in is the constant new inflection of Gothic material. Various stalwarts of the eighteenth-century plot (persecuted heroines, labyrinthine castles, young heroes) persist, as do certain structural relations, most notably, as Chris Baldick points out, the relation of the past to the present and the relation between history and geography (Baldick 1992: xix). However, Gothic is also dynamic and endlessly reinvents itself. In her essay Emma McEvoy discusses the development of the Gothic villain and the addition of new Gothic figures – Frankenstein's monster and the vampire, for example – during the Romantic period. Alexandra Warwick considers the course of Gothic in the Victorian era, following it into the confines of the bourgeois home, into the metropolis, and, in terms of its generic expeditions, into the forms of the sensation novel and detective fiction. Dickens, she argues, is crucial to the development of the Gothic in the period, his contribution lying 'not, however, simply in the emptying of the form, but in the construction of new possibilities for it'.

The chronological approach helps us to situate Gothic in terms of history. As in other fields of literary study, within Gothic studies there has recently been some revived interest in history as a lens through which to view Gothic, partially as a result of the influence of French theorist Michel Foucault. As Robert Mighall remarks 'That which is Gothicized depends on history and the stories it needs to tell itself' (Mighall 1999: xxv). The historical approach is both a more traditional way of looking at Gothic – Gothic has long been studied in terms of the history of ideas, placed somewhere midway between the eighteenth century proper and Romanticism – and one that is currently dominating critical investigation. Prominent examples of recent historicist readings of the Gothic (not all influenced by Foucault) include those of Victor Sage (1988), Kate Ferguson Ellis (1989), Robert Miles (1993), E. J. Clery (1995), Kelly Hurley (1996),

7

Robert Mighall (1999) and Catherine Spooner (2004). Indeed, in this book Warwick argues that Victorian Gothic is used 'explicitly to articulate the questions of the present . . . setting them in that same recognizable present', as she traces Gothic themes of ambivalent desires in the claustrophobic home, money, the city and the metamorphic body. Similarly, Robert Miles considers the engagement with and the re-moulding of the concept of Gothic in the works of eighteenth-century Whigs, dissenters and radicals.

The essays also consider Gothic within more traditional categories of period-isation – Romanticism, modernism, postmodernism and so on – demonstrating both how these categories can aid in reconceptualising Gothic and how Gothic exceeds and might help to rewrite the terminology of accepted literary histories. Catherine Spooner takes on the 'common-sense' view that modernism and Gothic are incompatible in a way that aids our understanding both of the Gothic in modernist texts and the (pre-)modernism in *fin-de-siècle* Gothic. For Spooner, the way such categorisation occurs is in some degree arbitrary, and related to the way criticism has constructed epistemological breaks. This also leads in turn to an interrogation of the way we categorise what Gothic is, so that in much twentieth-century writing, 'Gothic becomes, rather than the determining feature of the texts, one tool among many employed in the service of conjuring up interior terrors'. In related fashion McEvoy considers how examining Gothic through the lens of Romanticism and vice versa might aid our understanding of both, and of the dialogic interplay between them. Both Miles and McEvoy suggest that perhaps our understanding of the terms Gothic and Romantic is at times unnecessarily sundered; indeed, Miles points out, for some eighteenth-century writers Romantic poetry was a kind of Gothic. For Miles, Gothic was a style, an aesthetic revolution which made certain works possible.

This section commences with the essay by Miles which focuses on the changing fortunes of the term 'Gothic' in the eighteenth century, examining the political connotations of a word which was, at one point, associated with Germans and British liberties, and was adopted as a useful political mythology by the Whig party. Miles stresses the ambivalent and often contradictory origins of a concept and an aesthetic that has continued to elicit ambivalent and contradictory responses. As such, he sets the tone for the rest of the volume, which seeks to emphasise the complexity and variety of Gothic in all its forms and throughout its history.

WORKS CITED

Baldick, Chris (1992) 'Introduction', *The Oxford Book of Gothic Tales*, Oxford: Oxford University Press.

Clery, E. J. (1995) *The Rise of Supernatural Fiction, 1762–1800*, Cambridge: Cambridge University Press.

Ellis, Kate Ferguson (1989) *The Contested Castle: Gothic Novels and the Subversion of Domestic Ideology,* Chicago, IL: University of Illinois Press.

Hurley, Kelly (1996) *The Gothic Body: Sexuality, Materialism, and Degeneration at the Fin de Siècle*, Cambridge: Cambridge University Press.

Mighall, Robert (1999) *A Geography of Victorian Gothic Fiction: Mapping History's Nightmares*, Oxford: Oxford University Press.

Miles, Robert (1993) *Gothic Writing 1750–1820: A Genealogy*, London: Routledge.

Sage, Victor (1988) *Horror Fiction in the Protestant Tradition*, Basingstoke: Palgrave Macmillan.

Spooner, Catherine (2004) *Fashioning Gothic Bodies*, Manchester: Manchester University Press.

3

EIGHTEENTH-CENTURY GOTHIC

ROBERT MILES

Writing on Franz Kafka, Jorge Luis Borges argues that every significant writer invents his or her own precursors. A paradoxical feature of this law of criticism is that the phenomenon strengthens with the writer's originality. Franz Kafka's style is startling and new; critics therefore search for influences; as they do, hidden aspects of earlier writers emerge that appear to anticipate the later 'original'. The process is reciprocal. Calling *Bleak House* Kafkaesque brings out the Kafka in Dickens, and vice versa. Literary history is thereby altered: new lines of affiliation become set, obscuring the appearance of things prior to the arrival of the strong writer (Borges 1964).

The conventional history of eighteenth-century Gothic is the story of Ann Radcliffe and her precursors. Anna Laetitia Barbauld and Sir Walter Scott both edited a series of British novels and as such were decisive figures in the canonisation of the newly emerging form. Both agreed that Ann Radcliffe was the founder of her own style of romance. Barbauld, who was first to make the claim, may speak for both:

> Though every production which is good in its kind entitles its author to praise, a greater distinction is due to those which stand at the head of a class; and such are undoubtedly the novels of Mrs Radcliffe, which exhibit a genius of no common stamp.
>
> (Barbauld 2002: 450)

Radcliffe was the best-selling novelist of the 1790s, earning copyright fees several times those of her nearest competitors; her imitators filled the bookshops, so that the Gothic romance accounted for a third of novels sold; and as her reviewers agreed, her works were original, startling and powerful. In accordance with Borges' law, readers set out to find her precursors. The assessment of the age's leading critic, William Hazlitt, reflects the orthodoxy that quickly arose. 'The *Castle of Otranto* (which is supposed to have led the way in this style of writing) is, to my notion, dry, meager, and without effect', he writes in 1818. *The Recess* and *The Old English Baron* were 'dismal treatises'. Only in Radcliffe do we find 'the spirit of fiction or the air of tradition' (Hazlitt 1907: 165). Clara Reeve's *The Old English Baron* (1777) was a professed imitation of Horace Walpole's *Otranto* (1764), and both influenced Sophia Lee's *The Recess* (1783–5), but until Radcliffe, imitations of Walpole's 'experiment' were few and scattered. Radcliffe was the first to invest the new subgenre of terror fiction with the feel of the classic (Hazlitt's 'air of tradition'), and as such *Otranto* was trans-formed from originator to precursor.

When we regard eighteenth-century Gothic, it is easy to let our eyes run along the critical grooves that take us back from Radcliffe, to Lee, to Reeve, and from there to Walpole, whose *Otranto* is generally recognised as the first 'Gothic' novel. He also provided the new subgenre with its future name when he subti-tled the second edition 'A Gothic Story'. S. T. Coleridge sketches a more expan-sive view of the same genealogy in his hostile review of C. R. Maturin's Gothic play, *Bertram* (1816). It includes the German materials that flooded into 1790s London, such as the plays influenced by Schiller's electric *The Robbers*, or the novels Isabella Thorpe recommends to Catherine Morland as being perfectly 'horrid' in Jane Austen's *Northanger Abbey* (1818).[1] But as Coleridge argues in *Biographia Literaria* (1817), such materials are themselves imitations of English originals. Coleridge concedes that Schiller's *Robbers* started the so-called German drama, but Schiller himself had simply recycled English Graveyard poetry and the minutely self-reflexive introspections of Samuel Richardson's *Clarissa*, to which he added 'horrific incidents and mysterious villains', plus 'ruined castles, the dungeons, the trap-doors, the skeletons, the flesh-and-blood ghosts, and the perpetual moonshine of a modern author' (presumably Radcliffe), themselves 'the literary brood of the *Castle of Otranto*' (Coleridge 1983: II, 211). However, if we wish to see the eighteenth-century Gothic fresh, we need to look beyond Radcliffe and her precursors. And while Walpole's 'literary brood' is a particularly strong constellation, there were others that faded from sight, as Radcliffe's star waxed brighter.

One such constellation revolved around the dominant sense of the word 'Gothic', which was 'Germanic'. Focusing on the contemporary meanings of 'Gothic', our attention will naturally shift from literary to historical, political and ideological issues. *Germania*, by the Roman historian Tacitus, is the key text. According to Tacitus, the Goths were simply the most visible, and influential, of the German tribes. Tacitus provided an arresting, even charming, picture of a pre-modern society, where the Goths lounged around waiting for war, while the women worked. Nevertheless, from a Roman perspective, the Germans were unusual in holding women in high regard, viewing them as close and even sacred companions. The Goths worshipped the deep woods, the locus of their gods. They were, moreover, 'democratic', in that they elected their chiefs at a communal gathering, a Witan, or parliament. The Goths, and Tacitus, were important, because the English houses of parliament and traditions of constitu-tional monarchy were understood – at least by some – as having their origins in the Gothic Witan (Smith 1987: 26). As the French philosopher, Montesquieu, put it, in his hugely influential *Spirit of the Laws* (trans. 1750), the English derived their 'idea of political government' – that is, of constitutional monarchy – from the Germans, from their 'beautiful system . . . invented first in the woods' (cited in Clery and Miles 2000: 63).

Politically, eighteenth-century Britain was divided between Tories and

Whigs. Believing in the divine right of kings, Tories regarded the unbroken blood line of the monarchy as a sacred tie, whereas the Whigs argued that parliament was ultimately sovereign, and that the king ruled only so long as he abided by the compact inherent in the ancient or 'Gothic' constitution. For the eighteenth century the decisive event that tested the ideological differences between Whig and Tory was the deposition, in 1688, of the Catholic James II in favour of the Protestant William and Mary – the 'Glorious Revolution', as it was dubbed by the victorious Whigs. The followers of James, or Jacobites, did not go away, but tested the regime installed by the Whigs – ultimately, the House of Hanover – with two invasions, in 1715 and 1745. As a result of these constant challenges to the authority of the British crown Whig apologists worked to bolster the legitimacy of the Glorious Revolution through the vigorous development of a political mythology in which Britain's modern constitutional monarchy – the envy of Europe – was shown to derive, ultimately, from the Goths, and their 'beautiful system'. According to this mythology, Britons were Goths (that is, Anglo-Saxons), whose liberty-loving spirit was manifest in the evolution of their political institutions, from the Germanic Witan, to Magna Carta, to the Reformation, and onwards to the Glorious Revolution, the epoch of

> true liberty to England. The nation, represented by its parliament, obtained the Bill of Rights for the people, fixed the prerogatives of the crown, so long contested; and having prescribed to the Prince of Orange the conditions on which he was to reign, chose him for king.
>
> (Thompson 1791: 406)

In eighteenth-century Britain, taste generally filtered down from the aristocracy. As powerful Whigs invested ideological energy in the image of the Goth, Gothic things rose in aesthetic value. Nowhere was this more true than in architecture. Prior to the Gothic revival, 'Gothic' had been a synonym for barbarism. The benighted nature of the latter day Goths of the medieval period was supposedly epitomised by their churches – pointy, busy and strewn with gargoyles – and miserably primitive in comparison to the sleek lines of Greek and Roman temples. Lord Cobham, one of the richest and most powerful of mid-eighteenth-century Whig aristocrats, provides an example of the Gothic's changing fortune. Stowe in Buckinghamshire was the family seat of the Temple-Grenvilles. In order to attract and impress visitors, Cobham continued the practice of building follies in the grounds of the family estate (wittily called 'temples', punning on the family name) for the amusement of the cognoscenti. However, they also served as a form of political propaganda. Most drew upon the standard neo-classical imagery of political virtue. But in 1744 Cobham, through his architect James Gibbs, began work on a new folly in the Gothic style. The Gothic Temple, or Temple of Ancient Liberty as it was also known, was the 'ideological climax' of Lord Cobham's garden and a 'trumpet-call of Liberty, Enlightenment and the

Constitution'. The temple's vaulted ceilings were painted with the 'heraldry of Lord Cobham's spurious Saxon ancestry', and the building itself flanked by statues celebrating the Saxon deities (Robinson 1994: 98). Both testified to Cobham's bona fides as a true Saxon (or Goth), and therefore a true Englishman.

Lord Cobham's mortal political enemy was Sir Robert Walpole, Prime Minister and father of the future originator of the Gothic novel, Horace Walpole. Cobham and Walpole were both Whigs, the difference being that the latter was at the head of the faction that was in government, and the former at the head of the one that was out. In opposition Lord Cobham styled himself a 'patriot', lending the term its vogue. From Cobham's perspective Walpole was 'the Craftsman', a Merlin, a corrupt sorcerer who perverted the state to his own ends. By 'patriot', Lord Cobham meant that he was the true representative of the Gothic love of liberty embodied in the constitution (and therefore deserved to be in, just as Walpole deserved to be out).

Fashions go through cycles, then as now. Where the Augustan period favoured the light, airy, geometrical designs of the Palladian style, with its nods to the classical past, the fashion-leaders of the mid-eighteenth century lurched towards the exotic, such as the fad for 'Chinoiserie', or the Gothic. For Horace Walpole, the *sine qua non* of the latter style was 'gloomth'. After a visit to Stowe, and possibly inspired by Gibbs' Gothic Temple, Walpole set about giving his home, 'Chopp'd Straw Cottage' near Richmond, an extreme makeover. The well-heeled Walpole was able to command all the cosmetic arts of domestic architecture, as the science then stood. Through a judicious use of wallpaper, *papier maché*, and *trompe l'œil*, Walpole added a veneer of fretworks, pointed arches and battlements to transform his humble cottage at Strawberry Hill into a shrine of the faux-medieval. At the centre of it was a dimly lit staircase, the walls papered with imitation stonework, ancient and grey, which produced just the right shade of 'gloomth'. It was here on one of the ornamented balustrades, in the crepuscular light, that Walpole claimed to have had a waking vision of the giant hand that was to become the animating presence of *The Castle of Otranto*. From his redoubt at Strawberry Hill Walpole titillated and shocked the coteries of the fashionable world with a series of Gothic *jeux d'esprit* issued through his private press. Apart from his counterfeit 'Gothic story', Walpole produced *The Mysterious Mother* (1768), an incestuous drama so disturbing that Frances Burney retired to bed with a headache after an incautious – aborted – public reading, and *Richard the Third* (1768), a mischievous work of medieval history.

Mouldering castles were not the only source of fashionable gloomth: grave-yards also served. Hervey's *Meditations among the Tombs* (1746), Gray's *Elegy in a Country Churchyard* (1751) and Young's *Night Thoughts* (1752) formed the nucleus of what became known as the 'Graveyard' school of poetry. The Augustan Enlightenment was calmly secular and quietly deistical in outlook. The mid-century, by comparison, was already showing signs of the Great

Awakening – the Evangelical revival that would shake up England's religious Establishment, led by the Methodistical Wesleys. Where the Augustans favoured grim stoicism, the mid-century preferred theatrical, Calvinist panic. For the Graveyard school 'gloomth' concealed not just the ghostly presence of usurped princes, but *memento mori* calling the wayward soul to prayer. The turn to Gothic was religiously inflected throughout the eighteenth century. Thus, for instance, the influential Anna Laetitia Aikin (later Mrs Barbauld), in her 1773 essay, 'On Monastic Institutions', nods towards the reflex Enlightenment view that would condemn monkish superstition before advancing its saving grace: medieval monks may have been wrongheaded, but at least they were motivated by a strong religious impulse. Perhaps owing to this turn to religion, mid-century Britain found the aesthetics of terror congenial, whether arising from medita-tions in a country graveyard, or the sublime in nature. In his influential *On the Sublime and the Beautiful* (1757) Burke theorised that in all cases a sense of terror underlay our experience of the sublime, provided the viewer was safely accommodated. A sight of nature's vastness from the top of a mountain would be sublime; the same view from the perspective of someone falling down it would be simple terror. For this reason Burke's sublime is always oxymoronic: a dreadful pleasure. In the same volume as the essay on monastic institutions, Anna Laetitia Aikin and her brother John successfully married Burke's aesthetic of terror to religious awe and the medieval ghost story through the essay, 'On the Pleasure Derived from Objects of Terror', which provided the theory, and the story fragment, 'Sir Bertrand' (1773), which supplied the practice.

In the areas of politics, the arts and religion, 'Gothic' developed different shades of meaning, some of which were complementary, and others not. Up until the French Revolution Gothic largely maintained its positive value in polit-ical discourse. Thus the journal *Common Sense*, from 1739, comments approv-ingly that our 'old *Gothick* constitution had a noble Strength and Simplicity in it, which was well enough represented by the bold Arches, and solid Pillars of the Edifices of those Days'. The anonymous author wrings three different senses out of the word 'constitutional': the nation's political charter; the individual's make-up; and built fabric. Thus the writer enters 'those old hospitable *Gothick Halls* . . . with a Constitutional Sort of Reverence', regarding their hallowed arms as 'the Terror of former Ministers, and the Check of Kings', possibly the very same that 'had procured the confirmation of *Magna Charta*' (Clery and Miles 2000: 60). For the writer, 'Gothick' is the binding mark of Englishness, the defining essence of an Englishman's constitution, whether that of his body, his house, his nation or its charter. To rub it in, he contrasts the robust Gothick Hall with the effeminate, foreign, Italian villas of a new corrupt political class. Readers would have understood the quip about Italian villas as a reference to Sir Robert Walpole's recently built Palladian mansion in Norfolk, allegedly funded by the spoils of office.

The eighteenth century was a period of growing nationalism throughout Europe. As in many other areas, England was in the vanguard. Gothic rose on the nationalist tide. In architecture and the arts the Gothic style was increasingly identified with Englishness, an association that reached its apogee in the early decades of the next century, when the burnt-down Houses of Parliament were rebuilt in the high Gothic style. But if growing nationalism brought the political and architectural meanings closer together, it tended to divide them from Gothic's religious overtones. As Linda Colley has influentially argued, the eighteenth-century British identity that came to supplant the older ones of the home nations, was created in the forge of sectarian strife (Colley 1992). To be British was to be Protestant, with both identities drawing strength from deep wells of residual anti-Catholicism. The Catholic became the convenient other of 'British' identity. Britain's identity was of a modern, progressive nation transforming itself, and the world, through commerce and science, a process guided by the advanced condition of its constitution and government, in sharp contrast to Europe, figured as despotic, backward, feudal, Catholic and Gothic. Jane Austen has great fun with this self-conceit when she has the adolescent, naïve and thoroughly English Catherine Morland concede that while the Home Counties were indeed modern, she could not vouch for Britain's Celtic fringe, where, she suspected, European practices might still prevail, such as wife-murder (Austen 1995: 188). As British nationalism gathered strength in the eighteenth century, so did anti-Catholicism, a force that reached its height in 1780 when anti-Catholic sentiment spilled over into mayhem. The Gordon Riots, as they were called, ripped London apart in the biggest act of civil disobedience in the city's modern history.

Prior to the French Revolution, nationalist pressures pushed the various meanings of 'Gothic' in opposite directions. Insofar as the word meant pre-Reformation 'medievalism', it was negatively tarred with the Catholic brush. But insofar as it meant the cultural cradle of modern Englishness, it was positive. Moreover, the idealised meanings of political discourse – where the Goths were imagined as the original architects of the modern constitution – influenced aesthetics. Perhaps the most significant example of this was Bishop (Richard) Hurd's *Letters on Chivalry and Romance* (1762), which set out to prove, contrary to common assumptions, that medieval or chivalric (that is to say, Gothic) literature had an order or aesthetic of its own, one closer to the organic principles of nature, and possibly superior to the neat, orderly and artificial ones adopted by the previous generation of critics, unduly impressed by their French masters, who affected to despise the nation's early poets. Thus, according to Hurd, Spenser's *The Faerie Queen* (1590–6) was not the lengthy shapeless mess some assumed, but a work with its own organic principles, directly analogous to the designs of Gothic architecture. Walpole's self-defence in the preface to the second edition of *Otranto* is thus entirely typical. Walpole attacks Voltaire for having criticised Shakespeare for disrespecting the unities of dramatic composition. Shakespeare was superior to the French playwrights championed by Voltaire, argued Walpole, precisely because he did not follow mere rules: his genius was in his licence. Walpole's 'Gothic story' did no more.

James Mackintosh provides a late example of this confluence of nationalism and aesthetics. In his critique of *D'Allemagne* (1810), Madame de Staël's book on Germany, Mackintosh argues that the 'English nation' is 'the most illustrious of Germanic nations' and as such 'delights in a poetry more romantic and chivalrous' (Mackintosh 1813: 206).

> Nature produced a chivalrous poetry in the sixteenth century; learning in the eighteenth. Perhaps the history of English poetry reflects the revolution of European taste more distinctly than that of any other nation. We have successively cultivated a Gothic poetry from nature, a classical poetry from imitation, and a second Gothic from the study of our own ancient poets.
>
> (Mackintosh 1813: 207)

By 'Gothic poetry from nature' Mackintosh means the writing of the Elizabethan age, a period in which natural geniuses abounded; 'a classical poetry from imitation' refers to Augustan literature; while 'second Gothic' signifies a new generation of poets (Wordsworth, Southey and Coleridge) drawing inspiration from Shakespeare and other Elizabethans, England's 'ancient poets'.

It was the Victorians who dubbed this 'second Gothic poetry' 'Romanticism', and the tale of terror 'Gothic'. Thus we may say that it is an accident of literary history that we do not refer to the poetry of the early nineteenth-century as 'the Gothic revival', just as we do its architecture. Instead we call the Victorians' architectural medievalism 'Gothic', and their literary medievalism, 'Arthurian'. However, if Gothic had a positive connotation when signifying architecture, it came to have a negative one when referring to literature. The reason for this is twofold. First, the novel of aesthetic terror, principally associated with Ann Radcliffe, found itself increasingly proscribed as it came to be dominated by women writers. The fact that it was linked to unregulated modes of production, such as the prolific Minerva Press with its insatiable customer base in the rapidly proliferating circulating libraries, was also damning, as it played into cultural anxieties that the nation was being ruined by the female propensity for light reading. Second, its increasing reliance on sex and violence (for which Matthew Lewis's *The Monk* (1796) was the convenient lightning rod) was associated by hostile critics with the excesses of the French Revolution. According to this view, the horrors of the Terror had jaded the public imagination. To use one of the critics' own favourite metaphors, the tale of terror was a literary form of 'Spanish fly', used to rouse a public imagination enervated through excess. Thus, while the poems and novels of the period shared the general taste of Gothicism, the later retrospective classifications of literary history dubbed the one Romantic, and good, the other Gothic, and bad.

The meaning of Gothic thus differs, depending on the context. During the half-century prior to the French Revolution it was largely a positive term, increasingly associated with primitive (which is to say, vigorous and vibrant) English virtues, including the religious revival. The reverse side of this usage was a mounting hostility to the backward feudal practices of Catholic Europe. The early Gothic novel was able to sustain this ambiguity by incorporating within itself a contrast between progressive and regressive forces, the one implicitly English and Protestant, the other explicitly European and Catholic. Ann Radcliffe's penultimate romance, *The Italian* (1797), provides an excellent example of this. A good abbess is contrasted with a bad one; the former is essentially Protestant and English in sensibility – one of her distinguishing characteristics is that she permits freedom of conscience on religious matters, which was itself the mantra of Protestant dissenters – whereas the latter is despotic, irreligious and vindictive: in other words, Catholic. As French Revolutionary violence produced political reaction, Gothic novelists found it increasingly difficult to have it both ways: both idealising and criticising the feudal past. Superstitious Catholics were no longer the object of national paranoia, but Freemasons were, especially those known as the Illuminati, allegedly a secret brotherhood of promiscuous radicals flooding out of Germany intent on fomenting bloody revolution across Europe, including England. The most significant purveyor of this myth of secret revolutionary brotherhoods was again Edmund Burke (Deane 1988). His antidote to the mad dreams of political visionaries, prescribed in his *Reflections on the Revolution in France* (1791), was the spirit of chivalry, by which he meant the feudal manners of the Goths. This political cult of chivalry survived into the Victorian period as Arthurian romance, which was explicitly understood as a bulwark against the revolutionary energies dangerously unleashed during the 1790s.

The importance of Burke's move was clearly understood by radicals such as William Godwin, whose anti-Gothic novel, *Caleb Williams* (1794), sets out to 'deconstruct' chivalry as instrumental to the state terror of reactionary Britain. Whereas there had been a compact between aristocratic Whig interests (such as the Walpoles) and middle-class dissenters (such as the Aikins and Godwin), to support the progressive and aesthetic meanings of Gothic, prior to the Revolution, the compact did not survive the reaction. For dissenters and radicals, 'Gothic' now meant feudal, and bad; whereas the aristocratic interest understood 'Gothic' as meaning feudal, and good (especially when burnished by Burke as the English traditions of 'chivalry'). Meanwhile the tale of terror was increasingly populated, not by scheming monks, but by nefarious Freemasons (*Horrid Mysteries* (1796), recommended by Austen's Isabella Thorpe, being a perfect example). This cleavage in the meaning of 'Gothic' after the Revolution (which we can designate through the shorthand, chivalry/Gothic) is one of the most puzzling aspects of the eighteenth-century context to the rise of the Gothic – the fact that the word means one thing relative to buildings, and quite another when applied to fiction. In effect, the positive, idealised meanings of Gothic were channelled into chivalry and architecture, while the glamorously negative ones were poured into the Gothic novel, so that it soon gained a reputation much like Lord Byron's, of being mad, bad and dangerous to read.

NOTE

1 Although not published until 1818, *Northanger Abbey* was largely written in the 1790s, and as such reflects the literary scene of the mid-decade.

WORKS CITED

Austen, Jane (1995) *Northanger Abbey*, ed. Marilyn Butler, Harmondsworth: Penguin.

Barbauld, Anna Laetitia (2002) *Selected Poetry and Prose*, ed. William McCarthy and Elizabeth Kraft, Peterborough, Ontario: Broadview.

Borges, Jorge Luis (1964) 'Kafka and his Precursors', in *Other Inquisitions 1937–52*, trans. Ruth L. C. Simms, intro. James T. Irby, Austin, TX: University of Texas Press.

Clery, E. J. and Robert Miles (2000) *Gothic Documents: A Sourcebook, 1700–1820*, Manchester: Manchester University Press.

Coleridge, S. T. (1983) *Biographia Literaria, or Biographical Sketches of my Literary Life and Opinions*, ed. James Engell and W. Jackson Bate, 2 vols, in *The Collected Works of S. T. Coleridge*, ed. Kathleen Coburn and Bart Winer, vol. 7, London: Routledge and Kegan Paul.

Colley, Linda (1992) *Britons: Forging the Nation 1707–1837*, New Haven, CT: Yale University Press.

Deane, Seamus (1988) *The French Revolution and Enlightenment in England, 1789–1832*, Cambridge, MA: Harvard University Press.

Hazlitt, William (1907) *Lectures on the English Comic Writers*, Oxford: Oxford University Press.

Mackintosh, James (1813) Review of *D'Allemagne*, by Madame de Staël, *Edinburgh Review*, xxii (October): 198–239.

Robinson, John Martin (1994) *Temples of Delight, Stowe Landscape Gardens*, Andover: Pitkin.

Smith, R. J. (1987) *The Gothic Bequest: Medieval Institutions in British Thought, 1688–1865*, Cambridge: Cambridge University Press.

Thomson, George (1791) *The Spirit of General History, from the Eighth to the Eighteenth Century*, Carlisle: n.p.

4

GOTHIC AND THE ROMANTICS

EMMA MCEVOY

The relation between what we call Romanticism and the Gothic tradition has exercised literary critics for many years now. Montague Summers, writing in 1938, was somewhat atypical in seeing the Gothic novel as primarily a Romantic and Catholic genre dealing with what is excluded from the prosaic, materialist-inclined, Protestant realist tradition (Summers 1938). For most twentieth-century critics who choose to theorise Gothic and its relation to literary Romanticism, Gothic was to be distinguished from Romanticism, and the opposition set up between the terms was a tool in the definition of the transcendence of Romanticism. In the 1920s Eino Railo in *The Haunted Castle* discussed Gothic as a crude, early version of Romanticism. This line of criticism was later taken up by Devendra Varma who declared that the Gothic was '"the leaf-mould" in which more exquisite and stronger plants were rooted' (Varma 1966: 3). In Railo's version, the significance of the Gothic lies in its provision of fodder for the Romantic imagination which Romantic poets will transform and spiritualise. According to Railo, Gothic phenomena implicitly discuss the psyche; however, the fact that the stuff of the psyche is presented in material terms (the haunted castle, etc.) becomes the grounds of the Gothic's inferiority to the Romantic, for the Romantic involves 'a setting aside of mere outward effects and the transference of psychological phenomena into the foreground' (Railo 1927: 177).

Gothic was commonly considered as a reaction against neo-classicism and a stage in the journey to Romanticism. Very few critics discussed Gothic on its own terms. Its assessment, in terms of literary worth, was defined by critical ideas about Romanticism, and the debate was dependent on accepted hierarchies and teleologies. One of the reasons why the whole issue is problematic is that in terms of periodisation 'High Gothic' is very nearly synchronic with the Romantic period, with most of the best-known works appearing in the period of the 1790s to the 1820s, apart from *The Castle of Otranto* (1764) and a handful of other texts.

A second wave of criticism of Gothic sought to break down the Gothic/Romantic opposition. Robert Kiely, in *The Romantic Novel in England*, discusses many Gothic novels as Romantic novels. Acknowledging the fact that the Gothic texts he discusses are contemporary with literary Romanticism, he considers the divide between them to be, instead, a question of genre: 'Two hundred pages of narrative fiction could not be written about a skylark or a butterfly; a novelist was supposed to write about people in community' (Kiely 1972: 23). For Kiely, the Gothic novel is what happens when Romantic writers take to prose, but is an ill-advised outlet for Romantic expression. In somewhat of a more celebratory vein, Nina Auerbach's *Romantic Imprisonment* read Gothic novels as Romantic novels illustrating the Romantic 'imagination of containment' (Auerbach 1985a: 7) and an influential collection of essays edited by G. R. Thompson in 1974 discussed Gothic as 'Dark Romanticism'. The description 'Dark Romanticism' has proved attractive to critics, as it has the advantage of stressing the kinship of many Romantic and Gothic texts of the period: the shared interest in subjectivity, the figure of the outsider, social sympathies, concepts of agency, will, the relation to the past, the nature of temporality, formal innovation, the divine, and what Steven Bruhm calls 'the fascination with physical pain, and . . . the implications of physical pain on the transcendental consciousness' (Bruhm 1995: xvi). A text like Charles Brockden Brown's *Wieland* (1798), with its interest in concepts of agency both supernatural and human, fascination, perception and synaesthetic experience is very definitely of the same world as the work of Wordsworth and Coleridge, and, despite a critical insistence on the aural/visual divide marking the difference between Romantic and Gothic texts, *Wieland* is by no means the only Gothic text of this period preoccupied with sound.[1]

In recent years many literary critics have been less uneasy with the application of the term 'Romantic' to Gothic texts. With changes in critical focus, the concomitant questioning of categories, terms and definitions, and the broadening of the canon, Gothic texts have been welcomed into Romantic studies. Gothic novels are regularly studied on Romantics courses and discussed in Romantic journals (interest in Gothic drama, however, tends to remain an academic speciality), and works by canonical Romantic writers are discussed in forums devoted to Gothic. The implications of this position for Gothic and Romantic studies are many. Gothic texts may be studied as Romantic texts without denying their part within the Gothic tradition. (And it is worth pointing out that such enduring features as the double and the uncanny have their basis in Gothic tradition rather than in mainstream canonical Romantic texts.) Canonical Romantic texts – such as Coleridge's *Christabel* (1816), Shelley's *The Cenci* (1819) and Byron's Oriental Tales (1813–14) (*The Giaour, The Bride of Abydos, The Corsair* and *Lara*) – can be seen as participating within the Gothic. The course of Gothic is bound up with the myth of Romanticism; Romantic texts indulge in dialogic interplay with the Gothic, and Gothic texts themselves comment on the phenomenon of Romanticism. Interplay between the terms allows us to conceive of writers in new ways, allowing us, for example, to consider Mary Shelley's *Frankenstein* (1818/31) as a text in dialogic debate with other variants of Romantic outsiders, as well as with other overtly Gothic texts. Discussion of Gothic in terms of literary Romanticism might eventually even help widen the terms of a debate which is still trapped within a terminology that insists on presuming that Gothic's main engagement is with eighteenth-century critical values.

The recent historicist contribution to the debate, Michael Gamer's

Romanticism and the Gothic (2000), re-explores the Gothic/Romantic opposition. Rather than repeating the value judgements of the early critics who tended to see Gothic as a debased form, Gamer instead considers the ways in which (mostly first-generation) Romantics theorised and reacted to Gothic. For Gamer, in the 'ostentatious rejection' of Gothic (amongst other literary forms and aesthetics) 'we can trace the processes by which romantic ideology is constituted' (Gamer 2000: 15). Gamer's thesis provides a useful framework for thinking about the way in which Romantic writers situate themselves in relation to the Gothic. It serves to remind us that it is precisely in this period (particularly from the late 1790s onwards) that we see Gothic become established, a literature with a past, as it were. There is a perception of Gothic as a tradition and different writers orientate themselves differently in relation to it. Many writers see themselves purely as Gothic writers – Maturin, in a letter to Scott, puts himself in the line of descent from the 'Conjuror Lewis' (Sage 2000: 82), although his writing, seen with the benefit of hindsight, shares much material with the work of canonical Romantic writers. First-generation Romantics Coleridge and Wordsworth, Gamer argues, deliberately distanced themselves from Gothic, though he notes that the 'same years [in which this happened] witness from these same writers the production of their most gothic-influenced works' (Gamer 2000: 11). Indeed Coleridge, despite the critical distancing, emerges as the canonical Romantic writer with the most interesting contributions to make to Gothic, and in *Christabel* provides one of the most thorough-going explorations of the Gothic aesthetic.

Second-generation Romantics were much more embroiled in Gothic: Mary Shelley was the daughter of William Godwin, and we know that Byron and the Shelleys in particular were avid readers of Gothic.[2] Not only that, but they also wrote Gothic. Percy Bysshe Shelley published two Gothic novels in his teens (*Zastrozzi* (1810) and *St Irvyne* (1811)). Byron reinvented the Gothic hero and was also a patron of Gothic, as it were, lending support to Maturin and helping to get his drama *Bertram* (1816) produced, as well as being instrumental in the publication of Coleridge's *Christabel*. Further than this, the lives of the circle had been – and were to continue to be – subject to Gothicisation. Lady Caroline Lamb wrote an account of her affair with Byron portraying him as the Gothic villain of her novel *Glenarvon* (1816); Peacock employed the trappings of Gothic for his satirical portraits of Byron, the Shelleys and Coleridge in *Nightmare Abbey* (1818).

The story of the ghost story competition initiated at the Villa Diodati, involving Byron, Percy Bysshe Shelley, Mary Godwin and John Polidori, and responsible for the genesis of Mary Shelley's *Frankenstein* and Polidori's 'The Vampyre' (1819) (and Byron's 'Augustus Darvell' (1819)) has been told many times and has entered the repertoire as a Gothic set-piece. There have been some notable film depictions of the seminal scene,[3] but it was framed as Gothic long before *Bride of Frankenstein* (1935) employed it as its own Frankensteinian frame. Mary Shelley does so in the introduction to the second edition of the

novel in 1831, but the author of 'Extract of a Letter from Geneva, with anecdotes of Lord Byron, etc.' which prefaced Polidori's 'The Vampyre' when it
appeared in the *New Monthly Magazine* in 1819, had already done this, in a
description which features Percy Bysshe Shelley as the hysterical male who after
a recitation of a German work and part-way through Lord Byron's rendering of
the then unpublished *Christabel*, runs from the room and is discovered 'leaning
against a mantle-piece with cold drops of perspiration trickling down his face . . .
his wild imagination having pictured to him the bosom of one of the ladies with
eyes' (Polidori 1998: 240).

The relation between these second-generation canonical Romantics and the
Gothic is interesting. One could argue that Shelley finds Gothic attractive
precisely because he sees it as 'old hat'. Gothic provides a lexicon for a new
perspective on history and becomes almost a trope in itself within much of
Shelley's work: an undesirable mirror for the old (and still present) regimes to
examine themselves in. Byron's involvement with the Gothic, however, is ultimately more extensive.

The period from approximately 1790 to the 1830s is a rich one for Gothic. In
this period its generic provenance is enlarged, with Byron and Coleridge, in
particular, composing Gothic narrative poetry, Byron and Shelley continuing
the unperformable play tradition initiated by Walpole with his *The Mysterious
Mother* (1768), and the transformation of the Gothic fragment into the Gothic
short story. Gothic at this point is ripe for redefinition, and although many
highly enjoyable works continued to pour forth in the Walpole mould, in others
we see a determined taking on and redefinition of Gothic motifs. Gothic moves
to new locales and takes on contemporary material – moving into Regency
drawing-rooms and going on the Grand Tour ('The Vampyre'), inhabiting the
London of the 1790s (*Caleb Williams*, 1794), taking on developments in science
(*Frankenstein*), engaging with social philosophies and a 'new kind of philosophical history' (*St Leon*, 1799) (Clemit in Godwin 1994: viii), with politics at the
meta-level (P. B. Shelley's *The Cenci*), with Calvinist theological controversy
(*Confessions of a Justified Sinner*, 1824) and, as noted in terms of the Byron/
Shelley circle, overlapping with the biography and autobiography of living
people.

Many of the Gothic texts of the period are characterised by their experiments
with time – featuring moments that stretch to eternity, years that are traversed
in seconds – and their radical dislocation of chronology. A feature often, though
not always, associated with this temporal experimentation is the use of extremely
complex framing structures (see in particular *Melmoth* (1820) and *Frankenstein*).
Gothic in this period sees the exploration both of extreme subjectivities and of
the problematic nature of sympathy in relation to selfhood. It is the period in
which we see horror take centre-stage: many of these texts are filled to repletion
with violence, imprisonment, torture, murder, parricide, sex, rape, incest and
cannibalism by novelists whom *The Edinburgh Review* (reviewing Maturin's
Melmoth the Wanderer in 1821) called 'a numerous class of caterers to the public,

ready to minister to any appetite, however foul and depraved' (Anon. 1821: 359). There is somewhat of a commodification of horror and the sublime. Charlotte Dacre in her *Confessions of the Nun of St Omer* (1805) coins the word 'enhorrored' (Dacre 1805: III, 169), and Percy Bysshe Shelley gives us his hero 'sublimed' 'by the maddening fire of voluptuousness' (Shelley 1986: 87–8) in his Dacre-influenced *Zastrozzi*.

Many of the Gothic figures we associate most strongly with the period are born from deliberate collapses and reversals of earlier Gothic. Known material and endless plagiarisms have become so well known as to reward new input, so Lewis's *The Monk* (1796) makes mileage from the fact that hero–villain–victim are wrought together in the figure of Ambrosio. Charlotte Dacre's *Zofloya* (1806) gives us a heroine–villain. The pursuer and pursued change places in *Caleb Williams* (1794) and *Frankenstein* (1818). Victor Frankenstein collapses both the son and father figures in himself. The figure of the vampire might be said to collapse the roles of Satan, the hero, the villain and the victim into one. In this period also we see – in the different permutations of the wandering Jew, the alchemist in possession of the philosopher's stone, the vampire, or the individual who has entered into a Faustian pact – a variety of representations of the mortal immortal, tortured and elevated by his (and occasionally her) sense of sublime aloneness. There is also a marked interest in Protean figures, capable of assuming a variety of shapes both physical and spiritual. Hogg's devilish Gil-Martin is one of the most notable, but there are many others. Rosalina, in Catherine Smith's *Barozzi* (1815), appears as a page-boy, 'dreaded sorceress' and, when she plucks off her 'veil of mystic figures and long false hair' (Smith 2006: 136), the long-lost mother of the heroine; the monster of *Frankenstein*, himself an assemblage of body parts, adapts himself to the confines of a hovel adjoining the De Laceys' cottage and cuts a sublime figure in the arctic wastes; the biloquist Carwin of Charles Brockden Brown's *Wieland* with his seeming power to enter the most impossibly small and intimate of places is perhaps one of the most radically disturbing, in so much as his shape-changing mirrors his amoral sidestepping of the intellectual and moral concerns of the rest of the novel.

A new focus on interiority is integral to nearly all the developments of the period. Radcliffe's concern with the processes of perception and the way perception creates our sense of reality becomes its main mode of narration; novels such as *Romance of the Forest* (1791) and *Mysteries of Udolpho* (1794) are focused through a frequently terrified female protagonist (*The Italian* (1797) takes on a similarly beleaguered male sensibility) and achieve their effects through our empathetic response. As readers, we become subject to the terrors of a world which to a large extent is created by the mind of the protagonist. Texts such as *Caleb Williams* and *Nun of St Omer* take the process even further, giving us first-person narratives through which to experience the story, creating, in the former, a paranoid protagonist whose paranoia is, unfortunately, borne out by events in the real world. It is notable also that both of these texts significantly lower the age limit of the Gothic protagonist. Gothic texts have been notable for protagonists just out of adolescence but *Caleb Williams* gives us a hero whose story commences in boyhood, whilst Dacre's *Nun of St Omer* contains an unprecedented extended portrait of an unhappy, neglected, misunderstood childhood that looks forward to *Jane Eyre* (1847).

One of the most characteristic – and charismatic – figures of the period is the hero–villain. The centrality of the sublime villain has ever been a staple feature of Gothic texts with the Manfreds, Montonis, Schedonis and Vatheks commanding our attention: figures of awe, imperious, a law unto themselves, a danger to the young females (and males) around them, outfacing the supernatural with dangerously flashing eyes (of Vathek we learn that 'when he was angry, one of his eyes became so terrible, that no person could bear to behold it' (Beckford 1995: 29)). All the sublime villains noted above are in positions of power, acting from within the system, as it were (even when illegitimately and unjustly), and, with the exception of Vathek, they are all older men, or more explicitly, father figures.

The figure of the sublime Gothic villain is reworked again and again, but some general tendencies start to emerge from approximately the 1790s onwards. The villain moves centre-stage. (John Moore's *Zeluco* (1786) remains there for most of two volumes though he is eventually displaced by the female he has been victimising.) He is in many texts no longer a father figure. These sublime villains of the Romantic period tend to be young (even when they are, like Melmoth, actually over a century old), often explicitly sexually desirable, living out a life that provokes our desire in many respects. Most importantly he or she is no longer just a villain. The years 1790–1830 give us a whole crop of hero–villains, and these younger Satanic heroes are often portrayed from within. Many texts demand empathy with the agonised villain who is now also a warped hero (or, in the case of Victoria in *Zofloya*, a heroine[4]), and we are asked more explicitly to focus through his or her desire and passion. Most significantly, many of these heroes and heroines have fallen beyond the pale. They are outsiders and tend not to be associated with institutionalised power (indeed this is the journey that that pivotal character Ambrosio makes in *The Monk*). They have journeyed outside the prison house of normal society, although many, like Melmoth, are knocking on the prison doors, desperate to get back in. Many of these hero–villains do not even directly victimise females: the Giaour and Melmoth are both remarkably faithful lovers, although they are also both examples of what Mario Praz calls the 'Fatal Man' and 'diffuse all round them the curse which weighs upon their destiny' (Praz 1933: 74–5).

Byron's Giaour is resolutely in the Gothic tradition, possessed of what the Turkish narrator calls his 'evil eye' (*The Giaour* l. 612), his face marked with woe, his curse, like Cain's, written on his brow. The very form of the poem – discontinuous, achronological, framed and narrated by a variety of speakers – carries on the tradition of Gothic fragmentation and bears strong similarities to works such as *Frankenstein*, *Melmoth* or *Justified Sinner*. The Giaour carries many of the previous aspects of the Gothic within himself, collapsing, one might say, much of the former *mise-en-scène* and its terrific implications into one sublime and overbearing personage. He has created his own dark history; he is the sublime ruin (he is specifically referred to as a ruined tower (*The Giaour* ll. 878–82) and his stoniness is a running metaphor in the poem). The Giaour is a man haunted by himself, and his very aspect 'pale as marble o'er the tomb' (*The Giaour* l. 238) signifies his contagious deathliness. He endows himself with a Gothic past in one moment that collapses time, when in an instant 'o'er his soul / Winters of memory seemed to roll, / And gather in that drop of time / A life of pain, an age of crime. / . . . Though in Time's record nearly nought, / It was eternity to thought' (*The Giaour* ll. 261–4 and 271). However, the Byronic hero's supremely passionate sensibility, although it spurns social bonds, temporality and morality, nevertheless proves to be his own prison, his doom, reinventing for him that which he would cast away. The hero–villain's relations with his prison are, like those of many Romantic Promethean figures, curiously validating. As Byron's Prisoner of Chillon declares 'My very chains and I grew friends' (*The Prisoner of Chillon* l. 389).

The social relations of the Satanic outsider are (as indeed might be expected) imbued with a strange irony. Nina Auerbach, writing of vampires, has noted that, in the early nineteenth century they 'were not demon lovers or snarling aliens . . . but singular friends' (Auerbach 1995b: 13). What is most surprising about these sublimely alone outsiders is not their aloneness but their cravings for friendship. Despite being possessed of 'a soul that soared to a sightless distance above the sphere of pity' (Godwin 1994: 397), the hero–villain lets us know 'We loathe what none are left to share: / Even bliss – 'twere woe alone to bear' (*The Giaour* ll. 941–2).

In numerous texts the sublime figure of power acts as a rebuke to and constitutes a rejection of the communal, softening impulses of sensibility. Godwin's *St Leon* (1799) is one of the earliest to take on explicitly the social relations and philosophies of the sublime outsider. St Leon, the titular protagonist, notable for his social impulses and energetic philanthropy, is a being cursed with immortal life, who outlives his wife and ends up in a bizarrely complicated Oedipal situation with his own son. He attempts a friendship with another sublime outsider, Bethlem Gabor, a Hungarian nobleman (and – at over six feet tall, with one cheek shot away and three fingers missing on one hand – one of the first Gothic characters to have a very specific physical portrayal). The relationship between St Leon and Gabor, needless to say, is doomed to disaster: Gabor is dedicated to misanthropy and, unnoticed by St Leon, becomes more and more exasperated by the latter's 'senseless liberalities'. In retrospect, after Gabor has imprisoned and tortured him, St Leon realises 'It seems I inflicted on him a daily torture by my daily efforts for the dissemination of happiness' (Godwin 1994: 401).

Sympathy proves problematic in Coleridge's *Christabel*, a text which pre-eminently deserves the description 'dark Romanticism'. Christabel's encounter with the demonic female outsider Geraldine, who shares her bed and tries to steal the love of her father, is damned by what Coleridge calls 'forced unconscious sympathy' (*Christabel* l. 609). *Christabel* is a nightmare about the nature or even the very possibility of selfhood. Merely through looking, Christabel is doomed to double the appearance of the evil Geraldine, taking on her facial expressions whilst unable to utter a word. A similar reworking of sympathy as Gothic contagion may be found in the passage about the parricide's torture by the mob in *Melmoth* and in the lines in *The Giaour*, 'As if that eye and bitter smile / Transferred to others fear and guile –' (*The Giaour* ll. 848–9).

Social relations are recast with the use of the image of 'feeding' in a number of texts. *Melmoth* is replete with images of social relations as cannibalism (the child who sells his blood to the surgeon to raise money for his starving family, the lover who starts eating his mistress's shoulder, the family who allow the tetchy grandfather to consume all the bread while they starve). All these instances (like Byron's use of the image of the Pelican's 'rash devoted breast' (*The Giaour* l. 955) which she rends in order to feed her young) stress the part of generosity and unselfishness in fostering such cannibalism. The most extended use of the image of feeding in the period, however, is in the figure of the vampire.

The Gothic hero joins with the Byronic hero, and then comes out again on the other side by courtesy of Polidori's story 'The Vampyre', which engages in some deft intertextuality with the work of Byron and provides an illuminating take on the Byronic hero. Polidori's story not only takes up the vampiric fate which one of the narrators of *The Giaour* wishes on the protagonist (*The Giaour* ll. 755–86), but also provides a comment on the inherent vampirism of the Byronic hero. Doomed to feed off the mere mortals who surround them, to sustain their sense of overlordship, these hero–villains are the direct forefathers of Hannibal Lecter. 'The Vampyre', like *Melmoth* (Maturin 1989: 256) and *Christabel* (ll. 583–612), is one of a series of Gothic texts that deliberately reverse the trope of the withering eye, discussing it in terms of the victim, deprived not of life (as happens in *Vathek*) but of will, self-control and sense of individuation. In Polidori's story the flashing eyes of the vampire indicate not power and depth of soul, but precisely the opposite: 'the dead grey eye, which, fixing upon the object's face, did not seem to penetrate, and at one glance to pierce through to the inward workings of the heart; but fell upon the cheek with a leaden ray that weighed upon the skin it could not pass' (Polidori 1998: 3).

In the work of Edgar Allan Poe we find a writer who goes one step further than Polidori and presents us with a vision of Romanticism itself Gothicised. Poe may be considered a kind of *über*-Romantic whose speciality is the reification of Romantic concerns which he places within the Gothic. He insistently picks up on key Romantic tropes and preoccupations: the voluptuous interior of 'The Masque of the Red Death' (1842) reflects back on Keatsian medievalism and the cult of the beautiful object: stories such as 'The Oval Portrait' (1842) and 'The Fall of the House of Usher' (1840) cast a skewed look at the artist and the artistic process; the poem 'The Haunted Palace' (1838) renders the thing of beauty a particularly nasty thing of horror. Poe expresses Radcliffean rapture over Lewisean content, rehearsing the latter's fascination with mortality and dead maidens. In a tale such as 'The Pit and the Pendulum' (1842) he transforms the Gothic short story, exploring the experience of a moment through the intense focus of terror. In tale after tale he explores the subjective nature of terror, blurring the subject/object divide, and gives us characters who, like the narrator of 'The Black Cat' (1843), are complicit with their Gothic settings. It is in such explorations of the uncanny, as in his extended use of the double, that Poe points forwards to Victorian Gothic.

It is in the Romantic period that many Gothic figures are born – Frankenstein's monster, the double, the mortal immortal and the vampire – and each of them from concerns that we recognise as Romantic. Gothic and Romantic texts share similar subject matter and must be seen as in dialogic debate with each other. This does not mean that we have to collapse the two terms, however. Both Gothic and Romantic writers are aware of what the Gothic is, how Gothic tropes and structures may be deployed, and how flexible Gothic can be. Permeability characterises the relation of the Gothic tradition to Romanticism and the relation of Romanticism to Gothic.

NOTES

1 For further discussion of the aural/visual divide in relation to Gothic and Romantic aesthetics see Townshend (2005).
2 See Douglass Thomson's website: www.georgiasouthern.edu/~dougt/gothic.htm.
3 See in particular James Whale's *The Bride of Frankenstein* (1935), Ken Russell's *Gothic* (1986/7) and Gonzalo Suárez's *Rowing with the Wind* (1988).
4 For more on female Romantic outsiders see Craciun (2003).

WORKS CITED

Anon. (1821) 'Review of *Melmoth, the Wanderer*', *The Edinburgh Review*, 70: 353–62.
Auerbach, Nina (1985a) *Romantic Imprisonment: Women and Other Glorified Outcasts*, New York: Columbia University Press.
—— (1995b) *Our Vampires, Ourselves*, Chicago, IL: University of Chicago Press.
Beckford, William (1786/1995) *Vathek and Other Stories*, ed. Malcolm Jack, Harmond-sworth: Penguin.
Bruhm, Stephen (1995) *Gothic Bodies: The Politics of Pain in Romantic Fiction*, Philadel-phia, PA: University of Pennsylvania Press.
Byron, George Gordon, Lord (1967) *Byron: Poetical Works*, London: Oxford University Press.
Coleridge, Samuel Taylor (1993) *Poems*, ed. John Beer, London: J. M. Dent.
Craciun, Adriana (2003) *Fatal Women of Romanticism*, Cambridge: Cambridge Univer-sity Press.
Dacre, Charlotte (1805) *The Confessions of the Nun of St Omer: A Tale*, 3 vols, London: J. F. Hughes.

Gamer, Michael (2000) *Romanticism and the Gothic: Genre, Reception, and Canon-Formation*, Cambridge: Cambridge University Press.

Godwin, William (1994) *St Leon: A Tale of the Sixteenth Century*, ed. Pamela Clemit, Oxford: Oxford University Press.

Kiely, Robert (1972) *The Romantic Novel in England*, Cambridge, MA: Harvard University Press.

Maturin, Charles (1989) *Melmoth the Wanderer*, ed. Douglas Grant, Oxford: Oxford University Press.

Polidori, John (1998) *'The Vampyre' and Other Tales of the Macabre*, ed. Robert Morrison and Chris Baldick, Oxford: Oxford University Press.

Praz, Mario (1933) *The Romantic Agony*, trans. Angus Davidson, London: Oxford University Press.

Railo, Eino (1927) *The Haunted Castle: A Study of the Elements of English Romanticism*, London: Routledge.

Sage, Victor (2000) 'Irish Gothic: C. R. Maturin and J. S. Le Fanu', in David Punter, (ed.), *A Companion to the Gothic*, Oxford: Blackwell.

Shelley, Percy Bysshe (1986) *Zastrozzi and St Irvyne*, ed. Stephen C. Behrendt, Oxford: Oxford University Press.

Smith, Catherine (2006) *Barozzi*, ed. James D. Jenkins, Chicago, IL: Valancourt Press.

Summers, Montague (1938) *The Gothic Quest: A History of the Gothic Novel*, London: The Fortune Press.

Thompson, G. R. (ed.) (1974) *The Gothic Imagination: Essays in Dark Romanticism*, Pullman, WA: Washington State University Press.

Townshend, Dale (2005) 'Gothic Visions, Romantic Acoustics', in Robert Miles (ed.), 'Gothic Technologies: Visuality in the Romantic Era', *Romantic Circles: Praxis*, December, available at www.rc.umd.edu/praxis/gothic/townshend/townshend.html.

Varma, Devendra (1966) *The Gothic Tale*, New York: Russell and Russell.

5

VICTORIAN GOTHIC

ALEXANDRA WARWICK

In his introduction to a reprint of Charles Eastlake's 1872 book on Gothic architecture, Mordaunt Crook writes:

> Trying to track down a chronological watershed between the survival and revival of Gothic is like chasing a will o' the wisp. For the Gothic style was resuscitated several times before it was dead, and it lingered unconscionably long in certain traditionalist areas.

(Crook 1970: 29)

A suitably Gothic extended metaphor in itself, Crook's comment also points to some of the problems inherent in periodising a form that escapes anything but the loosest of definitions. It also raises the question of whether Gothic is, or ever has been, dead. In one sense it might be said to have had a relatively short life: from about 1764 to the high-water mark of production of Gothic literature in 1800. In that year it accounted for some 38 per cent of novels published, and occupied what Robert Miles calls 'a plateau of market dominance' from 1794 to 1807, declining thereafter (Miles 2002: 42). Yet clearly Gothic did not die; indeed, in the popular imagination the Victorian is in many ways *the* Gothic period, with its elaborate cult of death and mourning, its fascination with ghosts, spiritualism and the occult, and not least because of the powerful fictional figures of the late century.

In attempting to periodise Gothic, we could also speculate on another death that did not happen, that of Queen Victoria. Her long reign, and the self-identification of her subjects and their age as 'Victorian', gives the semblance of coherence to the years between 1837 and 1900, but had she died in the 1850s or 1860s we would now think of the nineteenth century as having a rather different chronology. In historical practice, something like a breaking-up of the 'Victorian' has long been in place, where reference to mid- or high Victorian indicates the period from 1850 to the 1870s broadly characterised by economic prosperity and liberal reform, and the late Victorian, from 1880 onwards, as a time of growing social uncertainty and varied challenges to Britain's economic and imperial position. Rather more recently in literary studies the *fin-de-siècle* has been somewhat separated from the rest of the century, evolving into a distinct field of study in itself and characterised by attention to the articulation of social and political 'crises'. Indeed, this period has seemed to dominate recent work in Victorian studies, and it is clear that the steep rise of critical interest in

29

the Gothic since about 1990 is connected to, arguably even driving, this reorientation. Is it possible then to differentiate this Gothic century, and to suppose a watershed between the survival and revival of Gothic in the span of 'Victorianism' between the Romantics and modernism?

The survivals of eighteenth-century and Romantic Gothic are perhaps relatively easy to locate. Despite the decline in the market there was still a good deal of popular fiction that drew on familiar conventions: William Harrison Ainsworth, for example, whose early work in the 1830s and 40s was, as he described his best-seller *Rookwood* (1834), 'in the bygone style of Mrs Radcliffe' (Gilbert 1998: 1). Ainsworth continued to write and to be widely read through the 1850s and 60s, as did his contemporaries Edward Bulwer-Lytton and G. P. R. James. Their novels were best-sellers in the 1830s and 40s and, like Ainsworth, they drew freely on a range of existing models and all were heavily influenced by Sir Walter Scott, Ann Radcliffe and Matthew Lewis.

Even writers more frequently associated with realism, such as Elizabeth Gaskell and George Eliot, wrote 'Gothic' tales. Eliot's 'The Lifted Veil' (written in 1859) reflects her preoccupation with questions of vision and cognition, refracted through the topical subjects of mesmerism and clairvoyance. Gaskell's stories, originally published anonymously, and mainly in Dickens' *Household Words* and *All the Year Round*, are folkloric and archaic. 'Disappearances', for example, which appeared in 1851, is interesting as a contemporary version of folklore, as it recounts a number of what are effectively urban myths surrounding the unexplained disappearances of people.

While all of the variously Gothic works of the earlier part of the century have their own interest, and the eighteenth-century form continues to survive for much longer, the significant shift to what I would describe as the Victorian Gothic revival begins in the 1840s. The shift can be summarised as the translation of Gothic to new locations: first to a bourgeois domestic setting, and second to the urban environment. Of principal importance in the former is the work of the Brontë sisters, which draws on their childhood and adolescent reading of *Blackwood's Magazine*. *Blackwood's* had a 'distinctive style of hair-raising sensationalism [that] took shape in its tales of terror and guilt' (Baldick 1995: xiii) and the Brontës' novels contain a number of images and characters that can be traced to their earlier reading. The characters are frequently versions of those found in late eighteenth-century models: the confined and threatened woman; the ambivalent figure of a dynamic anti-hero; the weak and ineffectual hero. They are not crude reproductions, however, and the Brontës' distinctive contribution is to create claustrophobic psychological dramas that represent sadomasochistic relations between men and women. In contrast to the emphatic Victorian development of the idea of the home as a place of peace, safety and protection, the Brontës' domestic spaces, and the state of marriage or family life that the spaces embody, are terrifyingly ambiguous. The novels are full of images of doors and windows, with women inside prevented from leaving and the same women outside, barred from entering. Their desire to be inside or outside switches constantly through the narratives, and the consequences are shown as potentially fatal to the women. The ambivalent desires are associated with Gothic images: the crazed laughter from the attic in *Jane Eyre* (1847); the desperate ghost in *Wuthering Heights* (1847); the dead nun in *Villette* (1853). The Brontës' novels take up the questions of gender that are apparent in earlier Gothic, but within the highly wrought drama of the stories the heroines are modern women seeking a place for themselves in a world that is hostile to them.

Anne Brontë's *The Tenant of Wildfell Hall* (1848) is a precursor to the sensation fiction of the 1860s that further elaborates the domestic space as a place of nightmares. Sensation fiction is in many ways the nineteenth-century equivalent of the late eighteenth-century Gothic: mass circulation, regarded as a low form and as mentally and morally dangerous, particularly to its largely female readership. The 'sensation' was in both content and form, representing scandalous events such as bigamy, madness and murder, but also exposing the reader's nervous system to a series of shocks strung on a high-tension narrative thread. Sensation fiction owed a good deal to the explosion in cheap newspapers after the repeal of the tax on printed materials in 1855, and when the Matrimonial Causes Act of 1857 made divorce rather easier the availability of salacious and scandalous stories increased. The language of Gothic, of sensation, terror, shock, and its characters are translated into a bourgeois domestic arena. The revelations in reportage and fiction that exposed the interiors of what Wilkie Collins in 1852 called the 'secret theatre of home' (Collins 1990: 76) contained not the visceral grotesqueries of grinning skeletons but the social horrors of the sadistic relations of men and women in ordinary life, and the disturbance of gender roles where women are active and often dangerous.

Wilkie Collins' *The Woman in White* (1860), for example, contains the strange figure of Marian. From the bizarre first description of her, she carries an erotic charge that the ostensible heroine does not, and her actions are crucial in the defeat of the villains. The final scenes of the novel are purged of Gothic intrusion, but Marian's awkward presence is still inassimilable. She fares better than the heroines of Mary Braddon's *Lady Audley's Secret* (1862) and Mrs Henry Wood's *East Lynne* (1861), however. Their awkwardness is shown as immorality and criminality, and they end, respectively, dead in a French mad-house and 'a barred name' with a gravestone marked only by initials. The threat that they represent to the middle-class home has to be contained; for the femmes fatales by death, and for Marian by her sterile suspension as a 'good angel'.

If the Brontës' work marks the beginning of one of the two strands of the Gothic revival, the second is inaugurated by that of one of their less-remembered contemporaries: G. W. M. Reynolds, whose vast serial production *The Mysteries of London* and its sequel were published in weekly instalments from 1844 to 1856. Although Reynolds' serial was not highly regarded in literary terms by his contemporaries, it is crucial in the shift that it makes towards the location of Gothic in the urban present of nineteenth-century London. Indeed, it has been suggested that the rambling and not always coherent nature of the narrative is a product of the material itself, and that Reynolds' writing deliberately represents the divergent and conflicting elements of the city without striving for formal resolution or aesthetic consistency (Thomas in Reynolds 1996: xiii). The narrative opens in 1831, and while there are recognisably conventional persecuted maidens, mysterious doubles and monstrous villains, its more important consequence is to make Gothic the texture and experience of the modern city, particularly its inhabitants. *The Mysteries of London* has the effect, as Gertrude Himmelfarb observes, 'of gothicizing poverty, making it seem barbarous, grotesque, macabre' (Himmelfarb 1984: 452).

Although Charles Dickens was disdainful of both Reynolds and his work (Maxwell 1992: 166), the similarities between them are perhaps closer than Dickens would have liked to acknowledge.

> Taken with Henry Mayhew's recording of the detail of street life in his *Morning Chronicle* letters of 1849, and with Dickens' apocalyptic vision of London in *Bleak House*, [*Mysteries*] completes a literary triptych representing the culture of the metropolis from three distinct perspectives at an epochal moment of social and political transition.
>
> (Thomas in Reynolds 1996: vii)

It is Dickens who accomplishes the most important transition from the survivals of eighteenth-century Gothic to a revived form that is adapted and renovated in response to the conditions of contemporary experience. There is not necessarily a strictly chronological development through his work, but the transitional nature of his use of the Gothic can be seen in the mixing of tropes and figures in the novels. For example, in *Great Expectations* (1860), a relatively late work, Miss Havisham is a character from an earlier mode. She is a wronged woman, in fact something like the ghost of the young Gothic heroine: a barely surviving remnant of herself and of a character-type from earlier fiction. Estella initially appears as the new version of Miss Havisham, a heroine confined and awaiting rescue, but the set of characters is broken: the promised villain Magwitch turns out to be nothing of the kind; Pip the putative hero comes, as he imagines, to rescue the imprisoned maiden but he is shown not only to fail in his endeavour, but to have entirely mistaken the nature of the task set him. The narrative of *Great Expectations* promises an older conventional form of Gothic that is then denied. Dickens' contribution to Gothic is not, however, simply in the emptying of the form, but in the construction of new possibilities for it.

It is Dickens who makes use of, and indeed establishes, a metropolitan sensibility that distinguishes a new Victorian Gothic. There are older uses of the word metropolitan in an ecclesiastical context, but all uses of it to denote a particular urban subjectivity date from the mid-nineteenth century. In fact the *Oxford English Dictionary* credits Dickens with the coinage of the term 'metropolitaneously': meaning to act in a metropolitan manner. Dickens mirrors, of course, the population patterns of mid-century Britain where the majority were concentrated in urban areas, and more than a tenth of the whole population in London. It is, however, more than a simple reflection of the demographic changes, but an articulation of the new forms of social relations inaugurated by capitalism. Georg Simmel writes in 1903 that the city is the seat of and dominated by the money economy. Money 'becomes the common denominator of all values; irreparably it hollows out the core of things, their individuality, their specific value and their incomparability. All things float with equal specific gravity' (Simmel 1997: 178). If money is the abstraction of social relations then the metropolis is the spatial equivalent of that abstraction. Karl Marx's own recourse to Gothic imagery is striking. In *Capital* (1867), for example, he cites spiritualism and table-rapping to emphasise what he sees as the mystical nature of the commodity form, the essentially non-material nature of exchange value, its spectralisation (Marx 1867: 164).[1]

In *Great Expectations* there is a stark representation of such spectralised relations, in which the expectations of the title are simultaneously financial, social, romantic and generic, and all of which are denied. The novel opens with the secure location of Pip in a still-feudal environment. His home-life, though not idyllic, is grounded in family and communal relations, and his future career as a blacksmith seems equally assured. This is interrupted by two Gothic promises – the marsh scene with Magwitch and Miss Havisham's house, in which the familiar triangle of villain, hero and heroine appears to be set up. Instead of the expected chivalric and heroic events, the relations between the characters become abstracted through the operations of money. Money is the ghost in *Great Expectations*: possessed of an absent presence, mysterious in origin, its influence governs all social and narrative relations and, as Simmel notes, hollows out their specificity. The Gothic form of the eighteenth century is similarly hollowed in Dickens' text, but in place of those essentially feudal relations is a new Gothic, of urban capital, where the spectral form is money. Dickens compounds the Gothic relations of urban capitalism by representing them as secrets embedded in the city, in the papers of its law courts, the letters, tokens and documents hidden by individuals. These secrets are only revealed by death.

Although it is of course demonstrable that eighteenth-century and Romantic Gothic were deeply concerned with issues of contemporary political and social life, these were rehearsed in terms of the past in the locations and conditions of medieval Europe. The revival of Gothic, the point at which it could be said to be 'Victorian', is the moment at which it is being used explicitly to articulate the questions of the present, and setting them in that same recognisable present. The anxiety of the legacies of the past remains, intensified by the self-consciousness of modernity.

At the same time as Dickens is making the city the form of abstracted social relations, the city itself was becoming visibly Gothic in the development of its architecture. Architecture has always been more closely related to Gothic than any other literary form, not simply because of its naming, but because of the crucial significance of the built environment which functions so frequently as a metaphor for dynastic, physical or psychic crisis. The surviving Gothic architecture of the early nineteenth century was religious and distinctly non-urban, and the Romantic aesthetic had already rendered the ruins of places like Tintern Abbey as sublime fragments of a lost past. Although through the influence of architects like A. W. N. Pugin Gothic was the style of the large majority of newly built or renovated churches, revived Gothic in its most spectacular form is resolutely secular.[2] Legislation in 1829 had lifted social and political restrictions on Catholics, and despite a resurgence in numbers and continued prejudice, particularly against the Irish, Catholicism was no longer viewed with almost superstitious fear. John Ruskin's emphatically non-religious insistence on the Gothic style as representing a right moral feeling of mental and physical freedom was hugely influential, and his 1853 book *The Stones of Venice* was instrumental in constructing a vision of a reconstituted civic sphere that was more than just an idealised medievalism.

Just as Dickens' urbanised and contemporised Gothic does not nullify its imaginative hold, the same is true of Gothic architecture. The de-coupling of explicit religious meaning from architectural form has the effect of diffusing the signifiers of Gothic throughout the urban context. Between its narrative and material revivals, Gothic moves into a new set of contemporary arenas: city streets, slums, docks, scientific laboratories and, perhaps most conspicuously, the ordinary bourgeois home. After mid-century Gothic is not so much political and dynastic as individual and social, and it becomes increasingly difficult (if it were ever possible) to distinguish anything like a single form of Gothic as the interrelationships between it and other generic fiction grow more complex and tangled. Science fiction, for example, can be seen as developing out of Victorian Gothic, particularly in H. G. Wells' 'scientific romances' written in the 1890s: *The Time Machine* (1895); *The Island of Dr Moreau* (1896); *The Invisible Man* (1897) and *The War of the Worlds* (1898). Wells' importance is that he Gothicises not just the present, but the future, a trope that is still observable, even ubiquitous, in the late twentieth and twenty-first centuries. Yet another form, the detective story, emerges from the knot of Gothic and sensation fiction, and the legacy can be traced from Edgar Allan Poe through Conan Doyle to Raymond Chandler's Los Angeles noir of the 1940s. The detective story, with its emphasis on the power of rationality, would seem an unlikely inheritor of Gothic, but its narrative efficacy and its fascination for the late Victorians lie in the same place – the rendering of urban modernity as Gothic.

By the end of the century the city has become its Other, dominantly figured as labyrinth, jungle, swamp and ruin, and described as blackened, rotten, shadowed and diseased. Most importantly perhaps, this city of dreadful night is populated by others who threaten to overrun or undermine the fabric of the imperial metropolis. These others are partly Himmelfarb's Gothic poor, evolved now in such a way that their class difference is imagined as biological and even racial difference. The criminal too is represented with a similarly increasing insistence on his/her physiological difference, and seen as embodying the survival of atavistic qualities of the savage human, even of the animal. After Darwin, the scientific notion of evolution through natural selection is transferred into the widest possible range of reference, becoming a complex metaphor for ideas of change and progress in any number of discourses. Increasingly, those ideas develop along pessimistic and alarmist lines, where a confidence in the process of natural selection to preserve the best is undermined by a suspicion that not all that persists through time is necessarily positive, and that far from evolution guaranteeing a steady march to perfection, it more strongly implies the possibility of retrogression, of degeneration. Evidence of retrogression in the natural world is quickly extrapolated into the condition of humanity and society, and we can see this in the characteristic concerns of late-century fiction. Rehearsed through contemporary theories of biology, medicine, anthropology, sociology, sexology and psychology, as Kelly Hurley puts it: 'in place of a human body stable and integral, the *fin de siècle* Gothic offers the spectacle of a body metamorphic and undifferentiated' (Hurley 1996: 3).

The metamorphic body is apparent in the changing representation of the vampire through the course of the century. In John Polidori's 'The Vampyre' (1818), the vampire is little more than a rakish seducer, and by the time of James Malcolm Rymer's sprawling pot-boiler *Varney the Vampyre; or, The Feast of Blood*, eventually published as one volume in 1847, the vampire is physically repellent, but no shape-shifter. Only with J. Sheridan le Fanu's 'Carmilla' (1872) does the human–vampire form lose its coherence. Carmilla, like her anagrammatic name, is capable of physical reformations. As well as the beautiful woman, she appears as a cat-like creature, a spectre and a mass of black mist. By 1897 and the publication of *Dracula*, the vampire is fully metamorphic and, more importantly, he is contagious – able to induce physical transformation in the bodies of others. Dracula, like so many of the other abhuman figures of late-Victorian Gothic – in Wells' *The Island of Dr Moreau*, Arthur Machen's *The Great God Pan* (1894), Richard Marsh's *The Beetle* (1897), Oscar Wilde's *The Picture of Dorian Gray* (1890), R. L. Stevenson's *Strange Case of Dr Jekyll and Mr Hyde* (1886) and H. Rider Haggard's *She* (1887) – can be seen as symbolic of more than physical anxiety. These narratives have convincingly been read as rehearsing contemporary questions of gender, sexuality, immigration and imperial power,[3] but if they are so firmly fixed in the issues of late-Victorian Britain why have they transcended that historical moment in such a way that they are recognisable to millions who have never read the novels? The figures of the *fin-de-siècle* fictions become more than fictional, as Iain Sinclair suggests: 'They got out into the stream of time, the ether; they escaped into the labyrinth. They achieved an independent existence' (Sinclair 1998: 129). The earlier work of Dickens and the Brontës has enabled the Gothic to come home, from the cultural, geographical, religious and chronological margins to permeate every area of Victorian life: domesticity, the family, the streets, the empire, the future. Sinclair's novel, *White Chappell, Scarlet Tracings* (1987), takes the Whitechapel murders of 1888 as its subject, and it is perhaps at that moment when the imaginative force of Gothic transcends the fictional and interweaves with the real. It is the real but mythic character of Jack the Ripper who blurs the boundaries of Gothic fiction. The murders seem to knot together the Gothic threads – the othered urban poor (including the alien Jew), the labyrinthine city, sexual pathology, the atavistically savage and questionably human criminal. The metamorphic body appears in the starkest of terms in the grotesquely mutilated bodies of the prostitute victims and the immateriality of the murderer apparently capable of vanishing into the fabric of the city. From this point, Jack the Ripper, Dorian Gray, Jekyll and Hyde, Dracula, the Invisible Man and Sherlock Holmes swirl in the popular imagination, condensed into a definitive Gothic code of a foggy, gas-lit cobbled street, threatened by an unseen malevolent presence. The enduring power of this image is that it connotes our modern anxieties about the existence of the self in the modern urban landscape and the relation of the self to the others who inhabit it.

The instant recognition of the same image as visual shorthand for Victorian London is partly the legacy of another nineteenth-century invention, the cinema, but it is perhaps to that other darkened space of dreams, the unconscious, that we owe the continued grip of Gothic on our imagination. As Stoker, Wells, Wilde, Machen, Blackwood and the others are producing their novels, the last of the great Victorian Gothic writers is beginning his work, not in London, but in Vienna. Sigmund Freud is concerned from his earliest writing to articulate and analyse excess – that which is more than the conscious or the rational. In this he mirrors the impulse of eighteenth-century Gothic to counter (or indeed to complete) the project of the Enlightenment by bringing apparently unaccountable mental experience within the bounds of rational inquiry. Indeed, his much-used essay on the uncanny opens by suggesting that it begins from the point at which theories of the sublime become inadequate. Freud's theories of the structure and processes of the psyche have been used more than any other to read the Gothic, yet it is equally plausible to reverse the terms of the analogy, and to use the Gothic to read his work. If Gothic can be thought of as interrogating the anxiety of the influence of the past on the present, then Freud's work can also be defined in these terms, persistently concerned with the question of what is dead, what survives and how things are revived. In his explicit articulation of the Victorian idea that we are, individually and collectively, haunted from within and by ourselves, Freud revives the Gothic will o' the wisp and provides a new impulse for it to live again in the twentieth century.

NOTES

1 Among the hundreds of possible examples: St Pancras Hotel (1868–74), Manchester Town Hall (1868–77) and the Law Courts in the Strand (1874–82). For detailed discussion of Victorian Gothic architecture see Hunt (2004).
2 Marx also repeatedly draws an analogy between capital and vampirism. This has been

picked out by later commentators: see, for example, Moretti (1988). Derrida's reading in *Spectres of Marx* (1993) has also been influential: see, for example, Wolfreys (2002); Robbins and Wolfreys (2000).

3 See, for example, Walkowitz (1992); Brantlinger (1988); Mighall (1999); Malchow (1996); Smith (2004).

WORKS CITED

Baldick, Chris and Robert Morrison (1995) (ed. and intro.) *Tales of Terror from Blackwood's Magazine*, Oxford: Oxford University Press.

Brantlinger, Patrick (1988) *Rule of Darkness: British Literature and Imperialism 1830–1914*, New York: Cornell University Press.

Collins, Wilkie (1990) *Basil*, Oxford: Oxford University Press.

Crook, J. Mordaunt (1970) 'Introduction', to Charles Eastlake, *A History of the Gothic Revival*, Leicester: Leicester University Press.

Gilbert, R. A. (1998) 'W. Ainsworth Harrison', in Marie Mulvey-Roberts (ed.), *A Handbook to Gothic Literature*, Basingstoke: Macmillan.

Himmelfarb, Gertrude (1984) *The Idea of Poverty*, London: Faber and Faber.

Hunt, Tristram (2004) *Building Jerusalem: The Rise and Fall of the Victorian City*, London: Weidenfeld and Nicolson.

Hurley, Kelly (1996) *The Gothic Body*, Cambridge: Cambridge University Press.

Malchow, H. L. (1996) *Gothic Images of Race in Nineteenth-century Britain*, Stanford, CA: Stanford University Press.

Maxwell, Richard (1992) *The Mysteries of Paris and London*, Charlottesville, VA: University of Virginia Press.

Mighall, Robert (1999) *A Geography of Victorian Gothic Fiction*, Oxford: Oxford University Press.

Miles, Robert (2002) 'The 1790s: The Effulgence of Gothic', in Jerrold E. Hogle (ed.), *The Cambridge Companion to Gothic Fiction*, Cambridge: Cambridge University Press.

Moretti, Franco (1983) *Signs Taken for Wonders*, London: Verso.

Reynolds, G. W. M. (1996) *The Mysteries of London*, ed. and intro. Trefor Thomas, Keele: Keele University Press.

Robbins, Ruth and Julian Wolfreys (eds) (2000) *Victorian Gothic*, Basingstoke: Palgrave.

Simmel, Georg (1997) 'The Metropolis and Mental Life', trans. Hans Gerth, in *Simmel on Culture: Selected Writing*, London: Sage.

Sinclair, Iain (1998) *White Chappell, Scarlet Tracings*, London: Granta.

Smith, Andrew (2004) *Victorian Demons: Medicine, Masculinity and the Gothic at the Fin de Siècle*, Manchester: Manchester University Press.

Walkowitz, Judith (1992) *City of Dreadful Delight: Narratives of Sexual Danger in Late-Victorian London*, London: Virago.

Wolfreys, Julian (2002) *Victorian Hauntings*, Basingstoke: Palgrave.

6

GOTHIC IN THE
TWENTIETH CENTURY

CATHERINE SPOONER

Gothic is sometimes positioned as a kind of counter-narrative to the major high-cultural movements of the twentieth century: a principally popular form, the stuff of cult readership and mass-market paperbacks, its sensationalism at odds with the serious, avant-garde experimentalism of modernism and postmodernism. The common-sense view is that modernism, in its emphasis on the contemporary world and high value on accurately recreating interior consciousness, was inimical to Gothic and that therefore in the first half of the twentieth century the genre was in decline. Postmodernism, on the other hand, with its embrace of genre fiction, pastiche, sensationalism and spectacle, provided a much more sympathetic climate for Gothic's revival. Yet both modernist and postmodernist texts have a rich and complex relationship with Gothic, one that goes beyond straightforward rejection or exploitation as a 'popular' genre. Modernism and postmodernism both took a variety of different forms, often contradictory, and cannot be reduced to a single formula: neither, then, can their relationship with Gothic.

The positioning of certain 'Gothic' writers outside of this high-cultural narrative is also potentially reductive. The work of Daphne du Maurier, whose best-selling novels such as *Jamaica Inn* (1936) and *Rebecca* (1938) have principally been read in terms of mainstream popular fiction, has recently been reassessed as having more in common with her avant-garde contemporaries than previously thought. Alison Light, for instance, suggests that 'Du Maurier . . . made entertainment out of modernist anxieties . . . to suggest that an existential "anguish" at the instability of subjectivity is at the heart of *Rebecca* is not as preposterous as it might first sound' (Light 1991: 191). Other 'Gothic' writers, such as American horror writer H. P. Lovecraft, deliberately located themselves within alternative literary traditions. Kuranes, the dreamer of Lovecraft's fragmentary short story 'Celephaïs' (1920), for example,

> was not modern, and did not think like others who wrote. Whilst they strove to strip from life its embroidered robes of myth, and to shew in naked ugliness the foul thing that is reality, Kuranes sought for beauty alone.
>
> (Lovecraft 1999: 24)

For Lovecraft, horror writing and fantasy offered an antidote to the modern world – in itself a new development, in sharp contrast to what Baldick and

Mighall have called the 'Whiggish', progressive attitude to the past found in earlier Gothic (Baldick and Mighall 2000). But despite this deliberate anti-modernism, Lovecraft shares influences such as Poe and Machen with many of his more explicitly modernist contemporaries. He is obsessed with the immeasurably ancient, with beings beyond time – and his attempts to construct mythologies structuring our world recall, albeit in a different register, the experimentation with myth of Yeats and Eliot. Gothic writers do not work in a vacuum, but participate, even if obliquely, in wider literary developments.

GOTHIC AND MODERNISM

Famously, in 1924 Virginia Woolf wrote in a critical essay that 'On or about December, 1910, human character changed' (Woolf 1988: 421). Like many commentators of the period, she sought to identify an epistemological break, a shift in ways of knowing and understanding the world, whereby the stifling influences of the Victorian period could be jettisoned in favour of a self-conscious attention to the 'modern'. With this disavowal of the past implicitly came a dismissal of the Gothic. For the intelligentsia of the early twentieth century, it became fashionable to reject Gothic along with other nineteenth-century baggage. Woolf's date is convenient for our purposes: following the end of the Edwardian period there was a relative dearth of Gothic literature (although in the cinema Gothic narratives thrived) until much later in the century, with the revival of interest in popular literary forms in the 1960s. Gothic and modernism have consequently been considered incompatible: in the brash new world of motor travel, aviation, female emancipation, accelerated consumption and global warfare the standard Gothic props of medieval castles and fainting maidens seemed creaky and hollow.

Yet recent scholarship has challenged the notion of an epistemological break '[o]n or about December, 1910', suggesting that the modernists paid a greater debt to the Victorians, and that the Victorians were more modern, than the modernists themselves liked to acknowledge (Meisel 1987). So too can we challenge the notion that Gothic and modernism do not mix. Woolf herself, in a review of Edith Birkhead's *The Tale of Terror* (1921), does not so much reject Gothic as suggest that in the modern period its terms have been renegotiated: 'It is at the ghosts within that we shudder, and not at the decaying bodies of barons or the subterranean activities of ghouls' (Woolf 1988: 307). While this still suggests a value judgement, privileging the 'subtler' ghost stories of the present over the clunky machinery of the past, it also points to a modernist understanding of Gothic as interior drama rather than dramatic spectacle. In this light, much of the Gothic literature of the *fin-de-siècle* anticipates the themes and concerns, as well as the formal experimentation, which the central figures of modernism were to adopt (Woolf's own example, Henry James's *The Turn of the Screw* (1898), is illustrative). The line between the *fin-de-siècle* and the modernist period proper is by no means secure, and critics are constantly redrawing it.

Kelly Hurley argues that *fin-de-siècle* Gothic novels 'engage in narrative experimentation more consistently than their mainstream contemporary counterparts' and 'can be seen as on a continuum with such twentieth-century movements as "high" modernism and surrealism' (Hurley 2001: 129–30). Bram Stoker's *Dracula* (1897), which in its multi-voiced narrative and emphasis on contemporary technologies is what Jennifer Wicke calls 'a liminal modernist artifact' (Wicke 1992), illustrates this continuum particularly well. *Dracula* is one of the literary fragments jumbled together in the final, apocalyptic section of T. S. Eliot's *The Waste Land* (1922), 'What the Thunder Said': a mysterious woman plays music on the strings of her long black hair, and bats crawl down a wall head first, as Jonathan Harker sees Dracula do. In Eliot's poem, Dracula's Transylvanian castle is suggestively mapped onto the Chapel Perilous of the Holy Grail legend, recalling the myth of blood-drinking and resurrection that structures both stories, linking them through a shared dynamic of ruin and rebirth. In Eliot, however, the physical horror presented by Stoker's Count is transmuted to a symbol of spiritual dereliction.

Traces of Gothic, then, can be found in some of the cornerstone texts of high modernism. James Joyce's *Dubliners* (1914), with its oppressive city streets and spoiled priests, Joseph Conrad's *Heart of Darkness* (1899), with its claustrophobic jungle and cannibal threats, or Eliot's *The Waste Land* with its cast of tarot readers, femmes fatales and the walking dead, invoke familiar Gothic concerns in a new register. These texts cannot conveniently be labelled Gothic in the same way as the novels of Walpole, Radcliffe and Lewis: they have an entirely different sensibility and ambition. Gothic becomes, rather than the determining feature of the texts, one tool among many employed in the service of conjuring up interior terrors. These texts contain Gothic incidents, episodes, imagery, moments, traces: Gothic, we might say, haunts them.

This is particularly clear in the work of Elizabeth Bowen. Bowen's fiction characteristically centres upon the loneliness and lost innocence of young middle-class women as they come of age in polite society. Her novels are elegant, restrained and melancholy – not the conventional stuff of Gothic fiction. However, she also wrote a number of ghost stories, including 'The Demon Lover' (1941), in which a woman returns to her empty London house in the middle of the Blitz, to discover a letter from a lover who died in the previous war, threatening to return to keep a mysterious promise extracted twenty-five years earlier. In addition to the motif of the return from the dead, Bowen exploits the uncanniness of the wartime city, eerily silent, and the bombed houses 'meet[ing] her look with their damaged stare' (Bowen 1999: 666). This Gothic sensibility is also shared by her longer fiction. In a crucial moment in *The Death of the Heart* (1938), the heroine's consciousness is refracted through the space of an empty lodging house:

> The front top bedrooms here were like convent cells . . . Their walls were mouldy blue like a dead sky, and looking at the criss-cross cracks in the ceiling one thought

of holiday people waking up . . . These rooms, many flights up, were a dead end: the emptiness, the feeling of dissolution came upstairs behind one, blocking the way down. Portia felt she had climbed to the very top of a tree pursued by something that could follow.

(Bowen 1998: 196)

Houses in Bowen are haunted spaces, but in the sense that they provide a framework for articulating the sense of loss and disappointment of those within them. Portia's disillusionment with her boyfriend Eddie is figured in terms of architectural dereliction and Gothicised entrapment. Momentarily, she is positioned within the tradition of the Gothic heroine, a revelation that transforms the way we read her isolation within other houses in the rest of the novel. *The Last September* (1929), a novel set in one of the embattled 'Big Houses' of the Anglo-Irish Protestant ascendancy in 1920, shortly before Irish independence, similarly ends with the house's conflagration and ruin. Bowen's writing is not Gothic in any straightforward sense, but it is haunted by spectres of a tradition of Irish Gothic encompassing Maria Edgeworth and J. Sheridan Le Fanu.

For American writers, whose national tradition has always been much more overtly Gothic, as Leslie Fiedler provocatively suggested in *Love and Death in the American Novel* (1960), the tension between Gothic and modernism does not seem to be so great. William Faulkner's novels, set in the murky, overheated world of America's Deep South, have long been recognised as reworking Gothic conventions: *Sanctuary* (1931), a sensational novel written for money, recasts the imprisoned Gothic heroine as a spoiled Southern society girl who falls among bootleggers and is forced into a brothel; *Absolom, Absolom* (1936) and *Go Down, Moses* (1942) are peopled by characters 'locked into the tragic repetitions of their personal pasts – repetitions that recur through the generations . . . in a landscape cursed by the twin specters of slavery and the Civil War' (O'Donnell 1995: 32). Djuna Barnes' *Nightwood* (1937) also pays an explicit debt to Gothic conventions, which may be one reason why it was left out of the modernist canon for many years, despite its initial critical success and its championing by T. S. Eliot. It is a novel about a society in decay: a society on the verge of the Second World War. It is shockingly modern in both its style (deliberately oblique and fragmented) and subject matter (sexually transgressive bohemians leading a cosmopolitan lifestyle in Paris, Berlin and America). Yet it is also a novel in which characters are trapped by the past, whether like Nora, haunted by a vague childhood trauma and unable to move on from a failed love affair; like Felix, obsessed by historical monuments and antiques; or like Robin, dressed in clothes refashioned from antique garments and enslaved by feral, atavistic urges to abandon herself to the night. Taking place in a series of darkened interiors – grand parties, seedy hotel rooms, cheap bars, chapels, the circus tent – it revisits the landscape of urban Gothic, presenting it as a site of psychic and social unease. The novel also characteristically narrates its preoccupation with the past in terms of costume – diffusing the 'deeper' material of the damaged psyche into outward trappings, in a manner that Eve Sedgwick has described as quintessentially Gothic (Sedgwick 1986).

Nightwood presents a world in which identity is performative, constructed through dress, and yet in which dress conveys dislocation and disquiet. It is a twilit novel peopled with liminal beings, a cast of misfits and freaks, living on borders and between states. Each of the main characters is ill at ease in their own skin: Felix Volkbein, for example, a Jew in Europe on the brink of Nazi tyranny, inhabits the subject position of the stock Gothic character, the Wandering Jew, 'for the step of the Wandering Jew is in every son' (Barnes 1963: 20); Matthew O'Connor is a transvestite who feels himself a woman in a man's body, and who appears in one memorable scene tucked up in bed 'in a woman's flannel nightgown . . . [his] full gun-metal cheeks and chin framed in the golden semi-circle of a wig with long pendent curls that touched his shoulders . . . heavily rouged and his lashes painted' (Barnes 1963: 117). Identities are fake, facades: 'Doctor' Matthew O'Connor is not a real doctor; Baron Felix Volkbein is not a real aristocrat, his ancestral portraits being 'reproductions of two ancient and intrepid actors' (Barnes 1963: 19). In the nocturnal, carnival world of the novel, however, there are no 'real' identities behind the numerous disguises. A dominant trope is provided by the circus, where performativity structures the freaks' and artistes' identities. The Duchess of Broadback, a trapeze artist, has become her costume: 'She seemed to have a skin that was the pattern of her costume: a bodice of lozenges, red and yellow . . . one somehow felt they ran through her as the design ran through hard holiday candies . . . The stuff of her tights was no longer a covering, it was herself; the span of her tightly-stitched crotch was so much her own flesh she was as unsexed as a doll' (Barnes 1963: 27–8).

In Barnes and Faulkner, perhaps, we can detect the crux of the modernist relationship with Gothic: both are preoccupied with the passing of time, with history and its relation to the present, with personal, psychic histories – but Gothic texts characteristically refigure this preoccupation through a different lexicon, a lexicon of sensation and horror at odds with the realist impulse of much modernist writing. Modernist texts may draw on this horror in order to articulate moments of spiritual crisis: Kurtz's infamous dying words in *Heart of Darkness*, 'The horror! The horror!', uttered deep within the claustrophobic imperial nightmare of the Congo, are representative in this respect (and were, in fact, used by Eliot as an epigraph for an early draft of *The Waste Land*). They are not, however, interested in exploring its effects for their own sake, as more self-consciously Gothic writers do.

GOTHIC AND POSTMODERNISM

The intense concern with time that structures both Gothic and modernist narrative is sensitively explored by Angela Carter's *post*modern short story 'The Lady of the House of Love' (1979), which revisits Woolf's moment of epistemological rupture and frames it in explicitly Gothic terms. A British tourist on a cycling holiday in Eastern Europe on the eve of the First World War encounters an ancient female vampire. She is locked into the repetitive patterns of an ancestral curse, endlessly going through the motions. But this historical scene is, significantly, set round about the moment that Woolf claimed that human relations, and therefore consciousness, changed. Carter relocates what Robert Miles has called the 'Gothic cusp' (Miles 1993: 32) – the moment of hesitation between barbarism and enlightenment – to the moment of modernism's epistemological break. The vampire is a vestigial survival in a forgotten pocket of a rapidly modernising Europe. Carter's hero, 'rooted in change and time', collides with 'the timeless Gothic eternity of the vampires, for whom all is as it has always been and will be, whose cards always fall in the same pattern' (Carter 1981: 97). Armed only with his bicycle, 'in itself some protection against superstitious fears, since the bicycle is the product of pure reason applied to motion', the hero dispatches the vampire with a chaste kiss, before Carter drily concludes, 'Next day, his regiment embarked for France' (Carter 1981: 97, 108). Gothic horrors are superseded by those of modern warfare; the curt conclusion suggests that death in the trenches is a more pressing fear than bloodsucking fiends.

Yet the modern is essential to the functioning of Carter's story: 'Gothic eternity' has only a limited narrative potential, being based on endless repetition; it is inimical to the art of story-telling. 'Change and time' are necessary requirements of narrative. 'Can a bird sing only the song it knows, or can it learn a new song?' is the story's repeated refrain (Carter 1981: 103). As it proves, the bird can only sing the song it knows, the vampire cannot change her tune, for a new song equals death. The bird and the vampire are trapped not only by their animal nature but also by a concept of time that only permits cyclical repetition. History is only meaningful to those who die; the Gothic tale can only narrate its own vanquishing. The paradox of Carter's story, however, is that in revisiting the vampire tale she writes it afresh: Gothic, it seems, is not doomed to cyclical repetition, but perfectly capable of change and variation.

Carter's narrative signals a shift in the relationship between Gothic and 'high' culture. Postmodernism presents few of the problems that modernism does in relation to the Gothic: as noted above, its embrace of the popular, of genre fiction, of sensation and spectacle, allowed plenty of room for the Gothic to flourish. Allan Lloyd Smith (1996) lists multiple coincident concerns between Gothic and postmodern texts, including indeterminacy; surfaces/affectivity; nostalgia/archaism/history; pastiche/reflexivity; criminality/the unspeakable/excess; and science/technology/paranoia. The ascendancy of what Linda Hutcheon calls 'historiographic metafiction' – or, self-conscious historical fiction – laid the past open for Gothic rewriting (Hutcheon 1998). Where the past disrupts modernist Gothic as anachronistic vestige or psychic trace within the present, postmodernist fiction often replays contemporary critical concerns within historical settings. Although historiographic metafiction is not always written in the Gothic mode, its concern with marginal voices, untold tales, and the difficulties history has in getting told lends itself naturally to Gothic treatment. Patrick McGrath's *Martha Peake* (2000), for example, opens with the line, 'It is a black art, the writing of a history, is it not?', presenting his narrative as an occulted account in more ways than one (McGrath 2001: 3). The novel revisits the original moment of the Gothic by placing its eponymous heroine at the centre of the American Revolution, and piling up Gothic clichés including Cornish smugglers, a hunchbacked, alcoholic, incestuous father, a sinister aristocratic scientist with a museum of anatomy, an unreliable narrator and a gloomy, marsh-ridden mansion. More self-consciously Gothic than any 'original' Gothic novel ever was, it exists as a kind of simulacrum of the Gothic, a book that, like Umberto Eco's account of the film *Casablanca*, rounds up all the clichés and allows them to converse (Eco 2000).

Although Gothicised historiographic metafictions plunder indiscriminately from multiple historical eras, from the Middle Ages of Umberto Eco's *The Name of the Rose* (1980, trans. 1983) to the brink of the twentieth century in Angela Carter's *Nights at the Circus* (1984), it is the Victorian era which appears to figure most prominently as a new version of Miles' 'Gothic cusp'. If, in the early Gothic novels, this enabled novelists to dramatise the struggle between the Gothic past and the progressive new era to which they themselves belonged, then in contemporary fiction the Gothic cusp is frequently relocated to the nineteenth century. The Victorian era thus is newly revealed as site of struggle between incipient modernity and an unenlightened past. In Peter Carey's *Jack Maggs* (1997), for instance, a rewriting of Dickens' *Great Expectations* (1861), this struggle is dramatised in terms of Empire, so that the convict Jack Maggs, newly returned from Australia, is initially in thrall to the British juridical and social system, as well as his own demons, but ultimately overthrows them to become one of the founding fathers of a new nation. However, these postmodern rewritings are permitted an insight not available to eighteenth-century Gothic novelists: as Foucault demonstrates, we may have dismissed the barbaric modes of punishment or enclosure once meted out to the criminal and the insane, but modernity finds new ways to discipline and control us. It need not be the barbarous past that imprisons us, but the mechanisms of Enlightenment itself, that expose us to constant surveillance and the total functioning of power. Sarah Waters' *Affinity* (1999) is set in Millbank Prison, a structure built along the lines of Bentham's Panopticon, the model prison that Foucault uses as a metaphor for the total functioning of power. In the Panopticon, physical restraint becomes redundant as each inmate is subjected to constant surveillance, to the extent that they internalise its mechanism and voluntarily conform. Waters Gothicises this space, making it representative of a repressive code of gender, sexuality and class that ultimately haunts the contemporary reader more effectively than the spirits evoked by the medium Selina Dawes. Postmodernist Gothic reveals the Victorians, so eagerly cast aside by the likes of Lytton Strachey, Virginia Woolf and Ezra Pound, as the repressed material of modernity.

It is not only a particular relationship with history, however, but also with geography, that distinguishes postmodern Gothic. For Fredric Jameson, 'A certain spatial turn has often seemed to offer one of the more productive ways of distinguishing postmodernism from modernism proper', with space becoming privileged over the modernist concern with time (Jameson 1991: 154). Mervyn Peake's *Gormenghast* trilogy (1946–59), which exists on the border between modernism and postmodernism and somewhat askew of either, may dramatise the conflict between a decaying feudal order and upstart modernity, but it does so within the bounds of an enormous fantasy castle, whose arcane geographies are the most memorable feature of the books. It is not just the prominence of location that is significant in postmodern Gothic, but also its destabilisation and derealisation. David Punter and Glennis Byron suggest that:

> What we find in the numerous conjunctions of Gothic and the postmodern is a certain sliding of location, a series of transfers and translocations from one place to another, so that our sense of the stability of the map is – as indeed it has been since the first fantasy of a Gothic castle . . . forever under siege, guaranteed to us only by manuscripts whose own provenance and completeness are deeply uncertain.

> (Punter and Byron 2004: 51)

Postmodern Gothic has seized on the idea of the found manuscript, revisited in Emma Tennant's *The Bad Sister* (1978), Alisdair Gray's *Poor Things* (1992) and Mark Z. Danielewski's *House of Leaves* (2000), among others. *House of Leaves* literalises Punter and Byron's observation on the instability of the map – its central narrative describes a house whose shifting interior dimensions exceed its exterior ones, and in which ultimately a labyrinth opens up which defies exploration or explanation. This labyrinth, significantly, is configured in the space of the text itself, so that narratives within narratives, convoluted footnotes, different typefaces and words arranged in 'concrete' form across the page force the reader physically to enact the process of exploration, flicking backwards and forwards and even turning the book upside-down in order to follow its path. The 'manuscripts' through which the story is relayed to us are comprised of academic musing, lurid confession, delusional letters and anonymous editorial, all with crucial gaps both literal (deletions, damaged pages) and figurative (missing information), and of dubious provenance and authority. Recalling the moment of revelation from Borges' short story 'The Garden of Forking Paths', 'to no one did it occur that the book and the maze were one and the same thing' (Borges 1970: 50), *House of Leaves* is both a book that enables the reader to re-enact the disorientation it describes, and the ultimate 'ghost of the counterfeit' (Hogle 2000), a Gothic simulacrum with no original.

The development of Gothic in the twentieth century, then, is bound up with an interrogation of the crucial elements of revenant history and claustrophobic space that have always been defining features of Gothic. Twentieth-century texts are rarely naïve in their exploitation of Gothic conventions, and whether writing in the 'popular' horror tradition of Lovecraft and Stephen King, or the 'high'-cultural one of Bowen, Barnes, Carter and Danielewski, they signal their debt to previous generations of Gothic writers. It is sometimes only by reading them in the light of these previous generations – for example, in the case of Bowen – that their Gothic aspect emerges. Nevertheless it is simplistic to say that Gothic is merely a counter-tradition to the high-cultural narrative of the twentieth century – if anything, the opposite is true, and by the opening decade of the twenty-first century Gothic has become one of the most crucial and widely used modes in contemporary fiction.

WORKS CITED

Baldick, Chris and Robert Mighall (2000) 'Gothic Criticism', in David Punter (ed.), *A Companion to the Gothic*, Oxford: Blackwell.

Barnes, Djuna (1963) *Nightwood*, London: Faber and Faber.

Borges, Jorge Luis (1970) *Labyrinths*, London: Penguin.

Bowen, Elizabeth (1998) *The Death of the Heart*, London: Vintage.

—— (1999) *Collected Stories*, London: Vintage.

Carter, Angela (1981) 'The Lady of the House of Love', in *The Bloody Chamber*, London: Penguin.

Eco, Umberto (2000) '*Casablanca*: Cult Movies and Intertextual Collage', in David Lodge with Nigel Wood (eds), *Modern Criticism and Theory: A Reader*, rev. edn, London: Longman.

Fiedler, Leslie (1982) *Love and Death in the American Novel*, rev. 3rd edn, New York: Stein and Day.

Hogle, Jerrold (2000) 'The Gothic Ghost of the Counterfeit and the Progress of Abjection', in David Punter (ed.), *A Companion to the Gothic*, Oxford: Blackwell.

Hurley, Kelly (2001) 'The Modernist Abominations of William Hope Hodgson', in Andrew Smith and Jeff Wallace (eds), *Gothic Modernisms*, Basingstoke: Palgrave.

Hutcheon, Linda (1998) *A Poetics of Postmodernism: History, Theory, Fiction*, London: Routledge.

Jameson, Fredric (1991) *Postmodernism, or the Cultural Logic of Late Capitalism*, London: Verso.

Light, Alison (1991) *Forever England: Femininity, Literature and Conservatism Between the Wars*, London: Routledge.

Lovecraft, H. P. (1999) 'Celephaïs', in *The Call of Cthulu and Other Weird Stories*, ed. S. T. Joshi, London: Penguin.

McGrath, Patrick (2001) *Martha Peake*, London: Penguin.

Meisel, Perry (1987) *The Myth of the Modern: A Study in British Literature and Criticism After 1850*, New Haven, CT: Yale University Press.

Miles, Robert (1993) *Gothic Writing 1750–1820: A Genealogy*, London: Routledge.

O'Donnell, Patrick (1995) 'Faulkner and Postmodernism', in Philip M. Weinstein (ed.), *The Cambridge Companion to William Faulkner*, Cambridge: Cambridge University Press.

Punter, David and Glennis Byron (2004) *The Gothic*, Oxford: Blackwell.

Sedgwick, Eve Kosofsky (1986) *The Coherence of Gothic Conventions*, rev. edn, London: Methuen.

Smith, Allan Lloyd (1996) 'Postmodernism/Gothicism', in Victor Sage and Allan Lloyd Smith (eds), *Modern Gothic: A Reader*, Manchester: Manchester University Press.

Wicke, Jennifer (1992) 'Vampiric Typewriting: *Dracula* and its Media', *ELH*, 59(2): 467–93.

Woolf, Virginia (1988) 'Gothic Romance' and 'Character in Fiction', in Andrew McNeillie (ed.), *The Essays of Virginia Woolf,* vol. 3: *1919–1924*, London: The Hogarth Press.

Part II
GOTHIC LOCATIONS

7

GOTHIC LOCATIONS

CATHERINE SPOONER AND EMMA MCEVOY

This section is informed by one of the newest areas of academic study of the Gothic: the exploration of location and of national tradition. Loosely speaking, it represents an attempt to map out the geographies of Gothic fiction through an emphasis on the countries and regions it originates from and/or depicts. In doing so, it hopes to demonstrate both the global diversity of anglophone forms of the Gothic and some of the features that these diverse texts share.

The following essays largely choose to approach Gothic geographies through national traditions rather than spatial tropes – in other words they look at the transformations that Gothic undergoes when transplanted from its English origins into a variety of other global environments, rather than exploring such familiar settings as ancestral houses, decrepit castles, precipitous mountains and windswept moors. Interestingly, although this approach would seem to privilege geography over history and space over time, many of the essays in this section are among the most historicist in this volume. Definition of national identity or literary tradition is bound up with the historical forces that shaped that identity or that tradition. Moreover the diasporic spread of Gothic from England to Scotland, Ireland, North America, Australasia and beyond is inescapably the movement of colonial expansion. Whether framed in terms of struggle with England's central rulership, the legacies of imperialism, or those of slavery, each of these modes of 'national Gothic' are structured by a common narrative of the buried past that rises up to haunt the present.

There are two significant effects of thinking about Gothic in this context. The first of these is a repeated concern, in many of these essays, with the notion of dialogue – of 'writing back' both to oppressors and to the 'traditional' Gothic novel itself. 'Writing back' is a concept we readily associate with postcolonial writing, explored here in essays by Coral Ann Howells, Ken Gelder, and James Procter and Angela Smith. For Howells and Gelder, Canadian and Australian Gothic offer a flexible medium for both the exploration of white settler fears, and contemporary indigenous writers' revisioning of diverse forms of 'haunting'. Procter and Smith challenge simplistic divisions between 'colonial' and 'postcolonial' Gothic, suggesting that colonial-era texts by Dickens and Kipling 'offer a critique of the empire from within', while not quite achieving the 'Janus-faced' political complexities of contemporary writers. From a somewhat different political and historical perspective, Teresa A. Goddu also utilises the theme of 'writing back' in her detailed analysis of Hannah Craft's *The Bondwoman's Narrative*, demonstrating that American Gothic bears indelible traces of the country's dark history of slavery, and that this national narrative is used not only by white Americans to explore their guilty heritage, but also by black Americans in 'complex and revisionary ways' to delineate their oppression.

As Richard Haslam and Angela Wright demonstrate, 'writing back' is also strongly associated with a 'pre-postcolonial' tradition in Scotland and Ireland, where writers exploited a Gothic idiom in order to negotiate national identities separate from that of England, and the terms of the Gothic itself. Haslam turns to the tradition of critical writing on Irish Gothic, noting that 'the term "Irish Gothic" generates as many questions as it appears to answer'. He stresses the 'political intricacy' of Irish Gothic and issues a firm warning to critics against the tendency to 'allegoresis', that is the tendency to read Irish Gothic works as if they were providing an allegory of the political situation. For Haslam this tendency is reductive and fails to do justice to the wealth and complexity of the many and varied texts of the Irish Gothic tradition. Angela Wright's essay avoids the charge of allegoresis as she seeks to uncover the political heritage of Scottish Gothic. Wright examines the relation between historical and Gothic fiction in the Scottish tradition and finds a recurring concern within Scottish Gothic with the 'process of uncovering histories'. She notes that 'Graves, castles, manuscripts and inscriptions are all warmly-contested sites of authenticity and authority' and suggests that 'national curation becomes the collective enterprise of Scottish Gothic'.

The other effect of thinking about Gothic in terms of space is one identified by Robert Mighall in his seminal book *A Geography of Victorian Gothic Fiction: Mapping History's Nightmares* (1999), which pioneered a geographical approach to Gothic. Mighall shows how in Gothic fiction, space characteristically becomes historicised and history becomes spatialised. Mighall's essay for this volume enables contrasts between two favourite Gothic locations, London and New Orleans, by exploring the significance of the urban environment to Gothic. If many of the other essays in this section emphasise the terrors of the wilderness, then Mighall shows that the metropolis has its own Gothic conventions.

This section does not claim to be comprehensive. We have, for the most part, chosen to focus on locations where the production of the narrative and the national identity of the writer are bound up with the geographical setting, such as America and Scotland, rather than the fantasised Mediterranean and Oriental locations of the earliest English Gothic novels. We have also, regretfully, chosen to confine analysis to anglophone traditions. There are distinct and important modes of Gothic associated with French, German and other European literatures, and latterly with Japanese literature and film, but for reasons of space and linguistic consistency we have had to exclude them.

We hope that the approaches outlined here will inspire readers to go on to explore the significance of their own chosen Gothic locations. As Freud suggests in his essay on 'The Uncanny' (1919), there is a particular class of the frightening associated with what is closest to home. Study of Gothic locations is about broad national traditions, but it is also about the specificity of place: the particular fears associated with Tasmania or Tennessee. As such, any collection of essays on Gothic locations can never hope to be comprehensive; rather, it offers a map with plenty of uncharted territory still to explore: in the words of the old sea-charts: 'Here Be Monsters'.

8

GOTHIC CITIES

ROBERT MIGHALL

The term 'urban Gothic' should be a contradiction in terms. For the first generation of Gothic novels it would have been. The Gothic depicted what the city
(civilisation) banished or refused to acknowledge, except in the form of thrilling
fictions. As Victor Sage explains, the 'paradigm of the horror-plot is the journey
from the capital to the provinces' (Sage 1988: 8). The sublime, rugged landscapes of southern France, Italy or Spain, the deep forests or craggy peaks of
Germany, were at the furthest remove from London or Bath; and were therefore the sanctioned preserve of terrors. Even when an incident takes place in
Rome or Madrid, the Protestant mind assumed that such cities institutionalised
unreason. Whilst Ann Radcliffe's *The Italian* opens just outside Naples around
the date of publication (1797), the first scene dramatises the outrage felt by an
English tourist who discovers that the law of 'sanctuary' (the protection of crimi-
nals on sanctified ground) still operates in this age of general reason.

However, within a generation, such divisions and disavowals collapsed. By
the early Victorian period, ideas of centre and margin were (ostensibly) overturned, as London, the very epicentre of the civilised world, became also, and in
time pre-eminently, one of the dark places of the earth. This essay provides
some coordinates of the urban Gothic geography. It focuses principally on
London and New Orleans as the quintessential Gothic cities: respectively, the
birth and current resting places of urban Gothic representation.

PLACE AND MEMORY

As the early Gothic banished horrors to the margins, so the Gothic entered the
capital initially by obeying similar rules, adapted to the circumstances of the
modern metropolis. The first wave of urban Gothic fiction followed the
emerging discourse of urban reform by focusing on the enclaves and subcultures
of 'outcast London'. G. W. M. Reynolds's *Mysteries of London* (1844–8) used
Gothic conventions to dramatise a deeply divided society. His description of an
area known as the 'Old Mint' establishes some of the key dimensions of urban
Gothic:

> The houses are old, gloomy and sombre . . . Most of the doors stand open, and
> reveal low, dark, and filthy passages, the mere aspect of which [. . . inspires fears]
> of being suddenly dragged into those sinister dens, which seem fitted for crimes of
> the blackest dye.
> This is no exaggeration.

> Even in the day-time one shudders at the cut-throat appearance of the places into the full depths of whose gloom the eye cannot entirely penetrate. But, by night, the Mint . . . is far more calculated to inspire the boldest heart with alarm, than the thickest forest or the wildest heath ever infested by banditti.
>
> (Reynolds 1846: II, 187)

The area is obscure (over the river), and has a distinctive character established through Reynolds's conscious evocation of set-piece Gothic sublimity. The urban version, however, surpasses the original. Its terrors are real, here, and now. There is also a measure of the 'historicity' essential to, if not the defining principle of, Gothic fiction, in Reynolds's depiction of this outrage. Reynolds continues: 'The Mint was once a sanctuary . . . and although the law has deprived it of its ancient privileges, its inhabitants still maintain them, by a tacit understanding' (II, 187). Reynolds points to a fundamental of Gothic representation: the persistence of historical memory. For the urban Gothic this meant the criminal past haunting the civic present. Contemporary London is thus no better, or rather no less Gothic, than Naples for Radcliffe, the last resting place of 'medieval' barbarism. As Reynolds remarked of West Smithfield: 'Civilisation appear[s] to have chosen particular places which it condescended to visit, and to have passed others by' (I, 22). The premise of Gothic fiction, dividing the civilised from the barbarous, the progressive from the retrograde or anachronistic, is here located in the metropolis of the modern world.[1]

FOG EVERYWHERE

It is incongruity – contemporary with, but being removed from the modern city – that creates the terrors of Reynolds's Gothic London. Its dangers derive from the proximity of these two distinct worlds. These divisions and segregations, however, started to blur or be overturned as the century progressed, enabling different forms of terror to be imagined. Charles Dickens's *Bleak House* (1854) plays a key role here. For if Reynolds, and indeed Dickens's own novel *Oliver Twist* (1837–8), portrayed a deeply divided London, *Bleak House* collapses the divisions between lawbound and outlawed, distant and the proximate. For the law itself is at the very centre of the urban labyrinth:

> The raw afternoon is rawest, and the dense fog is densest, and the muddy streets are muddiest, near that leaden-headed old obstruction, appropriate ornament for the threshold of a leaden-headed old corporation: Temple Bar. And hard by Temple Bar, in Lincoln's Inn Hall, at the very heart of the fog, sits the Lord High Chancellor in his High Court of Chancery.
>
> (Dickens 1996: 14)

We are used to talking about a work's 'atmosphere', something the Gothic has in abundance. Here the term is literal. Whilst the earlier Gothic novelists (following Shakespeare) exploited the sublime potential of storms – Maturin's

Melmoth rarely appears without the full artillery of the heavens accompanying him – Dickens adds fog to the Gothic meteorological repertoire. His fog-bound labyrinth, holding secrets at every turn, lays the foundations for a second wave of urban Gothic representation, best exemplified by Stevenson's *Strange Case of Doctor Jekyll and Mr Hyde* (1886). Stevenson's much-quoted description of foggy Soho as 'like the district of some city in a nightmare', guarantees the role of this element in late-Victorian urban horror. This 'great chocolate-coloured pall' (Stevenson 2002: 23) overhangs the literary, visual and cinematic imaginary, decades after the great pea-soupers have departed.

Fog is a supremely sublime element, bringing the essential 'obscurity' that Burke put at the very heart of terror. It also points to the problematic of visibility and knowledge with which the novella is obsessed. The fog obscures, but also reveals, the true character of the city. The 'London particular', was not always that particular about where it drifted, and could potentially lend 'nightmare' properties to any district. Its mobility and obscurity are emblematic of the terrors of the tale, and of late-Victorian urban Gothic. Fog makes certainty difficult, and yet reveals the city's sinister and menacing aspect: much like Jekyll's misty potion, and much like his house. Jekyll's mansion is the antithesis of the rookery hovel. Step round the corner, to what appears to be an altogether different district, and there is that sinister-looking door. The occult obscures both physical and urban 'physiognomy' here, as bodies and postcodes no longer provide reliable indexes to urban horror. Small wonder sightings started to imagine the Whitechapel murderer carrying a doctor's bag, and the police started looking in W1 rather than E1 for the Ripper. Small wonder we imagine the Ripper's crimes to be swathed in banks of swirling fog, despite the fact that he conducted most of his crimes under clear Whitechapel skies.

When Peter Ackroyd evokes the *fin-de-siècle* urban crimescape for his 1994 novel *Dan Leno and the Limehouse Golem*, it is with an archly anxious awareness of his own belatedness. As he doth protest: 'The notorious pea-soupers of the period, so ably memorialised by Robert Louis Stevenson and Arthur Conan Doyle, were quite as dark as their literary reputation would suggest' (Ackroyd 1994: 43).

As Reynolds and Dickens needed to challenge the conventions of the early Gothic when they situated it in the heart of London, so Ackroyd has to reassert the veracity of his own representations. This time it is to combat cliché rather than scepticism, as his own fiction creates a heavily mediated stage-set of urban Gothic horror: 'Some wreathes of it [fog] lingered about him as he walked into the great entrance hall, and for a moment he resembled some pantomime demon rising onto the stage' (1994: 43). Ackroyd's works offer one final turn of the urban Gothic screw for London, acknowledging and adapting versions of what went before. Ackroyd sees the Gothic skull beneath the modern skin of steel and glass. Haunted by absence rather than presence, his 'psychogeographical' London is a palimpsest of memories. His fiction performs a 'séance' for the city's dark voices, obsessively haunting many of the sites of historical resonance that fascinated the first wave of urban Gothicists. Thus, in Ackroyd's *Hawksmoor* (1985) the very foundations of the architect's churches (Spitalfields, Shoreditch, Shadwell, St Giles) are steeped in the blood of originary crimes that are re-enacted in the present day. Such emphases resurrect the logic of topographical 'survival' that informed Reynolds' and others' interest in the rookeries and former sanctuaries of London. The premise that first sanctioned a Gothic of the city returns in the arcane imaginings of this (post)modern heir to Dickens.[2]

So what makes the urban Gothic? For Gothic *of* a city rather than just in a city, that city needs a concentration of memories and historical associations. Ideally these would be expressed in an extant architectural or topographical heritage, as these areas provide the natural home for ghostly presences of imagined/projected meanings. Paris offers an interesting counterpart to London in this respect. Here the combined efforts of Mme La Guillotine and Baron Haussmann ensured it had a very different relationship with its past. Paris, even before the grand boulevards of Haussmann, was the model of a rational city, with a system of squares linked by broad thoroughfares. The labyrinthine Court of Miracles was but a legend when Hugo's *Notre Dame de Paris* was published (1831), and whilst Eugène Sue's *Mysteries of Paris* (1842) (Reynolds' immediate model) explores the Parisian underworld of the present day, the focus is far less topographical than in Reynolds or Dickens, relying on melodramatic incident and character rather than specific location to figure the horrors of criminality. An ordered visible city requires a different spatial model for its horrors. Horrors cannot lurk in isolated forgotten pockets, as they were once imagined doing in that chaotic collection of villages we call 'London'. So in Paris they hid underground. Hugo's *Les Misérables* (1862) literalises the idea of a criminal 'underworld', using the Parisian sewers as the dark and mysterious counterpart of the world above. *The Phantom of the Opera* (1910) reinforces this emphasis. Under the baroque splendour of the Opera are the cellars, complete with fiendish torture chamber. So when Anne Rice's vampires come to Paris, their natural home in the Théâtre des Vampires is an obvious recreation of Leroux's model. Subterranean Gothic has proved eminently useful for populating modern cities with terrors. Since Wells' Morlocks set the pattern, the freaks have gone underground, and come up at night to haunt the post-industrial cityscape. In T. E. D. Klein's 'Children of the Kingdom' (1984), and Whitley Streiber's *The Wolfen* (1978), mutant terrors lurk within and beneath the decaying infrastructure of the rational, grid-like New York City, and prey on the world that has swept them out of sight. Indeed, the fear of what lies beneath the ostensible modern sunlit world is most powerfully evoked in American Gothic fiction, and it is in the New World that the true successor to London is found. New Orleans is perhaps now the quintessential Gothic city, as responses to Hurricane Katrina sadly reinforced.

NEW WORLD, OLD FEARS

New World Gothic should be another contradiction in terms. As Nathaniel Hawthorne famously decreed, the Gothic, like ivy, needed ruins; and in America there is 'no shadow, no antiquity, no mystery, no picturesque and gloomy wrong' (Hawthorne 1990: 3). Of course his own works belie this claim. The Seven-Gabled House is as steeped in bad memories and buried crimes as any Italian castle or former urban sanctuary. 'Gloomy wrong', guilt and nemesis are the master-plots of American Gothic. It is a big paranoid country, guiltily aware that it has taken the land away from people, and taken other people away from their lands: hence the symbolic importance of land, and what lies beneath it, in fictions from Hawthorne to Stephen King. The Indian burial grounds that lie beneath the haunted edifices in *The Shining* (1980), and *The Amityville Horror* (1979) and *Poltergeist* (1982) entail indelible stains of guilty horror that erupt to damn the new masters of this nation. In New Orleans this guilt has another dimension, reflecting the peculiar history of the South.

PRE-AMERICAN CITY

New Orleans is the haunted house of un-American activities, an outpost of the Old World even up until relatively recently. *Deliverance* (1972) (set in North Carolina) and *Southern Comfort* (1981) (on the Louisiana swamps) follow similar plotlines: outsiders menaced by remote and regressive country folk who resent their intrusion. Whilst the inbred hillbillies of Carolina are scary in their own right, the Cajuns out on the swamps surrounding New Orleans have never conformed to the language and laws of America. This anomalous status within the newly formed union was what principally marked out New Orleans as a prime Gothic location. Edward King's picturesque travelogue, *The Great South* (1875) sums up the northern post-bellum attitude to the vanquished South in his introduction to New Orleans, the first port of call in his survey. For King, Louisiana typifies the conflict between 'the picturesque and unjust civilization of the past . . . and the prosaic leveling civilization of the present' (King 1875: 17). Of the French Quarter he asserts: 'This is not an American scene, and one almost persuades himself that this is Europe, although ten minutes of rapid walking will bring him to streets and squares as generically American as any in Boston, Chicago, or St Louis' (1875: 19). A familiar inference: that civilisation is partial, and that certain locations can occupy a different (earlier) temporal zone to the normative one of the observer. A similar (albeit more sympathetic) insistence on New Orleans being a place apart informs the works of George Washington Cable. Cable's *Old Creole Days* (1883) and *Strange True Stories of Louisiana* (1888) helped ensure that what King found 'picturesque' translated into the fertile ground for mystery and terror that the city has become. Cable's tale of 'The "Haunted House" in Royal Street' opens with an invitation to reverse the direction imagined by King. He invites his reader to turn from the

American Quarter, which shows that the city 'belongs to the living present, and has serious practical relations with these United States and this great living world and age' (Cable 1999: 192), and visit a particular house on Royal Street, associated with a 'strange true story'. It is this indeterminate status between now and then, New World and Old World, central and peripheral, that gives his tales and the pictures he paints of the city their resonance. This resonance echoes through its representation even today.

The tale he tells about the house originates from the 1830s, when, he claims: 'The Americans were just beginning in public matters to hold the odds. In private society the Creoles still held power, but it was slipping from them even there' (1999: 202–3). It is the private realm – what goes on behind the shutters of those old houses – that Cable explores in his tales. Ugly rumours start to circulate about what goes on in Madame Lalaurie's house. A fire breaks out, the populace seizes its chance to breach the privacy of the house, and terrible revelations emerge. The crowd finds emaciated slaves in chains, and the remains of others buried in the grounds: 'The most savage heart could not have witnessed the spectacle unmoved' (1999: 210). Madame Lalaurie flees, pursued by the mob, and escapes by schooner, perhaps to Paris. Back to the Old World where such 'gloomy wrongs' surely belong.

The horrors derive from the bad old days of slavery. Cable makes that clear; but the townspeople, who are part of that age and order, are horrified by what they discover. This transcends even the cruelty of those cruel days, partly exonerating the vanquished order by recognising, even then, acceptable and unacceptable levels of 'domestic discipline' (1999: 207). The memories linger, however. Rumours of ghosts replace those of cruelty, and set the house apart as haunted.

PRETERNATURAL CITY

New Orleans' allegiances make it a temporal and cultural anomaly, a breach in the fabric of time and space. Ghosts and other Old World demons naturally slip through, finding it a conducive port for entering the New World. Anne Rice, heir to Cable as the city's principal mythologiser, acknowledges this when Louis, her vampiric interviewee, recollects the world Cable shows in retreat:

> This was New Orleans, a magical and magnificent place to live. In which a vampire, richly dressed and gracefully walking through the pools of light of one gas lamp after another might attract no more notice in the evening than hundreds of other exotic creatures.
>
> (Rice 1977: 45–6)

It is a city made for vampires, then, and possibly now. For as (the 200-year-old) Louis continues:

even when the gas lamps went out and the planes came in and the office buildings crowded the blocks of Canal Street, something irreducible of beauty and romance remained; not in every street perhaps, but in so many that the landscape is for me the landscape of those times always, and walking now in the starlit streets of the Quarter or the Garden District I am in those times again . . . the moon that rose over New Orleans then still rises. As long as the monuments stand, it still rises.

(1977: 46)

This comes pretty close to providing a manifesto for New Orleans' urban Gothic status. The monumental record attests to its function (etymologically) as the marker of memories; the repository of pastness, through its relative antiquity. It makes it a place where a vampire might still feel at home. Rice is to Cable what Ackroyd was to Reynolds or Dickens. The fabric retains memories that make it the legitimate preserve of Gothic representation. After Transylvania it is now probably the place most readily associated with vampires. The Gothic is still a semi-official facet of the city's image.

Rice did not do this alone, of course. Her works built on fertile ground, renewing the city's pledge to the Gothic, and providing a highly popular focal point for a cultural and counter-cultural nexus of various histories, legends and traditions. There is the voodoo tradition that bubbles under, and infuses with the European references found in both Cable's and Rice's depiction of a melting-pot of cultures. *Angel Heart* (1987) and more recently *Skeleton Key* (2005) both exploited these traditions associated with the city and its environs. They stage powerful Gothic dramas that feed off the highly charged atmosphere of ancient magic and buried guilt that rises up from the swampy terrain surrounding the city. Both films look beyond the Quarter and even the city itself to tap into another important dimension to New Orleans' Gothic status: its geography.

PERIPHERAL CITY

If London Gothic was found initially in isolated vestiges nestling cheek-by-jowl within the modern fabric of the city, then New Orleans suggests a different spatial model. The Gothic is found on the edge. This goes for the city in relation to 'official' American identity (and especially Bible Belt America which it neighbours), and perhaps now applies within New Orleans itself. Whilst the Quarter and the Garden District can seem at times like tourist stage-sets, the hinterlands beyond, the swamps and bayous surrounding the city that have (until recently) provided the last refuge of the un-American, perhaps provide more potent grounds for Gothic imaginings.

As modernity started to lap up against even the picturesque 'Quarter', the Gothic was pushed even further out. Washington Cable's most famous Gothic tale 'Jean-ah Poquelin' shows this happening. Again, Cable situates his tale on the cusp:

In the first decade of the present century . . . when the Anglo-American flood that was presently to burst in a crevasse of immigration upon the delta had thus far been felt only as slippery seepage which made the Creole tremble for his footing.

(Cable 1991: 179)

The tale once more involves a house: 'an old colonial plantation-house half in ruin' (1991: 179) on the edge of the city. It belongs to Jean Marie Poquelin, a Creole 'adventurer', who has shut himself away with one last slave since his return from the Guinea coast many years before. His beloved brother had not been seen since the expedition they both set out on, and the chattering town suspects some 'witchery [or] devilish crime', and persecutes the old Creole. Jean's social isolation is figured topographically: the old house: 'stood aloof from civilization, the tracts that had once been its indigo fields given over to their first noxious wilderness, [had] grown into one of the horridest marshes within a circuit of fifty miles' (1991: 179). Jean's house is a final bastion of old civilisation. It stands against modernity and the expanding city on the one side, and the morass of a marshy nature that is slowly reclaiming what the retreating civilisation once attempted to achieve. Cable translates the House of Usher into historical allegory: 'The house was on a slightly raised spot, the levee of a draining canal. The waters did not run; they crawled, and were full of big, ravening fish and alligators, that held it against all comers' (1991: 180). The modern tide eventually has its way, compelling the house's secret inhabitants to retreat fully into this pre-civilised wilderness. The last we see of Jean-ah Poquelin is his dead body, held aloft by his loyal slave walking into the malarial swamps, accompanied by Jean's 'long-hidden brother – a leper, as white as snow' (1991: 209).

The Crescent City is surrounded by the waters from which it was reclaimed. In the swamps and the bayous lurk terrors, both natural and cultural. From escaped slaves or remote Cajun communities, to the snakes, alligators and leprous fevers Cable alludes to, the fauna and flora of these waterlands have for a long time been the repository for the unknown or the best-to-be-forgotten. Edward King's tour of 1874 moved from the Quarter to the swamp lands beyond, discovering a 'tract of hopelessly irreclaimable, grotesque water wilderness' (King 1875: 170). A heart of darkness and fearful ruination within the bright new Yankee republic. The swamp is a synecdoche for the vanquished order, to be claimed by modernity, or abandoned to the primal, fearful forces that lie just beyond or just beneath it.

This brings us back to where we started, with the originary definition of Gothic space as that which civilisation rejects or demonises. My cartography of urban Gothic would have ended here if Hurricane Katrina had not hit. When the hurricane made landfall on 29 August 2005, the symbolic geography I have been describing reasserted itself. It is difficult not to re-run Cable's Gothic allegory. Caught between the tide of 'civilisation' (American-style) and the fearsome forces of nature, the dispossessed (society's lepers) were left to the waters that reclaimed the city. Abandoned by God and by America, nature takes the city back to the swamp. This new Gothic did not find its setting in the pictur-esque French Quarter. The spectres emerged from the poor wards and housing projects existing beneath the waterline and the poverty line. Tales of rape, murder and cannibalism proliferated. As the mayor of Baton Rouge warned when his parish was to provide shelter: 'we do not want . . . that breed that seeks to prey on other people' (Yonge 2005). New Orleans's vampiric reputation obvi-ously preceded it. John Powers, writing in *LA Weekly*, looked back on a week of news coverage of the disaster and voiced a familiar refrain: 'put simply: this couldn't be America'. Maybe it is not. Powers' piece is entitled 'The Week of the Living Dead', comparing what was exposed by events to a 'George Romero horror movie where the living dead become a metaphor for everything white consumer society wants to repress – powerless black people, dying people' (Powers 2005). The Gothic is a natural form of reference here, as guilts and fears deeply lodged in the national psyche erupt from this city on the edges of that brave New World and those united states.

NOTES

1 For a much fuller exploration of how Reynolds, and his model Dickens, helped make London Gothic, see 'From Udolpho to Spitalfields', in Mighall (1999: 27–78).
2 On how the urban Gothic survives in the fictions of, amongst other, Ackroyd and Iain Sinclair, see Roger Luckhurst's 'Occult London', in Kerr and Gibson (2003: 335–40); on how criminal associations still haunt the topographical imaginary of London see my 'Crime and Memory in the Capital', pp. 371–6 of the same volume.

WORKS CITED

Ackroyd, Peter (1994) *Dan Leno and the Limehouse Golem*, Harmondsworth: Penguin.
Cable, George Washington (1991) *Old Creole Days*, Gretna, LA: Pelican.
—— (1999) *Strange True Stories of Louisiana*, Gretna, LA: Pelican.
Dickens, Charles (1996) *Bleak House*, ed. Nicola Bradbury, Harmondsworth: Penguin.
Hawthorne, Nathaniel (1990) *The Marble Faun*, ed. Richard H. Brodhead, New York: Penguin.
Kerr, Joe and Andrew Gibson (eds) (2003) *London: From Punk to Blair*, London: Reak-tion.
King, Edward (1875) *The Great South: A Record of Journeys in Louisiana, Texas, [etc.]*, Hartford, CT: American Publishing Co.
Mighall, Robert (1999) *A Geography of Victorian Gothic Fiction: Mapping History's Night-mares*, Oxford: Oxford University Press.
Powers, John (2005) 'Week of the Living Dead', *LA Weekly*, 8 September.
Reynolds, G. W. M. (1846) *The Mysteries of London*, 2 vols, London: George Vickers.
Rice, Anne (1977) *Interview with the Vampire*, London: Futura.
Sage, Victor (1988) *Horror Fiction in the Protestant Tradition*, Basingstoke: Macmillan.
Stevenson, Robert Louis (2002) *The Strange Case of Dr Jekyll and Mr Hyde and Other Tales of Terror*, ed. Robert Mighall, Harmondsworth: Penguin.
Yonge, Gary (2005) 'Murder and Rape – Fact or Fiction?', *The Guardian*, 6 September.

9

AMERICAN GOTHIC

TERESA A. GODDU

American Gothic, like Gothic more generally, is haunted by history. Instead of fleeing reality, Gothic registers its culture's anxieties and social problems. Often framed in terms of institutional power and oppression, Gothic records the pleasures and costs of particular social systems. Issuing from the context of New World slavery, American Gothic tells stories of racial desire and dread, of economic instability and anxiety. In eighteenth- and nineteenth-century US literature and beyond, the spectre of slavery often inhabits Gothic texts, conjuring forth how American Gothic's psychological and physical terror and its racialised narratives of darkness are grounded in the everyday realities of chattel slavery. From Poe's tales of terror to Toni Morrison's ghost story, *Beloved* (1987), the Gothic becomes the mode through which to speak what often remains unspeakable within the American national narrative – the crime of slavery.

Over and over again, American authors turn to the Gothic mode in order to disclose the ghostly origins of the nation as issuing from the oppressive social structure of slavery. Crevecoeur's mythic idyll of New World innocence, *Letters from an American Farmer* (1782), for example, is interrupted and destabilised by a Gothic scene of the living spectre of a caged slave being eaten alive by birds. Hawthorne's Gothic romance of hereditary sin, *The House of the Seven Gables* (1851), traces the family's illicit wealth both to their violent usurpation of Native American land and to their appropriation of the working-class labour of the 'blackened' Maule family, thereby exposing how the nation was built upon the stolen labour and property of racialised others. Poe's Gothic tale, 'The Black Cat' (1843), discloses the dangerous dependencies and murderous sentiments that lie uneasily at the heart of domestic slavery as well as the extent to which slavery undergirds the nation's most cherished domestic institution, the home. Frederick Douglass's *Narrative* (1845) rewrites the traditional trajectory of the American autobiography in Gothic terms when he describes slavery as a hell peopled by monstrous masters and as a nightmare from which he cannot awake. Similarly, Morrison's *Beloved* pictures American history as a haunted house, from which slavery's legacy of grief and horror cannot be exorcised. The United States, as many American Gothic texts argue, is built on economic exploitation and racial terror.

In focusing on slavery, the American Gothic also lays bare the unequal and fiercely competitive market structures that constitute the American myth of freedom and equality. Like the British Gothic, the American Gothic chronicles the rise of the market economy and an emerging middle-class subjectivity. However, in portraying a market economy where persons hold the status of property, the American Gothic necessarily views economic imperatives and class formation through the lens of race. In reading race as imbricated with class in the American Gothic, the critical commonplace – that the British Gothic is about class and that the American Gothic is about race – is complicated. If, as H. L. Malchow has shown, the British Gothic is also haunted by cultural and racial difference, the American Gothic unveils the racial affiliations that structure class formation. Hannah Crafts' *The Bondwoman's Narrative*, a slave narrative written as a full-blown Gothic novel, exemplifies not only how the curse of slavery hovers over the American Gothic, but also how its racialised narratives work to reveal the costs of capitalism even as they coalesce its class distinctions.

Recently recovered and published for the first time by Henry Louis Gates Jr in 2002, *The Bondwoman's Narrative*, a nineteenth-century fictionalised first-person account of slavery, deploys typical Gothic features: haunted houses and desolate ruins, family secrets and hereditary curses, persecuted heroines and evil villains, the oppression of tyranny and the spectacle of suffering.[1] The narrative's primal curse – 'the legend of the Linden' (Crafts 2002: 25) – exemplifies its vision of slavery as a Gothic institution. Lindendale, a southern plantation built by Sir Clifford de Vincent, a former British aristocrat, is haunted by one particularly vicious scene of punishment. Angered by Rose, an aged slave who refuses to kill her pet dog as he demands, Sir Clifford suspends her and the dog from a linden tree by iron hoops; they hang there under his cold, watchful eye until they become 'wan and ghastly' corpses (25). The linden tree is the sign both of the plantation's wealth – 'it had grown and flourished exceedingly under' Sir Clifford's management (20) – and of the violence of dispossession that undergirds Lindendale's prosperity: 'Many a time had its roots been manured with human blood' (21). The murder of Rose is representative of the systematic torture that sustains slavery; her death is particularly horrifying because it exposes the master's cruelty not simply as a quest for power but as a failure of feeling. His punishment is described as 'unnatural' and 'unmerited' (21). His 'appalling indifference' to suffering – he is unmoved by the woman's wailing, the dog's howling, the tree's creaking and his wife's entreaties – marks him, rather than the slave or the animal, as inhuman (23). While Rose's suffering and compassion for the dog emblematises the slave's martyrdom – her ability to maintain her spiritual values despite enduring bodily torture – the master's lack of humanity is reflected in his act of brutality toward the dog. In killing the dog, described as 'white and shaggy, with great speaking eyes, full of intelligence, and bearing a strong resemblance to those of a child', the master also murders his own humanity (21). Slavery, the narrative argues, transforms the master into a monster. Rose's dying curse, naturalised in the 'dull horrible creaking' of the linden tree (29), traces all of the family's misfortunes to the sin of slavery:

In sunshine and shadow, by day and by night I will brood over this tree, and weigh down its branches, and when death, or sickness, or misfortune is to befall the family ye may listen for ye will assuredly hear the creaking of its limbs.

(25)

The curse of slavery promises to haunt the family forever.

The 'legend of the Linden' encapsulates many of the key characteristics of American Gothic. First and foremost, it exemplifies how Gothic – like the linden tree whose eerie creaking conjures forth the torture of Rose as well as the mistreatment of innumerable others – is rooted in the violence and horrors of history. Despite its supernatural effects and its persecuted psyches, Gothic's terrors are neither imaginary nor individual. In exposing the materialist roots of Gothic, the 'legend of the Linden' also makes clear the structural affinity between the discourse of slavery and the conventions of the Gothic. The everyday realities of slavery are already coded in Gothic terms: slavery is a system of merciless horrors, a diabolical dungeon of bondage. In stating that her narrative is a 'record of plain unvarnished facts' (4), Hannah Crafts insists that the terrors she describes are actual rather than imaginary. By presenting the Gothic as a realistic mode, Crafts reveals its reliance upon slavery for its icon-ography and its haunting effects. Slavery provides American Gothic with its tools of terror as well as its anxiety and dread. The ominous creaking of the Linden tree, which echoes throughout Craft's narrative filling its interlocutors' 'bosoms with supernatural dread' (25), derives its force not from an imaginary or generalisable source but from the actual atrocities of slavery that it explicitly memorialises.

The 'legend of the Linden', then, underscores American Gothic's engage-ment with the project of documenting the horrors of history. Moreover, in bearing witness to slavery's atrocities, American Gothic enables the objects of terror and torture to haunt back. Sir Clifford may demonise Rose as an 'old witch' (23), turning her, through his brutality, into a living corpse – 'her rigid features assumed a collapsed and corpse-like hue and appearance, her eyes seemed starting from their sockets, and her protruding tongue refused to articu-late a sound' (23) – but as a ghostly spectre, who speaks in a 'deep sepulchral tone' (25), she is no longer mute. Her curse transforms her from a 'helpless object of [Sir Clifford's] wrath' (25) into a subject who can articulate the meaning of her own suffering. Refusing to be cut down from the tree, she intones: 'I will hang here till I die as a curse to this house, and I will come here after I am dead to prove its bane' (25). Turning herself into a ghost who will haunt the family's ancestral home, Rose transfers the slave's terror of possession to the master.

Rose's ghost story, like Crafts' narrative more generally, revises American Gothic's racialised discourse of demonised difference. In depicting Sir Clifford's cruelty and cold contempt as monstrous, Crafts demonises whiteness instead of blackness while also critiquing the distancing sensationalism of the Gothic mode. In this scene Crafts teaches her reader to identify with Rose, the compassionate witness, rather than Sir Clifford, the indifferent spectator. Even in her suffering, Rose gives the dog 'looks of unutterable tenderness' (24). Sir Clifford, on the other hand, remains insensible to his cruelty and uses terror as a form of enjoyment: sitting 'at the windows of his drawing room, within the full sight and hearing of their agonies', he drinks wine and discusses politics as he gives orders to prolong the torture (21). In this scene, Crafts rewrites Gothic's racialised narrative of titillation and revulsion, desire and dread, into one of sympathetic identification with the slave.

Throughout *The Bondwoman's Narrative*, Crafts utilises Gothic in complex and revisionary ways in order to articulate both the horror of slavery and the humanity of slaves.[2] Her central aim, as she states in her preface, is to portray 'the peculiar features of that institution whose curse rests over the fairest land the sun shines upon' and to show how 'it blights the happiness of the white as well as the black race' (4). Slavery, 'a thing so utterly dark and gloomy' (62), is a shadow that engulfs the entire nation. In the nation's capital, which also contains a slave market, there is 'Gloom everywhere' (162). The slave huts, 'old and ruinous with decay' and 'even older than the nation' (205), represent not just the atrocious living conditions of the slave but also the haunted origins and tainted inheritance of the nation. Built from 'sweat and blood and unpaid labor', the nation's wealth is morally bankrupt (14). Economic exploitation, Crafts' Gothic narrative argues, lies at the heart of the American experiment: slavery's shadow settles 'steadily down over the sumptuous habitations of the rich' even as it creeps 'through the cellars of the poor', promising to turn the American dream into a Gothic curse (162).

While Crafts' narrative makes clear how the legacy of slavery affects slaves, causing them to inherit 'toil and misery ... with no hope or possibility of anything better' (205), her Gothic tale is most interested in unveiling how the master class is also tyrannised by economic imperatives. The narrative obsessively repeats a story of white economic dispossession: Aunt Hetty, a kind northern woman who teaches Hannah to read, becomes 'poor through a series of misfortunes', exchanging the 'splendid mansion for the lowly cottage, and the merchant's desk and counting room for the fields of toil' (9); Mrs Bry, Lindendale's caretaker, is reduced 'to the extremity of accepting the situation of housekeeper' after her husband fails in business when he loses his 'India ship' (19); Mrs Wright, a white woman imprisoned for helping a slave to escape, loses her family to an epidemic while she is in jail and her property 'passed into other hands' (86). Lindendale itself becomes an 'impoverished house' (13) that is heavily mortgaged: its mistress, unable to pay her debts because 'the bank which contained [her] property broke' (38), must flee for her life or use her own body as collateral; the master, having slit his own throat, falls out of his 'easy chair' onto his face and stains his fine garments and carpet with blood (76). Even Sir Clifford's portrait is 'publicly exposed in the market and knocked down to the highest bidder' (199). Crafts fully exploits Gothic's generic concern with the transmission of property. In focusing on the lack of self-possession that accompanies the loss of property, Crafts extends the 'fear, the apprehension, the dread, and deep anxiety' that attend slaves who can have 'no certainty, no abiding confidence in the possession of any good thing' to everyone who participates in an economy that commodifies people as property (97). In a market economy inextricably intertwined with slavery, everyone is in bondage to insecurity, need, greed and reversals of fortune. The master can be reduced to the level of a servant, a prisoner, or even a slave.

Mr Trappe, the narrative's Gothic villain as masterful market manipulator, most fully articulates the narrative's drive to expose the shadow of slavery that lies at the heart of the US market economy. As a lawyer and a speculator whose line of business is trading in family secrets that concern hidden racial genealogies – 'No blood-hound was ever keener in scenting out the African taint than that old man' one character states (239) – Trappe is the embodiment of a market economy that traffics in human flesh. In Trappe's legalistic world, the market is a realm of contracts and bonds. Trappe's wealth depends upon his ability to manipulate while never untangling the complex web of connections between race and property in the United States. Like the market economy, he is greedy for 'bright gold' (101). He operates consistently and rationally and always without mercy, turning the situation to his own advantage and never indulging in 'barren speculation' (39). Trappe's actions – his extortion and relentless pursuit of Hannah's mistress, which causes her madness and death – expose the exploitation and violent forms of obsession and dispossession that sustain the market economy.

Trappe's descriptive association with 'blackness' – he has 'dark clothes, and darker eyes' and is depicted as a 'shadow darkening' the life of many (36, 34) – further marks the inextricable connections between the illegitimacy of the trade in slaves and the broader market economy. While Trappe's 'blackness' trades on Gothic tropes that racialise evil, Crafts rewrites this typical association by using it to demonise a wealthy white man rather than a black slave. Rather than uncouple 'blackness' from its Gothic referents, Crafts resituates the discourse in relation to the white body, thereby exposing the fictionality not only of race but also of the Gothic's racialised narratives of dread upon which racial discourse depends. Trappe's 'blackness' exposes to white culture its own illegitimacy: its complicity in the crime of slavery as well as its use of black bodies to project and proxy its own moral guilt. Described as a recluse as well as a shadow, Trappe is the secret self that haunts white culture. He is the respectable gentleman revealed as monster. '[D]omiciled in the family' (32) at both the plantation house and the cottage owned by sympathetic whites where Hannah takes refuge, he symbolises the market economy that lies at the heart of the home, both slave and free. Trappe rips apart the veil that separates the private domestic realm of sentiment from the public market of cold hard cash. Through Trappe, who 'strictly speaking . . . cannot be considered a slave-trader' but whose 'business is quite essential to trade' (116), Crafts erases the line between lawful and criminal acts. As Trappe shows, there is no distinction between legitimate and illegitimate trade, private and public spheres, or even slavery and freedom.

In defending his actions, Trappe makes this point explicitly: 'We are all slaves to something or somebody. A man perfectly free would be an anomaly, and a free woman yet more so. Freedom and slavery are only names attached surreptitiously and often improperly to certain conditions' (101). Trappe's self-defence hinges on his argument that the entire culture is complicit in his actions. He states:

> My conscience never troubles me . . . The circumstances in which I find people are not of my making. Neither are the laws that give me advantage over them . . . Whatever the law permits, and public opinion encourages I do, when that says stop I go no further
>
> (102)

While Trappe lays bare the institutional contexts of his atrocious actions in order to declare his innocence, Crafts does so in order to insist upon the public's monstrosity and their moral culpability. Her villain may be demonised, but in refusing to individualise him, his revelations becomes as much about the nation as himself.

Crafts' narrative underscores its desire to implicate its white readers in slavery's Gothic horror by casting Hannah's putatively white mistress, Mrs Vincent, in the conventional role of the persecuted Gothic heroine. Hunted by Mr Trappe, who discovers that her mother was a slave, Mrs Vincent becomes a petrified and passive victim: 'She seemed to be always looking for somebody and expecting something that never came' (33). As the white mistress exposed as a slave, Mrs Vincent represents the complex and intertwined genealogical lines of America's racial history. Moreover, her story materialises Trappe's assertion that everyone in a market economy – both white and black – is enslaved to external powers. Her hysteria about and repulsion of her state – death, she argues, would be preferable to being 'sold for a slave' (57) – mirrors the white reader's inability to face this truth fully. Indeed, Mrs Vincent ruptures a blood vessel and dies immediately after Trappe's speech in which he articulates his intent to sell her the next morning. Like Mrs Wright, another white woman who is 'the victim of mental hallucination' (82), imagining her prison a palace and herself a queen, or Sir Clifford's wife, who was never seen to smile after witnessing Rose's torture, declaring 'the sight of their agonies and the noise of their groans would haunt her to her dying day' (24), many of the white mistresses in Crafts' narrative are either reduced to insanity by the horrors of slavery or troubled by them forever. It is the white mistress, rather than the black slave, who remains hunted and haunted in this text.

Quite differently, Hannah, the house slave, who serves as Mrs Vincent's paradoxically 'light' double, helping her to run away and ministering to her through all of her tribulations, consciously refuses the role of persecuted heroine. She insists upon being a rational agent of her own destiny. Hannah states:

I seldom gave way to imaginary terror. I found enough in the stern realities of life to disquiet and perplex, without going beyond the boundaries of time to meet new sources of apprehension, and so I rested calmly in the assurance that whether spirit or man, angel or devil, or neither, it was nothing that could change my destiny, or affect in the least degree my happiness or misery.

(136–7)

Throughout the narrative, Hannah counters the irrational and superstitious forces of Gothic with rational thought and religious faith. Her fancy might paint a picture of Aunt Hetty, her benefactress, being 'immured in a dungeon for the crime of teaching a slave to read' but she quickly comes to a 'more rational and consistent manner of thinking' in which she concludes that 'they were happy whatever might be their condition' (13). Hannah refuses to be tormented by 'unnecessary fears' (63) or to place her destiny in any hands other than God's. While her mistress 'start[s] and shudder[s]', Hannah comforts her by reading the Bible (55). Indeed, the only time Hannah is truly frightened is during her escape, itself depicted as a trial of faith, when she loses her way with God: she is unable to overcome her terror of a leering corpse because 'Heaven seemed to have turned its face against me' (228).

In juxtaposing Hannah's rationality, agency and faith against Mrs Vincent's hysteria, guilt and fear, Crafts rewrites Gothic conventions – converting the dark lady to light double – in order to underscore the humanity of the slave and to forge an identification between slave and reader. In doing so, Crafts marks Hannah as embodying cherished middle-class characteristics: she is devout, 'industrious, cheerful, and true-hearted' (11). Crafts rewrites the slave narrative's conventional scene of the slave's entrance into literacy as an education in sentiment and sympathy. Aunt Hetty not only teaches Hannah to read but also cultivates her moral nature: as a slave, Hannah may not be rich or hold an 'elevated position in society' but she can do her 'duty, and be kind in the sure and certain hope of an eternal reward' (11). Class status, as Aunt Hetty's modest yet tasteful virtues suggest, resides in personal merit rather than economic capacity. As a middle-class, sentimental heroine negotiating a Gothic romance, Hannah models her readers' position and teaches them to sympathise with the tribulations of an 'other', specifically the slave. Crafts consistently situates Hannah in the position of reader/spectator. Like Trappe, Hannah is always watching others and figuring out their secrets. Unlike Trappe, however, Hannah's witnessing is sympathetic rather than aggressive; she becomes a 'repository of secrets' (11) due to others' confidence in her rather than an intrusive self-interest. She implores her mistress, for instance, to entrust her with her 'dreadful secret, that knowing I may more deeply sympathise with your woes and wrongs' (45). Moreover, by writing Hannah into the role of participant–observer – she seems strangely detached through much of the narrative, servings as the auditor to or witness of Lizzie's and Mrs Vincent's horror stories – Crafts provides her slave protagonist with the same privileges of the white middle-class reader: safety and security. It is her mistress, rather than Hannah, who is tormented. By the end of the narrative, Hannah is written completely into a middle-class subject position: she sits in her 'neat little Cottage' (244) with her aged mother and her affectionate husband, sustained by her faith and her work with children. Crafts' narrative, then, entwines two tales: a Gothic story of white dispossession and a sentimental narrative of black ascension to freedom and middle-class status.

Crafts' ability to revise the Gothic's racial narratives is not, however, fully successful. *The Bondwoman's Narrative*'s analysis of race does not evade assumptions of class.[3] Although Crafts' narrative shows how slavery's horrors loom over the entire nation, it does not extend humanity to all slaves. Rather her narrative differentiates – and demonises – slaves according to a familiar class structure, one that is structured by degrees of blackness. While she portrays the almost white house slave Hannah as an able decoder of Gothic's plots, she portrays black, lower-class slaves as stereotypically superstitious. Charlotte, a 'beautiful Quadroon' (122), for instance, is able to manipulate the Gothic by creating a diversionary ghost story (much like Cassy in *Uncle Tom's Cabin* (1852)) as a cover for her and her husband's escape; whereas the drunk old Jo, who Crafts depicts in the denigrating stereotypes of minstrelsy, is reduced to the 'most ludicrous state of terror conceivable' by that story – 'his eyes, large and glaring, seemed actually starting from their sockets, his teeth chattered and his whole frame trembled as with the ague' (137). Crafts repeats this class distinction in Hannah's own escape. After spending the narrative reluctant to claim her freedom, Hannah is compelled to '[run] for [her] life' (216) when she finally faces something that truly terrifies her: being reduced to the status of a field slave. Having lost her mistress's affections due to the evil undermining of Maria, a 'dark mulatto' with 'black snaky eyes' who is adept at the 'art of dissembling' (208) and who 'blacken[s]' (211) Hannah's reputation, Hannah is forced to work in the fields and is doomed to 'association with the vile, foul, filthy inhabitants of the huts' (211). Her soul is 'revolted with horror unspeakable' at the prospect of being condemned to receive one of them as her husband (211). Disgusted by the filth and impurity of the huts, as symbolised by the large pool of fetid black mud that stands in front of them, as well as the animalistic behaviour of their inhabitants, Hannah, frightened and anxious, escapes. She cannot stand to be 'brought down to their level' (215).

Crafts' reliance on Gothic's traditional narrative of racial loathing in the concluding section of her story is striking – and deeply disturbing – given her narrative's commitment to rewriting those conventions. As Robert Levine argues, it is as if she 'finally discovered the nightmare of slavery in the slaves themselves' (Levine 2002: 291). On the one hand, Crafts is careful to blame the degradation of the slave on a system that steals their humanity from them. She also offers a stinging class critique of slavery – and all 'false system[s]' (2002: 205) – that differentiate the great man from the poor man: the Constitution, she argues, 'asserts the right of freedom and equality to all mankind' and the Bible 'tells how Christ died for all; the bond as well as the free' (207). Yet, on the other hand, she 'blackens' and demonises lower-class field slaves and centres the climax of her narrative on her protagonist's racial fear and loathing. The sympathetic identification her narrative seeks to achieve for the racial 'other' is unavailable to lower-class slaves. The uncertain status of Crafts' authorial identity clouds the racial affiliations that lie at the heart of the narrative's anxiety but what Hannah's racial dread does unveil is the unease that accompanies Gothic's tale of class ascension. To claim her middle-class status fully, Hannah must not so much reject her status as slave but disassociate herself from its culturally constituted class characteristics. Throughout the narrative, Hannah actively refuses to claim her freedom, preferring instead to imagine her salvation as a form of service to and adoption into the white middle class. She tells Mrs Henry, whose hands are 'so white and soft and beautiful': 'You are so good, accomplished, and Christian-like, could I only have the happiness to be your slave, your servant, or –' (29). It is the loss of that status, specifically of her female virtue (marriage to a lower-class 'other' is figured as rape) that compels her finally to seek her freedom at the end: 'As I have observed before nothing but this would have impelled me to flight' (213). In her escape, Hannah claims her freedom in specifically middle-class terms. She is welcomed into Aunt Hetty's 'tidy and comfortable' cottage once again and then creates her own (235). To do so, Hannah must, like Aunt Hetty, who refuses association with the 'rude and profane habits' (235) of her neighbours, the miners, sever her connections to those who live in darkness. Class distinctions, as *The Bondwoman's Narrative* makes clear, trouble American Gothic as much as race and slavery.

The Bondwoman's Narrative, then, discloses the difficulty of characterising Gothic as either a conservative or radical mode. While American Gothic reveals what haunts the nation's cultural narratives, it also works to coalesce them. American Gothic can unveil the lasting legacy of slavery even as it perpetuates its culture's classed fictions of race. As Crafts' narrative demonstrates, Gothic remains stubbornly entrenched within a discourse of racial demonisation. The Gothic may be exorcised at the end of *The Bondwoman's Narrative* – the Linden bows to the axe, Lindendale is renovated, and Mr Trappe is violently assassinated, 'his schemes of wealth and ambition . . . suddenly terminated' (242) – but what continues to haunt Crafts' narrative is the disturbing revelation that even those texts most equipped to resist and rewrite Gothic's generic conventions can still fall into its racial traps.

NOTES

1 *The Bondwoman's Narrative* was most likely written in the mid-nineteenth century but was not published until 2002. Its authorship has not yet been fully authenticated. Gates argues that *The Bondwoman's Narrative* was written by a fugitive slave. William Andrews (2002), on the other hand, theorises that the possibly pseudonymous Hannah Crafts was a free black woman. Celeste-Marie Bernier and Judie Newman (2005) argue that Crafts may be a bonded white servant or an immigrant.

10

SCOTTISH GOTHIC

ANGELA WRIGHT

To attach a precise date to the genesis of 'Scottish Gothic' is an enterprise as perilous as the dating of its neighbouring counterparts 'English' and 'Irish' Gothic. Instead, in this exploration of what may constitute Scottish Gothic, I have chosen to examine two particular episodes in Scottish history that in turn created a particularly fertile territory in Scotland for the development of a Gothic aesthetic.

The most significant crises that the eighteenth century brought to Scotland were the Union between the parliaments of England and Scotland in 1707, and the Jacobite Rebellions of 1715 and 1745/6. These events were of course intimately connected: together, their shadows were cast over the literary impossibility of a coherent Scottish identity.[1] Some families sided with the Jacobite cause, others viewed Scotland as part of the Union, and there were those who remained undecided in their allegiances. With time and perspective, the nineteenth-century fiction of Walter Scott, James Hogg and Robert Louis Stevenson began to exhume this crisis in a particularly Gothic manner. To analyse their nation's fragmentation, these authors used recognisable Gothic tropes. Tales of haunted doubles, disowned sons and ineffectual heroes populate their fictional explorations of Scotland's fractured state.

Georg Lukács was not entirely correct when he argued for Sir Walter Scott as the first historical novelist (Lukács 1962: 50). Scott was undoubtedly influenced by Sophia Lee's novel *The Recess* (1785), and later by Jane Porter's engagement with history in her novels *Thaddeus of Warsaw* (1803) and *The Scottish Chiefs* (1810). Lee's *The Recess* has been read by Margaret Anne Doody as the 'first fully developed English Gothic novel' and one of the first 'recognizable historical novels' (Doody 1977: 559). This unchallenged location of Lee's fiction at the heart of two literary traditions suggests that it is quite possible to argue for the coterminous development of the historical and Gothic novel, and indeed for the symbiosis of their relationship. In *The History of Gothic Fiction* Markman Ellis argues that the Gothic is 'a mode for the apprehension and consumption of history' (Ellis 2000: 11). Whilst his argument neglects the Scottish dimension of the Gothic, it is especially pertinent to this. The analyses of Scotland's historical fragmentation undertaken by Scott, Hogg, and later Stevenson, is only made possible by their use of the Gothic.

True to the spirit of Gothic literature, however, my essay begins in a displaced location, south of the Scottish border. In order to examine the extent of Scotland's fragmented reputation in the eighteenth-century British psyche, it helps to begin with the preface to the first edition of *The Castle of Otranto* (1764). The location of the manuscript in 'the library of an ancient Catholic family in the north of England' is far from casual (Walpole 1996: 5). A remote and deliberately vague position on the cusp of England and Scotland permits Horace Walpole to freight the manuscript with a cluster of values that become of great significance to 'Gothic'. On the one hand, the specific identification of this ancient family seat as Catholic inaugurates what critics regard as the pervasive anti-Catholicism of the Gothic.[2] On the other hand, this 'ancient' and established family's carefully conserved library collection has secured the manuscript's transmission.

It is entirely fitting that the tensions between Walpole's imagined family's Catholicism and its antiquarian urge to safeguard past records are contained within 'the north of England', a border area that, by its proximity to Scotland, certainly gestures north towards an occluded space. Bound to England since the 1707 Union, Scotland was often referred to as 'North Britain' in the periodicals and press of the late eighteenth and early nineteenth centuries. The fiction and reports concerning Scotland throughout this period suggest that it remained an uncharted, confusing and hostile territory for writers. By way of example, in the *Anecdotes* of Samuel Johnson, Hesther Lynch Piozzi records her subject's well-known contempt for Scotland. She cites one particular example of a Scotsman asking Johnson for his opinion of Scotland:

> 'That it is a very vile country to be sure, Sir;' (returned for answer Dr Johnson.) Well, Sir! Replies the other somewhat mortified, God made it. 'Certainly he did (answers Mr Johnson again); but we must always remember that he made it for Scotchmen, and comparisons are odious, Mr S –; but God made hell'.
>
> (Piozzi 1786: 172)

Johnson's provocative retort is deliberately separatist: for him, Scotland was 'made' for 'Scotchmen', a discrete country best reserved for its natives.

In keeping with Johnson's infernal rendition of Scotland, the few glimpses of 'the north' gleaned in Gothic novels published in England are almost universally unflattering. Ann Radcliffe's first romance, *The Castles of Athlin and Dunbayne* (1789) portrays a feudal Scotland with two clans at war. Significantly, this was to prove Radcliffe's first and only attempt to locate her fiction in Scotland; thereafter she transferred her Gothic excursions to the much safer distance of Catholic Europe. Later, in 1818, Mary Shelley offered a brief glimpse of Scotland in *Frankenstein* when Victor travels to the Orkney Islands to create a companion for his creature. Shelley's description of Scotland emphasises the inhospitable: the cottagers surrounding Victor have 'been benumbed by want and squalid poverty' (Shelley 1998: 136). Victor remarks that his native Switzerland is 'far different from this desolate and appalling landscape' (136). Combined, these examples of Scotland's representation in Gothic fiction suggest that it was just as foreign and hostile a space as Spain, Italy or France: situations that Walpole, Radcliffe and others invoked in order to tell tales of persecution and religious tyranny.

When we turn to the Gothic fiction written by Scott and Hogg during the Romantic period, surprisingly we find confirmation of Scotland's inhospitable reputation. In Walter Scott's first novel, *Waverley, or 'tis Sixty Years Since* (1814), the eponymous English hero becomes entangled in the Jacobite uprising of 1745, and is variously imprisoned, attacked and robbed of his identity whilst in Scotland. *Guy Mannering, or the Astrologer* (1815), Scott's second novel, portrays its young hero Brown's (later discovered to be the heir Harry Bertram) entrance into Scotland from the pastoral serenity of the English Lake District as a rude awakening. Immediately beset by banditti, Brown and his friend Dandie Dinmont must fight to defend their lives and belongings.

James Hogg takes these national hostilities even further towards the conclusion of his 1824 novel *The Private Memoirs and Confessions of a Justified Sinner*. Hogg provides a playful self-portrait of himself as a surly shepherd who refuses the 'North British' editor's request to take him to see the eponymous sinner's grave. The editor of the tale records his impressions of Hogg thus:

> We soon found Hogg, standing near the *foot* of the market, as he called it, beside a great drove of *paulies*, a species of stock that I never heard of before. They were small sheep, striped on the backs with red chalk. Mr L–t introduced me to him as a great wool-stapler, come to raise the price of that article; but he eyed me with distrust, and turning his back on us, answered 'I hae sell'd mine.'
>
> I followed, and shewing him the above-quoted letter, said I was exceedingly curious to have a look of these singular remains he had so ingeniously described; but he only answered me with the remark, that 'It was a queer fancy for a woo-stapler to tak'.
>
> (Hogg 2002: 170)

Hogg portrays himself here as a suspicious, unreceptive shepherd who has no interest in sharing his knowledge and discoveries with strangers. At first glance, he seems the very embodiment of the provocative Scottish caricatures offered in earlier Gothic fiction.

Scott and Hogg's apparent confirmation of their nation's inhospitality may well cement the reader's equation of Scotland with a Gothic, hostile territory. As a national characteristic, however, this troubling hostility remains a superficial fictional trope in their works, one that exists in order to prompt larger questions. If we look more attentively, for example, at Hogg's refusal to accompany the editor to the grave in the extract quoted above, we can see that it is grounded in his immediate detection of the editor's poor and unnecessary pretence of being a wool-stapler. Why the editor and his companion choose to conceal his identity is an interesting question in itself, but what remains more compelling is Hogg the shepherd's immediate distrust of their lie. And justifiably so; as we discover in the pages to follow, the undeterred editor visits the sinner's grave, and in reopening the grave, destroys the body in order to secure the grave's concealed manuscript. The editor's lack of care for the corpse's preservation reveals a questionable disposition to separate a narrative from a wider national context; a work from a 'corpus'. This dubious disposition enables him to dismiss the sinner's private memoirs as those of 'not only the greatest fool, but the greatest wretch, on whom was ever stamped the form of humanity' (175). In the light of this easy dismissal of the 'confessions', it becomes essential to the integrity of Hogg's story that he inserts himself as a character who detects the fakery of the 'editor'. Like Walpole's first Gothic enterprise, *The Private Memoirs and Confessions of a Justified Sinner* is intimately concerned with the preservation and correct transmission of a manuscript.[3]

What truly justifies the reputation of Scott's and Hogg's works (and later authors such as Robert Louis Stevenson) as 'Scottish Gothic' is not their novels' superficial representation of Scotland as a wild, hostile space, but rather their careful excavation of Scotland's past. Like all Gothic fiction, Scottish Gothic is intimately concerned with the process of telling a tale. But through its minutely detailed attention to the artefacts which give rise to narratives, Scottish Gothic debates the process of uncovering histories. Graves, castles, manuscripts and inscriptions are all warmly contested sites of authenticity and authority. Such items are constantly argued over by masters and servants, editors and shepherds. Scottish Gothic is intimately concerned with distilling the right narrative from any story, with awarding equal attention to the stories of shepherds (as in Hogg) alongside the self-appointed narrators of the nation, such as the 'editor' of Hogg's tale and the lairds and antiquarians of Scott's fiction.

In *The Private Memoirs and Confessions of a Justified Sinner*, Hogg's appearance does not resolve the truth of the confessions; rather it serves to cast doubt upon the integrity of the editor's version. Likewise, Scott's novels are in places almost pedantically obsessed with the multiplicity of historical interpretations that have been freighted onto Scotland. They anticipate Hogg's later Gothic masterpiece *The Confessions* by arguing for a timely and orderly excavation of the past, whether that past be significant on the personal or national level. Scott's fiction qualifies as Gothic because he does not simply examine the history of his country, but instead revisits the processes of telling that history.

Scott displayed an apparent disdain for the Gothic in the first chapter to his anonymously published first novel *Waverley* (1814). There, he claimed (rather questionably) that the name chosen for his hero was 'uncontaminated' by literary precedent. He distanced himself in particular from the Gothic apparatus of Ann Radcliffe's *The Mysteries of Udolpho* (1794), launching a light-hearted attack on its ubiquitous Gothic paraphernalia:

> I have . . . assumed for my hero, WAVERLEY, an uncontaminated name, bearing with its sound little of good or evil, excepting what the reader shall hereafter be pleased to affix to it. But my second or supplemental title was a matter of much more difficult election, since that, short as it is, may be held as pledging the author to some special mode of laying his scene, drawing his characters, and managing his

adventures. Had I, for example, announced in my frontispiece, 'Waverley, a Tale of other Days,' must not every novel reader have anticipated a castle scarce less than that of Udolpho, of which the eastern wing had been long uninhabited, and the keys either lost, or consigned to the care of some aged butler or housekeeper, whose trembling steps, about the middle of the second volume, were doomed to guide the hero, or heroine, to the ruinous precincts?

(Scott 1898: I, 1–2)

Scott's overt critical distance from the Gothic is daring and deliberately disingenuous. His later critical assessment of Ann Radcliffe suggests that he took her fictional enterprise entirely seriously, so we cannot take this parody at face value (Scott 1968: 110).

Superficially, *Waverley* carries an ambition that is different to the Gothic. Scott states that 'the object' of his tale 'is more a description of men than manners', and hints at an attendant urgency in his novelistic shift of priorities (Scott 1898: I, 2–3). Whereas before novelistic emphasis could be placed upon 'manners', now 'men' must assume the central narrative stage; whereas before the medieval settings and fashions offered great decorative inspiration to Gothic novelists, 'who, meaning the costume of his hero to be impressive, would willingly attire him in the court dress of George the Second's reign, with its no collar, large sleeves, and low pocket-holes?' (I, 3). Scott's light-hearted attack on Hanoverian fashion only partially glosses a more serious attempt to shed light upon 'the period of my history' (I, 4). The occlusions in Chapter 1 are as revealing as the observations. *Waverley* becomes defined by what it is not; it is *not* a Gothic tale, nor a mere sentimental tale of 'manners'; it is not about medieval times, but a tale of 'sixty years since'. The costume of the character is discussed, but not the character himself. All of this careful literary preparation and exclusion accretes to tell us that the author wishes to examine 'the state of society in the northern part of the island'. Scotland is not specifically mentioned, although the narrative skeleton of the Jacobite Rebellion in 1745–6 could not be more bound up with national issues.

Of course, Scott's reference to 'the northern part of the island', rather than Scotland, reflects his own ostensibly pro-Union stance. But again this objective reference conceals a more intimate concern about the fate of Scotland. Whilst *Waverley* may not be a classic Gothic narrative of a displaced son returning to reclaim his birthright, it carries a Gothic secret at the heart of its narrative technique. The negatives compounded in the opening chapter suggest that the mourning for a lost nation lies at the heart of this tale. The inability to express this loss is what renders Scott's novel both Gothic and historical. His study morphs into a deliberately vague, labyrinthine examination of the Jacobite Rebellion. The novel's central hero becomes just as shadowy, unconvincing and ineffective as Radcliffe's Valancourt from *The Mysteries of Udolpho* (1794), and the plot becomes just as convoluted as the tales narrated by the guide in *The Italian*.[4]

Although *Waverley* ostensibly refuses to engage with the recognisable Radcliffean Gothic, by contrast *Guy Mannering* does. The tale of the lost fortune and kidnapped heir of the Bertram estate, Scott's hero Harry Bertram (initially Brown) returns from the dead in order to reclaim his family's inheritance. Having been kidnapped by pirates as a child, he has been raised in the Netherlands. His return is frequently referred to in specifically spectral terms: it is reported that the gypsy Meg Merrilies had impressed one of Bertram's few surviving relatives (his aunt) 'with a notion that the callant – Harry Bertram ca's she him? – would come alive again some day after a" (Scott 1898: II, 226) and both Mannering and Merrilies refer to him as 'the living image' of his father (II, 324 and 342). Brown/Bertram becomes an uncanny figure, both foreign and recognisably Scottish, simultaneously alive and dead.

Guy Mannering demonstrates Scott's indebtedness to the classic Gothic plot motif. A young, wronged laird, raised as a merchant and a soldier, returns to claim his ancestral home. As with Walpole's hero Theodore in *The Castle of Otranto* and Clara Reeve's Edmund Twyford in *The Old English Baron* (1778), Harry Bertram's first unwitting encounter with his ancestral home Ellangowan is as a stranger. The description of his unwitting return to his birthplace is replete with Gothic tropes. Like a Radcliffean heroine, Bertram admires the 'massive and picturesque effect of the huge round towers' that offer 'a double portion of depth and majesty to the high yet gloomy arch' (Scott 1898: II, 244).

What distinguishes *Guy Mannering* as a specifically Scottish Gothic novel follows Bertram's initial contemplation of the ruined house's (significantly called 'The Old Place') heraldry:

> 'And the powerful barons who owned this blazonry,' thought Bertram, pursuing the usual train of ideas which flows upon the mind at such scenes, – do their posterity continue to possess the lands which they had laboured to fortify so strongly? Or are they wanderers, ignorant perhaps even of the fame or power of their forefathers, *while their hereditary possessions are held by a race of strangers*? 'Why is it,' he thought, continuing to follow out the succession of ideas which the scene prompted, – 'why is it that some scenes awaken thoughts which belong as it were to dreams of early and shadowy recollection, . . . ? Is it the visions of our sleep that float confusedly in our memory, and are recalled by the appearance of *such real objects* as in any respect correspond to the phantoms they presented to our imagination?'
>
> (Scott 1898: II, 244, my emphasis)

'Real objects' prompt Bertram's memory, and help him discover the secret of his birthright. They are what resuscitate the uncanny 'phantoms' of his imagination, and lead him to surmise that his 'hereditary possessions are held by a race of strangers'.

Possessions and objects become of great significance to the project of Scottish Gothic; like the manuscript concealed by the corpse in Hogg's *Confessions*, they create the material impetus for the narrative, and stimulate the debates that eventually reveal hidden tales. In *Guy Mannering*, the impotency created by Bertram's father's death means that the few remaining friends and relatives cannot assist the young Bertram in his quest. 'Hereditary possessions' are the only clues to reveal the Gothic tale of usurpation.

Locally in *Guy Mannering*, the 'race of strangers' is represented by the usurper Gilbert Glossin, an aspirant factor who was instrumental in the childhood abduction of Bertram, and who has since purchased the family lands. When Bertram meets Glossin, the latter's ignorance of the family motto indicates that he is the true stranger, one who takes no interest in histories or contexts. When asked by Bertram to interpret the motto, Glossin replies, 'I am the worst person in the world to consult upon legendary antiquities' (Scott 1898: II, 247). Bertram's own contemplation of the heraldry of 'The Old Place' has imperfectly revived the memory of his family motto and childhood memories. But in the absence of Glossin's assistance, it is an anonymous washerwoman nearby who, hearing Bertram pick out a half-remembered tune from his childhood, confirms the memory for him:

> Apparently the tune awoke the *corresponding associations* of a damsel, who . . . was engaged in bleaching linen. She immediately took up the song:
>
>> 'Are these the Links of Forth, she said,
>> Or are they the crooks of Dee,
>> Or the bonny woods of Warroch Head
>> That I so fain would see?'
>
> 'By Heaven!' said Bertram, 'it is the very ballad! I must learn these words from the girl.'
>
> 'Confusion!' thought Glossin; 'if I cannot put a stop to this, all will be out. Oh, the devil take all ballads, and ballad-makers, and ballad-singers! And that d–d jade too, to set up her pipe!'
>
> (Scott 1898: II, 248, my emphasis)

Crucially, it is the washerwoman's assistance that evokes 'corresponding associations' about Bertram's homeland and family. The ballad becomes a shared, confirmed memory between him and the washerwoman. This episode assumes greater significance on the national level: Glossin's ill-tempered curse on 'all ballads, and ballad-makers, and ballad-singers' indicates his readiness to suppress a vital cultural memory. Immediately prior to the washerwoman's prompt, Bertram remarks to Glossin that 'those who brought me up discouraged all my attempts to preserve recollection of my native land' (Scott, 1898: II, 247). Through this passage, *Guy Mannering* suggests that Scotland's preservation is a vital, collective enterprise that must be shared between classes and generations.

Artefacts, ballads and manuscripts all participate in this fictional act of remembering. Through their 'corresponding associations', they discover the hidden secret at the heart of *Guy Mannering*. Collectively, they unite the fate of the individual character, Harry Bertram, with a larger national context. The preservation of these artefacts is not the sole province of the self-appointed curators of the nation. The contribution of washerwomen, gypsies and shepherds, Scott and Hogg argue, is vital to the recovery of the lost text, the reclamation of the nation's 'hereditary possessions' from a 'race of strangers'.

This national curation becomes the collective enterprise of Scottish Gothic. Blending classic Gothic motifs with a national oral tradition, Scottish Gothic fiction embarks upon the excavation of a nuanced, multilayered version of Scotland's history. Scott's third novel, *The Antiquary* (1816), confirms this. Again, it follows the classic Gothic plot of a young heir, Lovel, whose name echoes the true name of Reeve's hero Edmund Twyford in *The Old English Baron*. Lovel, abducted at an early age, has been raised in ignorance of his origins. The Gothic plot, however, takes a poor second place to *The Antiquary's* witty and serious contemplation of Scotland's ancient and recent history. Scott's eponymous antiquary, Jonathan Oldbuck, is a kind-hearted amateur curator of antiquities. He enjoys displaying his knowledge of remote and seemingly obscure artefacts, and demonstrates a keen appetite for debating and disputing any historical or literary discovery. Oldbuck's topics of debate range from the dubious location of an ancient Roman battlefield, to the warmly contested topic of the time, the authenticity of Macpherson's *Ossian* (1765).[5] As David Punter has persuasively argued, *The Antiquary* proves the impossibility of constructing 'a single, unified history of Scotland from the fragmentary and in some cases contradictory evidence still remaining' (Punter 1998: xxv).[6] Oldbuck's own complex origins (he is descended from a Flemish printer) render him a suitable – if flawed – challenger to the orthodoxy of certain Scottish narratives; he is not caught up in a national, romanticised myth of ancestry that erases the nation's shortcomings.

Scottish Gothic explores the reasons behind the inconsistencies of its nation's history and population. James Hogg's haunting tale of double identities and editorial aggression in *The Private Memoirs and Confessions of a Justified Sinner* allows neither reader nor characters consistent responses. Nor does the fiction of Sir Walter Scott: his opening chapter to *Waverley* is all too aware of its deceitful self-distancing from Gothic, and Waverley the character's very lack of 'contamination' is the problem with his unconvincing one-dimensional portrayal.

In the end, what draws us to these narratives are the flawed characters, the missed opportunities in Scotland's own fractured history. *The Antiquary* offers a prescient description of Oldbuck's neighbour and friend, Sir Arthur Wardor. Wardor's 'insincere Jacobitism' conveniently pays homage to the now-extinct Stuart family in Scotland whilst he is in practice 'a most zealous and devoted subject of George III' (Scott 1898: III, 33–4). This light observation belies the significance of the political message here: Wardor's loyalties are not truly divided. His insincere support of the Jacobite cause is overridden by his pragmatic obeisance to England's throne. This indicates a far larger crisis of identity, honour and consistency within Scotland in the nineteenth century. After the eighteenth century's severe testing of political allegiances in Scotland, the nation itself did not know whether 'North Britain' or 'Scotland' was its most fitting appellation.

Scottish Gothic undertakes the examination of its nation's identity crisis. The evident flaws of Scott's characters are writ large in Hogg's tale of schizophrenic obsessions between its protagonists and competing narrators. Later in the nineteenth century, Robert Louis Stevenson resumes this exploration of dual identities in many of his works, most famously *The Strange Case of Dr Jekyll and Mr Hyde* (1886). This theme gains added momentum in Stevenson's *The Master of Ballantrae* (1889), a tale of brotherly rivalry and madness similar to Hogg's *Confessions*. The crisis which precipitates the biblical struggle between two brothers competing for power is their politically expedient decision that the older brother (the eponymous Master) should go out and fight for the Jacobite cause in the 1745/6 Rebellion, whilst the younger one remains at home, displaying fidelity to the British monarch. Such understandably calculated decision-making is condemned, for it precipitates peculiarly Gothic crises of identity. As with *The Confessions*, *The Master of Ballantrae* concludes with a belated dispute over a grave (the eponymous Master's) that has already been plundered.

If we look to group these and other fictions together under the banner of Scottish Gothic, one consistent theme emerges: the novels explored here do not seek to explain or rationalise the inconsistencies in either Scotland or the characters that they describe. Nor, in contrast to the early Gothic novels that we examined at the beginning, do these texts seek to portray Scotland as a straightforwardly hospitable nation. Rather, they look for a way to exhume Scotland's past with care to both local and national contexts. Scott, Hogg and Stevenson are exacting curators of their nation's particularities and inconsistencies. By paying careful attention to ballads, servants' tales, manuscripts, artefacts and plundered graves, they suggest that parts of a complex and troubled history can be reclaimed from 'a race of strangers'. Scottish Gothic is concerned with correcting misguided and superficial judgements of its history, geography and people, such as those that Johnson and earlier Gothic novelists espoused. It demonstrates an anxiety that its 'real objects' or artefacts be honestly represented, that its 'hereditary possessions' are correctly transmitted to posterity, and that its protagonists are dissected with care and attention.

NOTES

1 For further analysis and exploration of this crisis, see Davis (1998) and Pittock (1991).
2 See the summary of this position offered by Baldick and Mighall (2000).
3 For further readings of the grave and burial in Hogg's novel, see Duncan (2003).
4 Michael Gamer (2005) explored the tensions inherent in the opening chapter's claims in more depth.
5 For further study of this, see Stafford (1988).

6 See his excellent 'Introduction' to the Penguin classics edition of *The Antiquary* (Punter 1998), where he begins by examining the Glenallan/Lovel Gothic narrative in further detail before proceeding to the problems that history poses in the novel.

WORKS CITED

Baldick, Chris and Robert Mighall (2000) 'Gothic Criticism', in David Punter (ed.), *A Companion to the Gothic*, Oxford: Blackwell.

Davis, Leith (1998) *Acts of Union: Scotland and the Literary Negotiation of the British Nation 1707–1830*, Stanford, CA: Stanford University Press.

Doody, Margaret Anne (1977) 'Deserts, Ruins and Troubled Waters: Female Dreams in Fiction and the Development of the Gothic Novel', *Genre*, 10: 529–72.

Duncan, Ian (2003) 'Authenticity Effects: The Work of Fiction in Romantic Scotland', *South Atlantic Quarterly*, 102(1): 93–116.

Ellis, Markman (2000) *A History of Gothic Fiction*, Edinburgh: Edinburgh University Press.

Gamer, Michael (2005) '*Waverley* and the Object of Literary History', Plenary Lecture delivered at 'Deviance and Defiance', the conferences of the International Gothic Association and NASSR, Montreal, August.

Hogg, James (2002) *The Private Memoirs and Confessions of a Justified Sinner*, ed. Peter Garside, Edinburgh: Edinburgh University Press.

Lukács, Georg (1962) *The Historical Novel*, trans. Hannah and Stanley Mitchell, London: Merlin.

Piozzi, Hesther Lynch (1786) *Anecdotes of the late Samuel Johnson, LL.D. During the Last Twenty Years of his Life*, London: T. Cadell.

Pittock, Murray (1991) *The Invention of Britain: The Stuart Myth and the Scottish Identity*, London: Routledge.

Punter, David (1998) 'Introduction', to Walter Scott, *The Antiquary*, ed. David Hewitt, London: Penguin.

Scott, Walter (1898) *The Waverley Novels*, Melrose Edition, 25 vols, London: Caxton.

—— (1968) 'Ann Radcliffe', in Ioan Williams (ed.), *Sir Walter Scott on Novelists and Fiction*, London: Routledge.

Shelley, Mary (1998) *Frankenstein, or the Modern Prometheus: The 1818 Text*, ed. Marilyn Butler, Oxford: Oxford University Press.

Stafford, Fiona J. (1998) *The Sublime Savage: A Study of James Macpherson and the Poems of Ossian*, Edinburgh: Edinburgh University Press.

Stevenson, Robert Louis (1990) *The Master of Ballantrae*, ed. Emma Letley, Oxford: Oxford University Press.

Walpole, Horace (1996) *The Castle of Otranto*, ed. E. J. Clery, Oxford: Oxford University Press.

11
IRISH GOTHIC

RICHARD HASLAM

'IRISH GOTHIC' AS 'TERMINISTIC SCREEN'

'[W]e can't say anything without the use of terms', notes Kenneth Burke, but our terms 'necessarily constitute a corresponding kind of screen; and any such screen necessarily directs the attention to one field rather than another' (Burke 1966: 50). In this essay, I treat 'Irish Gothic' as a 'terministic screen', while bearing in mind Burke's caveat that '[n]ot only does the nature of our terms affect the nature of our observations' but also that 'many of the "observations" are but implications of the particular terminology in terms of which the observations are made' (1966: 46). In this case, since the ductility of the descriptor 'Gothic' is matched only by that of 'Irish', the term 'Irish Gothic' generates as many questions as it appears to answer.

Here is the first one. When did 'Irish Gothic' enter the critical world? Its birth date remains obscure, but an early perambulation occurred in 1972, when John Cronin discerned in Somerville and Ross's *An Irish Cousin* (1889) 'a social novel struggling to break through the book's overlay of Irish Gothic' (27; cited in Kreilkamp 1998: 118). Alluding to Emily Brontë's *Wuthering Heights* (1847), Joseph Sheridan Le Fanu's *Uncle Silas* (1864) and Maria Edgeworth's *Castle Rackrent* (1800), Cronin implicitly defines 'Irish Gothic' as the creation of an 'atmosphere compounded of equal parts of Brontean Gothic, Le Fanu-like mystification, and Rackrentish disorder' (27; cited in Kreilkamp 1998: 118). Since Brontë was an Anglo-Irish emigrant's daughter, Le Fanu was both Anglo-Irish and Huguenot-descended, and Edgeworth was not Irish-born, Cronin's allusion raises questions about critical and national classification. For example, how are Irish Gothic works 'compounded' of different literary elements? And how should we gauge the relationship between the term's 'Irish' and 'Gothic' components? By exploring the changing parameters of 'Irish Gothic' over the past three decades, I hope not only to address such questions but also to contribute to a critical idiom that can do justice to the intricate liaisons between literary stances and historical circumstances.

IRISH GOTHIC IN THE 1980S

During this decade, 'Irish Gothic' most frequently implied narratives by three nineteenth-century Protestant writers: Le Fanu, Charles Maturin and Bram Stoker. For example, A. Norman Jeffares stated that Stoker's '*Dracula* [1897] was influenced, obviously, by Sheridan Le Fanu's vampire story 'Carmilla' [1871–72], and the *genre* in Ireland probably goes back to Maturin's *Melmoth the Wanderer* [1820]' (Jeffares 1982: 135–6, my italics). Like Cronin's comment on *An Irish Cousin*, Jeffares' observation raises questions that recur explicitly or implicitly in the critical dialogue. Should we terministically screen Irish Gothic as a genre, a subgenre, a tradition or an illusion? And how should we determine 'influence', whether literary or critical?

Let us begin with the question of critical influence. Julian Moynahan's 'The Politics of Anglo-Irish Gothic: Maturin, Le Fanu and the Return of the Repressed' (1982) significantly affected discourse about Irish Gothic. The essay's title first intimates the intellectual pleasure offered by the topic (the desire to disclose political phobias supposedly secreted within troubled texts); its subtitle then hints at the Freudian methodology selected for the uncovering. Many critics of Irish Gothic are intrigued by the story/history intersection, and a fair few apply psychoanalytic formulae. Allegory is frequently invoked during Freudian readings, since, as Frederick Crews notes, Freud's case studies exhibit an 'allegorizing tendency' (Crews 1995: 59), in which 'symptoms' are represented 'as allegories of repressed mental contents' (1995: 214). Critics employing a psychoanalytically inflected historicism attempt to extract the political contexts (allegedly) inscribed allegorically within literary texts. Aware of the procedure's potential reductionism, Moynahan performs an intricate methodological dance. Following a plot synopsis of Maturin's play *Bertram* (1816), he poses a question:

> Must we read this nonsense as coherent allegory? Of course not, but if we do here is the way it pretty much will go. If Sicily is Ireland, then Imogine is the familiar dolorous archetype of Ireland as unhappy woman beset or contested while Bertram is obviously the supplanted native aristocracy and St Aldobrand the English supplanter. At the roots of this fantasy there exists [sic] both fear of a native revival and restoration and some longing for it, except that the wish is colored by pessimistic dread.
>
> (Moynahan 1982: 48)

Admitting that *Bertram* should not be read as 'coherent allegory', Moynahan nonetheless does so. His justification? Even though Maturin is *not* 'deliberately squirreling away a political allegory in his Gothic melodrama', the play still functions allegorically because it has been written less by Maturin than by an hypostasised entity named 'the Anglo-Irish or Ascendancy literary imagination', which 'is ineluctably haunted, cloven into duality by the cleavage in Irish society between expropriated and expropiators' (1982: 48). However, Moynahan's decoding conflates the expressive practice of allegory with the exegetical practice of allegoresis. In allegoresis, a text with none of the conventionally accepted generic characteristics of theological, moralistic, historical, political, or personification allegory is read *as if* one were explicating a deliberately designed allegory. Irish writers have, of course, consciously used allegory (for example, in *aisling* poems), but this does not diminish the need for critics to distinguish between reading a designed allegory and designing an allegorical reading.[1] As we shall see, Moynahan's psychoanalytically historicising allegoresis offered a tempting model for subsequent interpreters of Irish Gothic.

Moynahan's essay spins out other influential strands, including the suggestion that Le Fanu's *Uncle Silas* explores 'the intricate, involuted "psycho-politics" of country-dwelling Anglo-Irish families, suffering a fearful and historic isolation and loneliness, in pride and obstinacy offering their children as sacrifice to that isolation and loneliness' (52), a theme that Margot Backus would later explore in the work of several authors. Moynahan also foregrounds Maturin's assertion in *The Milesian Chief* (1812) that he chose Ireland as setting

> because I believe it the only country on earth, where, from the strange existing opposition of religion, politics, and manners, the extremes of refinement and barbarism are united, and the most wild and incredible situations of romantic story are hourly passing before modern eyes.
>
> (Maturin 1979: I, v)

For Moynahan, Maturin's 'claim that early nineteenth century Ireland *is* a living Gothic may be admitted in part' (Moynahan 1982: 47), and the 'living Gothic' thesis would later be amplified by Luke Gibbons (2004: 23–4) and Siobhán Kilfeather (2004: 60). Finally, Moynahan's proposal that '[w]ith a little creative misreading, one could claim that the Gothic strain in . . . [Anglo-Irish] literature is a major one all the way through [1800–1944]' (Moynahan 1982: 44) foreshadows efforts by Roy Foster, W. J. McCormack, Siobhán Kilfeather, Margot Backus and Moynahan himself (1995) to expand the authorial range of the Irish Gothic imprint.

Whereas Moynahan's preferred term is 'Anglo-Irish Gothic', Seamus Deane's description of Maturin as 'the first of the Irish Gothic novelists' (Deane 1986: 99) provides an important source for that term's dissemination. Resisting allegorical or psychoanalytical applications, Deane nevertheless declares that the 'ruins in Maturin's wild Irish landscapes are . . . *emblems* of an alienation and a failure, which the destitution of the peasantry intensifies' (1986: 100, my italics). According to Deane, Maturin's 'hatred of Catholicism helps to explain the sense of homelessness which pervades his writings', whereas a 'less melodramatic but a more haunting sense of estrangement issues from the work of the greatest of Irish Gothic writers, Joseph Sheridan Le Fanu' (100). Deane also claims that during 'the nineteenth-century, the decay of Anglo-Irish society had been *expressed* in novels of an increasingly sinister tone'; that '[r]uined houses *consorted well with* stories of hauntings'; '[and that] ghostly presences were *readily available images* of guilt and loneliness' (205, my italics). As with Moynahan's allegoresis, Deane's terminology highlights the critical challenges involved in screening the interaction between literary texts and historical contexts.

Roy Foster's 'Protestant Magic', first published in 1989 and then reprinted in *Mr Paddy and Mr Punch* (1993), also searches for a suitable lexicon and syntax, as it extends 'the nineteenth-century *tradition* of supernatural fiction' (Foster 1993: 219, my italics) beyond Maturin, Le Fanu and Stoker to include W. B. Yeats and Elizabeth Bowen. According to Foster, 'the *line* of Irish Protestant supernatural fiction is an *obvious* one, though it has not been analysed as such' (220, my italics). The writers he assembles are:

> marginalized Protestants all, often living in England but regretting Ireland, stem-
> ming from families with strong clerical and professional colorations, whose occult
> preoccupations *surely mirror* a sense of displacement, a loss of social and psycho-
> logical integration, and an escapism motivated by the threat of a takeover by the
> Catholic middle classes.
>
> (220, my italics)

Thus, during the 1980s, a critical consensus emerged: Irish Gothic constituted a genre or tradition; its core authors were Maturin, Le Fanu and Stoker, although other Irish Protestants, like Yeats and Bowen, could be admitted; and its Faustian-pact plots and themes of ruin, haunting and disputed possession somehow mirrored, emblematised, or allegorised the repressed political anxiety and theological ambivalence of its authors.

In the 1990s, the quest for an adequate critical language would continue, and new authors would be incorporated into Irish Gothic. Yet, simultaneously, doubts would arise about the classification's plausibility.

IRISH GOTHIC IN THE 1990S: THE PROBLEM WITH TRADITION

Through *The Field Day Anthology* (1991), Irish Gothic achieved widespread terminological currency. Editing an 118-page section on the subject, W. J. McCormack incorporated work by Yeats and Bowen (as Foster had done) and extended the brand range to include material by Sydney Owenson, William Carleton, Oscar Wilde and (rather implausibly) J. M. Synge. However, he displayed surprising scepticism, stating that 'the Irish tradition of gothic fiction turns out, on examination, to be a slender one' (McCormack 1991: 833). In *Dissolute Characters* (1993), McCormack went further, referring to the '[c]ashiering' (2) of an 'uncertainly called' (viii), 'doubtful' (3), 'so-called' (3), and 'merely convenient' (10) 'Irish gothic tradition' (viii).

Let us pause a moment, then, to inquire: in what form – if any – does Irish Gothic exist? An answer requires precise wording – and even spelling – since terministic screens encode not only the selection of individual words but also the choice of upper case or lower case: McCormack's 'Irish gothic' is not quite Deane's 'Irish Gothic.' In *Dissolute Characters*, McCormack rejects what he labels a '*tradition* of Irish gothicism' (McCormack 1993: 10, my italics; see also

29 and 161). If we define 'tradition' as a 'long established and generally accepted custom or method of procedure, having almost the force of a law' (*OED*), we must agree with McCormack that there is no Irish Gothic tradition, solemnly passed down from Maturin to Le Fanu and so forth.

However, if we instead treat 'Gothicism' as a *mode*, we find a more flexible way to phrase and thereby frame the issue. As Robert Hume once observed, 'there is in an objective sense no such thing as *The Gothic Novel*; rather there are a variety of novels from different periods and countries which, on the basis of similarities, we may want to categorize as a group' (Platzner and Hume 1971: 273). It is more sensible, he maintained, to speak of 'a very loosely defined mode' than to assume that 'Gothic and Romantic are discrete entities which have an essential nature and real existence' (1971: 273). Fred Botting later revisited the point, arguing for a Gothic 'mode' that 'exceeds genre and categories' and is 'restricted neither to a literary school nor to a historical period' (Botting 1996: 14).

Via modes, we can establish more precisely the 'compounded' nature of Irish Gothic (Cronin 1972: 27). Some Irish authors use the Gothic mode extensively in one work (Maturin's *Melmoth*) but not in another (Maturin's *The Wild Irish Boy*). Or they splice the Gothic mode with other supernaturalist or quasi-supernaturalist modes, such as the ghost story (Bowen's *A World of Love*, 1955), the folkloric (Somerville and Ross's *The Silver Fox*, 1897), the theological (Le Fanu's 'Green Tea', 1869), the sensational (Le Fanu's *Uncle Silas*), or the mystagogical (W. B. Yeats' 'Rosa Alchemica', 1896). Writers can also combine within one work supernaturalist and more naturalist modes, such as the society novel (Oscar Wilde's *The Picture of Dorian Gray*, 1890/1), or the national tale (Sydney Owenson's *The O'Briens and the O'Flahertys*, 1827).

If a shift from *tradition* to *mode* provides one way to rethink Irish Gothic, Seamus Deane offers another. By proposing that James Clarence Mangan's *Autobiography* 'introduces us to a new genre – what we may call Catholic or Catholic-nationalist Gothic' (Deane 1997: 126), Deane challenged the consensus that Irish Gothic meant Anglo-Irish Protestant Gothic. However, any case for an Irish-Catholic-nationalist Gothic must address the intersection of supernaturalist mode with narrative tone, since Mangan produced not only the solemn Gothic of his *Autobiography* but also the parodic Gothic of 'Love, Mystery, and Murder' (1834) and the Romantic-ironic Gothic of 'The Man in the Cloak' (1838). The latter work increases considerably our awareness of intertextual complexity in Irish Gothic, since, as Patricia Coughlan notes (1987), it is a plagiarised adaptation of Honoré de Balzac's *Melmoth Réconcilié* (1835), which is itself a satirical sequel to Maturin's *Melmoth the Wanderer*. Because Mangan's story adopts a pro-Catholic stance, despite being published in the anti-Catholic *Dublin University Magazine*, it can also enlarge our understanding of Irish Gothic's political intricacy, without the need to import allegoresis.[2]

IRISH GOTHIC IN THE 1990S: *ALLEGORESIS REDUX*

Speaking of which, its methodological ploys re-emerged in the 1990s, primarily through critical engagements with *Dracula*. For example, Terry Eagleton's claim that *Dracula* was 'another allegory of the collapse of the gentry' (Eagleton 1995: 215) constituted another case of allegoresis masquerading as allegory. Acknowledging Eagleton, Seamus Deane declared that 'Dracula's dwindling soil and his vampiric appetites consort well enough with the image of the Irish landlord current in the nineteenth century' (Deane 1997: 90).[3] Subsequently, Bruce Stewart challenged these interpretations, arguing that '[i]f *Dracula* is an allegory of Irish historical events, it is surely more likely to be based on a reaction to the climate of terror engendered by Land League agitation than to the legacy of resentments caused by colonial dispossession' (Stewart 1999: 247). Stewart's reading drew upon Michael Valdez Moses, who had explicitly deciphered Dracula as Charles Stewart Parnell (Moses 1997: 69, 86, 101). Although Stewart and Valdez Moses disagreed with Eagleton and Deane about the puzzle's solution, all four nonetheless agreed that *Dracula* was an allegory. They thereby occulted their own allegoresis, through which (to paraphrase Oscar Wilde) they 'found in stones the sermons' they 'had already hidden there' (Wilde 1994: 1078).

Similar manoeuvres occur in Joseph Valente's 'revisionist Hibernian reading' of *Dracula* (Valente 2002: 5). Valente's ingenious explication bears comparison with medieval 'figurative' exegesis (i.e. allegoresis), which, as Graham Wood notes, seeks to 'resolve ... three problems: reception (those scandalized by some scriptural passages), biblical consistency, and textual obscurities' (Wood 2000: 13). Beneath the scandal of *Dracula*'s apparent racism, sexism and narrative inconsistency, Valente detects 'a carefully wrought stylistic and structural complexity that enacts a more tentative and progressive ideology' (Valente 2002: 5) – namely, 'to frame the so-called facts of race as the fantasy effects of race consciousness' (112). However, Valente faces the tricky task of persuading readers (i) that Stoker employed 'the kind of sophisticated, post-impressionistic strategies of representation ... [found in] early modernist artists such as Ford, Conrad, and the young James Joyce' (5–6); (ii) that he prophetically channelled the theories of Jacques Lacan and Slavoj Žižek; and (iii) that in *Dracula* – and *Dracula* alone – he transcended the reactionary gender, racial and imperial politics amply displayed in *The Snake's Pass* (1891), *The Mystery of the Sea* (1902), *The Man* (1905), *Lady Athlyne* (1908) and *The Lair of the White Worm* (1911).

Valente's methodology – 'a necessarily abrasive and unstable synthesis of psychobiographical and cultural studies approaches' (Valente 2002: 10) – finds echoes in the 'psycho-historical experiment' (Killeen 2005: 26) of Jarlath Killeen's *Gothic Ireland*, which aspires to 'prob[e] ... the internal geography of the [eighteenth-century] Anglican mind' (13). Like Moynahan's 'Ascendancy literary imagination' (Moynahan 1982: 48), Killeen's 'Anglican mind' is another hypostasised hostage trapped in psychoanalytic flights of fancy. To his credit,

Killeen acknowledges possible theoretical shortcomings: 'It could be said that I adopt an Eriksonian style, in that I attempt to understand a culture through a very limited number of texts and personalities' (Killeen 2005: 25). The problem for 'psycho-historian[s]' (27) like Killeen or Valente, however, lies equally with psychoanalysis itself. As Frederick Crews observed of Erik Erikson, 'With the concepts of resistance and denial ready at hand, the psychohistorian can place his central dramatic emphasis wherever he pleases' (Crews 1986: 10). Similarly, Frank Cioffi has urged 'that instead of seeing in "condensation", "displacement", "representation by the opposite", etc., etc., laws governing unconscious processes, we recognize them as recipes for the construction of associative chains to preselected termini' (Cioffi 1998: 110). Using such 'recipes', for example, *Dracula*'s 'stylistic and structural incoherence' and 'conservative racial politics' can be cooked into 'meticulous formal symmetries [intentionally organized] for the purpose of political critique' (Valente 2002: 5).

IRISH GOTHIC IN THE NEW MILLENNIUM

Although Irish Gothic is now an accepted category throughout Gothic studies, this is not necessarily the case in Irish studies.[4] True, *The Cambridge Companion to the Irish Novel* includes a chapter on Irish Gothic, but the 1400-page *Cambridge History of Irish Literature* allocates to the topic a mere three paragraphs.[5] Margaret Kelleher acknowledges that 'the Gothic *mode* with its distinctive anxieties is a significant form in nineteenth-century Irish writing', but she argues that the 'coherence and extent of such a *tradition* may be overstated' (Kelleher 2006: 472, my italics). The tension between these claims reinforces the hypothesis advanced in the present essay: Irish Gothic is more conceptually plausible when envisioned as mode rather than tradition.

A modalising perspective also assists the pursuit of Irish Catholic-nationalist Gothic beyond Mangan. Despite claims that the 'genre slumbered' (Loeber and Stouthamer-Loeber 2003: 8) between the publication of Maturin's *Melmoth* in 1820 and Le Fanu's *The Purcell Papers* in 1838–40, the following fiction appeared, all of which substantially incorporates the Gothic mode: 'The Fetches' (1825) and 'The Ace of Clubs' (1838) by John Banim; 'Crohoore of the Bill-Hook' (1825) and *The Ghost Hunter and his Family* (1833) by Michael Banim; 'The Lianhan Shee' (1830/3) by William Carleton; and 'The Barber of Bantry' (1835) by Gerald Griffin.

As noted above, we need to identify the significance of not only mode but also tone for Irish Gothic. Mangan's register of tones, which includes solemnity, parody and Romantic irony, provides us with new ways to recognise and contextualise the arch tone in Gerald Griffin's 'The Brown Man' (1827), the polemical tone in Carleton's 'Lianhan Shee', the jocular tone in Le Fanu's 'The Ghost and the Bone-Setter' (1838), and the alternation between earnest and parodic tones in Wilde's 'The Canterville Ghost' (1887) and between sarcastic and fearful tones in Wilde's *Dorian Gray* and Maturin's *Melmoth*. We also need to register the agency of rhetorical effect (or intended mood); as Robert Hume notes, 'the serious Gothic works were written with effect very much in mind – terror, horror, mystery in a more than frivolous sense – and hence "affective" groupings have some justification' (Platzner and Hume 1971: 274). Similarly, Victor Sage recommends conceptualising 'Le Fanu's Gothic ... not as a genre, but a rhetoric: a recurring set of designs on readers' security and pride in their own rationality' (Sage 2004: 4).

Using this rhetorical approach, we can trace more precisely the unique combinations of mode, tone and intended mood that distinguish individual works of Irish Gothic; in addition, we can reduce the critical temptation to make 'Gothic', via '[l]yrical flights of oratory, hasty generalizations, prophetic attitudes and recuperative manoeuvres', a term 'synonymous with almost everything' (Levy 1994: 7). A mode–tone–mood perspective also helps us to address questions about the many Irish-authored and Gothic-themed novels and novelettes published in London and Dublin between 1750 and 1829, uncovered through the pioneering work of the Loebers. For example, why is Thomas Leland's *Longsword* (1762) initially placed in the subgenre of 'historical fiction' but later classified as 'Irish Gothic' (Loeber and Stouthamer-Loeber 2003: 3, 8)? What does it mean to label *Longsword* and *The Adventures of Miss Sophia Berkeley* (1760) 'Irish Gothic' when they were published before the Gothic mode's generally accepted *terminus a quo* – Horace Walpole's *The Castle of Otranto* (1764)? Does *The Children of the Abbey* (1796) by Regina Maria Roche primarily exhibit the Gothic mode, with a soupçon of sentiment; or, despite some Gothic and ghostly trimmings, does it principally employ the sentimental mode of Samuel Richardson's *Pamela* (1740) and *Clarissa* (1747–8)?[6] And is Roche's tone principally directed at generating the rhetorical effect that Angela Carter identified as literary Gothic's central concern – 'provoking unease' (cited in Mulvey-Roberts 1998: xvii and 35)?

The mode–tone–mood framework can also assist us in identifying the introduction and modulation of Gothic effects in the work of twentieth- and twenty-first-century Irish writers. For example, Elizabeth Bowen's use of Gothic and ghostly modes is indebted to Le Fanu, as her prefaces to reissues of his *Uncle Silas* and *The House by the Church-Yard* (1863) reveal. However, by merging the Gothic mode with an arch tone in 'The Cat Jumps' (1934), a clinically detached tone in 'The Demon Lover' (1941), and a nostalgic tone in 'The Happy Autumn Fields' (1944), she creates variations in mood that are much more subtle than those of Le Fanu. In Flann O'Brien's *The Third Policeman* (1939–40; 1967) and Brian Moore's *The Mangan Inheritance* (1979), elements of the Gothic mode intersect with a bleakly humorous tone to create a distinctively fatalistic mood.

If Maturin, Le Fanu and Stoker are the (Protestant) power trio of early Irish Gothic, then the new (Catholic) triumvirate comprises Seamus Deane, John Banville and Neil Jordan. As the force behind *Field Day*'s 'Irish Gothic' section, Deane generated a relevant critical context for the publication of his novel–memoir *Reading in the Dark* (1996), a context later ramified by his coining of the term 'Catholic-nationalist Gothic' (Deane 1997: 126).[7] In his *Short History*, Deane astutely noted how John Banville's utilisation in *Birchwood* (1973) of Irish Gothic motifs from Le Fanu and Bowen 'restores to Irish fiction the principle of radical doubt' (1997: 225) previously exhibited in the work of Flann O'Brien and Samuel Beckett. Banville played further postmodern variations on Irish Gothic and ghostly modes in *Mefisto* (1986), *Ghosts* (1993) and *Eclipse* (2000). Whereas Mangan intertexes Maturin with Balzac, Banville adds Vladimir Nabokov to the palimpsestic mix: the references to Melmoth in Banville's *Mefisto*, *The Book of Evidence* (1989) and *Athena* (1995) also allude to Nabokov's *Lolita* (1955), whose narrator drives an 'Ocean Blue Melmoth'. And it is unsurprising that a Banville tribute adorns the Bloomsbury edition of Neil Jordan's *Shade* (2004), since Jordan's novel is a flamboyant homage not only to Le Fanu, Yeats and Bowen but also to Banville's postmodern rejuvenation of Irish Gothic motifs.

With Deane, Banville and Jordan, the creative future of Irish Gothic seems promising, but what of its *critical* prospects? Any significant theoretical rethinking, I have suggested, should consider the possibility of viewing Irish Gothic as a mode rather than a tradition; of recognising the shaping power of tone and mood; of avoiding allegoresis; and of submitting psychoanalytical methodologies to the vampire-vanquishing stake of Ockham's Razor. We may then be able to trace more confidently the interference patterns between literary forms and social formations, between Irish societies and Gothic anxieties, between imagination and situation.[8]

NOTES

1 For overviews of allegoresis, see Grondin (1994: 17–34) and Szondi (1995: 1–13).

2 See Haslam (2006).

3 Deane's 'consort well enough' echoes his previous verb choice: 'Ruined houses consorted well with stories of hauntings' (Deane 1986: 205). Declan Kiberd subsequently affiliated himself with the Eagleton–Deane reading of *Dracula* (albeit with reservations):

> Whether he [Dracula] is to be seen as a type of the absentee landlord running out of soil may be open to doubt, for his land at home is secure: but he does bear striking analogies to those ascendancy parasites who visited England in hopes of seducing society girls and sucking their financial blood.
>
> (Kiberd 2001: 385–6).

In a variation, Gregory Castle argued that 'Van Helsing and Dracula each embodies an aspect of Stoker's split and compromised Anglo-Irish identity in a double projection that allegorizes social anxieties and offers symbolic consolation for feelings of political illegitimacy and spiritual and cultural homelessness' (Castle 2002: 529).

4 Entries in various 'Companions' to Gothic have further validated Irish Gothic's terminological status. However, despite the membership drive promoted by Foster (2006), McCormack (1991), Kilfeather (2006), Deane (1997), Moynahan (1995) and Backus

(1999), most 'Companion' essayists (Kilfeather excepted) have rounded up the usual suspects – Maturin and Le Fanu. See, for example, Sage (2000) and Hennelly (2003); Punter (2002) deals only with Maturin. Although Punter and Byron's book lacks a separate entry on Irish Gothic, it does engage with a wider range of works and authors, including John Banville (2004: 84–5).

5 See Connolly (2006: 418) and (Kelleher 2006: 472). However, the volumes do examine individual authors such as Maturin, Le Fanu and Stoker in some depth.

6 Discussing Roche's *Children*, Siobhán Kilfeather notes 'the particular fusion of the sentimental and the gothic characteristic of much [late eighteenth-century] Irish fiction' (Kilfeather 1994: 37–8); see also McCormack (1991: 831–2) and Connolly (2006: 418).

7 On the influence of Mangan's *Autobiography* on Deane's novel, see Haslam (2000: 73–4). On the influence of Maturin's *Melmoth* on *Reading*, see Culver (2006).

8 I want to thank Ellen Crowell, Rich Fusco, Patricia Haslam, Siobhán Kilfeather, Emma McEvoy and Catherine Spooner for their helpful feedback on earlier drafts of this essay.

WORKS CITED

Backus, Margot Gayle (1999) *The Gothic Family Romance: Heterosexuality, Child Sacrifice, and the Anglo-Irish Colonial Order*, Durham, NC: Duke University Press.

Botting, Fred (1996) *Gothic*, London: Routledge.

Burke, Kenneth (1966) *Language as Symbolic Action: Essays on Life, Literature, and Method*, Berkeley, CA: University of California Press.

Castle, Gregory (2002) 'Ambivalence and Ascendancy in Bram Stoker's *Dracula*', in Bram Stoker, *Dracula*, ed. John Paul Riquelme, Boston, MA: Bedford/St Martin's.

Cioffi, Frank (1998) *Freud and the Question of Pseudoscience*, Chicago, IL: Open Court.

Connolly, Claire (2006) 'Irish Romanticism, 1800–1830', in Margaret Kelleher and Philip O'Leary (eds), *The Cambridge History of Irish Literature*, 2 vols, Cambridge: Cambridge University Press.

Coughlan, Patricia (1987) 'The Recycling of *Melmoth*: "A Very German Story"', in Wolfgang Zach and Heinz Kosok (eds), *Literary Interrelations: Ireland, England and the World*, 3 vols, Tübingen: Gunter Narr Verlag.

Crews, Frederick (1986) *Skeptical Engagements*, Oxford: Oxford University Press.

—— (1995) *The Memory Wars: Freud's Legacy in Dispute*, New York: New York Review of Books.

Cronin, John (1972) *Somerville and Ross*, Lewisburg, PA: Bucknell University Press.

Culver, Jennifer (2006) 'The Delight of Horror: The Irish Nationalist Gothic in Seamus Deane's *Reading in the Dark*', paper given at the American Conference of Irish Studies' national conference, University of Missouri – St Louis, 22 April.

Deane, Seamus (1986) *A Short History of Irish Literature*, London: Hutchinson.

—— (1997) *Strange Country: Modernity and Nationhood in Irish Writing since 1790*, Oxford: Clarendon Press.

Eagleton, Terry (1995) *Heathcliff and the Great Hunger: Studies in Irish Culture*, London: Verso.

Foster, J. W. (ed.) (2006) *The Cambridge Companion to the Irish Novel*, Cambridge: Cambridge University Press.

Foster, R. F. (1993) *Paddy and Mr Punch: Connections in Irish and English History*, London: Penguin.

Gibbons, Luke (2004) *Gaelic Gothic: Race, Colonization, and Irish Culture*, Galway, Ireland: Arlen House.

Grondin, Jean (1994) *An Introduction to Philosophical Hermeneutics*, trans. Joel Weinsheimer, New Haven, CT: Yale University Press.

Haslam, Richard (2000) 'Ghost-Colonial Ireland', *Bullán: An Irish Studies Journal*, 5.1: 63–80.

—— (2006) '"Broad Farce and Thrilling Tragedy": Mangan's Fiction and Irish Gothic', *Éire-Ireland*, 41(3/4): 215–44.

Hennelly, Mark (2003) 'Teaching Irish Gothic: Big-House Displacements in Maturin and Le Fanu', in Diane Long Hoeveler and Tamar Heller (eds), *Approaches to Teaching Gothic Fiction: The British and American Traditions*, New York: The Modern Language Association of America.

Jeffares, A. Norman (1982) *Anglo-Irish Literature*, Dublin: Gill and Macmillan.

Kelleher, Margaret (2006) 'Prose Writing and Drama in English, 1830–90: From Catholic Emancipation to the Fall of Parnell', in Margaret Kelleher and Philip O'Leary (eds), *The Cambridge History of Irish Literature*, 2 vols, Cambridge: Cambridge University Press.

—— and Philip O'Leary (eds) (2006) *The Cambridge History of Irish Literature*, 2 vols, Cambridge: Cambridge University Press.

Kiberd, Declan (2001) *Irish Classics*, Cambridge, MA: Harvard University Press.

Kilfeather, Siobhán (1994) 'Origins of the Irish Female Gothic', *Bullán*, 1(2): 35–45.

—— (2004) 'Terrific Register: The Gothicization of Atrocity in Irish Romanticism', *Boundary 2*, 31(1): 49–71.

—— (2006) 'Gothic Novel', in J. W. Foster (ed.), *The Cambridge Companion to the Irish Novel*, Cambridge: Cambridge University Press.

Killeen, Jarlath (2005) *Gothic Ireland: Horror and the Irish Anglican Imagination in the Long Eighteenth Century*, Dublin: Four Courts Press.

Kreilkamp, Vera (1998) *The Anglo-Irish Novel and the Big House*, Syracuse, NY: Syracuse University Press.

Levy, Maurice (1994) '"Gothic" and the Critical Idiom', in Allan Lloyd Smith and Victor Sage (eds), *Gothick Origins and Innovations*, Amsterdam: Rodopi.

Loeber, Rolf and Magda Stouthamer-Loeber (2003) 'The Publication of Irish Novels and Novelettes, 1750–1829: A Footnote on Irish Gothic Fiction', *Cardiff Corvey: Reading the Romantic Text* 10 (June), www.cf.ac.uk/encap/corvey/articles/cc10_n02.html.

McCormack, W. J. (1991) 'Irish Gothic and After (1820–1945)', in Seamus Deane (ed.), *The Field Day Anthology of Irish Writing*, 3 vols, Derry: Field Day.

—— (1993) *Dissolute Characters: Irish Literary History Through Balzac, Sheridan Le Fanu, Yeats and Bowen*, Manchester: Manchester University Press.

Maturin, Charles (1979) *The Milesian Chief*, 4 vols, New York: Garland.

Moses, Michael Valdez (1997) 'The Irish Vampire: *Dracula*, Parnell, and the Troubled Dreams of Nationhood', *Journal X*, 2(1): 67–111.

Moynahan, Julian (1982) 'The Politics of Anglo-Irish Gothic: Maturin, Le Fanu and the Return of the Repressed', in Heinz Kosok (ed.), *Studies in Anglo-Irish Literature*, Bonn: Bouvier Verlag.

—— (1995) *Anglo-Irish: The Literary Imagination in a Hyphenated Culture*, Princeton, PA: Princeton University Press.

Mulvey Roberts, Marie (ed.) (1998) *The Handbook to Gothic Literature*, New York: New York University Press.

Platzner, Robert L. and Robert D. Hume (1971) '"Gothic Versus Romantic": A Rejoinder', *PMLA* 86: 266–74.

Punter, David (2002) 'Scottish and Irish Gothic', in Jerrold E. Hogle (ed.), *The Cambridge Companion to Gothic Fiction*, Cambridge: Cambridge University Press.

—— and Glennis Byron (2004) *The Gothic*, Oxford: Blackwell.

Sage, Victor (2000) 'Irish Gothic: C. R. Maturin and J. S. Le Fanu', in David Punter (ed.), *A Companion to the Gothic*, Oxford: Blackwell.

—— (2004) *Le Fanu's Gothic: The Rhetoric of Darkness*, New York: Palgrave.

Stewart, Bruce (1999) 'Bram Stoker's *Dracula*: Possessed by the Spirit of the Nation', *Irish University Review* 29(2): 238–55.

Szondi, Peter (1995) *Introduction to Literary Hermeneutics*, trans. Martha Woodmansee, Cambridge: Cambridge University Press.

Valente, Joseph (2002) *Dracula's Crypt: Bram Stoker, Irishness, and the Question of Blood*, Urbana, IL: University of Illinois Press.

Wilde, Oscar (1994) 'The Decay of Lying', *Complete Works of Oscar Wilde*, Glasgow: HarperCollins.

Wood, Graham (2000) 'Allegory', in A. Hastings (ed.), *The Oxford Companion to Christian Thought*, Oxford: Oxford University Press.

12

GOTHIC AND EMPIRE

JAMES PROCTER AND ANGELA SMITH

In their audacious and controversial texts, *Empire* (2001) and *Multitude* (2004), Michael Hardt and Antonio Negri speak of a 'monstrous' (Hardt and Negri 2004: 192) formation that will eventually overcome an increasingly global and oppressive 'Empire'. They call this formation 'the multitude'. Unlike the people, the masses or the working classes, which Hardt and Negri suggest are redundant collective metaphors because they exclude or homogenise difference, the multitude refers to a chaotic, incoherent and excessive assemblage. Alluding to Bram Stoker's *Dracula*, Hardt and Negri describe the vampire as 'one figure that expresses the monstrous, excessive, and unruly character of the flesh' (Hardt and Negri 2001: 193) of the multitude in a global culture where conventional social bodies like the nation and family are disintegrating:

> It should come as no surprise, then, that vampires have become so prevalent in recent years in novels, film and television. Our contemporary vampires will turn out to be different. The vampires are still social outsiders, but their monstrosity helps others to recognize we are all monsters – high school outcasts, sexual deviants, freaks, survivors of pathological families and so forth. And more important, the monsters begin to form new, alternative networks of affection and social organization. The vampire, its monstrous life, and its insatiable desire has become symptomatic not only of the dissolution of an old society but also the formation of a new.
>
> (2001: 193)

While Hardt and Negri state their thesis as a radical break with traditional (postcolonial) theories of empire, their recourse to Gothic tropes of monstrosity, the vampiric and the deviant is, we shall see, entirely compatible with a strain of empire writing that first became prevalent in the nineteenth century.[1] The nodal point of the comparison also reveals, as the quotation implies, a crucial difference, which is the site of horror. Stoker in *Dracula* evokes an England in danger of contamination by the alien vampiric invader and his legions, reversing the supposedly ethical work of empire. Hardt and Negri, however, see that contaminating monstrosity within a plural society as a source of energy and resistance to the structures of empire. Their recognition of monstrosity as a recurring source of social anxiety within empire that might nevertheless be reclaimed as a positive resource of subversion characterises a more recent subgenre of late twentieth-century writing that we might call 'postcolonial Gothic'.

A provisional distinction could be drawn at this point between what Patrick Brantlinger calls 'imperial gothic' and so-called postcolonial Gothic. For

Brantlinger, imperial Gothic refers to writing from the late nineteenth and early twentieth centuries, from Rider Haggard's *King Solomon's Mines* (1885) to John Buchan's *Greenmantle* (1916) (Brantlinger 1988: 233–59). Imperial Gothic tends to express anxieties over the failure of religion through a fall from civilisation into barbarism and savagery. In Rider Haggard's romances and in many of Kipling's stories, for example, the civilised explorer or servant of empire is constantly threatened by entombment in the landscape or loss of self-control because of disease and excessive heat. Here the colonised culture is given Gothic treatment as being itself the source of barbarism, temptation and horror. In this context, 'postcolonial Gothic' would refer to writing *after* empire from, say, Jean Rhys's *Wide Sargasso Sea* (1966) to Arundhati Roy's *The God of Small Things* (1997). Postcolonial Gothic might be said to cite and write back to familiar Gothic texts (including imperial ones) in order to unsettle or in some way disturb their grand narratives of colonial mastery/degeneration, relocating the horror from the locus of the colonised to the violence and abuses perpetrated by empire.

Alternatively, the relationship between Gothic and empire might be said to confound the very term 'postcolonial', with its apparently Eurocentric emphasis on a chronological break that implies colonialism is over. As Judie Newman suggests:

> Postcolonial Gothic is ... Janus-faced. At its heart lies the unresolved conflict between imperial power and the former colony, which the mystery at the centre of the plot both figures and conceals. Its discourse therefore establishes a dynamic between the unspoken and the 'spoken for'.
>
> (Newman 1995:70)

Unspeakable instances of colonial horror repeatedly return to haunt and terrorise the postcolonial text to the extent that, as David Punter notes, 'its apparent insistence on a time "after", on an "aftermath"', exposes itself precisely to the threat of return, falls under the sign of repetition' (Punter 2003: 193).

Of course, just because a postcolonial text appears 'haunting' or 'uncanny', it does not mean it is Gothic, and it becomes necessary to check the capacious qualities of the Gothic (and postcolonial) if the affinities between empire and Gothic studies are to be regarded as anything more than merely rhetorical. In a special issue of *Postcolonial Studies* on 'Global/postcolonial horror', Ken Gelder notes '[t]he tropes of horror – spectralisation, the return of the repressed, uncanny (mis)recognitions, possession (and dispossession), excess, the "monstrousness" of hybridity – have lent a certain structural logic to postcolonial studies' (Gelder 2000: 35). Thus, when Fred Botting speaks of 'gothic excesses ... the fascination with transgression and the anxiety over cultural limits and boundaries' (Botting 1995: 8), he might just as easily be talking about 'postcolonial' excesses. The other, the outsider, the *unheimlich*, the revenant all become unhelpfully elastic concepts within this context, stretching just a little

too comfortably around both postcolonial and Gothic forms. It is worth emphasising here that there might be quite specific cultural and political reasons for
the related emergence of postcolonial and Gothic discourses from the late eighteenth century onwards. William Hughes and Andrew Smith have suggested
that Gothic and empire writing might be regarded together as specific responses
to the enlightenment period. Both Gothic and postcolonial texts work within,
while ultimately serving to undermine or question, 'post-enlightenment notions
of rationality' (Smith and Hughes 2003: 1). For example, while Gothic texts have
typically foregrounded the irrational, the repressed, the dispossessed, postcolonial texts have repeatedly worked to unpick Cartesian notions of the unified
subject in terms of a distinction between the human and non-human. Moreover,
and as we shall see, the Gothic obsession with otherness, monstrosity and the
non-human, its reproduction *and transgression* of racial binaries, possibly
explains the genre's seductiveness for many postcolonial writers. That transgression is evident in the use of the very term 'postcolonial Gothic', in that in the
eighteenth and nineteenth centuries a dominant meaning of 'Gothic' was that
which was quintessentially English. Even in its name, postcolonial Gothic seems
to have 'written back' to the empire, appropriating the signifier 'Gothic' and its
literary conventions to resist the work of empire. Gothic, a term that for many in
Britain's former colonies was the signifier of Englishness, becomes a means of
articulating the experience of other cultures repressed by the empire.

In an attempt to avoid easy generalisations, in what follows we offer a (neces-
sarily selective) chronological survey of some of the key texts to articulate both
Gothic and (post)colonial concerns in India, the Caribbean and England from
the nineteenth century to the present. In focusing on Dickens' *The Mystery of
Edwin Drood* (1870) and Kipling's 'The Man Who Would Be King' (1888) we
hope to problematise the distinction between imperial Gothic and postcolonial
Gothic. We suggest that these texts, written within the colonial period like
H. Rider Haggard's fiction, offer a critique of the empire from within.

Edward Said was the first theorist to explore, in a postcolonial context, the
binary, frequently racialised distinctions between the non-human and human
that were central to post-Enlightenment notions of identity as coherent and self-
contained. In his foundational text, *Orientalism* (1978), Said argues that the
Western imagination of the East has systematically served to legitimise the
process of colonisation since at least the eighteenth century. Said examines how
binaries such as civilised/savage, black/white, Christian/pagan, human/animal
were deployed in Western literature to master and control the Orient. More
than this though, he suggests, 'European culture gained in strength and identity
by setting itself off against the Orient as a sort of surrogate and even underground self' (Said 1978: 3). The Orient was not simply Other in this context, but
a projection of the *repressed* desires of the European *self*. To be savage, black,
animal or wild in orientalist terms was not necessarily negative then, but
frequently a site of ambivalent (often sexual) desire, eroticism/exoticism and
fantasy.

An image of the Orient provides the startling opening paragraph to Charles Dickens' last, unfinished, novel *The Mystery of Edwin Drood*: 'An ancient English Cathedral town? ... The well-known massive grey square tower of its old Cathedral? How can that be here! ... What IS the spike that intervenes, and who has set it up? Maybe, it is set up by the Sultan's orders ... It is so, for cymbals clash, and the Sultan goes by to his palace' (Dickens 1985: 37). The town of Cloisterham suggests by its name that it embodies the Christian values of empire and the Establishment but the reader's first encounter with it shows the cathedral invaded by the infidel, as scimitars flash, dancing girls strew flowers and infinite numbers of elephants pass in procession. This novel, like Rudyard Kipling's 'The Man Who Would Be King', interrogates contemporary assumptions about empire rather than single-mindedly expressing anxiety about threats to it; though its perspective is entirely British it in some ways anticipates the Janus-faced aspect of postcolonial writing.

The eroticised cathedral proves to be an opium dream of the choirmaster, John Jasper, who appears as a pillar of the community but probably murders his own ward, Edwin Drood (this is only implied as the novel is unfinished) and certainly stalks Drood's fiancée. His companion is often Durdles the stone-mason who is the same colour as the graves: 'With the Cathedral crypt he is better acquainted than any living authority; it may even be than any dead one' (1985: 67). The novel pivots on the claustrophobic decay of the cathedral and the unnatural cruelty of Jasper whose contact with Princess Puffer, the source of his opium, is masked by his respectable role. The object of horror is the physical disintegration of the iconic cathedral, symbolised by the decadence of its choir-master. The link between dusty Cloisterham, which is clogged and haunted by its own past, and empire is forged through the younger characters. Drood's effete remark that he is '[g]oing to wake up Egypt a little' (96) which he impertinently regards as 'an undeveloped country' (59) is undermined by the narrator's insis-tent irony about the colonial project. It mocks the mayor's penchant for national ditties that extol reducing 'to a smashed condition all other islands but this island, and all continents' (147). The narrator sardonically defines the local view of 'Natives' as 'nomadic persons, encamping now in Asia, now in Africa, now in the West Indies ... vaguely supposed in Cloisterham to be always black, always of great virtue, always calling themselves Me' (198). The significantly named Landless twins bring new but disruptive life to the town: 'An unusually hand-some lithe young fellow, and an unusually handsome lithe girl; much alike; both very dark ... something untamed about them both' (84–5). The narrator ruth-lessly analyses even the sympathetic Crisparkle's Orientalism: 'so his notes ran on – much as if they were beautiful barbaric captives brought from some wild tropical dominion' (85). The implication is that they are mixed-race immigrants from Ceylon (now Sri Lanka) whose power as catalysts exposes the dark and dusty mores of Cloisterham, rather as the oriental image at the beginning trans-mutes the cathedral.

Kipling's 'The Man Who Would Be King' can, like *The Mystery of Edwin*

Drood, be interpreted as a critique of colonialism rather than simply as an imperial Gothic expression of anxiety about its imminent disintegration. It is a story
told by the editor of the *Backwoodsman*, a daily newspaper for the members of
the Raj. Two former members of the Indian Army, both Freemasons, Peachey
Carnehan and Daniel Dravot, set off to create their own kingdom in Kafiristan.
Carnehan returns alone to tell the editor of his friend's death, the result of being
bitten by his intended bride. He produces Dravot's withered but crowned head
from a bag; when Carnehan dies soon afterwards, the bag has disappeared. The
Gothic theme in this story lies in its focus on the occult, comparable with the
much earlier necromantic experiments in Mary Shelley's *Frankenstein* (1818) or
the occult practices in Lewis's *The Monk* (1796). Carnehan and Dravot claim to
have found the lost white tribe descended from Greek colonists left behind by
Alexander the Great. They communicate through masonic gestures and arcane
emblems cut into rocks. Dravot asserts that his 'kingdom' is a kind of El Dorado,
the fabled city: 'the gold lies in the rock like suet in mutton. Gold I've seen, and
turquoise I've kicked out of the cliffs, and there's garnets in the sands of the
river, and here's a chunk of amber' (Kipling 1987: 265). After his death this
seems to be confirmed as his dried head is crowned by 'a heavy circlet of gold
studded with raw turquoises' (278).

By creating a parodic version of the colonial process the story unsettles the
assumed legitimacy of imperialism. Carnehan and Dravot are both magicians
and rogues. They disguise themselves as priests and traders but hidden in their
camel-bags are 20 rifles with ammunition; in the nineteenth century missionary
and trading activity frequently preceded territorial appropriation. Their success
in establishing themselves with the mysterious white tribe leads Dravot into a
grotesque version of imperialist rhetoric: 'I won't make a Nation . . . I'll make an
Empire! . . . When everything was shipshape, I'd hand over the crown – this
crown I'm wearing now – to Queen Victoria on my knees, and she'd say: "Rise
up, Sir Daniel Dravot"' (269). In a bizarre inflection of the Christian story,
Carnehan is crucified by his former subjects, and they regard his survival as 'a
miracle' (277). The narrator sees the two men as monstrous shape-shifters, but
the reader is left with the question of how to interpret the story of two working-
class heroes who over-reach themselves in the service of the empire, and is also
left to speculate about what happened to the crowned head.

In Jean Rhys's emphatically *post*colonial Gothic novel *Wide Sargasso Sea*
(1966) Antoinette tells her husband, 'There is always the other side, always'
(Rhys 1997: 82). Postcolonial texts, unlike those of Rider Haggard, are, as we
have said, characteristically Janus-faced, looking both ways and often apparently contradictory. Rhys wrote her prequel to *Jane Eyre* (1847) because she
thought, of Brontë's novel, 'That's only one side – the English side' (Wyndham
and Melly 1985: 297). The reader who knows *Jane Eyre* has the experience of
déjà vu when characters such as Mason and the young man to be married off to a
West Indian heiress appear, though there are also haunting absences, such as
the omission of the young man's name. The death of mad Mrs Rochester in the

canonical novel is prefigured uncannily in the death of the parrot in Antoinette's burning house: 'He made an effort to fly down but his clipped wings failed him and he fell screeching. He was all on fire' (Rhys 1997: 22–3). A suppressed awareness of colonial history as well as of *Jane Eyre* tantalises the reader. When Rochester (for it must be he) asks whether slaves were slaughtered in the village called Massacre his wife replies, 'Not slaves. Something must have happened a long time ago. Nobody remembers now' (39). Yet slavery is part of all the characters' experience; the incident implies that a willed amnesia on the part of former masters and slaves complicates Caribbean culture because their violent history is unspeakable. Part of that violence was the planters' sexual abuse of the slaves. Throughout the novel hints are dropped about the miscegenation that is so appalling to Rochester: 'For a moment she looked very much like Amélie. Perhaps they are related, I thought. It's possible, it's even probable in this damned place' (81). Antoinette is terrified of her own genetic history. When her aunt tells her that her hair will grow again after her illness Antoinette replies ominously, 'But darker' (25).

As in Freud's definition of the uncanny, what ought to have remained hidden keeps coming to light in flashes of revelation that are then suppressed by the text and the characters. When Antoinette says of her mother that there 'are always two deaths, the real one and the one people know about' (81), she is also unwittingly anticipating her own story. The cycle of repetition in the novel is the threat of return, the reiteration of unresolved barbarism. Antoinette's name resembles her mother's, Annette; both are used as counters in patriarchal and colonial power-play. Both go mad, which is the first death. What Antoinette asserts is that the binary oppositions parroted by Rochester are false. She does not only attack his platitudes in responding to his claim that slavery was a question of justice: 'I wrote it down several times and always it looked like a damn cold lie to me. There is no justice' (94). She also follows this with the accusation that what he sees as witchcraft and the dark arts, thought to be the preserve of the intimidating but illiterate black Christophine, are practised by Rochester himself: 'You are trying to make me into someone else, calling me by another name. I know, that's obeah too' (94). This prophecy is fulfilled at the end of the second part of the novel. Rochester looks at Antoinette and sees with satisfaction that she has become a zombie: 'She was only a ghost. A ghost in the grey daylight . . . The doll had a doll's voice, a breathless but curiously indifferent voice' (110). From one perspective he can be said to have practised obeah, which had been banned on pain of death in the West Indies by the colonial authorities since the implementation of the Jamaican Slave Laws of 1760; his cruelty has turned her into one of the living dead. The object of horror is the islands' unspeakable history and the patriarchal Englishman's rapacious destruction of what both repels and entices him: 'It was a beautiful place – wild, untouched, above all untouched, with an alien, disturbing, secret loveliness . . . "I want what it *hides*"' (54).

The narrative method of most of the postcolonial Gothic texts we discuss differs significantly from Dickens' and Kipling's authoritative narrators. In *Wide*

Sargasso Sea there are often incompatible versions of events and we are left not knowing, for instance, whether Antoinette has an affair with Sandi. The narrative voice shifts unpredictably and inexplicably; the reader sees 'the other side' and is left with unanswered questions such as what the relevance of the title is to the novel. Earlier, Newman was cited arguing that postcolonial Gothic hinges on the tension between the spoken and spoken for. She develops this argument in relation to the work of Eve Kosofsky Sedgwick, arguing that in both Gothic and postcolonial novels 'dire knowledge may be shared, but it cannot be acknowledged to be shared, and is therefore "shared separately", as the barrier of unspeakableness separates those who know the same thing' (cited in Newman 1995: 70). This argument provides a fruitful way into *Wide Sargasso Sea*, and into the secretive Gothic narratives of Arundhati Roy's *The God of Small Things* (1997) and Salman Rushdie's *Shame* (1983), our last two examples.

Shame evokes the dynastic, closed-off society of Pakistan through the stifling, claustrophobic spaces of an ancestral home called Nishapur (Sanskrit: 'night city'), a remote, labyrinthine mansion in which the windows only look inward. Nishapur belongs to the recently deceased Old Mr Shakil, a reclusive, aristocratic figure whose death leaves his three daughters financially destitute. After hosting a gala celebration at which one of the sisters falls pregnant, they too confine themselves to the house, thereby shrouding the shameful event in secrecy. The sisters remain behind the mansion's heavy, padlocked doors and 'gates of solitude' (Rushdie 1983: 18) for more than 50 years, even organising the construction of an external dumbwaiter with a false floor and concealed blades to protect their privacy. Omar, their son, is born on the deathbed of his grandfather, a four-poster, the mahogany columns of which are carved with serpents. Omar is an insomniac who wanders the corridors of the mansion at night, a trait that earns him the nickname 'Little bat' (the narrator also likens him to a wolf and Dracula (23)):

> He plunged deeper and deeper into seemingly bottomless depths of that decaying realm. Believe me when I tell you that he stumbled down corridors so long untrodden that his sandaled feet sank into the dust right up to his ankles; that he discovered ruined staircases made impassable by long ago earthquakes which had caused them to heave up into tooth-sharp mountains and also to fall away to reveal dark abysses of fear.
>
> (31)

At the end of the novel, 65 years later, Nishapur is the setting for a series of gruesome deaths. (Nishapur dominates the opening and close of the text, as if to reinforce the building's symbolic architecture of containment.) Last to die is Omar, decapitated by his wife Sufiya on the deathbed of Old Mr Shakil. Sufiya is the living embodiment of shame in the novel. Born with red cheeks, she carries her mother's shame at not having mothered a son, and by extension, the various and violent sexual and political repressions that are structuring absences in Rushdie's Pakistan. As Nishapur burns to the ground, the reader is reminded once more of Sufiya's intertextual affinities with Charlotte Brontë's Gothic novel, *Jane Eyre*: like Bertha Mason, Sufiya has also been confined to an attic, from which she strays at night. Elsewhere in *Shame*, Sufiya embodies other monstrous doubles, including Beauty and the Beast and Jekyll and Hyde. However, if Sufiya is described as 'the ghost of other stories', she is more than simply an intertextual 'play' upon Gothic tropes. For example, at one point we are told she 'grows out of the corpse' of Anahita Muhammed of East London, a girl murdered by her father for dating a white boy. She is also the ghost of an unnamed British Asian girl, attacked by a group of white youths on a late-night train. Most strikingly, perhaps, she is the embodiment of the British/Brixton riots of the early 1980s that the authorial narrator watches on television.

The extent to which houses constitute a barrier of unspeakableness in both these novels is notable. While the figure of the house has long been recognised as a 'motif of indigenization' (Tiffin 1986: 23) in nationalist literature, and as a site of unhomely dislocation in migrant writing (Bhabha 1994), few critics have commented on the peculiarly Gothic provenance of this trope in much contemporary postcolonial writing. For example, the 'disjecta membra' of Derek Walcott's 'Ruins of a Great House', like the 'spiteful' goings-on at 124 in Toni Morrison's *Beloved* (1987), register the unspeakable horrors of slavery. Similarly, Roy's 'History House', like Rushdie's 'Nishapur', contains taboo narratives that must remain private, or be 'shared separately' among those intimately involved.

In *The God of Small Things* the 'History House' (or 'Heart of Darkness' as it is frequently called) was once owned by an Englishman 'gone native', and has subsequently been transformed into a five-star hotel called 'Heritage'. The History House stands on the opposite side of the river to Ayemenem House, the family home which is also its double. In the novel's deathly opening, an abundance of fecund and fetid images of ripeness, over-ripeness and decay coalesce in the stifling image of a Gothic interior – 'Dissolute bluebottles hum vacuously in the fruity air. Then they stun themselves against clear windowpanes and die, fatly baffled in the sun' (Roy 1997: 1). Through these condensed, oddly incomplete sentences, Roy both sets the scene for Rahel's return to the unhomely childhood home (described as damp, overgrown, whispering) and foregrounds the failure of language to capture it. Inside the house 'in a room that had kept its secrets. It gave nothing away' (91), is her mute brother Estha. The buried secrets of Ayemenem are echoed in those of Heritage Hotel, where the past has been 'enclosed and converted' (127) into a hotel kitchen, but where 'something lay buried in the ground. Under grass. Under twenty-three years of June rain' (127). The two houses are haunted by a series of events: paedophilia; the suicide of the Black Sahib, 'Kurtz'; incest; the taboo touch of an untouchable; the brutal and excessive police violence meted out on Velutha's broken body. Embedded, rendered obliquely, deferred and dispersed through the narrative, these haunting events appear as both imperial and inbred legacies, without clear origin. As such they fulfil Eve Kosofsky Sedgwick's sense that in Gothic novels

'The story does get through, but in a muffled form, with a distorted time sense, and accompanied by a kind of despair about any direct use of language' (Sedgwick 1986: 14).

The muffled text that is haunting this essay and surfaces fleetingly in the previous paragraph is Joseph Conrad's *Heart of Darkness* with its charismatic Kurtz, the 'emissary of pity, and science, and progress, and devil knows what else' (Conrad 1985: 55). Kurtz's story indicates that we may all be monstrous, excessive and unruly; his is a 'soul that knew no restraint, no faith, and no fear' (108), not even belief in evil. His triumph, as the narrator Marlow sees it, is that his dying words, at 'that supreme moment of complete knowledge', are 'The horror! The horror!' (111). The Gothic horror of his own transgressive behaviour intersects with the horror of the colonial project, etched on the reader's memory by the human heads on Kurtz's fence and the exploited black shadows from the chain-gang. The novel's opening on the Thames invokes the cycle of repetition, that London too 'has been one of the dark places of the earth' (29). That imperial darkness is evoked in the links between London and Cloisterham in *Edwin Drood* and in Dravot's yearning to be knighted by Queen Victoria for his exploitation of the people of Kafiristan in 'The Man Who Would Be King'. Janus-faced as *Heart of Darkness* is, however, it does not prefigure the explosion of creative and often comic energy to be found in such novels as *Shame* and *The God of Small Things*. Their ability to unsettle grand narratives, to exceed conventional fictional boundaries, to shock, challenge and disrupt, to defy the imperial definition of the monstrous colonised subject, exemplify the dynamism of postcolonial Gothic texts from the empire on which the sun was not supposed to set.[2]

NOTES

1 This is not to deny the presence of earlier literature combining Gothic and imperial concerns. For instance, William Beckford's *Vathek* (1786) draws upon both the *Arabian Nights* and Walpole's *The Castle of Otranto* (1764).
2 The authors would like warmly to thank Dr Dale Townshend for his invaluable comments on an early draft of this chapter.

WORKS CITED

Bhabha, Homi K. (1994) *The Location of Culture*, London: Routledge.
Botting, Fred (1995) *Gothic*, London: Routledge.
Brantlinger, Patrick (1988) 'Imperial Gothic Atavism and the Occult in the British Adventure Novel, 1880–1914', in Fred Botting and Dale Townshend (eds) (2004) *Gothic Critical Concepts in Literary and Cultural Studies*, vol. 1, London: Routledge.
Conrad, Joseph (1985) *Heart of Darkness*, London: Penguin.
Dickens, Charles (1985) *The Mystery of Edwin Drood*, London: Penguin Classics.
Gelder, Ken (2000) 'Introduction: Global/Postcolonial Horror' and 'Postcolonial Voodoo', *Postcolonial Studies*, 3(1): 35–8.

Hardt, M. and Negri, A. (2001) *Empire*, Cambridge, MA: Harvard University Press.

—— (2004) *Multitude: War and Democracy in the Age of Empire*, London: Penguin.

Kipling, Rudyard (1987) *The Man Who Would Be King and Other Stories*, Oxford: Oxford University Press.

Newman, Judie (1995) *The Ballistic Bard: Postcolonial Fictions*, London: Arnold.

Punter, David (2003) 'Arundhati Roy and the House of History', in Andrew Smith and William Hughes (eds), *Empire and the Gothic: The Politics of Genre*, Houndmills: Palgrave.

Rhys, Jean (1997) *Wide Sargasso Sea*, London: Penguin.

Roy, Arundhati (1997) *The God of Small Things*, London: Flamingo.

Rushdie, Salman (1983) *Shame*, London: Picador.

Said, Edward (1978) *Orientalism*, New York: Vintage Books.

Sedgwick, Eve Kosofsky (1986) *The Coherence of Gothic Conventions*, rev. 2nd edn, London: Methuen.

Smith, Andrew and William Hughes (eds) (2003) *Empire and the Gothic: The Politics of Genre*, Houndmills: Palgrave.

Tiffin, H. (1986) 'New Concepts of Person and Place', in P. Nightingale (ed.), *A Sense of Place in the New Literatures in English*, St Lucia: University of Queensland Press.

Wyndham, F. and D. Melly (eds) (1985) *Jean Rhys: Letters 1931–1966*, Harmondsworth: Penguin.

13

CANADIAN GOTHIC

CORAL ANN HOWELLS

'The part of the country I come from is absolutely Gothic. You can't get it all down.'

(Munro 1973)

Alice Munro is a key figure in contemporary English–Canadian Gothic writing, and her comment on her own early fiction offers an intriguing introduction to this chapter.[1] For Munro, location is crucial: she sets most of her stories in her home place of small-town rural south-western Ontario, though what she emphasises is not its familiarity but its strangeness. This is a place so full of mysteries and secrets that even the most meticulous fictional documentation may fail to 'get it all down'. The key word here is 'Gothic' with its promise of the uncanny, scandalous secrets about sex and violence, forgotten histories and buried lives – all part of a fantastic subtext of repression, fear and desire. Munro acknowledged her debt to women writers of the American South, especially Eudora Welty, for they both shared a similar vision of place, where people's lives were like 'deep caves paved with kitchen linoleum' (Munro 1982: 249). So, are there distinctive qualities of Canadian Gothic fiction which mark its difference from American Gothic or European Gothic? And is Munro's domestic Gothic the only kind written in Canada? The answer to the first question is yes, and to the second no, as this chapter will illustrate. It begins with a brief historical overview of Canadian Gothic fiction by male and female writers, followed by critical analyses of four significant contemporary women's Gothic texts, for it is in these women's fictions that traditional Gothic anxieties over questions of identity and power are best articulated. There are noticeably fewer contemporary Gothic texts by male writers. Instead, men have made their distinctive contribution in film, where Mort Ransen's ghoulish *Margaret's Museum* (1995) and David Cronenberg's *Dead Ringers* (1988), *Crash* (1996) and *Spider* (2002) with their dismembered and monstrous bodies mark a mutation in Canadian Gothic towards 'the grotesque and the fantastic' (Edwards 2005: 162).[2]

OVERVIEW

The English–Canadian Gothic tradition begins in the mid-nineteenth century with Canadian-born John Richardson's nightmarish historical romance, *Wacousta; or, The Prophecy: A Tale of the Canadas* (1832) and Susanna Moodie's non-fictional immigrant memoir *Roughing it in the Bush; or, Life in Canada*

(1852). At that time, Canada was a remote colonial location far from British civilisation, a place of 'thick, impervious, rayless forests, the limits of which have never yet been explored, perhaps, by the natives themselves' as Richardson wrote (Richardson 1987: 6), and for Moodie a place of dread, 'the fitting abode of wolves and bears' (Moodie 1986: 467). Not surprisingly, the first Canadian Gothic was wilderness Gothic, emphasising not only location but also dislocation, refiguring the classic tropes of European Gothic in a New World context. It was a hybrid form existing 'at the imaginative frontier where the imported European imagination meets and crosses with the Native indigenous one' (Atwood 1995: 64). Wilderness features have been examined by later critics: Atwood in *Survival* (1972), Margot Northey in *The Haunted Wilderness* (1976), Gerry Turcotte in 'English-Canadian Gothic' (1998) and Justin D. Edwards in *Gothic Canada* (2005), though Edwards and Turcotte position the wilderness motif within an explicitly political argument relating Gothic discourse to anxieties over national identity and history. Those early texts are 'emergent nation' narratives, representing a new society suffering from an identity crisis, which has its uncanny repetitions in Northrop Frye's and Atwood's later questions, 'Where is here?' / 'Who are we?' and currently being refigured in Canada's evolving national ideology of multiculturalism.

Curiously, wilderness Gothic seems to go underground by the late nineteenth century, though the forest was still very much present in the animal stories of Ernest Thompson Seton and Charles G. D. Roberts, and in the British Columbia painter Emily Carr's autobiographical sketches in *Klee Wyck* (1941). It is resurrected by Atwood over a hundred years later, when she acknowledges both Moodie and Richardson as her predecessors, in *The Journals of Susanna Moodie* (1969), *Surfacing* (1972) and *Survival* (1972). Since then, wilderness Gothic has appeared in various revisionist forms in Atwood's writing up to *Oryx and Crake* (2003) and *The Tent* (2006):

> You're in a tent. It's vast and cold outside, very vast, very cold. It's a howling wilderness. There are rocks in it, and ice and sand, and deep boggy pits you could sink into without a trace. There are ruins as well, many ruins.
>
> (Atwood 2006: 143)

Wilderness has also been refigured in two recent novels from British Columbia: Gail Anderson Dargatz's *The Cure for Death by Lightning* (1996) and *Monkey Beach* (2001) by Aboriginal writer, Eden Robinson.

Gothic elements of a more domestic kind (with unhomely houses, family romance plots gone wrong, and grotesque images of violence) occasionally break the surface of a dominant tradition of literary realism from the 1920s and 40s with two prairie novels, Marta Ostenso's *Wild Geese* (1925) and Sinclair Ross's *As for Me and My House* (1941), though the fissures in realistic small-town fiction really occur with Alice Munro's stories in *Dance of the Happy Shades* (1968) and *Lives of Girls and Women* (1971). There were a cluster of 'Souwesto'

Gothic writers at that time: James Reaney with his 1970s dramas *The Donnelly Trilogy* and *Wacousta!*, Robertson Davies with his Deptford trilogy (1970–5) and Timothy Findley's *The Last of the Crazy People* (1967). However, Findley's most Gothic novel comes later with his urban Gothic *Headhunter* (1993), indebted to Conrad's *Heart of Darkness* and set in Toronto. Atwood's *The Robber Bride* (1993) is urban Gothic, employing traditional motifs like dark doubles and shape-shifters, a female vampire and magic mirrors, while it also chronicles Toronto's post-war social history and its contemporary multicultural ethos. Vampiric images pervade three other urban Gothics of this period: Kate Pullinger's *Where Does Kissing End?* (1992), Andrew Pyper's short stories in *Kiss Me* (1996) and Nalo Hopkinson's futuristic *Brown Girl in the Ring* (1998), where Toronto becomes a nightmarish labyrinth.

Though Atwood and Munro remain pre-eminent, the mid-1990s saw a neo-Gothic revival as a new generation of writers (mainly women) from diverse ethnic and racial backgrounds have come to prominence across Canada. Once again Gothic conventions are being renegotiated as these writers highlight issues of cultural difference, race, ethnicity, sexuality and national identity in a post-modern context which is still haunted by history and unquiet ghosts within individual psyches and collective memory. These neo-Gothic novels include not only Robinson's and Anderson Dargatz's already mentioned but also Barbara Gowdy's stories *We So Seldom Look on Love* (1992) and *Mister Sandman* (1995), Ann-Marie MacDonald's Maritime Gothic *Fall on Your Knees* (1996) set in Cape Breton Island Nova Scotia, and Aritha Van Herk's Western Gothic *Restlessness* (1998). A new phenomenon is the diasporic Gothic of Caribbean Canadian novelists Shani Mootoo's *Cereus Blooms at Night* (1996), Dionne Brand's *At the Full and Change of the Moon* (1999) and *What We All Long For* (2005), plus Sri Lankan-born Michael Ondaatje's *Anil's Ghost* (2000), all of which explore the legacies of violence hidden within colonial history.

MARGARET ATWOOD

Atwood has always been a Gothic writer, resurrecting and refashioning Gothic conventions throughout her 40-year-long career as poet, novelist and cultural critic. Here I shall consider an earlier and a later novel, *Lady Oracle* (1976) and *The Blind Assassin* (2000). *Lady Oracle* is a witty parody of women's popular Gothic romance, while *The Blind Assassin* (following the exotic Gothic of *Bodily Harm* (1981), the urban Gothic of *The Robber Bride* and the colonial Gothic of *Alias Grace* (1996)) tells twentieth-century Canadian history as Gothic tale, crossed with a dazzling variety of other genres including science fiction and modernist female romance. Both novels are fictive autobiographies told by female story-tellers, one of whom is a professional novelist and cult poet and the other an old woman writing her memoir at the end of her life. Curiously, for both these women life-writing is death-haunted, and it is with the writing process as Gothic activity that I am concerned here. As Atwood has commented, 'perhaps all writing . . . is motivated, deep down, by a fear of and a fascination with mortality – by a desire to make the risky trip down to the Underworld, and to bring something or someone back from the dead' (Atwood 2003: 140). Ghostly voices, dark doubles, suicides and death threats proliferate in these narratives which are themselves labyrinthine structures, endlessly doubling between real life stories and fictional reconstructions. These features produce uncanny effects, for ghosts figure the secret life of memory while split selves and dark doubles provide images for psychic repression and self-alienation, so that life-writing becomes a process which Terry Castle has described as 'the spectralization of the Other' (Castle 1988: 125). That blurring of boundaries between the real and the imaginary would account for a fascination with transgression as these narrators negotiate border crossings between dreams and waking, truth and lies, even between life and death. But Atwoodian Gothic is not entirely serious, and we should not neglect her ironic humour nor the ferocious delight with which her duplicitous story-tellers conduct their negotiations, not only with their dead but also with us, their living readers.

Lady Oracle opens with a voice speaking from beyond the grave: 'I planned my death carefully, unlike my life' (Atwood 1993: 7), though as we read, that first paragraph transforms itself into parody. We discover that the speaker is not dead after all, but is a Canadian living in disguise in Italy. (The speaker, Joan Foster, is only the first of Atwood's female trickster narrators and Iris Chase Griffen in *The Blind Assassin* is not quite the last.) Not only does Joan write Gothic romances, but she also tries quite disastrously to construct her real life like a Gothic plot, with herself as victim. In Atwood's ironic revisioning 'that allows for self-reflexivity and implicit critique' (Becker 1999: 152), Joan's elaborate plots fail. Her Costume Gothics turn out to be not escape fantasies but dark mirrors of her own life where she carries out complex negotiations with her memories and her mother's ghost. Yet writing does provide Joan with the illusion of escape, for she writes (always secretly) under different pseudonyms, cultivating a double life: 'The important thing was not the books themselves . . . It was the fact that I was two different people at once' (Atwood 1993: 213). However, a split self can quickly become a symptom of paranoia, as Joan discovers when she finds herself overnight a Toronto celebrity and media personality: 'It was as if someone with my name were out there in the real world, impersonating me . . . my dark twin . . . She wanted to kill me and take my place' (250–1).

Like her Gothic victims, Joan is motivated by fear – fear of the past, fear of blackmail, fear of losing her husband's love, and above all of being found out. Her staged death by drowning in Lake Ontario does not free her, and even her writing begins to look like another failed escape attempt. In Italy she finally decides to follow the heroine of her unfinished Gothic novel into the maze, only to discover that she is following the villainess instead. At the centre of the maze she finds four of her fictional heroines who all claim to be her doubles, and when the villain reaches for her throat, he becomes a shape-changing version of the men in her own life – altogether a multiple figuring of Joan's shifting identities and 'unspeakable' insecurities and sexual fears. However, violent Gothic fantasy is interrupted by the sound of real footsteps outside. Is it her husband or is it a murderer? (Are they one and the same?) When he appears, the man is only a newspaper reporter who has come for her life story, and, once translated into realism, Gothic terrors collapse. The novel has a comic ending, when Joan decides to return to Canada, to give up writing Gothics, and to write science fiction instead.

Lady Oracle is Gothic entertainment, but in *The Blind Assassin* Atwood leads her protagonist further into the psychological maze than ever before, as an old woman writing in small-town Ontario has to confront all she has repressed in her long life. The very title of this novel suggests skullduggery, though it is the death opening (not a faked one this time) which engages our interest. There are three suicides in the first 20 pages of Iris Chase Griffen's narrative, all close relatives of hers, and though Iris appears to be innocent, we cannot help speculating on her possible involvement. Is this another of Atwood's Ontario Gothic mysteries? The plot is so complicated with its three interlocking stories, and there are so many uncanny motifs (doubles, severed hands and surrealistically disembodied moving fingers with a life of their own) that we begin to suspect that this is a novel as obsessed with identity and writing as it is with identity and national history. In contrast with Joan, Iris is an amateur, though once she begins her memoir she writes incessantly. She already has her life story, just as she has her dead sister Laura's published novel *The Blind Assassin* and also Laura's hidden notebooks. Iris and Joan are involved in quests as devious as any Gothic heroine's, though for Iris writing is not escape but more like bleeding to death, as old wounds split open and her secret life spills out onto her handwritten pages. Though her motives for writing are initially unclear to her, she gradually realises the significance of memoirs and memorials: 'But what is a memorial, when you come right down to it, but a commemoration of wounds endured? Endured, and resented. Without memory, there can be no revenge' (Atwood 2000: 621). Hers is a very Gothic tale which is a confession as well as a private memoir and public memorial, for this is Iris's trip to the Underworld where she continues to negotiate with her dead.

Writing is an uncanny enterprise, as Atwood reminds us in her comment on identity and authorship in a chapter entitled: 'Duplicity: The jekyll hand, the hyde hand, and the slippery double' (Atwood 2003: 35). For Iris writing is certainly a double act, indeed a kind of ghost writing, for as she confesses, she is really a co-author – with her dead sister: 'Laura was my left hand, and I was hers. We wrote the book together' (627). Moreover, she reveals that it was she who wrote Laura's novel and the science fiction fable as well. The metaphor of the writer's split subjectivity becomes literalised here as a series of Gothic doubles, where borders blur between authorial identities as well as between overlapping plots. Iris leaves her memoir locked up in her old steamer trunk for her granddaughter to inherit after her death, which occurs as she finishes writing. So Iris becomes another Gothic voice, speaking from beyond the grave: 'By the time you read this last page, that – if anywhere – is the only place I will be' (637). Her life story, like Joan's, is an uncanny revisionist project bringing to light what has been assiduously repressed in an ambiguous mixture of truth and lies constructed through the artifice of fiction. Something close to home that seemed to be dead and buried might not be dead after all – just 'floating around loose, ignored but powerful, waiting to get in anywhere' (Munro 1982: 46).

NEO-GOTHICS

Turning now to two neo-Gothics, Eden Robinson's *Monkey Beach* (2000) and Ann-Marie MacDonald's *Fall on Your Knees* (1996), we find that they follow the traditional female Gothic plot of 'disclosure and reparation . . . where the weight of the past . . . may be escaped only when its secrets are brought to light through the process of discovering connections between past and present' (Williams 1995: 171). However, these authors' emphasis on disclosing the hidden histories of oppression suffered by racially marginalised non-white immigrants and Aboriginal people in Canada adds a subversively political dimension to the old plots. MacDonald, who is of Scottish–Lebanese descent, and Robinson, who belongs to the Haisla nation, write from the marginalised position of 'Others' in white Canadian society, and their female protagonists' quests to retrieve what has been repressed, forgotten or deliberately hidden raise social and ethical issues which refigure Gothic endings. Instead of the satisfying closure of 'reparation' and 'escape' from the past, these novels end with a celebration of inheritance restored; the main issue here is not 'reparation' but 'reconciliation' where looping back to the past contains the promise of new beginnings and hopes for a different future.

Fall on Your Knees is a regional and historical novel set in a small mining town in Atlantic Canada, with its declining coal industry and its mixed population of immigrants from all over Europe, the Lebanon, the United States and the Caribbean. However, the appeal of this novel is distinctly Gothic, for beneath its surface realism, like the black coal underground, runs the suppressed history of one Scottish–Lebanese family over three generations, from the first mixed-race marriage of James Piper to Materia Mahmoud in 1900 up to the 1960s. By then, most of the family are dead and the two surviving members meet far away in Harlem, New York, where at last the family tree is spread out and the secrets of the past are brought to light. It is the making of this history and the process of its recovery which form the main plot, as MacDonald's story-telling method peels back layers of deceit and half-truths to reveal a long history of patriarchal tyranny, domestic violence and sexual abuse, silenced mothers, rebellious daughters and women's failed escape attempts. This is domestic Gothic where the unhomely home hides the secret scandal at the centre of the novel (a story of incest and illegitimacy, and of a daughter's live burial before the mercy-killing by her own mother).

Interwoven with domestic Gothic is the theme of race relations in Canada, with its cluster of social taboos around sexual desire for the Other. James Piper becomes obsessed with perpetuating the imperialist myth of white superiority and the hidden scandal of his own mixed marriage. 'He doesn't hate blacks, he just doesn't want them near his bloodline' (MacDonald 1997: 359). However, this is family history retold from a feminine perspective where rebellious daughters defy patriarchal authority. Kathleen, the eldest daughter, falls in love with a black pianist called Rose in New York, only to be raped by her father when he discovers her doubly transgressive love affair, and her sister Frances seduces a black Nova Scotian to be the father of her child. All this is revealed at the end when Frances's mixed race illegitimate son delivers the family tree to Lily, who is the product of James's incestuous union with Kathleen and who has escaped to New York to become the partner of Rose, her dead mother's lover. So, the daughters resist their white father's master narrative in their own relationships, while the family tree provides the documentary evidence for their hidden multi-racial inheritance. As Lily comments: 'Look. We're all in it' (565). Indeed, from another angle, the novel could be read as national allegory where the country's repressed history of non-white immigrants and mixed-race relations returns to unravel Anglo-Canadian myths of whiteness, an appropriate revisionary stance in contemporary multicultural Canada.

But most uncanny is Frances's quest to discover the secret of Lily's parentage, with which she feels intimately and anxiously connected. That connection, which it takes her most of the novel to disinter, has its origins in her repressed traumatic childhood memory of the night of Lily's birth, when Frances accidentally caught sight of Kathleen's mutilated body up in the attic with two new babies between the dead woman's legs. Horror is compounded when Frances drowns one of the babies in the creek while trying to christen them, and as MacDonald reports, these events are stowed away in Frances's 'cave mind'. It is not possible here to trace the tangled web of dreams, fantasies and story-telling by which Frances accomplishes her mission to the psychic Underworld 'to bring someone or something back' to consciousness, 'a mission so secret that even she does not know what it is' (116). Frances's quest does succeed in restoring Lily's true history, just as in a manner of speaking she gives Lily back her dead brother in the person of her son who brings the family tree to New York. Doubled identities and uncanny returns ironically reverse tragic history here to produce a happy Gothic ending.

Monkey Beach represents a return to the original Canadian wilderness Gothic, now told from a contemporary Aboriginal perspective, which gives a very different view of questions of inheritance, history and identity from white or ethnic-minority writing. Robinson's haunted wilderness of forests and rivers on the north-west coast of British Columbia is not an alien place; instead it is full of ancestral ghosts, and her protagonist's visit to the watery Underworld is a quest to retrieve a lost tradition of Native spirituality belonging not just to herself and her own family but to her Native community. As an Aboriginal writer educated in English in Canadian schools, Robinson is caught between two different cultures and belief systems, and it is from this liminal position that her heroine Lisa Marie Hill, a young Haisla woman, tells her first-person narrative. As a result, familiar Gothic motifs are defamiliarised and recontextualised, and it is the fascinating interplay between Aboriginal and white representations of the uncanny that I shall sketch here.

This is a girl's growing-up novel when she enters into her inheritance. The plot moves on two different levels, for Lisa (like her Native foremothers) has the gift of second sight, seeing in 'double exposure – the real world, and beyond it, the same world, but whole' (Robinson 2000: 265). Robinson creates parallel spatial and temporal realities – material space and also the symbolic space of myth and spirituality. In her fiction the boundaries between them are insistently blurred, and her narrator lives on that borderline, slipping unexpectedly through the grid of the everyday into a parallel plane of subjectively apprehended reality. At the realistic level, Lisa's quest is for her lost brother Jimmy who is feared drowned on a fishing trip, but it is also a psycho-spiritual quest which leads her through the labyrinth of repressed memories in her desire to retrieve her Aboriginal inheritance. This is the novel which comes closest to literal negotiations with the dead: 'You don't have to be scared of things you don't understand. They're just ghosts' (265), though it is symptomatic of Lisa's in-between position that she oscillates between belief in the spirit world of Native mythology and an edgy scepticism. Her parodic comments on her dreams ('I used to think that if I could talk to the spirit world, I'd get some answers. Ha bloody ha' (17)) strike against her desire to believe, and there are so many references back to her own body and feelings (images of open-heart surgery and heartbreak) that a conventional psychological reading of her experience is possible.

Even the visionary ending on Monkey Beach which is the goal of her quest is fraught with ambiguity. Lisa's fragmented narrative mixes the realism of her exhaustion and near-drowning with dreams of desire and dread and uncanny returns as she watches the ghost dance on the beach and speaks with her beloved dead. This is followed by her slow awakening in a liminal space filled with echoes – the howl of the Sasquatch of Aboriginal legend who has haunted the margins of this text, 'not quite human, not quite wolf, but something in between', and a mechanical sound from the modern world, 'I hear the sound of a speed boat', which are the final words of the novel. Like *Wacousta*, *Monkey Beach* is a hybridised narrative on the imaginative frontier between the European and the Native imagination, though now the emphasis has shifted and the Aboriginal story-telling imagination is primary.

Residual phenomena haunt every nation's literature, though as this brief sampling has shown, there are distinctive features of Canadian Gothic which emerge out of its colonial history, its traditions of regional difference, and its ethnically and racially diverse postcolonial present. Canada has always been a borderline case (like so many Gothic protagonists), colonised by two European nations, now officially bilingual and for a long time strategically deaf to the other voices (non-English or French) inside its borders, and overshadowed by its powerful neighbour to the south. The Canadian trope of unhomeliness ('If you are Canadian, home is a place that is not home to you' (Sugars 2004: xiii)) resonates through its Gothic fictions. Sublime landscapes are refigured differently here, from the sea-battered coast of Nova Scotia across the northern Ontario bushlands and the western prairies to the ancient forests of British Columbia. Though there are no feudal castles and ruined monasteries nor decadent Southern mansions, nevertheless those traditionally Gothic spaces are transformed into humbler forms of entrapment in unhomely homes and claustrophobic small towns, while city streets become psychological labyrinths inhabited by dissident and alienated outsiders. Wilderness Gothic may be *the* Canadian mode but even that is being constantly refigured, for the Gothic is a shapeshifting genre and peculiarly appropriate to Canada's constant revisioning of its national narrative and its own (or disowned) history. And it is Atwood the Canadian literary icon who gives perhaps the best definition of Gothic as 'the lure of the unmentionable – the mysterious, the buried, the forgotten, the discarded, the taboo' (Atwood 2005: 218).

NOTES

1 In this chapter I shall not consider francophone Quebec writers like Marie-Claire Blais and Anne Hébert whose remarkable Gothic novels come out of a very different historico-cultural context.
2 See Edwards (2005: 151–64) for a fuller analysis of this neo-Gothic trend.

WORKS CITED

Atwood, Margaret (1969) *The Journals of Susanna Moodie*, Toronto: Oxford University Press.
—— (1972) *Survival: A Thematic Guide to Canadian Literature*, Toronto: Anansi.
—— (1993) *Lady Oracle*, London: Virago.
—— (1995) *Strange Things: The Malevolent North in Canadian Literature*, Oxford: Clarendon Press.
—— (2000) *The Blind Assassin*, London: Virago.
—— (2003) *Negotiating with the Dead: A Writer on Writing*, London: Virago.
—— (2005) *Curious Pursuits: Occasional Writing 1970–2005*, London: Virago.
—— (2006) *The Tent*, New York: Nan A. Talese.
Becker, Susanne (1999) *Gothic Forms of Feminine Fictions*, Manchester: Manchester University Press.
Castle, Terry (1988) *The Female Thermometer: Eighteenth Century Culture and the Invention of the Uncanny*, Oxford: Oxford University Press.
Edwards, Justin D. (2005) *Gothic Canada: Reading the Spectre of a National Literature*, Edmonton: University of Alberta Press.
MacDonald, Ann-Marie (1997) *Fall on Your Knees*, London: Vintage.
Moodie, Susanna (1986) *Roughing it in the Bush; or, Life in Canada*, London: Virago.

14

AUSTRALIAN GOTHIC

KEN GELDER

Australia was colonised and settled by the British – towards the end of the eighteenth century – at precisely the moment at which the Gothic novel emerged as a clearly defined genre back home. Its colonisation also followed the Gothic revival in architecture in Britain, which was to influence large-scale metropolitan architecture in Australian cities later on: for example, in the 1860s reconstruction of Sydney's St Mary's Cathedral or the Great Hall at Sydney University with its distinctive kangaroo gargoyle, or the ANZ Bank (the 'Gothic Bank') which was built in Melbourne in the 1880s (Randles 2006: 151, 158). As for the architecture of the Gothic novel itself, however, there were those who thought that Australia was simply too new to accommodate it. Around the time Sir Edmund Thomas Blacket was designing Sydney University's neo-Gothic Great Hall, the immigrant journalist Frederick Sinnett wrote a foundational literary essay, 'The Fiction Fields of Australia' (1856), in which, paraphrasing Milton's 'Il Penseroso' (1633), the Gothic novel in Australia was cast, perhaps with some regret, as a sheer impossibility:

> No storied windows . . . cast a dim, religious light over any Australian premises. There are no ruins for that rare old plant, the ivy green, to creep over and make his meal of. No Australian author can hope to extricate his hero or heroine, however pressing the emergency may be, by means of a spring panel and a subterranean passage, or such like relics of feudal barons.
>
> (Sinnett 1856: 9)

Australia may well have seen few old ruins by this time. Even so, it soon became the site of what Tom Griffiths has called an 'antiquarian imagination' which – through the early work of colonial collectors of 'curiosities', naturalists, amateur archaeologists, ethnologists and historians – infused the newly settled country with a remarkable sense of the ancient (Griffiths 1996). In colonial Australian fiction, this found one sort of expression in a fascination with the 'timelessness' of Aboriginal people, as well as in fantasies about the discovery of a Lemuria (a lost or forgotten civilisation) that revealed settler Australians' proximity to vibrant prehistorical forces: as in George Firth Scott's *The Last Lemurian* (1898), which finds a lost race of people in the Australian desert, or J. D. Hennessey's *An Australian Bush Track* (1896), where a group of settler entrepreneurs discover the remnants of a great civilisation in a place called 'Zoo-Zoo land' somewhere in northern Queensland. There are at least two ways of understanding these strange Gothic romances: first, through their creation of what

Melissa Bellanta has called a 'fabulated' nation, full of wonders and strangeness, luxurious and Edenic, even utopian (Bellanta 2004); and second, as a means of eliding (or at least, sublimating) both the depressed and dispossessed predicament of actual Aboriginal people by this time, and the harsh, austere realities of settler life in the bush.

Colonial explorers in Australia could find themselves caught somewhere between the acknowledgement of harsh bush realities and flights of fancy that saw the interior landscape rendered picturesque. John McDouall Stuart's early 1860s account of the region to the north of Chamber's Pillar, where the hills 'resemble nothing so much as a number of old castles in ruins', imports Gothic architecture into Australia as a kind of phantom image, Sinnett notwithstanding (cited in Ryan 1996: 77). Roslynn Haynes has noted that the vastness of the Australian interior was also not untypically perceived by explorers as a Gothic place of confinement. The 'most alarming prospect faced by the inland explorers, coming from the confines of heavily populated Britain and Europe', she writes, 'was that of void. This was particularly true of the desert with its repeated vistas of empty horizontal planes under a cloudless, overarching sky. It therefore seems paradoxical that this vast expanse of apparently empty space was so frequently described, in their accounts, in Gothic terms of enclosure and entrapment' (Haynes 1999: 77). A diary entry from Captain Charles Sturt, who was keen to discover an 'inland sea' in the desert interior of the country, reveals 'no-doubt conscious echoes' of Wordsworth as it chronicles the 'absolute loneliness of the desert' and the 'stillness of the forest', the silence of which is broken only by the 'melancholy howl' of wandering native dogs (cited in Haynes 1999: 79).

Gothic tropes seemed to lend themselves all too readily to the colonially perceived Australian interior. In 1876, the Melbourne novelist and journalist Marcus Clarke wrote a preface to a new edition of a book of poetry by Adam Lindsay Gordon, a colonial writer, adventurer and renowned horseman, whose increasing debts had driven him to suicide six years earlier. Clarke drew on Edgar Allan Poe to acknowledge Gordon's melancholic condition and then transferred it – as what he famously called 'Weird Melancholy' – onto the Australian landscape itself, in an escalating sequence of Gothic horror images:

> The Australian mountain forests are funereal, secret, stern. Their solitude is desolation. They seem to stifle, in their black gorges, a story of sullen despair. No tender sentiment is nourished in their shade . . . The sun suddenly sinks, and the mopokes burst out into horrible peals of semi-human laughter. The natives aver that, when night comes, from out of the bottomless depth of some lagoon the Bunyip rises, and, in form like monstrous sea-calf, drags his loathsome length from out the ooze. From a corner of the silent forest rises a dismal chant, and around the fire dance natives painted like skeletons. All is fear – inspiring and gloomy.
>
> (Clarke 1876: 645–6)

This lurid passage sees the Australian bush, Aborigines and monstrosity – through a uniquely Australian creature, the bunyip – yoked together under the

exaggerated sign of the Gothic. For the literary critic Andrew McCann, Clarke
sublimates an 'Aboriginal presence' into the perceived melancholia of the bush,
producing a racist stereotype that – along with the primal bunyip – casts
Aborigines back into the remote past in order for readers to experience them
solely as 'an object of aesthetic pleasure' (McCann 2005: 172–3): an already
'vanished race' that barely exists outside of the Gothic imagination. This interpretation is persuasive, but it plays down the significance of melancholy itself, a
sensibility imprinted onto the bush so often in colonial writing as to make it
paradigmatic. We can perhaps recall Freud's famous essay on the subject,
'Mourning and Melancholia' (1917), which had seen melancholy – in contrast to
mourning – as the result of one's refusal to properly acknowledge or confront
the loss of the thing one had loved. That lost object is then transferred to the self
or ego, so that the melancholic is typically self-reproaching. For Freud, it is as if
'the shadow of the [lost] object fell upon the ego' (Freud 1917: 258). It is
certainly worth thinking about Clarke's projection of Gordon's melancholy onto
the Australian landscape, with the strange accompanying images of monstrous
birth (the bunyip rising up from the depths, sliding 'from out the ooze') and
animated death (the natives 'painted like skeletons'). What has vanished in the
midst of all this, however, is Gordon himself: the suicided settler–adventurer.
Clarke's Gothic description may not so much subscribe to the consoling racism
of a 'vanished race' as register the loss of a certain kind of colonial optimism,
expressed through Gordon's own 'manly admiration for healthy living' to which
Clarke had paid tribute (Clarke 1876: 644). A shadow has fallen over the colonial ego, we might say, in which case it could well be that Clarke's account gives
expression to the 'Weird Melancholy' of settler colonialism itself.

A brief discussion of three colonial Australian short stories might help to
clarify this point. W. Sylvester Walker's 'The Mystery of Yelcomorn Creek' was
published in the *Centennial Magazine* in March 1890. An old man who now lives
alone at the end of a boundary fence tells a story about his search for opals in
Queensland's interior, helped by Bobbie, an Aboriginal tracker. They discover a
lost valley that seems like 'the Garden of Eden' (Walker 1890: 96): so that this
story appears at first to be another lost race or Lemurian romance. But the
narrator hears an unearthly cry suggesting 'a sort of quivering despair' (98); and
soon he stumbles across a series of bloodstained Aboriginal graves. Phantom
Aboriginal warriors appear and the narrator faints away. When he recovers, he
leaves the valley – without a single opal – and seals the entrance. So here is a
colonial Gothic tale in which a settler discovers a massacre site, a difficult-to-
find place that testifies – after the event – to the fact of colonial violence, even
though the story also refuses properly to acknowledge this fact through its
distancing Gothic tropes and its affiliation to the lost race romance genre. To
return to Freud, this story does not mourn its Aboriginal characters (including
Bobbie, who is also killed) but it does generate a certain melancholic effect that
sees a once ambitious colonial prospector subsequently retreat into old age and
self-absorption on the edge of the frontier.

The colonial writer and explorer Ernest Favenc's story, 'Doomed', published in the *Australian Town and Country Journal* in April 1899, intensifies that melancholic effect as it introduces five 'eager, young, and hopeful' men in the Australian bush: youthful settler–adventurers, rather like Adam Lindsay Gordon (Favenc 1899: 35). On a whim, one of them shoots and kills a pregnant Aboriginal woman beside a waterhole. The five men then each die as if cursed, with the Aboriginal woman and her baby – born after death, as it were – haunting their final visions. This story is much closer to the realities of colonial violence than Walker's. There is no expression of guilt or remorse here, however, just a sense that – no matter how casual an act of colonial violence might be – all settlers are implicated. The melancholy of the story is registered not only through the loss of Aboriginal lives (which, typically for colonial Australian Gothic fiction, are nevertheless reanimated after death) but also through the *effects* of that loss, in particular the dissolution of youthful colonial optimism: as if this, more than anything else, is colonialism's lost object.

The third colonial story, Rosa Praed's 'The Bunyip', was published in a collection titled *Coo-ee: Tales of Australian Life by Australian Ladies* in 1891. We have already seen the bunyip in Marcus Clarke's description above, and in fact the creature was well known by the 1860s, with collectors like Reynell Eveleigh Johns expressing interest in it alongside his fascination for extinct animals like the New Zealand moa and the dodo (Griffiths 1996: 35). For Praed, the bunyip is local and all too familiar:

> Everyone who has lived in Australia has heard of the bunyip. It is the one respectable flesh-curdling horror of which Australia can boast. The old world has her tales of ghoul and vampire, of Lorelei, spook, and pixie, but Australia has nothing but her Bunyip.
>
> (Praed 1891: 271)

It seems to work as an effect on people's lives, for better or worse: as Praed evocatively puts it, the creature 'deals out promiscuously benefits and calamities from the same hand' (274). The problem is that, although Aborigines seem especially familiar with it – referring to it as 'Debil-Debil' and avoiding the waterholes it is supposed to frequent – no settlers ever seem to have seen the bunyip with their own eyes. The story then turns to the business of colonial settlement as two brothers travel up country to meet a dray 'loaded with stores and furniture for the new home to which we were bound' (277). These are colonials who are yet to settle: colonials who are as yet to occupy a home. The group make camp beside a 'dark swamp' and soon 'the talk got to eerie things . . . and as we talked a sort of chill seemed up creep over us' (280). They hear a strange cry, like that of a child 'in dire distress' (281), and wonder about the possibility of a child lost in the bush, another not uncommon Gothic trope in colonial Australian writing (see Pierce 1999). Going in search of the child, the men are unexpectedly disoriented: 'Though we tried to move in the direction of the voice, it was impossible to determine whence it came, so misleading and fitful and will-o'-the-wisp was the sound' (283). Finally, the colonials find the body of a dead young girl whom they identify as Nancy, from a station ominously called Coffin Lid. But she has been dead for some time, a fact which leads the narrator to wonder if the cry they heard was 'the Bunyip, or little Nancy's ghost' (286). What is striking about this story is that these would-be settlers are themselves the victims of an effect – frightened, disoriented and possessed by nothing more than a sound, by something no one has actually seen. This all occurs as they prepare themselves for settlement, for the occupation of their colonial properties. But occupation is not allowed to happen in this story. We might say that occupation is replaced by *preoccupation*, by a bothersome sense of something that is already there before them. In one sense, this is a typically colonial Gothic representation of the mis-recognition of Aboriginal inhabitation, elliptically or dimly revealed through an occulted bush full of unseen 'presences'. But in another sense, it offers these preoccupied settlers – even before they properly arrive – a melancholic glimpse of their own future: where the entry into colonial occupation is tied to an untimely death and the loss of innocence.

Another kind of colonial melancholia played itself out in relation to Australia's penal history, where lost innocence was a readily available trope for convict narratives chronicling the journey to and arrival in the new world. Australia's greatest colonial Gothic novel was Marcus Clarke's *His Natural Life* (1874), which returns us to the themes of 'enclosure and entrapment' noted above through its melodramatic treatment of the émigré convict experience. Its hero, Richard Devine, is a quintessentially innocent man, unjustly transported to Australia to experience all the brutalities of penal life in the colonies, in particular the penal settlement at Port Arthur in Tasmania. Devine – who changes his identity to become the convict Rufus Dawes – survives the ending of this novel, but a revised version published under title *For the Term of his Natural Life* (1885) saw Devine/Dawes and his beloved Sylvia drown in each other's arms during a cyclone: a much bleaker ending that refuses to give the characters a productive colonial future. Port Arthur was established as a penal colony in 1830 when Tasmania was still known as Van Diemen's Land, modelling its formidable layout on the panopticon at Pentonville prison in London. It soon became notorious for its brutality, psychological as well as physical, as it built its disciplinary regime around rigid routines and prisoner anonymity and isolation. In a first-hand account of his own convict experiences there, *Old Convict Days* (1899), William Derrincourt described Port Arthur as 'the Abode of Horror'. Clarke had described the penal settlement and its environs as a 'natural penitentiary', surrounded by natural hazards such as the Devil's Blow-Hole as well as the nearby 'Island of the Dead' where convicts who had died at Port Arthur were buried. The entrepreneur and forger Henry Savery, who published Australia's first novel, *Quintus Servinton*, in 1831 – a semi-autobiographical account of his own convict experiences – had himself died while incarcerated at Port Arthur, in 1842. By the time Clarke wrote *His Natural Life*, however, Port Arthur was no longer a penal colony and had begun to fall into disrepair. In a series of news-paper articles about the site published in Melbourne's *The Argus* in July 1873, Clarke gave Australia's recent convict history a familiar sensibility:

> The history of 'Convict Discipline' in these colonies is a melancholy one . . . the prisons and barracks erected at such cost in various parts of the colonies have been pulled down or abandoned to other uses, and intelligence has at last reached us of the final dismantling of the last relic . . . the 'Natural Penitentiary' of Port Arthur.
>
> (Clarke 1873: 511)

We have seen Frederick Sinnett's claim that colonial Australia had no Gothic ruins. But the 'relic' of Port Arthur casts its own shadow upon the colonial scene. The literary critic David Matthews reproduces Clarke's sentiments in these much more recent comments on *His Natural Life*: 'Convictism, the ruined monu-ments of which could still be seen on the landscape, was Australia's own equiva-lent of castellated culture, a repressed and melancholic past' (Matthews 2006: 9). For John Frow, in his essay 'In the Penal Colony' (1999), Port Arthur is 'a memorial . . . its ruined traces bearing ambiguous witness to a whole system of punishment, involuntary exile and unfree labour which has come to represent the foundational moment of the Australian nation'. Frow also writes about the mass murderer Martin Bryant, who shot and killed 35 people at Port Arthur – by this time, a tourist destination – on 28 April 1996. The question of how this terrible event should be memorialised in turn preoccupies those involved, a matter that Frow expresses in typically Gothic terms:

> Nobody uses Bryant's name, but his denied presence is everywhere. Nobody knows the forms which will lay the ghost. Nobody knows what kind of monument will insert this story into the other story for which this site is known, into that other past which is barely available for understanding.
>
> (Frow 1999: n.p.)

For Jim Davidson, the re-naming of Van Diemen's Land as Tasmania in 1856 saw this off-shore Australian state 'determined to be born again'. But in spite of this, he notes, Tasmania remains a 'landscape containing presences. Perhaps these are more correctly styled absences, not yet fully expiated – the slaughtered Aborigines, the downtrodden convicts, and hunted species like the diminutive Tasmanian emu and the Gothically named Tasmanian Tiger' (Davidson 1989: 307). This is enough to encourage Davidson to coin the term, 'Tasmanian Gothic', accounting for the island's traumatic past as well as its often defiantly proclaimed sense of isolation and difference from mainland Australia. When he visited Australia in 1871 and 1872, Anthony Trollope declared that Tasmania 'already had the feel of an old country' (cited Davidson 1989: 316); a common mainland corollary of this view, however, is that Tasmania is 'backward'. More recent examples of the Tasmanian Gothic include Roger Scholes' award-winning film, *The Tale of Ruby Rose* (1987), set in the Tasmanian highlands in

1933; and the novelist Mudrooroo's hallucinatory *Master of the Ghost Dreaming* series which begins in 1991 with a novel that returns to the early colonial experience from an Aboriginal perspective.

It would be possible to identify a contemporary indigenous Gothic subgenre in Australia that includes Mudrooroo's novels, as well as (for example) Sam Watson's *The Kadaitcha Sung* (1990), which also returns to the colonial scene where it chronicles a history of brutal violence and exploitation in the midst of which it stages a pre-colonial struggle between *kadaitcha* spirit men. Some of the work of Aboriginal artist Tracey Moffatt might also be termed indigenous Gothic: such as the short film *Night Cries: A Rural Tragedy* (1989), where an Aboriginal woman lives out her confinement nursing her dying white mother in an isolated homestead amidst a series of vividly baroque, traumatic recollections; or *BeDevil* (1993), the first feature film directed by an Aboriginal woman. *BeDevil* consists of three ghost stories built around sites that are inhabited by very different kinds of spirits: a black American soldier from the Second World War who haunts a swamp, a young white girl killed on a railway track, and two Aboriginal lovers who haunt a warehouse earmarked for property development by greedy investors. These ghosts have each been dislocated or, in the case of the young Aboriginal lovers, dispossessed. Yet they also seem more a part of their place than ever before, condemned to remain there and to possess those who try to live there later on. In fact, those who come afterwards to these sites are drawn to the hauntings and held by them, as if transfixed. Elsewhere, Jane M. Jacobs and I have drawn on the verb 'solicit' to describe this particular spectral effect, with its overtones of allure and attraction as well as anxiety and alarm (Gelder and Jacobs 1998: 21–2). But *BeDevil* also cuts to scenes which show modern Australians away from these sites enjoying themselves, at leisure, playing 'innocently' and freely in the sun, frolicking in those Australian places that seem to be unaffected by shadows. This is one aspect of the film's post-colonialism where, in contrast to Ernest Favenc's colonial Gothic story, implication is much less absolute. On the other hand, postcolonial 'innocence' can also look like wilful disavowal: as if, this film seems to suggest, some haunting is good for you.

Australian cinema has explored the Gothic since the early 1970s. The film critics Susan Dermody and Elizabeth Jacka in fact mark the emergence of Australian Gothic in cinema with Peter Weir's 1971 black comedy, *Homesdale* (Dermody and Jacka 1988: 50). A better-known and more lyrical example of the Australian Gothic in film, however, is Weir's *Picnic at Hanging Rock* (1975), the story of the disappearance of three girls and their teacher in the bush on St Valentine's Day, 1890 – based on the 1967 novel by Joan Lindsay. Mysterious experiences in the bush remain a stock theme of the Australian Gothic, especially those involving inexperienced metropolitan travellers who find themselves stranded in some remote and often deranged outback location. The Canadian director Ted Kotcheff's film *Wake in Fright* (1971) – based on Kenneth Cook's 1961 horror novel – was the first of a number of films drawn to what Jonathan

Rayner has called the 'Gothic rural community', where the outback town 'is portrayed as the repository of warped or degenerate tendencies', a place defined by exaggerated violence, aggressive masculinity, misogyny, xenophobia and corruption (Rayner 2001: 28). Greg McLean's *Wolf Creek* (2005) is a more recent example of a Gothic rural horror film, with its two female British tourists coming to grief (their male Australian companion survives) after their car breaks down beside a meteorite crater and they are hoodwinked by a crazed outback hunter who has set up camp in a remote abandoned mining site.

For these characters, the Australian interior is again a place of Gothic 'enclosure and entrapment'. But the horizontal openness of the landscape can also be exploited for its Gothic effects. George Miller's *Mad Max* (1979) and its two sequels presented a near-future dystopian vision of a 'primal' Australian outback striated with straight endless roads and inhabited by lawless, threatening gangs of bikers, carjackers and petrol-heads who constantly fight with and elude the police. Miller has astutely noted, 'The Americans have a gun culture – we have a car culture . . . Out in the suburbs it's a socially acceptable form of violence. That's the wellspring a film like this has' (cited in O'Regan 1996: 105). The menacing black car on the highway came to symbolise *Mad Max*'s Gothicness, with the horror of road in the film linked precisely to its straightness: as if violent unpredictable encounters there are the inevitable result of perfect visibility, of seeing all too clearly. Ross Gibson has written about the 'Horror Stretch', tracing actual murder cases and disappearances at various locations along the highways of northern Queensland in his study, *Seven Versions of an Australian Badland* (2002). The 1975 murders of Noel and Sophie Weckert enable him to offer a kind of archaeology of horror that takes him back to 'many more murder-scenes from the bloody past of Australia's colonial frontier', thus demonstrating that 'history lives as a presence in the landscape' (Gibson 2002: 50). Some contemporary Australia films, and some novels too, have staged a return to the colonial scene in order to animate its violence all over again: for example, Kate Grenville's novel *Secret River* (2005), which tries to recreate the mindset of a colonial settler involved in the massacre of Aborigines; or *The Proposition* (2006), a film directed by John Hillcoat and written by Nick Cave, Australia's best-known Goth songwriter and performer, which cast itself as a 'real' account of the stark brutality of colonial experience. Built upon its dispossession and killings of Aboriginal people and its foundational systems of punishment and incarceration, the colonial scene – we might even say, the 'ruins of colonialism', to draw on the title of a book on the subject (Healy 1997) – continues to shadow Australian cultural production and helps to keep the Australian Gothic very much alive.

WORKS CITED

Bellanta, Melissa (2004) 'Fabulating the Australian Desert: Australia's Lost Race Romances, 1890–1908', *Philament: The Online Journal of the Arts and Culture*, issue 3, April: www.arts.usyd.edu.au/publications/philament/issue3_Critique_Bellanta.htm.

Clarke, Marcus (1873) 'Port Arthur', in Michael Wilding (ed.), *Marcus Clarke*, St Lucia: University of Queensland Press, 1976.

—— (1876) 'Adam Lindsay Gordon', in Michael Wilding (ed.), *Marcus Clarke*, St Lucia: University of Queensland Press, 1976.

Davidson, Jim (1989) 'Tasmanian Gothic', *Meanjin*, 48(2): 307–24.

Dermody, Susan and Elizabeth Jacka (1988) *The Screening of Australia*, vol. 2: *Anatomy of a National Cinema*, Sydney: Currency Press.

Favenc, Ernest (1899) 'Doomed', *Australian Town and Country Journal*, April.

Freud, Sigmund (1917) 'Mourning and Melancholia', in Angela Richards (ed.), *The Penguin Freud Library,* vol. II: *On Metaphsychology*, trans. James Strachey, Harmondsworth: Penguin Books, 1991, pp. 245–68.

Frow, John (1999) 'In the Penal Colony', *Australian Humanities Review* (April): www.lib.latrobe.edu.au/AHR/archive/Issue-April-1999/frow3.html.

Gelder, Ken and Jane M. Jacobs (1998) *Uncanny Australia: Sacredness and Identity in a Postcolonial Nation*, Carlton, Victoria: Melbourne University Press.

Griffiths, Tom (1996) *Hunters and Collectors: The Antiquarian Imagination in Australia*, Melbourne: Cambridge University Press.

Haynes, Roslynn (1999) *Seeking the Centre: The Australian Desert in Literature, Art and Film*, Cambridge: Cambridge University Press.

Healy, Chris (1997) *From the Ruins of Colonialism: History as Social Memory*, Melbourne: Cambridge University Press.

McCann, Andrew (2005) *Marcus Clarke's Bohemia*, Carlton, Victoria: Melbourne University Press.

Matthews, David (2006) 'Marcus Clarke, Gothic, Romance', in Stephanie Trigg (ed.), *Medievalism and the Gothic in Australian Culture*, Carlton, Victoria: Melbourne University Press.

O'Regan, Tom (1996) *Australian National Cinema*, London: Routledge.

Pierce, Peter (1999) *The Country of Lost Children: An Australian Anxiety*, Melbourne: Cambridge University Press.

Praed, Rosa (1891) 'The Bunyip', in P. Martin (ed.), *Coo-ee: Tales of Australian Life by Australian Ladies*, London: Richard Edwin King.

Randles, Sarah (2006) 'Rebuilding the Middle Ages: Medievalism in Australian Architecture', in Stephanie Trigg (ed.), *Medievalism and the Gothic in Australian Culture*, Carlton, Victoria: Melbourne University Press.

Rayner, Jonathan (2001) *Contemporary Australian Cinema: An Introduction*, Manchester: Manchester University Press.

Ryan, Simon (1996) *The Cartographic Eye: How Explorers Saw Australia*, Melbourne: Cambridge University Press.

Sinnett, Frederick (1856) 'The Fiction Fields of Australia', in John Barnes (ed.), *The Writer in Australia: A Collection of Literary Documents, 1856 to 1964*, Melbourne: Oxford University Press, 1969.

Walker, W. Sylvester (1890) 'The Mystery of Yelcomorn Creek', *Centennial Magazine*, March.

Part III

GOTHIC CONCEPTS

15

GOTHIC CONCEPTS

EMMA MCEVOY AND CATHERINE SPOONER

The essays in this section examine concepts that are important to the Gothic –
the uncanny, the abject and haunting, for example – and critical approaches to
the Gothic. We have chosen to concentrate on concepts that have been the
subject of a substantial tradition of theorising and critical writing. Of course
there are many other key tropes and thematics – religion, vampires, doubles, for
example – and with reference to these we encourage you to use the comprehensive index at the back of the book. In the case of the essays on femininities,
masculinities and queer Gothic our selection has been made on the grounds that
the subject matter encompasses both traditional Gothic thematics and a significant critical tradition. Gothic children is perhaps a less conventional theme, but
is quickly becoming an important area of study. All the essays provide a useful
set of tools for approaching Gothic, working as they do by providing examples of
critical readings as well as discussing the critical traditions themselves. They
come from a variety of critical and theoretical traditions – including gender
theory, queer theory, psychoanalysis and deconstruction.

David Punter's essay on the uncanny discusses definitions and descriptions of
the uncanny from Freud onwards, as well as considering contemporary criticism
of the uncanny. For Punter, the very 'notion of the uncanny permits a rethinking
of what we might term the "unsaid" of Gothic' and exceeds or supplements the
insights that we might find in context-based historical criticism. Kelly Hurley's
essay on the abject and the grotesque also seeks to expand the boundaries of
critical investigation as she combines the theorising of Kristeva on the abject
and Bakhtin on the grotesque, and reminds us of Kristeva's interest in Bakhtin's
theories of carnival. Hurley insists on the celebratory aspects of topics more
usually discussed in terms of Gothic anxieties as she discusses how we may
'relate Bakhtin's idea of a joyous, rejuvenating "carnivalesque" to what seems to
be the relentless negativism of Gothic horror'.

The essays by Sue Walsh on Gothic children and Andrew Smith on hauntings
consider Gothic subject matter in relation to a variety of critical approaches.
Andrew Smith picks up on a favourite Gothic trope which is susceptible to readings from a range of critical traditions. He suggests a number of ways in which to
read the ghost, not only in psychoanalytic terms but also in social and historical
ones. Sue Walsh uses her deconstructive reading of the text 'The New Mother'
to demonstrate by example, and takes much other Gothic criticism to task for its
reading of the child within the Gothic text. She argues that critics want to produce the child as a version of the unconscious, suggesting through her reading of

'The New Mother' that the Gothic text is often far more wary of these pitfalls and resists such easy pigeon-holing.

The essays on femininities, masculinities and queer Gothic all trace a critical tradition in relation to Gothic texts and all have contributions to make to these critical debates. Alison Milbank discusses a range of texts and examines, in the shape of the Radcliffean 'explained supernatural', a phenomenon that has vexed critics for many years. Milbank makes a welcome contribution to the debate, reintroducing metaphysics and adroitly sidestepping some of the simplistic binaries that have characterised much previous critical writing. Brian Baker's and Ellis Hanson's essays come from newer critical approaches and provide lucid, comprehensive surveys of queer theory and the study of masculinities in relation to the Gothic. Baker's essay considers fragmented masculine subjectivities from Henry Jekyll to Hannibal Lecter, and argues that Gothic 'from its very inception, uncovers pre-existing fault-lines in the masculine subject'. Hanson discusses both the contributions of queer theory to Gothic criticism (its major contribution he finds to be in its 'historicising, Foucauldian challenge to the pathologising topologies of psychoanalysis') and the contributions of Gothic to queer theory. Appropriating the persona of Jane Austen's Catherine Morland, he investigates and celebrates the queer pleasures to be found within the Gothic, discussing the possibilities for 'the creative transfiguration of the self through the readerly pleasures of fear and abjection'.

Despite the difference in style, approach and subject matter in these essays, a common set of critical influences tends to resurface – among them Freud, Kristeva, Michel Foucault, Eve Kosofsky Sedgwick and Terry Castle – suggesting that, for contemporary critics, there is a key body of writing that continues to inform our understanding of the Gothic. As the writers in this volume engage in diverse ways with this critical material, important debates emerge – about sexuality, transgression, the body and the supernatural, for example. These debates often complement or echo those found in the more historical approaches found in the preceding two sections. The focus on identity politics in the essays on gender and sexuality, for example, could be expanded by recourse to many of the essays in the 'Locations' section, particularly Teresa Goddu's discussion of race in American Gothic. Similarly the essays on hauntings and the uncanny explore in greater depth concepts found, for example, in Alexandra Warwick's essay on Victorian Gothic or Catherine Spooner's on Gothic in the twentieth century. Although these debates can provide no easy answers to what Gothic 'is' or even what it 'does', they will hopefully offer a selection of routes into the Gothic, opening up new critical vistas, or reopening old ones.

16

THE UNCANNY

DAVID PUNTER

It is conventional – and perhaps inescapable – to begin any consideration of the concept of the 'uncanny' by referring to Freud's essay under that title of 1919. Before doing so, however, it is worth recording some of the meanings ascribed to the word in the *Oxford English Dictionary*, which include 'mischievous', 'malicious', 'careless', 'incautious', 'unreliable', 'not to be trusted', 'partaking of a supernatural character' and 'mysterious, weird, uncomfortably strange or unfamiliar'. The earliest usage of the word recorded in the *OED* is in 1596; but it is the last sense on which Freud picks up, and which provides the clearest link to the Gothic. Here the *OED* cites three exempla, all from the nineteenth century, and they are all of interest. The first is from Bulwer-Lytton: 'If men, gentlemen born, will read uncanny books . . . why they must resolve to reap what they sow'; the second is from Emerson, speaking of Stonehenge: 'We walked in and out, and took again and again a fresh look at the uncanny stones'; and the third is from Mary Braddon, who refers to a 'slate quarry under the cliff' as 'a scene of uncanny grandeur'.

The first of these references situates us in a realm of the magical, the supernatural, but with clear undertones of what we might call 'black magic', of the danger inherent in dealings with matters which are 'unfamiliar', which might threaten the 'normal' world inhabited even by 'gentlemen', those most conventional of societal participants. The second refers us to a world of the ancient, of indecipherable signs from the past, of something which might once have been understood but whose meaning now eludes us; also, in the 'again and again', it might remind us of a primal *topos* of the uncanny, the phenomenon of déjà vu. The third effects a connection between the uncanny and the sublime; we might deduce that this slate quarry evokes feelings in us – feelings of respect, admiration, even awe – but exactly what the source of those feelings might be remains again elusive, an image which continues to trouble us even if we cannot be certain whence that troubling derives.

It would be, then, against this background that we might situate Freud's sustained attempt to get to grips with quite what this sense of the 'uncanny' might mean. Famously, he begins his essay by stating that the exploration of the uncanny might seem an unusual endeavour for a psychoanalyst, because it abuts onto the category of the aesthetic, but goes on to say that in fact aesthetics has been powerless to expound the quality of the uncanny.

It is undoubtedly related to what is frightening – to what arouses dread and horror; equally certainly, too, the word is not always used in a clearly definable sense, so that it tends to coincide with what excites fear in general. Yet we may expect that a special core of feeling is present which justifies the use of a special conceptual term. One is curious to know what this common core is which allows us to distinguish as 'uncanny' certain things which lie within the field of what is frightening.

(Freud 1955: 219)

At this point we need to remind ourselves, of course, that the exact term to which Freud is referring is not the English 'uncanny' but the German equivalent, 'unheimlich', and it is from this position that he goes on to probe the precise connotations of the term. For, as he says, 'unheimlich' – meaning literally 'unhomely' – is itself in a sense an uncanny word. Through adducing his own catalogue of examples, he demonstrates that there is a remarkable convergence between that which is 'unheimlich' and that which is apparently its opposite, 'heimlich', 'homely'. To put it very simply: because that which is 'heimlich' is in fact also 'surrounded', 'secret', 'kept close to home', then it also becomes 'unheimlich', incapable of full description, unknown to those who are outside the magic walls. Thus the uncanny comes to partake of secrecy, of that which is held away from general advertisement or interpretation, and it is this thought which leads Freud to reliance on a splendid maxim of Schelling's: '"Unheimlich" is the name for everything that ought to have remained . . . secret and hidden but has come to light' (Freud 1955: 224).

This remains the crucial point in the definition of the uncanny: namely, that it represents a feeling which relates to a dialectic between that which is *known* and that which is *unknown*. If we are afraid, then more often than not it is because we are experiencing fear of the unknown: but if we have a sense of the uncanny, it is because the barriers between the known and the unknown are teetering on the brink of collapse. We are afraid, certainly; but what we are afraid of is at least partly our own sense that we have *been here before*. It is perhaps easy to guess how Freud pursues this argument: namely into the idea that the uncanny is occasioned when an event in the present reminds us of something in the (psychological) past, but something which cannot be fully remembered, a past event, or situation, or feeling, which should have been locked away or buried but which has emerged to haunt the current scene.

In the service of his analysis, Freud offers a critique of a story by E. T. A. Hoffmann, 'The Sandman' (1817); but rather than rehearse that critique, what is perhaps more valuable is to note that 'The Sandman' remains at the end of the day – and even at the end of Freud's remarks on it – a remarkably inexplicable story. It is a story, we might say, which places the reader in an untenable position: it appears to supply some clues to meaning, but there is nevertheless something withheld; it is as if there might be some key to the tale, but this key is never placed in the reader's hands. And thus, perhaps, it might be with the Gothic: the boundaries between the 'heimlich' – the socially acceptable and explicable – and the 'unheimlich' – that which lies beyond the bounds of human reason – never become clear, and we are invited to accept a version of events which is, in the strict sense, 'super-natural', not relating to our normative experience but none-theless suggesting another realm which we have perhaps only experienced in dream, in haunting, in our sense of something which exists in our everyday life but nevertheless continues to remind us of something archaic, something which indeed lies within our psyche but at a level so deep that we know it only phantas-mally, only as something which leaves its imprint as it continues to surge upwards and threaten our everyday lives, even as it reminds us of something which, perhaps, we have *once* known but only in the remote past, whether that past be considered historically or psychologically.

In order to translate this more fully into literary terms, we can have recourse to three recent moments in the discussion of the uncanny. The first occurs in the book *Introduction to Literature, Criticism and Theory* by Andrew Bennett and Nicholas Royle. The uncanny, they say, 'has to do with making things *uncertain*: it has to do with the sense that things are not as they have come to appear through habit and familiarity, that they may challenge all rationality and logic' (Bennett and Royle 1999: 37). It is, however, possible, they claim, to 'suggest a few forms that the uncanny takes', and in fact they list ten: (1) 'strange kinds of repetition', a category which includes the double or doppelgänger and the expe-rience of déjà vu; (2) coincidence and the sense that things are 'fated' to happen; (3) animism and (4) anthropomorphism, which are, we might say, clearly related examples of uncanny shape-changing; (5) automatism – in a sense another example of shape-changing insofar as it refers to the process whereby 'what is human is perceived as merely mechanical'; (6) 'a sense of radical uncertainty about sexual identity' – one of the examples they use is Virginia Woolf's *Orlando* (1928), where the protagonist changes gender as s/he moves through different historical epochs; (7) the fear of being buried alive; (8) silence, perhaps a contentious idea, but with some force if one considers instances where silence substitutes for the possibility of a response; (9) telepathy, which Bennett and Royle take to refer crucially to the 'thought that your thoughts are perhaps not your own, however private or concealed you might have assumed them to be'; and (10) death – in the sense of something which 'at once familiar . . . and abso-lutely unfamiliar, unthinkable, unimaginable', a point of ending which is always in some sense simultaneously 'survived' as the record of a life, real or fictional, continues to 'live on'.

Clearly, this is not meant to be an exhaustive list (Bennett and Royle 1999: 37–40); indeed, the very notion of an 'exhaustive list' would be alien to the uncanny, if such a notion would suggest the possibility of a complete quasi-Linnaean categorisation of human experience. According to the logic of the uncanny, such experience continually overflows the bounds of reason; it suggests other realms which hover just beyond the reach of our conventions and assump-tions, it asserts the irreducible presence of the 'ghost in the machine', and thus relates directly to the Gothic and its insistence on forms of knowledge which run counter to everyday expectations. There are many recent fictions – Russell Hoban's *The Medusa Frequency* (1987) and *Angelica's Grotto* (1999) would be two of them – which have effectively 'modernised' this process, to show how, however refined the machines may have become in an age of e-connectedness, some kind of ghost continues to hover, and indeed to manifest itself even in the very heartland of the so-called 'new' technologies, and especially the 'tele-technologies' – those which have to do with communication and manipulation 'at a distance'. And, of course, it is with ambiguities of technological advance that many older classic Gothic texts, *Frankenstein* (1818) and *Dracula* (1897) primary among them, have been principally preoccupied.

In 2003 Royle published a book simply called *The Uncanny*, which, perhaps surprisingly – or indeed uncannily – is the first book-length general study of the uncanny to appear. It is a dense and challenging work, and there is certainly no possibility of summarising it here, but perhaps a sense of it can be gleaned from part of the opening paragraph of the first chapter, 'The Uncanny: An Introduction':

> The uncanny entails another thinking of beginning: the beginning is already haunted. The uncanny is ghostly. It is concerned with the strange, weird and myste-rious [as the *OED* has already reminded us, in what we might think of as an uncanny premonition], with a flickering sense (but not conviction) of something supernatural. The uncanny involves feelings of uncertainty, in particular regarding the reality of who one is and what is being experienced. Suddenly one's sense of oneself . . . seems strangely questionable. The uncanny is a crisis of the proper: it entails a critical disturbance of what is proper (from the Latin *proprius*, 'own'), a disturbance of the very idea of personal or private property including the proper-ness of proper names, one's so-called 'own' name, but also the proper names of others, of places, institutions and events. It is a crisis of the natural, touching upon everything that one might have thought was 'part of nature': one's own nature, human nature, the nature of reality and the world.
>
> (Royle 2003: 1)

These are grand claims indeed: what is asserted here, in part following Lacan's analysis of the *méconnaissance* of subjectivity, that process whereby the ego always and inevitably 'misconceives' itself as central to the universe, is that below, or athwart, the 'grounding' of our conceptions and self-conception – below, indeed, the 'conception' of the self – there is another force at work, which serves to undo, or to have already undone, the sureties by which we try to live. To deny the uncanny, then, would be to subscribe to a 'myth of origins'; the uncanny comes to remind us that there is no obvious beginning, to life or to thought, that we are composed of prior traces, some of them available for conscious memory but most of them sunk in a primal past which is not recover-able by conscious means but which continues to influence, and perhaps even determine, our sense of our place in the world.

In 2005, in an essay called 'New Versions of the Uncanny', to be found in *The*

Influence of Post-Modernism on Contemporary Writing, I developed some of these thoughts on the uncanny, and especially on the specifically contemporary forms it might take (Punter 2005: 131–53). I was particularly concerned there with nine other ways of attempting to 'classify' the uncanny, particularly as it appears in contemporary writing, and no doubt thus in response, in some form, to contemporary experience.

To take a first example: by the 'uncanny of virtual locality' we may wish to refer to the increasing sense that the human subject is no longer located in a single place at a single time (if, indeed, s/he ever has been). A crucial example here would be Bret Easton Ellis's *Glamorama* (1998), which reflects and develops a sense that from the evolution of the placeless and directory-less mobile phone to the ascendancy of the worldwide web, the possibility that we can be certain that the person with whom we are communicating occupies a specific location has been continuously eroded; alongside this goes an 'uncanny awareness of multiplicity', an awareness that earlier ideas about the 'doubleness' of the psyche may now be radically insufficient as we emerge into a world where the individual – or his or her surrogate – may be occupying *many* different 'scenes' at once – only one, perhaps, in the body, but many others according to the technological extensions, the range of prostheses, available. This we can see as an extension of the Gothic logic of the 'apparition', which challenges the very notion of 'appearance' as conventionally understood and suggests that we can never fully understand the rules according to which anything is 'made manifest'; the ghost, the demon, may appear at any time and command our attention, beckon us to worlds which we may have preferred to disown or disavow.

This leads, we might say, to a 'morphological uncanny': a version of the uncanny which dissolves our sense of physical shape, so that – in the realm of internet chat-rooms, for example – we can choose to appear in any guise we wish. There is no longer a certain link between psychic presence and physical form, as so many chat-room disappointments clearly demonstrate; our bodies, as relayed through the electronic media, become strictly 'supernatural', engineered ghosts of our physical selves – just as, for those who can afford it, the body itself becomes uncannily pliable, an enactment of a stance towards the world as much as an efflorescence of the body with, or into, which we may have been born. A key literary exemplar here would again be Hoban's *Angelica's Grotto*.

These uncertainties of place and space, I suggest, are also now necessarily inflected by what I have termed the 'diasporic uncanny', a phenomenon which is marked by the appearance of ghosts in so many writers deemed to be 'postcolonial', from Derek Walcott and Salman Rushdie to Pauline Melville and Chitra Banerjee Divakaruni. Here we find a literary reflection of what it might feel like to have no 'place' of one's own, to be part of an 'effect of history'; this, of course, can be summarised and addressed in political terms, under the rubrics of the postcolonial, of imperial invasion, or post-imperial dislocation, as in the works of, for example, Jamaica Kincaid, but alongside this attempt to recover – or to recover from – the exigencies of past history there lies also a more profound effect of displacement, an uncanny absence of origin which forbids entirely any attempt at a convincing and unitary notion of origins. There is a sense in which the very notion of 'English literature' is itself under siege as the past exportation of the language and the culture returns to haunt us and to relay the 'different' ghosts of colonised or settled lands back into the literary mainstream.

This is a further example, then, of the ways in which there is always something *there before* our attempts to marshal our selves around a rationally convincing centre; but at the same time, there is also something 'outside', which I have described as the 'uncanny of the streets'. From Edgar Allan Poe to Doris Lessing, the 'domestic', *heimlich* self has been under pressure, indeed under siege, from uncanny urban forces which are less than fully explicable, which appear to move along lines and trajectories, indeed whole geographies of their own – geographies traced, in the emblematic case of London, by Peter Ackroyd, Martin Amis and Iain Sinclair among others. This uncanny, then, would be a sense that wherever life is going on, it is always going on 'elsewhere', responding to a set of imperatives which are always 'different' from what we might have imagined. The uncanny of the streets is the klaxon in the night, the unidentifiable telephone call, the surge of noise in the dark hours, that fear of strangeness or the other which on the one hand renders 'home' a place of embattled refuge, while on the other it reminds us of a life going on 'elsewhere' in some location which we can no longer define or explain. In the traditional Gothic, of course, this sense of the 'elsewhere' was powerfully conjured in terms of exotic locations, barbaric castles, roving bands of banditti; as the whole concept of 'exotic' comes under revision, is increasingly seen as a late effect of imperialism, so the dangers there enshrined gather outside our very doors and threaten to render us strangers in a realm where we feel we have the right to be 'at home'.

The 'uncanny of translation' is a term I take to be related to this sense of the 'elsewhere', the otherness of experience. The arrival of literatures in English from many parts of the globe might reasonably be taken to signify a beneficial sharing of experience; but alongside this, I would argue, there also lies a profound sense of the *unheimlich*, of all that is *not* told in English, of all that might be understood if only language were not a barrier as well as a facilitator. In some African novels written in English, for example those of Chinua Achebe, we find glossaries provided to account for words which are, in a powerful sense, 'untranslateable'; this, clearly, is a device of 'naturalisation', designed to reassure, but it carries with it precisely the opposite effect, of hinting at realms of experience which can never be fully relayed in English, in a language already compromised by its association with empire; more importantly, though, it points to a sense in which the 'literary', strictly understood, is always an act of translation, an attempt to render in language that which, in the end, resists linguistic appropriation – and here we may find ourselves circling round to Bennett and Royle's view that the literary itself is co-essential with the uncanny, that in the relaying and 're-marking' of experience it inevitably suggests the irreducible complexity of experience, the ghostly hauntings which will forever elude categorisation.

And this issue of language, of what language(s) we ostensibly speak or understand, would have a bearing too on what I have termed the 'uncanny of the commodity': that sense, so well documented by theorists from Baudrillard on, that our part of the story of the world is but a small one, that it is the commodities themselves, as in, for example, Don DeLillo's fiction, which are actually telling the story of which we are mere effects. This may operate at the level of the individual commodity; but also, just as some classic Gothic fictions point to the idea of a 'different plot' – stemming from the alchemists, the 'illuminati', the Rosicrucians – which in fact exerts a hidden control over individual lives, so the commodity points us towards the sense that the levers of power are operated 'elsewhere', by a set of overweening corporate entities, by what used to be known as the 'military/industrial' complex, but which may now be most visible in the constant intrusion of Coca-Cola, McDonalds, or Levis, as the true story of what holds the world together. This may seem a long way from the Gothic; but insofar as the Gothic was, in its heyday, frequently concerned with the hidden operations of the power and the subjection and victimisation of the subject, there is a clear link between the ghosts of Gothic and the ghostly appearance – or apparition – of the corporate logos which provide the watermark on the script of the world.

My final category is the 'uncanny of the monumental', by which I mean to refer to 'the cults of the famous and the dead', and by extension to the 'supernatural' Western worship of 'celebrity'. Interestingly, the very concept of celebrity has been usefully analysed as having its origin in the very Gothic moment of the late eighteenth and early nineteenth centuries, and specifically in the cult – which one might also term a sacrificial quasi-religion – of Byron. That which haunts, we might say, looms 'monumentally' larger than life, as it does at the apparent origin of all Gothic fiction in the giant forms of Walpole's *Castle of Otranto* (1764); it reduces our own concerns to the petty and the mundane as it sets up images of a 'different' kind of life before which we can only prostrate ourselves.

What, then, to return to the 'originary' question, *is* the uncanny. One simple formulation would be to say that it is contained in the link between 'premonition' and the fulfilment of that premonition. Dreams, Freud famously observed, are not, despite the opinions of ancient commentators on dream, omens; but although that may be factually true, it does not prevent cultures from believing in, wishing for, and then being terrified by, the sense that dreams do sometimes come true. A cardinal modern Gothic example would be from the work of Stephen King, and specifically in his book *Pet Sematary* (1983). Here there is a wish that what has died – a pet, in the first instance, and then a child – might return from the dead. And return they do; but not in the form we may have constructed in our ever-hopeful imagination, but rather precisely as that which is indeed already dead and which should no longer be allowed to walk the earth.

The uncanny suggests that this notion of 'what might be allowed' is fundamentally unstable; that there is no irreducible law which has the strength to permit or to forbid such 'returns', however unwelcome or misshapen they might be. Thus the uncanny, at root, suggests the uncontrollable nature of memory, of trauma, of haunting; it serves to remind us that we cannot, at the end of the day – or during the watches of the night – exorcise the ghost.

That the Gothic is structured around ghosts goes, one might say, without saying, but the notion of the uncanny permits a rethinking of what we might term the 'unsaid' of Gothic. The persecutions of Radcliffean heroines may indeed have a basis which we can term 'historical', 'cultural' and so on, in the sense that they relate to the specific conditions of the times – to power relations, gender relations, organisations of the social world. But they also have a relation to phenomena which, if not 'eternal', nonetheless trouble the fabric of time, suggesting to us that our attempts to organise history in terms of specific periods or epochs may in fact be merely a simulacrum, that we are composed of the past and that we cannot control the moments at which it signifies its presence in the form of upheavals, transformations or phantoms which cannot be reduced to the order of daylight and which instead suggest to us that the apparent 'present' is in fact a flickering screen on which are, from time to time, writ images from a world which antecedes us and which also constantly threatens us with its unpredictable moments of recapitulation.

WORKS CITED

Bennett, Andrew, and Nicholas Royle (1999) *Introduction to Literature, Criticism and Theory*, 2nd edn, Hemel Hempstead: Prentice Hall Europe.

Freud, Sigmund (1955) 'The "Uncanny"', in *The Standard Edition of the Complete Psychological Works of Sigmund Freud*, ed. James Strachey *et al.*, 24 vols, London: Hogarth Press and the Institute of Psycho-Analysis, 1953–74, vol. XVII.

Punter, David (2005) *The Influence of Post-Modernism on Contemporary Writing: An Interdisciplinary Study*, Lampeter: Edwin Mellen Press.

Royle, Nicholas (2003) *The Uncanny*, Manchester: Manchester University Press.

17

ABJECT AND GROTESQUE

KELLY HURLEY

En route to an isolated New England seaport to conduct a bit of antiquarian research, the narrator of H. P. Lovecraft's 'The Shadow Over Innsmouth' (1936) surreptitiously studies his bus driver, an Innsmouth man, and is overcome by 'a wave of spontaneous aversion which could be neither checked nor explained'. The driver is marked by strange gill-like creases running down the sides of his neck, scaly grey-blue skin, 'a narrow head, watery-blue eyes that seemed never to wink, a flat nose, a receding forehead and chin, and singularly undeveloped ears' (Lovecraft 1982: 254). Nor is the bus driver atypical in his repulsive appearance, the narrator will learn after becoming stranded in Innsmouth that night and watching its seemingly deserted streets fill with 'uncouth, crouching shapes'. Some generations back Innsmouth's human population mated with vaguely anthropoid sea-creatures, 'fabulous monsters . . . half ichthyic and half batrachian in suggestion' (Lovecraft 1982: 285, 252), and their loathsome fish–frog–human descendants, at various stages of transformation into bodies more suited to water than land, now creep and shamble and hop through the streets of Innsmouth and swarm in its waters.

Compare Lovecraft's description of Wilbur Whateley, the offspring of a human woman and an otherworldly entity, in 'The Dunwich Horror' (1929). Wilbur is 'semi-anthropomorphic' above the waist, and 'teratologically fabulous' below, furred and tailed, with saurian limbs and a 'rudimentary eye' on each hip (Lovecraft 1982: 114–15). Lovecraft's bizarre creatures are first of all characterised by their hybridity. They violate categories, most notably (and alarmingly) breaking down the distinction between human and inhuman, human and animal. Related to that hybridity are bodies both excessive – Wilbur's nine-foot height, his 'abdomen [from which] a score of long greenish-grey tentacles with red sucking mouths protruded limply' (Lovecraft 1982: 115) – and kinetic, always in the process of transformation into still more fabulous, still more loathsome forms. Such bodies are grossly, stickily material, like Wilbur's which leaks a 'foetid . . . greenish-yellow ichor', or the fish–frog–humans' which reek of 'the most nauseous fishy odour imaginable' (Lovecraft 1982: 114, 257). Finally, these admixed beings arouse abhorrence and a disgustful curiosity in those who come into contact with them. The narrator of 'Innsmouth' finds the town's denizens 'abominably repellent', and yet they are also oddly compelling, drawing him with a 'half-hypnotic fascination' (Lovecraft 1982: 282, 284).

Lovecraft's monsters, like those of Gothic horror generally, are both grotesque and abject. Dictionaries list a number of meanings for 'grotesque', including fantastical, hideous, ludicrous, bizarre, distorted, incongruent and unnatural, and I will have recourse to all of these in this essay, but I am especially interested in Mikhail Bakhtin's discussion of the grotesque in his *Rabelais and his World* (1965; Eng. trans. 1968). For Bakhtin the grotesque involves an act of degradation: 'the lowering of all that is high, spiritual, ideal, abstract' to 'the material level' (Bakhtin 1984: 19). In other words, Bakhtin associates the grotesque with the human body in all its coarse, clumsy earthiness and changeful mortality, focusing on the material *thingness* of the human subject rather than intellect or spirit. The word 'abject' (etymologically, 'cast off' or 'cast away') has similar connotations, being used as a synonym for debased, degraded, humiliated, despicable and so forth. But here I will be more concerned with psychoanalytic critic Julia Kristeva's understanding of the term in her *Powers of Horror: An Essay on Abjection* (1980; Eng. trans. 1982). For Kristeva the abject is 'the in-between, the ambiguous, the composite'. Any phenomenon that 'disturbs identity, system, order' and that 'does not respect borders, positions, rules' (Kristeva 1982: 4) elicits queasiness and horror because it reminds one of traumatic infantile efforts to constitute oneself as an ego, or discrete subject, from out of an undifferentiated pre-Oedipal state, and of the fragile nature of an ego that remains threatened by and yet attracted to the possibility of dissolution.

Both Bakhtin and Kristeva share a preoccupation with gross materiality, of obvious relevance to Gothic horror, a genre which 'abounds in images of . . . the corpse, whole and mutilated', and of 'an array of bodily wastes such as blood, vomit, saliva, sweat, tears and putrefying flesh' (Creed 1993: 10). Kristeva writes of the 'loathing' felt towards 'a piece of filth, waste, or dung . . . defilement, sewage, and muck', the 'cesspool', the 'wound with blood and pus', the 'sickly, acrid smell of sweat, of decay' (1982: 2–3). The body's secretions and excretions are abject, breaching the boundary between the (seemingly self-contained) body and the external world. They are also foregrounded in Bakhtin's grotesque body, a body that 'copulates, defecates', breaks into boils, urinates, sweats, 'overeats' and retches (Bakhtin 1984: 319). For Bakhtin this grotesque body is a richly comic body. Not attempting to transcend the flesh, it is invigorated and renewed by its embrace of the earthly. For Kristeva the grotesque–abject body is a body of fear, but fear tempered with fascination. The abject is like the Frankenstein monster, 'the filthy mass that moved and talked' (Shelley 1992: 142). One cannot bear to look upon it, but cannot bring oneself to look away from it either.

Mary Shelley's monster is one of Kristeva's 'composites'. Victor Frankenstein painstakingly combines bits and pieces of dead human bodies in hopes of forming a harmoniously unified being, but his finished creature is a heterogeneous atrocity whose disparate body parts are in 'horrid contrast' to one another (Shelley 1992: 56). And as an animate corpse capable of articulate speech and complex thought, the monster blurs the boundary between death and life, between 'mere' matter and matter infused with sentience and spirit. Shelley's monster is liminal: it exists at the *limen* or threshold between two opposing conceptual categories, and so can be defined by both and neither of them.

Liminality is a key attribute of the grotesque–abject, and social anthropologist Mary Douglas's study of human pollution behaviours, *Purity and Danger* (1966), is especially helpful in understanding liminality and its relevance to Gothic horror. Noting that '[d]efilement . . . cannot occur except in view of a systematic ordering of ideas' (Douglas 1966: 41), Douglas argues that entities perceived as 'impure' within a given culture are those which trouble a culture's conceptual categories, particularly the binary oppositions by means of which the culture meaningfully organises experiences. The anomalous or interstitial phenomenon – the wild man, the dog-faced boy, the hermaphrodite – is troubling because it undermines such crucial binarisms as nature and culture, human and animal, male and female. Kristeva, working from Douglas in part, writes that the abject (the in-between, the interstitial) is 'the place where meaning collapses' (1982: 2). Dead–alive, Frankenstein's creature eludes, exceeds, and thereby profoundly disturbs human understanding.

Chimaeras, sphinxes, centaurs, griffins, harpies, satyrs: these fabulous monsters of antiquity are all admixed beings, like the Sphinx with her lion's body, wings and woman's head. Modern literary and filmic monsters also 'specialize in . . . categorical interstitiality and categorical contradictoriness' (Carroll 1990: 32). The 'beast people' in H. G. Wells' *The Island of Dr Moreau* (1896) and the werewolves in *The Wolf Man* (1941) and *The Howling* (1981) collapse the distinction between human and animal. Cyborgs like those in the *Terminator* films are simultaneously human and machine, organic and inorganic. The eponymous monster of Richard Marsh's *The Beetle* (1897) shifts sexual as well as species identity, changing from man to woman and back again. The doppelgänger or double – Dr Jekyll's Mr Hyde, the alien 'body snatcher' – breaks down the boundary between self and other. The category of the 'undead' includes not only the Frankenstein monster or golem, but also the vampire, the zombie and the mummy. Demons breach the border between the supernatural and terrestrial spheres when the immaterial demon takes physical form, as a particularly repulsive one does in M. R. James's 'Casting the Runes' (1911). 'What he touched [under the pillow] was . . . a mouth, with teeth and hair about it, and, he declares, not the mouth of a human being' (James 1987: 146).

Etymologically speaking, the word 'grotesque' has to do precisely with such admixtures. 'Grotesque' (*la grottesca*) was derived from the Italian *grotta* (cave) in the late fifteenth century, and used to describe an unusual style of ornamentation found in newly excavated first-century Roman structures like the Domus Aurea (Golden House) of Nero. Grotesque ornamentation featured plant, animal and human forms interwoven fantastically, each form blending into its neighbouring ones so that no form was finished or discrete, and all appeared to be in a continuous state of flux and becoming, almost as if 'giving birth to each other' (Bakhtin 1984: 32). Its critics deplored this 'wilful rejection of proper continuities in the representation of objects' (Trodd *et al.* 1999: 4). That is, in its refusal to render individual figures in their distinctness and perfection, and its

blurring of the boundaries between types of organism generally, grotesque ornamentation was seen as violating both classical aesthetic norms and the laws of
nature. Nonetheless the grotesque style quickly became popular in sixteenth-
century Italy and across Europe, as artists experimented with the 'turbulent
entanglement' of unlike objects and the 'monstrous fusion of human and
nonhuman elements', aggravating the grotesque effect by the practice of asym-
metry and disproportion (Kayser 1966: 21, 24).

Bakhtin delights in the representational strategies of grotesque ornamentation, celebrating the idea of a human body without proper boundaries, a body
that is composite, unfinished and surreally disproportionate. Bakhtin's
grotesque body 'is not separated from the rest of the world. It is not a closed,
completed unit; it . . . outgrows itself, transgresses its own limits' (Bakhtin 1984:
26). It is a hyperbolic body, and Bakhtin emphasises 'the *positive* hyperbolism' of
the grotesque (45; emphasis added).

> [Bakhtin] images the human body as multiple, bulging, over- or under-sized, protu-
> berant and incomplete. The openings and orifices of this carnival body are empha-
> sised, not its closure and finish. It is an image of impure corporeal bulk with its
> orifices (mouth, flared nostrils, anus) yawning wide and its lower regions (belly,
> legs, feet, buttocks and genitals) given priority over its upper regions (head, 'spirit,'
> reason) . . . [This body] is always in process, it is always *becoming*, it is a mobile and
> hybrid creature, disproportionate, exorbitant, outgrowing all limits, obscenely
> decentered and off-balance.
>
> (Stallybrass and White 1986: 9; emphasis in text)

In its metamorphic exuberance, the grotesque body 'protrudes, bulges, sprouts,
or branches off'; it 'seeks to go out beyond . . . [its own] confines' and link itself
'to other bodies or to the world outside' (Bakhtin 1984: 320, 316–17).

Such images of a grotesquely metamorphic body are of course common to
Gothic horror, albeit in a less comic, more uncanny register. In Dean Koontz's
Midnight (1989), a loose rewriting of *The Island of Dr Moreau*, human beings are
technologically enhanced so as to be able to reshape themselves into any form
that appeals to them. Most turn into 'regressives' like Wells' beast people,
but those who choose to become cyborgs make their bodies permeable and
'flexible as gelatin' (Koontz 1989: 329) in order physically to conjoin with their
computers.

> [Coltrane] was connected to the VDT by a pair of inch-thick cables that looked less
> metallic than organic, glistening wetly in the amber glow. They extended from
> within the bowels of the data-processing unit . . . and into the man's bare torso
> below his rib cage, melding bloodlessly with the flesh . . . The meat of his upper
> arms ended smoothly two inches above the elbows; from those stumps, bones
> thrust out as cleanly as robotic extrusions from a metal casing. The skeletal hands
> were locked tightly around the cables, as if they were merely a pair of clamps. . . .
> [Sam] saw the bones were not as well differentiated as they should have been but

had half melted together. Furthermore, they were veined with metal. As he watched, the cables pulsed with such vigor that they began to vibrate wildly.

(325)

Nor does Coltrane's amalgamation with his machine produce a neatly self-contained entity. *Midnight*'s cyborgs sprout new limbs, new and unheard-of body parts, 'pale, oily tentacles' and 'segmented, wormlike probe[s]', as they attempt to link themselves to and subsume other humans (330, 331).

The 1978 *Invasion of the Body Snatchers*, a remake of the 1956 film in which an alien plant species parasites, replicates and destroys its human hosts, features a scene that is almost reminiscent of classical grotesque ornamentation, wherein human forms and foliage, fruit and flowers are seamlessly intermingled. While Matthew (Donald Sutherland) sleeps, tendrils from a hairy, watermelon-sized 'pod' creep over his body, absorbing his vital essence. Soon a flower attached to the pod opens stickily, wetly, and gives 'birth' to Matthew's replicant, which emerges near-grown, snorting and writhing as it attempts to free itself from a cocoon of web-like filaments. In the story 'Fungus Isle' (1923), spores from a parasitic species of fungus invade the digestive tract, lungs and skin – 'the [fungoid] growth had already ... worked in its horrid development so as to penetrate the skin and spread out into the living red flesh below' – and transform human beings into 'ghastly' admixed creatures whose face, '[l]egs, body, and arms were ridged and mottled and fringed with fungus-like growths' (Fisher 1991: 116–17, 111). Brian Lumley's 'Fruiting Bodies' (1993) also explores the possibility of such a melding between human and exotic fungus: '[Garth] leaned half out of the wall like a great nodding manikin, his entire head a livid yellow blotch, his arm and hand making a noise like a huge puffball bursting underfoot' (Lumley 1993: 44).

How do we reconcile such unsettling images with the idea of the hilariously fluid and variable body that Bakhtin celebrates? The work of Wolfgang Kayser, who focuses on the 'ominous, nocturnal, and abysmal features' of the grotesque in literature and art (Kayser 1966: 18), might seem more appropriate here. Kayser shows how grotesque phenomena, like the automaton in E. T. A. Hoffmann's 'The Sandman' (1816), serve to alienate and unhinge those who encounter them. Grotesque affect is like Sigmund Freud's 'uncanny', the familiar defamiliarised: 'apparently meaningful things are shown to have no meaning, and familiar objects begin to look strange' (Kayser 1966: 61). While grotesquerie might arouse startled laughter, the more significant response is 'surprise and horror, an agonizing fear in the presence of a world which breaks apart' in unexpected, even impossible ways, as it does in Gothic horror (Kayser 1966: 31). Bakhtin rightly remarks that Kayser writes 'in the spirit of existen-tialism' (Bakhtin 1984: 50). For Kayser the grotesque seems to be a correlate to the confusion, the incongruence, the whirling heterogeneity of modern life. He emphasises 'a feeling of helplessness and disparagement before an increasingly absurd and fantastically estranged world' (Kayser 1966: 78). Composite and admixed phenomena are maddening, estranging, so that one should not be surprised when Hoffmann's protagonist is driven insane, when Professor Rice faints at the sight of Wilbur Whateley's furred, scaled, and tentacled nakedness (Lovecraft 1982: 114), or when Garth's fungoid body sends Lumley's narrator into hysterics (Lumley 1993: 44–5).

For Kayser the grotesque involves contradictions that are not reconciled, moments of disjunction and rupture that are not smoothed over. As in Edgar Allan Poe's 'The Masque of the Red Death' (1842), all is 'phantasmagoric' and fearsomely distorted; 'beautiful, bizarre, ghastly, and repulsive elements' are drawn together 'into a *turbulent* whole' – that is, a whole which has neither organic unity nor stasis (Kayser 1966: 79; emphasis added). Bakhtin would agree, but add that contradiction, distortion, turbulence and incompleteness should be relished rather than feared. Bakhtin relates the grotesque to the medieval carnival, the uproarious festival of the common people.

> As opposed to the official feast, one might say that carnival celebrated temporary liberation from the prevailing truth and from the established order; it marked the suspension of all hierarchical rank, privileges, norms, and prohibitions. Carnival was the true feast of time, the feast of becoming, change, and renewal. It was hostile to all that was immortalised and completed . . . to all pretense at immutability. [Carnival] sought a dynamic expression; it demanded ever changing, playful, undefined forms.
>
> (Bakhtin 1984: 10–11)

'Carnival is presented by Bakhtin as a world of topsy-turvy, of heteroglot exuberance, of ceaseless overrunning and excess where all is mixed, hybrid, ritually degraded and defiled' (Stallybrass and White 1986: 8). The carnival world was a world turned upside down, where a jester might be crowned king or elected pope (Bakhtin 1984: 81), and a servant could safely jeer and toss refuse at her master.[1] During carnival, ritual defilement – being rolled in the mud, smeared with excrement – was experienced as regenerative rather than degrading, and provoked laughter rather than rage. Carnival meant reconnecting with the earth and earthiness. It involved the indulgence of appetite, the boisterous celebration of the body in all its gross animality.

How, then, does one relate Bakhtin's idea of a joyous, rejuvenating 'carnivalesque' to what seems to be the relentless negativism of Gothic horror – its focus on abomination, bodily torment and death? Among other things, Bakhtin can help us account for what one might call the *gleeful excessiveness* of Gothic horror. The genre specialises in not just admixture but multiple and aggravated admixture; think of Lovecraft's 'ichthyic' and 'batrachian' human beings, or Wilbur Whateley's phantasmatic body. Gothic horror unfolds its uncontrollable and prolonged metamorphoses without apology or restraint, and unconcernedly piles its bloody, eviscerated, suppurating bodies one atop another.[2]

Gothic horror is a highly self-conscious, self-reflexive genre that tends to call attention to its own conventions (Brophy 1986), conventions which are in any case easily parodied and burlesqued, as we see in the *Scream* and *Scary Movie* franchises. Moreover, the genre delights in outrageously disgusting embodiment for its own sake, featuring over-the-top climaxes such as in 'Innsmouth', when its narrator is nearly overwhelmed by a carnivalesque mob of 'flopping, hopping, croaking, bleating' monstrosities (Lovecraft 1982: 290). Thus Gothic horror texts often feature plot devices that allow for the endless multiplication of grotesque embodiments. Stephen King's *It* (1986) features a shape-shifting alien whose repertoire of monstrous forms is limited only by the imagination of its victims – in other words, is endless. And while in *Midnight* metamorphoses unfold through an often banal logic (the regressives wish to be free of their human responsibilities; the cyborgs prefer the cold emotionlessness of machinic subjectivity), it is also true that metamorphosis is represented as wildly anarchic, opportunistic, metonymic. It is triggered by random and contingent events or associations (cued by sounds, smells, the presence of objects like the computer) and it develops according to the script the would-be xenomorph happens to have available and have in mind. A cinemaphile priest turns himself into the creature from *Alien* (1979); a fan of 'fifties bug movie[s]' equips himself with 'clacking mandibles and multifaceted eyes', a 'mouth framed by small pincers' and a razor-sharp serrated stinger (Koontz 1989: 373).

In her 1966 essay on Bakhtin, Kristeva comments approvingly on the *surreal* quality of the carnivalesque. Kristeva is interested in the idea of carnival not so much on Bakhtin's terms as for its compatibility with theories of the unconscious (Kristeva 1986: 41). With its maskings and gay impostures, its reversals and overturnings, its transgression of all boundaries, its exuberant staging of preposterous events, carnival is not unlike dream-work. Dream-work also deals in distortions and disguises; it proceeds according to the illogic of an unconscious that is indifferent to narrative order or coherency and condenses the dreamer's heterogeneous thoughts and desires into single bizarre images or events. As something that accesses and channels (but does not try to control) unconscious human depths, carnival, for Kristeva, is a source of artistic creativity. The idea of the Bakhtinian carnivalesque would continue to influence Kristeva's work, including *Powers of Horror*, which describes a kind of dark carnival of the soul.

Here and in her earlier *Revolution in Poetic Language*, Kristeva is concerned with the infant proto-subject – the human subject before ego-formation, before Oedipality, before the acquisition of language – and with what happens within 'the body of the subject *who is not yet constituted as such*' (Kristeva 1984: 25; emphasis added). This proto-subject experiences itself as a 'motility': as waves of instinctual and destructive energy that break, then are held in stasis (arrested by 'the constraints of biological and social structures'), then break, and so on (25, 28). The external world is no less indistinct, vaguely perceived as a place of indifferentiation and flux. Nor is this external world understood as such by the proto-subject. Crucially, the proto-subject does not experience *itself* as an integrity, neither as a subjective integrity (a self, an ego) nor a bodily integrity. It knows no boundaries: it cannot distinguish its own waves of sensation from the movements around it, its own body from the field of objects that surround it – including, most importantly for Kristeva, its mother.

Eventually the impulse towards self-differentiation overtakes the proto-subject. But self-differentiation is achieved at great cost. Clearing out a space upon which it will construct an 'I', the proto-subject attempts to identify what is 'not-I' and then repudiate and expel it as 'other'. However, since 'I' and 'not-I' have not been (and as yet cannot be) counter-distinguished, this is also an agonising and convulsive moment of self-repudiation, self-expulsion. 'I spit *myself* out, I abject *myself* within the same motion through which "I" claim to establish *myself* . . . During the course in which "I" become, I give birth to myself amid the violence of sobs, of vomit' (Kristeva 1982: 3; emphasis in text). One experiences *oneself* as the vile matter that must be cast off.

The infantile experience of abjection remains accessible to the fully formed subject as a kind of 'phantom' or 'somatic memory' (Hogle 2002: 51), mani-festing itself as both physical nausea and Sartrean existential nausea. In Kristeva the 'abject' on the one hand refers to any admixed phenomenon that, by virtue of its admixture, recalls this sickening experience of entrapment at the border between identity and non-identity. The human corpse, for example, is 'the utmost of abjection', the human subject voided of all its specialness and particu-larity, 'death infecting life' (Kristeva 1982: 4). The protagonist of the zombie novella 'Naming of Parts' describes his once-beloved undead sister as a 'slab of meat . . . Her eyes showed none of his sister, her expression was not there, he could not *sense* her at all' (Lebbon 2004: 317, 332; emphasis in text).

Secondly, an 'abject' also resembles but is not quite an 'object'. The content of the 'abject' is always loathsome, a point of particular interest for studies of Gothic horror. The self defines itself against both its 'abjects' and objects, and both serve as vehicles for intolerable ideas and affects that must be repressed, displaced and projected elsewhere. Such ideas especially include indifferentia-tion and materiality in *Powers of Horror*, since for Kristeva the belief that one is, or has, a discrete and integral 'self' is only an illusion that one works to maintain with great energy. And since in abjection 'the subject rejects the flux of physical matter in order to [try to] secure the boundaries of its own identity' (Constable 1999: 173), the gross materiality of embodiment serves as both metaphor and aggravation of the self's indifferentiation, whether feared and actual. We attempt to repress and 'expel those unwanted objects which remind us of our origins and our fate' (Stacey 2003: 260) – birth and death, the wet bloody such-ness of material existence.[3]

Thus Gothic horror often describes the dynamism and '[a]ggressive vitality' of mere matter (Trodd *et al.* 1999: 4), the unexpected, unwelcome liveliness of *stuff*. Clouds of spores and thick damp masses of fungus surround the humans in 'Fungus Isle', choking them with 'their resistless life energy, their will, their *will* to live, and their determination to add our lives to their own' (Fisher 1991: 105;

emphasis in text). Mere matter may take on its own kind of sentience, as occurs in the post-apocalyptic story 'Looking for Jake' (1998).

> In the cracks of buildings and the dark spaces under abandoned cars little knots of matter are self-organising into grease-stained chip wrappers, broken toys, cigarette packets, before snapping the tiny umbilicus that anchors them to the ground and drifting out across the streets . . . [E]very morning sees a fresh crop of litter, each filthy newborn piece marked with a minuscule puckered navel.
>
> (Miéville 2005: 9)

Or mere matter may become voracious, like the slime-entity in *Midnight*: 'Suddenly a score of lipless, toothless mouths opened in that fluid form . . . Its need was so intense that it pulsed and writhed' (Koontz 1989: 354, 463). The zombie, that blank-eyed 'slab of meat', is characterised most of all by its mind-less appetency.

And yet, as Steven Shaviro writes, zombies 'exercise a perverse, insidious fascination'. Zombies 'are not radically Other so much as they serve to awaken a passion for otherness and for vertiginous disidentification that is already latent within our own selves' (1993: 96, 99). The self is drawn towards the prospect of indifferentiation, dissolution, blank mindless embodiment, even as it struggles to keep it at bay. The abject fascinates. It 'simultaneously beseeches and pulver-izes the subject'. Abjection is a 'vortex of summons and repulsion' (Kristeva 1982: 5, 1), like the slime-entity which purses its many lipless mouths to shrill for prey and then opens them wide to receive it. Just as Bakhtin helps us understand the paradoxical hilarity of the violently horrific, Kristeva helps us understand the paradoxical attraction of the repulsive.

NOTES

1 As Stallybrass and White argue, *Rabelais and His World* is much more than an aesthetic study, and can be read as a political indictment of authoritarianism, dogmatism, and officiousness in general. 'Carnival, for Bakhtin, is both a populist utopian vision of the world seen from below and a festive critique, through the inversion of hierarchy, of the "high" culture' (1986: 7). On this point, see also Russo 1994: 61–2.
2 In a discussion of special-effects technologies in contemporary film, Brophy coins the word 'horrality' (a combination of 'horror, textuality, morality, [and] hilarity') to denote this almost Bakhtinian quality of Gothic horror (1986: 3).
3 Working closely from Kristeva and with films like *The Birds* (1963), *The Brood* (1979), and *Alien*, Creed is especially concerned with Gothic horror's 'construction of the maternal figure as abject' in its representations of motherhood, birth, and death (Creed 1993: 11). See also Russo, who discusses the stereotypical conflation of femininity with the 'earthly, dark, material, immanent, visceral . . . [A]ll the detritus of the body that is separated out and placed with terror and revulsion . . . on the side of the feminine [is] down there in that cave of abjection' (1994: 1–2).

WORKS CITED

Bakhtin, Mikhail (1984) *Rabelais and his World*, trans. H. Iswolsky, Bloomington, IN: Indiana University Press.

Brophy, Philip (1986) 'Horrality – The Textuality of Contemporary Horror Films', *Screen*, 27(1): 2–13.

Carroll, Noel (1990) *The Philosophy of Horror or Paradoxes of the Heart*, London: Routledge.

Constable, Catherine (1999) 'Becoming the Monster's Mother: Morphologies of Identity in the *Alien* Series', in A. Kuhn (ed.), *Alien Zone II: The Spaces of Science-Fiction Cinema*, New York: Verso.

Creed, Barbara (1993) *The Monstrous-Feminine: Film, Feminism, Psychoanalysis*, London: Routledge.

Douglas, Mary (1966) *Purity and Danger: An Analysis of the Concepts of Pollution and Taboo*, London: Routledge and Kegan Paul.

Fisher, Philip M. (1991) 'Fungus Isle', in S. Dziemianowicz, Robert E. Weinberg and Martin H. Greenberg (eds), *Famous Fantastic Mysteries*, New York: Gramercy Books.

Hogle, Jerrold E. (2002) *The Undergrounds of 'The Phantom of the Opera': Sublimation and the Gothic in Leroux's Novel and its Progeny*, Basingstoke: Palgrave.

James, M. R. (1987) *'Casting the Runes' and Other Ghost Stories*, Oxford: Oxford University Press.

Kaufman, Philip (dir.) (1978) *Invasion of the Body Snatchers*.

Kayser, Wolfgang (1966) *The Grotesque in Art and Literature*, trans. U. Weisstein, New York: McGraw-Hill.

Koontz, Dean (1989) *Midnight*, New York: Berkley Books.

Kristeva, Julia (1982) *Powers of Horror: An Essay on Abjection*, trans. L. Roudiez, New York: Columbia University Press.

—— (1984) *Revolution in Poetic Language*, trans. M. Waller, New York: Columbia University Press.

—— (1986) 'Word, Dialogue and Novel', in T. Moi (ed.), *The Kristeva Reader*, New York: Columbia University Press.

Lebbon, Tim (2004) *Fears Unnamed*, New York: Leisure Books.

Lovecraft, H. P. (1982) *The Best of H. P. Lovecraft: Bloodcurdling Tales of Horror and the Macabre*, New York: Del Rey Books.

Lumley, Brian (1993) *'Fruiting Bodies' and Other Fungi*, New York: Tor Books.

Miéville, China (2005) *Looking for Jake: Stories*, New York: Del Rey Books.

Russo, Mary (1994) *The Female Grotesque: Risk, Excess and Modernity*, New York: Routledge.

Shaviro, Steven (1993) *The Cinematic Body*, Minneapolis, MN: University of Minnesota Press.

Stacey, Jackie (2003) 'She Is Not Herself: The Deviant Relations of *Alien Resurrection*', *Screen*, 44(3): 251–76.

Shelley, Mary (1992), *Frankenstein: or, the Modern Prometheus*, ed. M. Hindle, New York: Penguin.

Stallybrass, Peter and Allon White (1986) *The Politics and Poetics of Transgression*, Ithaca, NY: Cornell University Press.

Trodd, Colin, Paul Barlow and David Amigoni (1999) 'Uncovering the Grotesque in Victorian Culture', in C. Trodd, P. Barlow and D. Amigoni (eds), *Victorian Culture and the Idea of the Grotesque*, Aldershot: Ashgate.

18

Hauntings

Andrew Smith

The spectre is an absent presence, a liminal being that inhabits and gives shape to many of the figurations of trauma that characterise the Gothic. The spectre is also a strangely historical entity that is haunted by the culture which produced it. This contribution will explore how reading ghosts helps to illuminate historical and national contexts. It will also explore how the ghost has been interpreted psychoanalytically, and as a figure that can be related to models of subjectivity. The texts explored here form a highly selected history of the ghost story, but they have been chosen on the basis that they provide representative examples of the different contexts (critical, cultural, economic and national) in which the ghost can be discussed.

First, it is important to note that the intangibility of the ghost can be read as a counterpoint to more palpable monstrous bodies (demons, vampires, zombies, ghouls and so on). In the late eighteenth century this is exemplified by the different approaches of Ann Radcliffe and Matthew Lewis. In more abstract terms it also corresponds to the differences between the 'female Gothic' and 'male Gothic' traditions.[1] Radcliffe's ghosts illustrate how an overwrought (and therefore Gothic) imagination can become overly stimulated by fantastical ideas. In *The Mysteries of Udolpho* (1794) and *The Italian* (1797) Radcliffe's ghosts expose the provenance of imaginative and emotional excess. Her ghosts are bogus, employed by villains to dupe superstitious 'heroes' and thus doubly spectral – the ghost of a ghost as it were. Such ghosts participate in the female Gothic's language of subtle and implied terrors. In contrast Lewis, in *The Monk* (1796), whilst using images of the supernatural, focuses on the explicit physicality of horror. Ambrosio, Lewis's anti-hero, is fascinated by sexual pleasure and is prepared to barter his soul in order to gain access to the virtuous Antonia. The body, its appearance, passions and appetites underpin Lewis's quasi-pornographic imagery – creating a dialectical 'other' to Radcliffe's world of imaginative and emotional excess.

However, Radcliffe's ghosts are not just tricks of the imagination; they can also be related to models of subjectivity. Terry Castle has argued that Radcliffe's use of spectrality in *The Mysteries of Udolpho* implicates a model of subject-formation which anticipates Freud's notion of the uncanny. Castle notes that during the enforced separation between Emily St Aubert and her suitor, Valancourt, both entertain anxieties that the other may be dead. This suggests that the subject is haunted by feelings of loss in which the living are falsely construed as dead. There are also instances when the dead (such as Emily's father) retain a hold over the living. Castle therefore argues that Radcliffe does not so much explain away the supernatural as conceptually relocate it: 'It is diverted – rerouted, so to speak, into the realm of the everyday' (Castle 1995: 124). Such a move redeems the imagination from excess because it suggests the presence of a sensibility that enables us to imaginatively empathise with others and so provides the bridge between 'self and other' (125). This leads Castle to conclude 'that a crucial feature of the new sensibility of the late eighteenth century was, quite literally, a growing sense of the ghostliness of other people' (125). Ghosts are thus projections of our innermost anxieties and this blurring of physical and psychological realities becomes reworked in Freud's idea that the self is ghosted by the subconscious; or, as Castle puts it, 'Ghosts and spectres retain their ambiguous grip on the human imagination; they simply migrate into the space of the mind' (135).

Ghosts are not just the spirits of the dead; rather they are, in 'high' Gothic texts, ciphers for models of subjectivity which refer to culturally specific notions of psychological trauma. For Castle 'high' Gothic represents a cultural shift in which the meaning of death is fundamentally changed because it is no longer part of a logically understood cosmology, as it had been in the Middle Ages, but rather indicates how the self becomes ghosted by images of projection. We can see this in Mary Shelley's 'On Ghosts' (1824), where she reminisces about a visit to a house of a deceased friend:

> He had been there; his living frame had been caged by these walls, his breath had mingled with that atmosphere, his step had been on those stones, I thought: – the earth is a tomb, the gaudy sky a vault, we but walking corpses.
>
> (Shelley 2000: 282)

Shelley's evocation of the living dead and a life haunted by death develops Radcliffe's model of ghosting and helps to support Castle's theory of an emerging, quasi-Freudian model of subjectivity.

Freud's 'The Uncanny' (1919) has made an important contribution to a critical understanding of the post-Romantic Gothic. If ghosts conflate self with other, then Freud reworks this as a conflation between *heimlich* (the homely) and the *unheimlich* (the uncanny). Initially, Freud opposes these terms, associating the *heimlich* with domesticity and the *unheimlich* with the wild and the untamed. However, he concludes that '*unheimlich* is in some way or other a subspecies of *heimlich*' (Freud 1985: 347). This is because the home is the place where Oedipal anxieties are generated and is thus not such a safe place after all. Indeed because it is the site where sexual trauma is generated it becomes truly *unheimlich*. Freud argues that such trauma is repressed but is made visible in the desire to repeat certain types of activity, because such a repetition compulsion represents an urge to reclaim past traumas in order to lay them to rest. Freud suggests that this repetition of the past constitutes a moment of spectrality in which the past (or the dead) comes back to life, so that 'Many people experience the feeling in the highest degree in relation to death and dead bodies, to the return of the dead, and to spirits and ghosts' (364). This entails a modification of Romantic spectrality, because he demonstrates that uncanny experience involves a necessary projection of inner anxieties: 'The uncanny is that class of the frightening which leads back to what is known of old and long familiar' (340).

For Castle, the Freudian analyst explains the haunted world of the patient's unconscious, but because such projections 'are ghostly in nature, the products of the unconscious also stand outside any purely human control' (Castle 1995: 184). The ghost therefore remains irrational because it cannot be rationally understood, even whilst the image of the ghost captures the fragile, because liminal, sense of modern subjectivity. This failure of science means that 'Seen in historical terms, as an offshoot of the radically introspective habit of mind initiated in the late eighteenth century, psychoanalysis seems both the most poignant critique of romantic consciousness to date, and its richest and most perverse elaboration' (Castle 1995: 139). However, the idea that reading ghosts enables us to decode a covert history of subjectivity is not the only theoretical approach available to us.

So far ghosts have been considered as forms that underpin certain models of subjectivity which have their roots in eighteenth-century Gothic. In the Victorian period a new strand enters into the ghost story which refers, covertly, to economic realities. In both contexts the ghost represents that which haunts a culture: its formulation of the self and its troublesome economy. Marx in *Capital* (1867) uses an alternative account of haunting in order to explain commodity fetishism (and the intricacies of surplus value). Marx in a discussion of the labour spent in the production of a table notes that:

> A commodity appears, at first sight, a very trivial thing, and easily understood. Its analysis shows that it is, in reality, a very queer thing, abounding in metaphysical subtleties and theological niceties ... Yet, for all that, the table continues to be that common, everyday thing, wood. But, so soon as it steps forth as a commodity, it is changed into something transcendent. It not only stands with its feet on the ground, but, in relation to all other commodities, it stands on its head, and evolves out of its wooden brain grotesque ideas.
>
> (Marx 1984: 435)

Marx's point is that one needs to make the labour which produced the table visible; by doing so one can generate a scepticism about the economic system which would be the starting point for radical thought. However, the idea that the economic system makes people ghostly can be tracked back, in a non-Marxist fashion, to late eighteenth-century texts. Mary Poovey has noted that the period was characterised by new forms of economic activity (such as, for example, the emergence of the Stock Exchange) and by the prevalence of paper money. The effect of this was to make wealth appear to be intangible, subject to seemingly occult fluctuations in the market, and present only as promissory notes (bank notes) which can be redeemed for 'real' money (gold and silver), but which themselves are little more than facsimiles of money. Poovey has noted that 'Making the system seem trustworthy – making it imaginatively visible – was the work of journalists and novelists who write about financial matters' (Poovey 2003: 3). This new, seemingly spectralised economy influenced the ghost story in the nineteenth century and supports a reading of ghosts in Charles Dickens and J. H. Riddell which explains why their ghost stories so often make links between money and spectrality.

Dickens, in *A Christmas Carol* (1843), represents Scrooge's world as dominated by his inability to empathise with the plights of others. Written during a period of acute economic depression (in a decade known as the 'hungry forties'), the tale suggests that Scrooge becomes depersonalised by hoarding wealth. His wealth is both there (hoarded) and not there (not in circulation), a fact that formulates an implicit language of spectrality that is linked to the construction of the ghosts.[2] Ultimately the tale implies, somewhat paradoxically, that the problem is solved if Scrooge puts money back into the system and himself back into social circulation.

Scrooge's ghosts represent different aspects of his life and are there to help him. Scrooge's invaded domestic space suggests that the ghosts have an intimacy with the subject because they are linked to his inner life. It is tempting to account for this in psychoanalytical terms; however, there are also implied links between ghosts and more material issues. As Poovey notes, journalists like Dickens were trying to find a new idiom through which to explain the workings of the economic system. Such writing 'was an attempt to understand and interpret something that was only partially visible and constantly in a state of change' (Poovey 2003: 4), and this is hinted at in Scrooge's account of the first spirit:

> its belt sparkled and glittered now in one part and now in another, and what was light one instant, at another time was dark, so the figure itself fluctuated in its distinctness: being now a thing with one arm, now with one leg, now with twenty legs, now a pair of legs without a head, now a head without a body: of which dissolving parts, no outline would be visible in the dense gloom wherein they melted away. And in the very wonder of this, it would be itself again; distinct and clear as ever.
>
> (Dickens 1985: 68)

Within the context of the tale and its economic obsessions the protean, shifting, form represents a desire to make the system visible. In this instance the occult fluctuations of the ghost unconsciously represent the unpredictable nature of the economy during a time of economic depression (which has turned Scrooge into a miser). Dickens's ghosts are not so intangible after all and this oblique relationship between ghosts and money is developed in the 1870s by J. H. Riddell.

J. H. Riddell (or Charlotte Riddell) wrote many novellas about ghosts as well as a number of novels focusing on the financial sector of London.[3] Her *The*

Uninhabited House (1875) is a parody of materialism. The novella centres on a haunted house (River House) and the legal practicalities of letting it out to tenants. A solicitor's clerk, who narrates the tale, stays in the house in an attempt to discover its secret. It is revealed that the house is haunted by the ghost of the Scrooge-like Mr Elmsdale. One tenant describes how they saw 'a man . . . seated counting over bank-notes. He had a pile of them before him, and I distinctly saw that he wetted his fingers in order to separate them' (Riddell 1971: 31). This physical ghost, with his wetted fingers and attachment to money, re-emphasises the links between presence and absence, between money and spectrality. Like the bank note itself, money is there but not there. The drama concerns how and why Elmsdale was murdered by a Mr Harringford whom Elmsdale had attempted to ruin financially. After Elmsdale's murder Harringford becomes wealthy, but his wife and family die and he becomes conscious that the money is a curse. As in *A Christmas Carol* the solution appears to be in the 'proper' redistribution of wealth which happens when he leaves his wealth (he is gravely ill and dies) in a will to Elmsdale's daughter, who marries the narrator. Money is thus dangerous in these tales; its improper use conjures up a ghostliness which is inherent to money.

Structurally speaking, the ghost story has often appeared to critics to be highly formulaic and oddly reassuring. M. R. James's tales, for example, have been seen by critics such as David Punter (1996: 86–90), Clive Bloom (1993: 64–71) and Julia Briggs (1977) as little more than exercises in formalism. James's tales were published in various collections between 1904 and 1931 (when the complete collected tales were produced). Often his tales centre on vacationing academics who discover old manuscripts or artefacts which bring to life their occult subject matter. However, James's dons rarely respond with horror but with curiosity and a disdain for superstition, and are represented as strangely unempathetic.[4] In 'The Mezzotint' (1904), for example, the dons are unmoved by the tale of child abduction and murder played out in a mezzotint (a form of engraving) that they are contemplating purchasing for their college museum. Their very lack of emotional engagement with the drama of abduction and murder subtly suggests that they are responsible for generating the horror within James's tale. As one of them comments on seeing the unfolding drama of the mezzotint 'it looks very much as if we were assisting at the working out of a tragedy somewhere' (James 1970: 46), which implicates their dispassionate amorality as part of the problem. James's 'The Dolls' House' (1925) subtly forces the reader to share in the type of amoral voyeurism of the dons in 'The Mezzotint', as it structurally distances them from the emotional turmoil suffered by Dillet when he purchases a haunted dolls' house that plays out a murder every night. This type of moral vacuity can be read as a critique of the impersonality of a modernist outlook. This sense of emptiness is not just central to modernism; it is also developed within the ghost story. We can see it, for example, in the post-First World War tales of E. F. Benson (one of James's auditors at Cambridge where James read his tales aloud at Christmas). In Benson's 'Expiation' (1923) the narrator notes of the vicar that tells the tale that 'his communication was very impersonal. It was just a narrating voice, without identity, an anonymous chronicle' (Benson 1986: 53).

Such tales should be seen within their national contexts. Shirley Jackson's *The Haunting of Hill House* (1959), for example, examines the experiences of many white middle-class American women in the 1950s who felt trapped within domestic spaces and unable to develop a model of identity that was independent of family life. This was a plight which Betty Friedan explored in *The Feminine Mystique* (1963). Friedan famously referred to the issue as 'the problem that has no name', thus using a language of spectrality in order to account for how the 'problem' which haunted the lives of many women had been rendered invisible. Jackson's novel centres on the 32-year-old Eleanor Vance who had looked after her recently deceased mother for 11 years. Eleanor becomes involved in a psychic experiment in the supposedly haunted Hill House, where the ghostly activities appear to implicate Eleanor's projected feelings of loss and guilty sense of freedom. It is within the house that Eleanor initially develops a sense of identity that is free from her mother's influence: 'what a complete and separate thing I am, she thought, going from my red toes to the top of my head, individually an I, possessed of attributes belonging only to me' (Jackson 1999: 83). However, although the death of her mother is a liberation she is unable to free herself from her influence as the 'ghost' leaves messages scrawled on the wall such as 'HELP ELEANOR COME HOME' (Jackson 1999: 146). Eleanor is forced by the other participants in the experiment to leave and she commits suicide by crashing her car into a tree in the grounds of Hill House. It is a moment of liberation and self-destruction, her final thoughts being 'I am really doing it' (245), followed by '*Why* am I doing this? Why am I doing this? Why don't they stop me?' (246). The novel can be read as a female Gothic narrative which explores feelings of liberation which are ultimately compromised by an inability to envision an alternative existence, and as such captures the representative anxieties of women of a certain class at the time.

Whilst it would be banal to state that ghosts bring the past back to life, spectrality does become a means through which to explore history. Toni Morrison's *Beloved* (1987) uses the ghost of a child as a means of evoking the history of a family and the history of slavery. Beloved had been killed by her mother, Sethe, when she and her children had been about to be recaptured after escaping from their plantation. In killing her child she asserts ownership over her and sees this as preferable to the slow death offered by slavery. The child returns, but her story makes it unclear whether she is there to haunt Sethe (and so punish her) or whether she is there to keep alive the past of slavery which Sethe and the others are still compelled to confront, even in a tale set in the post-slavery era. How to represent the past is one of the central concerns and the figure of the ghost is used to raise questions about making visible that which a culture has lost or has been forced to forget. Memory, and more importantly Morrison's coinage 'rememory', are key terms in the novel as it explores ways in which the past can be evoked. These themes are repeatedly focalised through Sethe for whom 'the future was a matter of keeping the past at bay' (Morrison 1997: 42), a strategy that becomes undermined by the arrival of Beloved (and before that Sethe's lover Paul D., whom she had known in the past). Initially Beloved is unable to account for where she has come from and Sethe's question to her 'You disremember everything?' (118) reflects her own wilful suppression of the past. Morrison suggests that the ignoble history of slavery cannot and should not be forgotten because it ghosts the lives of generations of African Americans. The concluding lines appear to complicate this with the repeated refrain that this is 'not a story to pass on' (275) interwoven with images of forgetting. However the refrain also refers to how histories become lost, and the novel represents a version of the past that one should not 'pass on' or overlook. Finally, as always, the ghost, like the history of slavery, is there but not there, spectrally shaping the lives of today's African Americans.

Ghosts are historical beings because they are messengers about the preoccupations of a particular age. Radcliffe's ghosts are inevitably quite different to Morrison's. However, this is not to say that we cannot observe literary continuities within ghost stories, as Radcliffe and Jackson, for example, have much in common. Ghosts are never just ghosts; they provide us with an insight into what haunts our culture. Ghosts, of course, cannot die and as such are a persistent reminder of what a culture can only express in oblique terms. Making visible what it is that haunts the ghost is thus the crucial challenge for contemporary Gothic criticism.

NOTES

1 The term 'female Gothic' was first used in 1976 in Ellen Moers' *Literary Women* (Moers 1978).
2 See Smith (2005).
3 These include *City and Suburb* (1861), *Mitre Court* (1885) and *The Head of the Firm* (1892). Her Gothic novellas are *Fairy Water* (1873), *The Uninhabited House* (1875), *The Haunted River* (1877) and *The Disappearance of Mr Jeremiah Redworth* (1878), as well as the collection of tales *Weird Stories* (1884), which includes many ghost stories.
    Please also note that the discussions of Dickens, Riddell, M. R. James, Jackson and Morrison are developed in Smith (2007).
4 See Smith (2004) for a development of these ideas.

WORKS CITED

Benson, E. F. (1986) 'Expiation', in *The Tale of an Empty House and other Ghost Stories*, Guernsey: Black Swan.

Bloom, Clive (1993) 'M. R. James and his Fiction', in *Creepers: British Horror and Fantasy in the Twentieth Century*, ed. Clive Bloom, London: Pluto.

Briggs, Julia (1977) *The Rise and Fall of the English Ghost Story*, London: Faber and Faber.

Castle, Terry (1995) 'The Spectralization of the Other in The Mysteries of Udolpho', in *The Female Thermometer: Eighteenth-Century Culture and the Invention of the Uncanny*, Oxford: Oxford University Press.

Dickens, Charles (1985) *A Christmas Carol* in *The Christmas Books*, vol. 1, ed. Michael Slater, Harmondsworth: Penguin.

Freud, Sigmund (1985) 'The "Uncanny"', in *Art and Literature: Jensen's* Gradiva, *Leonardo Da Vinci and Other Works*, vol. 14 of the Penguin Freud Library, trans. James Strachey, ed. Albert Dickson, Harmondsworth: Penguin.

Friedan, Betty (1992) *The Feminine Mystique*, Harmondsworth: Penguin.

Jackson, Shirley (1999) *The Haunting of Hill House*, London: Constable.

James, M. R. (1970) 'The Mezzotint', in *The Collected Stories of M. R. James*, London: Edward Arnold.

Marx, Karl (1984) *Capital*, in *Karl Marx Selected Writings*, ed. David McLellan, Oxford: Oxford University Press.

Moers, Ellen (1978) *Literary Women*, London: The Women's Press.

Morrison, Toni (1997) *Beloved*, London: Vintage.

Poovey, Mary (2003) *The Financial System in Nineteenth-Century Britain*, Oxford: Oxford University Press.

Punter, David (1996) *The Literature of Terror*, vol. 2: *The Modern Gothic*, rev. 2nd edn, London: Longman.

Riddell, J. H. (1971) *The Uninhabited House*, in *Five Victorian Ghost Novels*, ed. E. F. Bleiler, New York: Dover.

Shelley, Mary (2000) 'On Ghosts', in E. J. Clery and Robert Miles (eds), *Gothic Documents: A Sourcebook 1700–1820*, Manchester: Manchester University Press.

Smith, Andrew (2004) 'M. R. James's Gothic Revival', special issue of *Diegesis* on 'Horror', ed. Gina Wisker, 7: 16–22.

—— (2005) 'Dickens's Ghosts: Demonic Economies', in special issue of *Victorian Review* on 'Literature and Money', 31(2): 36–55.

—— (2007) *Edinburgh Critical Guide to Gothic Literature*, Edinburgh: Edinburgh University Press.

19

GOTHIC FEMININITIES

ALISON MILBANK

As soon as the features of what we now call Gothic fiction began to be recognised as comprising a new genre in the 1790s, their feminine qualities were emphasised. The two most effective parodies of the new mode, Jane Austen's *Northanger Abbey* (1818) and Eaton Barrett's *The Heroine; or, Adventures of a Fair Romance Reader* (1813), reveal the centrality of the persecuted maiden, who is pursued by a rapacious tyrant or imprisoned in a mouldering castle or monastery, where she uncovers the secrets of the past before escaping to freedom and recognition as the true heir. The potency of this female protagonist is such that not even her most satirical presentation is safe from Gothic incursion, so that Catherine Morland's comic fantasies of General Tilney's murderous propensities are eventually justified when he behaves like a fictional tyrant in throwing her out of Northanger Abbey. Similarly, although Barrett's Cherry Wilkinson, or 'Cherubina' as she calls herself, causes universal havoc by her attempts to interpret the world as a Gothic novel, having her innocent father immured as a lunatic, she does actually end up imprisoned in a libertine's mansion, like Adeline in Radcliffe's *Romance of the Forest* (1791), and escapes by means of a revolving fireplace and a passing ghoul. Gothic heroines always cause the downfall of the patriarchal figures or institutions that seek to entrap them, and their fears are never merely imagined.

When Gothic fiction came to modern scholarly attention in the 1970s and 80s, its rise coincided with the second wave of feminism, and criticism was often driven by feminist concerns. The Gothic heroine thus became a proto-feminist in her resistance to patriarchal control, and Kate Ferguson Ellis located in the Gothic novel an awareness of the contradictions inherent in the separation of the feminised private home from the masculine public sphere, so that Emily St Aubert fleeing Montoni's redoubt in *The Mysteries of Udolpho* (1794) became an avatar for later women escaping the confines of domesticity. After an early flurry of Freudian readings in which the Gothic heroine might be seen as a hysteric, or in erotic thrall to the father, attention turned to her search for a lost maternal origin in studies influenced by the psychoanalytic theory of Jacques Lacan and Julia Kristeva. Radcliffe's *A Sicilian Romance* (1790) for example, described the travails of Julia Mazzini, who discovers the mother she had long supposed dead, imprisoned in the vaults beneath her father's palazzo. Critics also played with the ambiguities in the mother/daughter relation, and the girl's difficulties of achieving individuation and her own separate sense of identity.

My examples of Gothic heroines have all been taken from the novels of Ann

Radcliffe – 'mother Radcliff [sic]' as Keats called her in a letter of 1819 (Keats 1970: 214). As Gothic criticism developed, it seemed that one could trace the development of a specifically 'female' Gothic, not only in terms of plot but also authorship. From the beginning, women were prominent in novel writing, and Marie Mulvey Roberts lists 57 women in about a hundred authors represented in the important Sadleir–Black Gothic novel collection (Otto *et al.* 2003). One important publisher of Gothic romance, the Minerva Press, specialised in fiction by women, often anonymous, following in the tradition of Charlotte Reeve, Ann Radcliffe and Sophia Lee (Blakey 1939). Ellen Moers (1976) made an early critical attempt to discern a female Gothic tradition beyond the 1790s, and included Mary Shelley's *Frankenstein* and Emily Brontë's *Wuthering Heights*. Sandra Gilbert and Susan Gubar's influential *The Madwoman in the Attic* (1979) also interpreted a whole range of nineteenth-century woman writers as Gothic heroines in their attempts to escape the power of the male literary canon to establish their own place in the pantheon, and to struggle with their repressed female energies, as Charlotte Brontë's Jane Eyre did with the original 'mad woman in the attic', the lunatic Bertha Mason.

A third strand of femininity is located in the Gothic reader who, like most imagined readers of fiction, is held to be female. Austen's Catherine spends much time perusing *The Mysteries of Udolpho* and is wild to discover what is behind the black veil; Barrett's Cherry Wilkinson's misadventures are caused by omnivorous consumption of Gothic fictions. There was, indeed, a symbiotic relationship between Gothic readers and writers, with the former becoming the latter. The *Lady's Magazine* solicited stories from its readers, and many a Minerva Press production was authored by 'a Lady'. Yet men of the stature of the poet Shelley (*Zastrozzi*, 1810) and the politician Lord John Russell (*The Nun of Arrouca*, 1822) wrote Gothic fiction in their youth, suggesting that Gothic was not just the preserve of the female young, although women were held to be particularly at risk of reading without critical distance. Henry Tilney in *Northanger Abbey* appropriates his sister's copy of *Udolpho* and reads it cover to cover, but he is able to renarrate it as parody to tease and confuse Catherine Morland, who takes it all too literally.

Yet, although the journal *Gothic Studies* published a special issue on the 'Female Gothic' in 2004, there has been a definite turning away from straightforward feminist interpretations as taking too essentialist an approach to the nature of gender, while psychoanalytic readings have given way to more historically contextualised approaches. Two of the most substantial studies in relation to femininity have been, first, Terry Castle's chapter on Radcliffean Gothic in *The Female Thermometer* (1995) and, second, E. J. Clery's *Women's Gothic* (2000), a study of female Gothic writers from Charlotte Reeve to Charlotte Dacre. Different as they are, both studies move 'female Gothic' out of the ghetto to show texts not just reacting to social processes but intervening in the public debates of their day. Castle's article interprets the dreamy atmosphere and tendency of the heroine's thoughts to produce the subject of her reflections to her sight as indicative of a response to the spectrality of all human experience in the post-Enlightenment period. Clery's book situates Gothic fiction in relation to debates about the nature of tragedy and the passions in eighteenth-century aesthetics and, in particular, among the bluestocking circles around Sarah Siddons, the actress. Here we have an historical grouping of female writers engaged in the intellectual concerns of a specific period, rather than a vague and ahistorical 'female Gothic'. Clery's study is particularly important in showing that the first 'wave' of Gothic by women writers did have a coherent and shared intellectual project, from the 1773 essay by Anna Aikin (later Barbauld), 'On the Pleasure Derived from Objects of Terror', which links the 'paradox of the heart' of enjoying tales of ghosts, goblins or murderers, to the pity and terror evoked by tragedy, to Radcliffe's posthumous essay comparing and contrasting the effects of terror and horror (Radcliffe 1826).

In the rest of this chapter, I would like to follow Clery in attending to a specific intellectual project among writers of female Gothic, and Castle in attending to post-Enlightenment theories of psychology and aesthetics, particularly as they developed in nineteenth-century Gothic writing. And in so doing I hope to justify the remarks made earlier about the reality of the Gothic heroine's fears and her Gothic reading of reality.

One element of female Gothic writing that has perplexed critics is its use of the explained supernatural. It evokes a spiritual world through unexplained ghostly visions and sounds, yet finally provides a natural origin for all the effects. Sometimes the explanation is awkward or belated: the most celebrated example is the mystery behind the black veil about which Catherine Morland was so concerned. Emily St Aubert faints as soon as she lifts it, without giving any explanation, and the reader is left to imagine all sorts of horrors before the tame, even off-hand, explanation given at the very end of the novel: that it was a wax image of a skeleton, made as an act of penance for a previous owner of Udolpho.

Later women writers imitate Radcliffe's explained supernatural quite closely, and emphasise her stress on the nature of perception. First, they continue the focus on female subjectivity through free indirect narration, which gives access to the heroine's thought processes and gives her perspective on events a privileged status in the narration. Second, such novels contain an interest in the relation of the heroine to the natural world, as a series of vistas are presented to her sight: sublime and lofty mountain landscapes, and the castles, chateaux and abbeys of the past. The heroine views these structures both from outside but also from within their labyrinthine complexities, and similarly the narration will move from viewing the heroine from outside, as a figure in the landscape, and from within her mind. The narrative mechanics of the inside/outside point of view have been crucial in interpretation of this Gothic femininity: does this collapse the world inside the mind, and the novel become a purely phantasmal revival of images in the brain, as Castle suggests? Or is Radcliffean Gothic about the rigidity of female virtue as it seeks to maintain a hysterical fixity in relation to sexual desire?

My own interpretation of this Radcliffean Gothic viewpoint seeks to show that it both promotes the validity of the heroine's perceptions and a philosophy that underpins them. It explores a middle way between philosophical idealism, in which the mind is primary, and its perceptions, as it were, create the world, and a crude materialism that can find no mediation between the self and the world beyond.

It is Terry Castle's opinion that this naturalising of the supernatural is the obverse of the supernaturalising of the natural, which occurs once the transcendent had been dethroned in the Enlightenment, and it was thought possible to explain phenomena without recourse to God. Her argument has an elegant reversibility, and makes some sense seen in relation to the way in which the philosopher, Immanuel Kant (1781) divided our perception of reality between the phenomena – the nature of objects as we perceive them – and the noumena, which are their aspects to which we have no access: the things-in-themselves. Since things-in-themselves are ungraspable, this does in a sense render them oddly spectral and unreal. Yet this does not really account for the deliberate way in which the supernatural holds sway in Radcliffe's writing for most of the narrative, so that the impression the reader takes away is not exactly one in which the ghostly has been trounced. Certainly the heroine learns to fear human rather than spectral threats in the 'female' Gothic novel, unlike the 'masculine' tradition of the transgressive hero, who is punished by an all too real supernatural force, like Matthew Lewis's *The Monk* (1796), in which the eponymous hero is seduced and finally destroyed by a demon.

The explained supernatural has something to do with Radcliffe's Whig radicalism that seeks to challenge the tyranny of feudal times, and send her virtuous and enlightened heroine and hero off into a progressive future, having validated their destruction of the old order. Yet as a devout Christian she evidently believed in the supernatural, and she puts such a belief into the mouth of the exemplary governess of the Mazzini children, Madame de Menon, in *A Sicilian Romance*: 'Who shall say that any thing is impossible to God? We know that he has made us, who are embodied spirits; he, therefore, can make unembodied spirits' (Radcliffe 1993: 36). A posthumously published story, *Gaston de Blondeville* (Radcliffe 1826), contains an unexplained ghostly visitation, although elsewhere characters are praised for their resistance to superstition. One might argue that here she is being Kantian in aiming to separate things we can know from those we cannot, and educating her heroines in the distinction between phenomena and noumena. She was evidently influenced by Schiller's story, *The Ghost Seer* (1795), in which the protagonist is made to believe in the supernatural origin of effects which are in fact the machinations of a Vatican agent. Radcliffe's *The Italian* (1797) made its hero Vivaldi the victim of supernatural terrors and deliberately staged effects, while the heroine is never troubled by such fears. Ellena, however, is no materialist but one who finds a relation to God through the sublime and uplifting effects of nature. As she reflects: 'Here, the objects seem to impart somewhat of their own force, their own sublimity to the soul. It is scarcely possible to yield to the pressure of misfortune while we walk as with the Deity, amidst his most stupendous works' (Radcliffe 2000: 75). Whereas crafty monks create sinister voices to mislead Vivaldi by concealing their own participation, Ellena finds the created, artistic character of natural effects a true and open mediation between herself and the divine. So the false supernatural is unmasked as a human attempt to ape divine power and agency, while the true supernatural is revealed in the interplay between human and non-human nature.

Furthermore, this cluster of tropes – the perceiving female subject, the Gothic structures and natural wonders opened to her gaze and presence, and the explained supernatural – are imitated by a succession of later writers such as Charles Brockden Brown, *Wieland* (1798), Wilkie Collins in *The Woman in White* (1860), J. Sheridan Le Fanu in *Uncle Silas* (1864) and Henry James in *The Turn of the Screw* (1898), thus showing the importance of their association. The Victorian writer Charlotte Brontë is a particularly clear example of a Radcliffean imitator. She uses Gothic motifs in all her novels and makes direct reference to *The Italian* in *Shirley* (1859), which also imitates its plot by reuniting the heroine with her long-lost mother, and in her two most famous novels, *Jane Eyre* (1847) and *Villette* (1853) she reproduces all three elements of the 'female' Gothic plot. *Jane Eyre* takes its heroine to imprisoning structures like Lowood School, with its tyrannous and hypocritical clerical overseer, and old houses such as Thornfield, which famously has its owner's lunatic first wife secreted in the attic. The heroine and first-person narrator's subjectivity is presented in the imagined landscapes and forms of her sketches. She believes Thornfield haunted as she wakes in the night before her wedding to find a spectral presence tearing her bridal veil, only to have her fears rendered actual in the discovery of Rochester's bigamy and his imprisoned wife. Later Jane hears a supernatural maternal voice: 'my daughter, flee temptation' and leaves Thornfield's Gothic thrall for Mother Nature and freedom on the moors. Just when she is succumbing to her cousin's demand that she marry him so that she can act as an aid to his missionary work in India, she hears another voice:

I saw nothing: but I heard a voice somewhere cry –
'Jane! Jane! Jane!' – Nothing more.
'Oh, God! What is it?' I gasped.
I might have said, 'Where is it?' for it did not seem in the room – nor in the house –
nor in the garden: it did not come out of the air – nor from under the earth – nor
from overhead. I had heard it – where, or whence, for ever impossible to know!
(Brontë 1969: 536)

This voice is recognisable as that of her master and would-be husband, Edward Rochester. It is therefore 'natural', and the reader later learns that, at many miles distance, Rochester did indeed call in anguish on Jane. Yet although she understands this at once and sternly denies 'superstition' and 'miracle', the voice sends her to prayer and direct access to 'a Mighty Spirit; and my soul rushed out in gratitude at His feet' (537). The 'explained supernatural' works both like and unlike that of Radcliffe. Brontë's heroine is not deceived by ghostly effects as is Emily St Aubert, but again an encounter with 'nature' brings the heroine to direct access to the transcendent. Here, however, this is not so much by means of a sublime landscape of power but a human voice. Hitherto, Rochester, the ultimate Romantic doomed hero, had usurped the place of God in Jane's life and had indeed had resort to all sorts of stratagems, such as cross-dressing as an all-knowing fortune teller, to gain power over her. By means of the needy voice, however, he leads Jane beyond him to the divine, and afterwards she is able to act: the voice 'had opened the doors of the soul's cell, and loosed its bands' (539). No longer will Rochester lord it over her but she famously will marry *him*, blinded and maimed as he has become through trying to rescue his mad wife from the fire she set to destroy his house.

Despite, however, the immediate insight into the natural basis of the voice, Jane Eyre has no means of understanding how it is heard or whence it comes. The extract quoted above makes every 'natural' explanation impossible. Yet she knows it is real and actual. This double experience that sets one in an interpretive quandary has been analysed in detail by the narrative theorist Tzvetan Todorov in his book *The Fantastic*:

> In a world which is indeed our world, the one we know, a world without devils, sylphides, or vampires, there occurs an event which cannot be explained by the laws of this same familiar world. The person who experiences the event must opt for one of two possible solutions: either he is the victim of an illusion of the senses, of a product of the imagination – and laws of the world then remain what they are; or else the event has indeed taken place, it is an integral part of reality – but then this reality is controlled by laws unknown to us . . .
>
> The fantastic occupies the duration of this uncertainty. Once we choose one answer or the other, we leave the fantastic for a neighbouring genre, the uncanny or the marvellous. The fantastic is that hesitation experienced by a person who knows only the laws of nature, confronting an apparently supernatural event.
>
> (Todorov 1973: 25)

The tales that form the texts under discussion in Todorov's study of the fantastic are all from the period following the Enlightenment in the late eighteenth and nineteenth centuries, and so are exactly coterminous with the rise of the Gothic. In a Todorovian reading, the state of hesitation over the reality of one's perceptions is thus not a clumsy device for the assertion of rationalism over superstition but an exploration of the complex nature of reality, and a means of mediating between the world and the self. Jane Eyre is in the classic state of hesitation, since her senses tell her she is really hearing a voice, but her reason tells her that it is impossible. She is thus brought directly up against the limits of the empirical validation of the real. Indeed, the real is now supernaturalised, not in a ghostly sense of being rendered unreal and spectral, but as *more* than natural, or rather the natural rests on the supernatural. Later the reader and

Jane learn that Rochester did actually call for her at that moment, yet the mechanism whereby the message reached her remains impossible. So the actual phenomenal world of her experience is indeed a Gothic and fantastic one that requires a supernatural origin, just as Ellena's mountains took their power from a divine source.

A celebrated article by Robert Heilman (1958) about Charlotte Brontë, praises her work for internalising the conventions of the supernatural. Instead of cumbersome ghostly stage machinery, he notes a turn into the self as an uncanny space. I have already shown that Jane Eyre's 'inner' voice has an external validation but his argument might be held to be truer of Brontë's later novel, *Villette* (1853). Lucy Snowe travels abroad like Emily St Aubert, and like Ellena Rosalba finds herself in a convent school, although one now under lay leadership. Repeatedly a spectral nun haunts the convent, appearing first in the attic to which Lucy resorts to enjoy some imaginative freedom like Ellena in the convent turret:

> Something in that vast solitary garret sounded strangely. Most surely and certainly I heard, as it seemed, a stealthy foot on that floor: a sort of gliding out from the direction of the black recess haunted by the malefactor cloaks. I turned: my light was dim; the room was long – but as I live! I saw in the middle of that ghostly chamber a figure all black or white; the skirts straight, narrow, black; the head bandaged, veiled, white.
>
> Say what you will, reader – tell me I was nervous, or mad; affirm that I was unsettled by the excitement of that letter; declare that I dreamed: this I vow – I saw there – in that room – on that night – an image like – A NUN.
>
> (Brontë 1984: 351)

The reader as well as the protagonist hesitates to understand the event described. The language of the narrator lurches from the certain to the unsure: 'as it seemed'. This emphasis on the impossible spectre provokes the fantastic, and the reader is left in this quandary throughout the novel because the nun is viewed by Lucy on later occasions. She addresses the nun on one occasion, and later sees her with a witness. However, reaching the school dormitory late one night after a thoroughly fantastic evening in a drugged state, during which she glides about unseen like the spectral nun herself, Lucy returns home to encounter the nun lying on her own bed. Fired up by her recent adventure, Lucy advances:

> In a moment, without exclamation, I had rushed on the haunted couch; nothing leaped out, or sprung, or stirred; all the movement was mine, so was all the life, the reality, the substance, the force; as my instinct felt. I tore her up – the incubus! I held her on high – the goblin! I shook her loose – the mystery! And down she fell – down all round me – down in shreds and fragments – and I trode upon her.
>
> (Brontë 1984: 681)

It transpires that the 'nun' had been a pupil's lover using the disguise to gain access to the school. So here is a truly explained supernatural, and one that Heilman interprets in terms of the uncanny, by which the mystery now lies in the protagonist's psychology, not the supernatural.

The effect is, however, more complex than a mere dethronement of the supernatural. A psychological interpretation had already been suggested, as befits the fantastic. The first sighting accompanied Lucy's reading of a cherished letter from Dr John, whom she loved in vain, and could be interpreted as an effect of the repression of erotic desires for an unattainable object. The second accompanied her burial of letters from that same sender. The third came just as Lucy and M. Paul met in the garden where she was recalling her feelings for Dr John as not yet buried. The resolution of the fantastic in this instance, however, is not in terms of the uncanny through repression, nor of the marvellous, but in terms of the justification of Lucy's experience: she really *did* see what she described. The nun appeared to stand for Lucy because Lucy's experience was that of a poor governess in a school of nubile and prosperous young women: she was like a nun in her enclosure, sexlessness and poverty. In reality, however, the nun stood for love and freedom, finally announcing the elopement of the young lovers, and presaging Lucy's running away from the school with M. Paul to live her own independent life. Supernatural elements still remain in the novel, such as the banshee wail before death and disease, the voice telling Lucy to leave 'this wilderness', and most of all the storm that may or may not drown M. Paul at the end of the novel. His ship is christened the 'Paul et Virginie' after the doomed lovers in a tale by Bernardin de Saint-Pierre, but the novel ends without inform- ing the reader whether all on the ship are lost or not. Brontë therefore leaves her reader in the hesitation of the fantastic, although in tones weighted towards the tragic, and thus towards the uncanny coincidence of ship name and its fate.

What *Villette*'s employment of the fantastic moment of hesitation reveals about the use of the explained supernatural generally in this heroine-centred Gothic narrative, is that it opens an imaginative space in which anything may be imagined, and no possibility is closed. This has both feminist and philosophical liberatory potential. For paradoxically what the Gothic plot offers the heroine is enclosure as a validation of her value and significance, so that she may become aware of her imprisonment and escape to freedom. But it offers also a philo- sophical pleasure as it brings her, through the fantastic and the openness to the supernatural, up against the limits of perception and the nature of reality beyond those limits. The space of the fantastic allows the presence of the noumena some expression, and mediates between the self and things-in-themselves, so that in some sense the heroine is liberated from the prison of Kantian sense impres- sion. In explaining the supernatural, the Gothic plot bestows not just the heir- ship of the ruinous patriarchal castle on the heroine, but also the key to the supernatural origin of existence. It is no wonder that the Gothic mode has attracted its female readers over the centuries, because the Gothic heroine, reading the world correctly, really does inherit the earth – as she glimpses something of the nature of reality itself.

WORKS CITED

Aikin, Anna Laetitia and John Aikin (1773) 'On the Pleasure Derived from Objects of Terror', in *Miscellaneous Pieces in Prose*, London: J. Johnson.

Blakey, Dorothy (1939) *The Minerva Press 1790–1820*, London: Oxford University Press.

Brontë, Charlotte (1969) *Jane Eyre*, ed. Jane Jack and Margaret Smith, Oxford: Clarendon Press.

—— (1984) *Villette*, ed. Herbert Rosengarten and Margaret Smith, Oxford: Clarendon Press.

Castle, Terry (1995), *The Female Thermometer: Eighteenth-Century Culture and the Invention of the Uncanny*, New York: Oxford University Press.

Clery, E. J. (2000) *Women's Gothic: From Clara Reeve to Mary Shelley*, Tavistock: Northcote House.

Ellis, Kate Ferguson (1989) *The Contested Castle: Gothic Novels and the Subversion of Domestic Ideology*, Urbana, IL: University of Illinois Press.

Gilbert, Sandra and Susan Gubar (1979), *The Madwoman in the Attic: The Woman Writer and the Nineteenth-Century Literary Imagination*, New Haven, CT: Yale University Press.

Heilman, Robert (1958) 'Charlotte Brontë's New Gothic', in *From Jane Austen to Joseph Conrad*, ed. R. C. Rathburn and Martin Steinman, Minneapolis, MN: University of Minnesota Press.

Kant, Immanuel ([1781] 1999) *Critique of Pure Reason*, ed. Paul Guyer and Allen W. Wood, Cambridge: Cambridge University Press.

Keats, John (1970) *Letters of John Keats: A New Selection*, ed. Robert Gittings, Oxford, Oxford University Press.

Moers, Ellen (1977) *Literary Women*, London: W. H. Allen.

Otto, Peter, Alison Milbank and Marie Mulvey-Roberts (2003) *Gothic Fiction, Rare Printed Books from the Sadlier–Black Collection of Gothic Fiction at the Alderman Library, University of Virginia on Microfilm*, Marlborough, Wiltshire: Adam Matthews.

Radcliffe, Ann (1826) *Gaston de Blondville or the Court of Henry III*, London: Henry Colburn.

—— (1993) *A Sicilian Romance*, ed. Alison Milbank, Oxford: Oxford University Press.

—— (2000) *The Italian, or The Confessional of the Black Penitents*, ed. Robert Miles, Harmondsworth: Penguin.

Todorov, Tzvetan (1973) *The Fantastic: A Structuralist Approach to a Literary Mode*, trans. Richard Howard, Cleveland, OH: Case Western Reserve University Press.

20

GOTHIC MASCULINITIES

BRIAN BAKER

In the fields of film and literary criticism, the last 25 years have seen a major development in studies of masculinity. The analyses of gender produced by the rise of a feminist critical practice in the late 1960s resulted in a renewed focus upon what might once have seemed a monolithic male subject, aligned with discourses of domination. From the pioneering work of Richard Dyer (1992) and Steve Neale (1993) in analysing the male screen icon; through the rise of queer criticism and such illuminating (and indeed revolutionary) works by Jonathan Dollimore (1991), Judith Butler (1990) and particularly Eve Kosofsky Sedgwick (1985) (whose use of the concept of 'homosociality' has been massively influential, and who has also written directly on the Gothic); to analysts of constructions of 'hegemonic' and subordinated masculinities in post-war fiction and film, such as Lynne Segal (1997), Steven Cohan (1997), Robert J. Corber (1993) and David Savran (1998), it is now a commonplace in critical works on masculinities to assume a fragmented, plural, performative or anxious subject (or range of subjectivities), constructed (incompletely) by contemporary cultural discourses.

Accordingly, Gothic masculinities have, in the last ten years or so, been the focus of a historicising mode of criticism, which understands the representations of masculinity, 'manliness' and sexuality through contested cultural fields. For early Gothic, the discourses of Enlightenment and Romanticism have been investigated as crucial influences; in the Victorian period and 'second wave', *fin-de-siècle* Gothic, empire, degeneration, sexology and medicine have all provided vital avenues of enquiry. Kelly Hurley, in *The Gothic Body* (1996), investigates the impact of degeneration discourse on Gothic texts of the *fin-de-siècle*; and Andrew Smith, in *Victorian Demons* (2004), focuses on degenerationist theories, medicine and disease, and the space of London through which to approach what he calls 'the often problematic relationship which exists between models of deviancy and apparently "normative" gender scripts' in relationship to masculinity (Smith 2004: 6). Cyndy Hendershot, in *The Animal Within* (1998), deploys a range of historically grounded readings of Gothic texts from the 'first wave' to the present, connecting masculinity and the Gothic to science, psychoanalysis and imperialism. Hendershot states that 'the Gothic exposes the others within and without that give the lie to the notion of such a category as stable masculinity' (Hendershot 1998: 1), a vital insight for my argument in this chapter. The presence of the threatening Other and, more importantly, the divided or fractured masculine subject in *fin-de-siècle* Gothic, is, I would acknowledge, produced by historically situated cultural forces, but my intention is to push the sense of the 'split' subject further back, to suggest that the Gothic, from its very inception, uncovers pre-existing fault-lines in the masculine subject.

Robert Miles, in his article 'The Eye of Power: Ideal Presence and the Gothic Romance' (1999), uses the work of Michel Foucault to investigate early Gothic, particularly in terms of visibility and power. Miles cites Foucault's own interview/essay 'The Eye of Power', in which Foucault identifies the Gothic romance and its 'whole fantasy-world of stone walls, darkness, hideouts and dungeons' as a kind of 'negative of the transparency and visibility which [the Enlightenment] aimed to establish' (Foucault 1980: 154), a visibility made most manifest in Bentham's panopticon. Following Foucault's and Miles's implication of the Gothic with the discourses of the Enlightenment, I would like to suggest that a 'split' in Gothic masculinity, which can be found most explicitly in Stevenson's *Strange Case of Dr Jekyll and Mr Hyde* (1886), is the result of a fundamental paradox at the heart of post-Enlightenment constructions of the subject, which are themselves often universalised as male. I will argue that the traces of the Enlightenment discourses in which one can situate early Gothic texts can also be found in the constructions of the masculine subject in late Victorian Gothic, and in contemporary horror fictions which self-consciously deploy Gothic themes and ideas. I will first, however, for rhetorical purposes and in full knowledge that all binaries are Derridean 'violent hierarchies', propose a dyad at the heart of the post-Enlightenment subject which can ultimately be diagnosed in the fragmented masculine figures in Gothic texts, a dyad which can be seen in later theorisations of self and other. This dyad is the principle of 'reason' opposed to, and implicated with, the imperative of 'passion'.

I should stress that I am following a critical and theoretical practice that understands the subject to be a construct, brought into being by certain historical forces, rather than suggesting some kind of originary, 'whole' self that pre-exists the moment of splitting. In Foucauldian terms, the construction of the unitary, rational Enlightenment subject is at the expense of the expulsion of elements which might destabilise this construct: the 'mad', the non-rational, the 'passionate'. The dominance of reason (in the form of medical, juridical and scientific discourses) not only expels the non-rational but seeks to understand the Other through rational means, to return the Other to the realm of reason through science, medicine, penology, psychology and other explicatory systems. The Cartesian cogito implies a reasoning, thinking subject (*Homo sapiens*), and thereby one in which the 'passions' (excessive emotion, transgressive desire, 'madness') are controlled or expelled. My proposed dyad, reason/passion, alternatively suggests that, as Henry Jekyll proposes in Stevenson's *Strange Case of Dr Jekyll and Mr Hyde*, 'man is not truly one, but truly two' (Stevenson 1999: 76). The expulsion is incomplete: 'passion' is implicated in 'reason'.

Masculine figures that inhabit this implicated reason/passion dyad, whose excessive or transgressive actions place them outside the discourses of reason, can be found in literature from Macbeth, to Milton's Satan, through the eighteenth-century libertine (especially in the writings of Sade), and in the Romantic (or Byronic) transgressive hero whose intellect and 'passion' places him outside normative social or ethical bounds. The relationships between the Enlightenment, Romanticism (in its various forms) and the Gothic is a complicated one that I do not have space here to pursue. However, rather than understanding any of these modes or forms of discourse to be in opposition to one another, I would again stress a model of mutual implication. For instance, Peter Gay argued that 'the limits of rational inquiry into ultimate mysteries, the impotence of reason before the passions, were ... themes that haunted the Enlightenment' (Gay 1973, cited in Day 1996: 67). Within Enlightenment discourse, despite the elevation of rationality and critical intelligence, there are some areas of experience or knowledge which are incommensurable with reason. Reason's 'impotence before the passions' finds a place for the mysterious, the Other, within the ambit of rationality; not only 'silencing' the non-rational, as Foucault argued, by exposure to discourses of reason, but allowing it to remain unexpelled *within* rationality. For the relationship between Romanticism and the Gothic, Robert Miles posits this crucial point:

> If one were to summarize the source of critical interest in the early Gothic, one might say that it is stimulated by the question of whether the Gothic is a late expression of eighteenth-century culture or whether the genre begins with – is the beginning of – modernity [or put more narrowly] whether the Gothic is a 'dark' variety of Romanticism or whether it is tied up in the logic of the late Enlightenment.
>
> (Miles 1999: 10)

Peter Gay and Aidan Day's connection of Enlightenment and Romanticism(s) helps overcome an overstated sense of epistemic break between the two; perhaps Miles's question is unanswerable because of what I have proposed as a mutual implication of one discourse in another. The paradox at the heart of the unitary subject of the Enlightenment and after, the unacknowledged implication of 'reason' and 'passion', 'rationality' and 'madness' (created by the incomplete expulsion of the abject, the Other) is made visible in the split or fractured masculine subject of the Gothic. Gothic texts trace the fragmentation of the unified subject, making visible the fracture lines that are always present within the formation of post-Enlightenment subjectivity.

In terms of the modes of Gothic and horror (which I will deal with here in a kind of generic continuum, albeit acknowledging that the two are not identical), the work of constructing the self and other also takes place in gender terms. The Enlightenment subject is, by implication, a masculine subject. Abjection, Julia Kristeva's term, works as a means of separating self from other, the centre from the margin, the human from the non-human. Barbara Creed explains thus:

> In *Powers of Horror*, Kristeva argues that the constitution of acceptable forms of subjectivity and sociality demands the expulsion of those things defined as

improper and unclean. Whatever is expelled is constituted as an abject, that which 'disturbs identity, system, order' . . . A crucial aspect of the abject is, however, that it can never be fully removed or set apart from the subject or society; the abject both threatens and beckons. The abject constitutes the other side of seemingly stable subjectivity.

(Creed 1986: 121)

The process of abjection is crucial to the constitution of the unitary (masculine) subject. The abject, the excluded, help define the boundaries of the subject. The construction of the abject is dependent on the creation of taboos, the operation of which defends unitary subjectivity from a dangerous, destabilising plurality. Creed suggests that horror films are full of images of abjection, and watching them 'signifies a desire not only for perverse pleasure (confronting sickening, horrific images . . .) but also a desire, having taken pleasure in perversity, to throw up, throw out, eject the abject (from the safety of the spectator's seat)' (Creed 1986: 46). As Creed notes, however, that which is abjected is never truly expelled: it 'both threatens and beckons'. The boundary between self and other remains blurred: as Hendershot notes above, in the Gothic there are others within as well as others without. As Jonathan Dollimore writes, in his *Sexual Dissidence*, with regard to transgression and perversion: *'the absolutely other is inextricably within'* (Dollimore 1991: 182, italics in original).

In Stevenson's *Strange Case of Dr Jekyll and Mr Hyde*, the lines between self and monstrous Other are similarly blurred. While Jekyll/Hyde's fractured subjectivity is ranged against the seemingly unified masculine subjectivities of Utterson, Lanyon and others, Jekyll's 'Full Statement of the Case' at the end of the text indicates an alternative understanding of subjectivity: '[M]an will be ultimately known for a mere polity of multifarious, incongruous and independent denizens' (Stevenson 1999: 76). The linguistic slippages in the text, where both Hyde and Jekyll are both 'I', and Hyde's usurpation of the position of 'originary' (whole) subject from Jekyll, destabilise a reading of the narrative that posits Hyde as simply a manifestation of desire, some kind of (whole or originary and atavistic) 'beast within'. Hyde is an abject being, however, and displays the signs of his abjection on his body. He is 'pale and dwarfish, he gave an impression of deformity without any nameable malformation, he had a displeasing smile, he had borne himself to the lawyer with a sort of murderous mixture of timidity and boldness' (41). The text seems to invite a reading in terms of a psychological depth-model: Hyde as Jekyll's inner double, the alter ego who satisfies all Jekyll's repressed or unacknowledged desires. I would argue that the text presents instead a radically disrupted masculine subject, where the 'originary self' does not, in fact, exist. Hyde demonstrates the impossibility of removing utterly the other from the self, 'passion' from reason, abject from subject. This dangerous plurality of selves proposed by Henry Jekyll himself suggests that the subject is, in fact, only one of many 'denizens', and has no more claim to be an originary 'self' than the seemingly secondary, abject Hyde. Hyde, the abject, 'beckons and threatens' Jekyll, offering the fulfilment of desire, but the probability of destruction. Hyde is the violent return of the forces that divide reason from unreason, played across the very body of Jekyll/Hyde, resulting ultimately in the destruction of both.

The continuum upon which Gothic and horror reside helps us to understand the continuity of interest these texts show in issues of subjectivity and gender. I would argue that figures of the 'monstrous masculine' (to coin a Kristevan phrase), once the province of the Gothic, now appear prevalently in the horror texts of popular fiction and film. In this light, I wish to turn, for the majority of this chapter, to one of the most memorable monsters from late twentieth-century horror, Dr Hannibal Lecter, the increasingly central focus of Thomas Harris's novels *Red Dragon* (1982), *The Silence of the Lambs* (1989) and *Hannibal* (1999). Jonathan Demme's 1991 film adaptation of *The Silence of the Lambs*, with its dungeon- or castle-like imagery of incarceration, and emphasis on bodily transformation and horror, indicates the interpenetration of Gothic and 'slasher' horror modes in popular texts.

Harris's Gothicised monstrous male is the serial killer/psychiatrist Dr Hannibal Lecter, whose subjectivity inhabits the 'split' reason/passion dyad I proposed earlier, and as such indicates the longevity (or recurrence) of the disruptions in subject-formation I outlined above. The figure of the serial killer, particularly important to the imaginary of late twentieth-century America, but also to a range of popular literature and filmic modes (including horror and the police procedural), inherits the Gothic preoccupation with destabilised subjectivities. As I will outline below, the 'split' subjectivity of the serial killer and the rational detective offer representations of non-normative and normative formations of gender and subjectivity, an opposition which is then itself destabilised. As an example, where an abjected Dracula is positioned against the normative masculine subjects of British society (Arthur Holmwood, Dr Seward) in Stoker's *Dracula* (1897), effecting a division between self and other, subject and abject, Dr Hannibal Lecter is increasingly positioned against the abjected serial killers Francis Dollarhyde (in *Red Dragon*) and Jame Gumb (in *The Silence of the Lambs*), whose 'gender distress' (Clover 1992) is manifested in their desire to transform themselves, in the latter case physically, into the other sex. This is because, as I shall outline below, Harris increasingly places Lecter in the centre of the narratives, transforming him into a heroic (and I will argue Romantic) self, signifying a strange turn away from the 'split subject' and towards a rather less troubling and disrupted form of subjectivity.

One of the ways in which Thomas Harris's texts indicate the blurring of the self/other binary, thereby destabilising unitary subjectivity, is by emphasising a continuum between the investigating agent (Will Graham or Clarice Starling) and their source of knowledge, Dr Lecter. This is a version of the Gothic trope of the double. In fact, Graham and Starling's recourse to Lecter's mode of insight – he can understand the serial killers not because of his medical training, but because he is one himself – signifies the limits of rational discourse when faced with the seemingly inexplicable actions of the serial killer. In *Red Dragon*, Lecter emphasises the doubleness of himself and Will Graham when he tells the fleeing investigator: 'Do you know how you caught me, Will? . . . The reason you caught me is that WE'RE JUST ALIKE' (Harris 2000: 75). In *Manhunter*, Michael Mann's 1986 adaptation of *Red Dragon*, Graham (William Petersen) flees Lecter's cell at the run after this dialogue scene (filmed almost in its entirety by Mann), running not only from his nemesis but from the fatal recognition of his own similarity to, rather than difference from, Dr Lecter. In Demme's *Silence of the Lambs*, shots in which Lecter's face is reflected in near-superimposition on Clarice Starling's, in the Perspex of Lecter's cell, signify the same doubling.

Lecter, the 'monster' (as he is called in all three novels) is, perversely, increasingly placed in the role of the hero, particularly in *Hannibal*, where the narrative of the novel finds perverse resolution in the 'romance' between Lecter and Starling. Lecter's isolation is undone at the end of *Hannibal* through the transgressive 'romance' with Starling, and he seems to achieve his own space of peace and tranquillity. The 'Satanic' traces of the Gothicised Romantic (or Byronic) hero, the destructive individual, are turned into the hero of romance: rescue, seduction and the creation of the *Reich der Zwei*. In the first of the novels, *Red Dragon*, in an analogous way to the positioning of the abject Dracula against the legitimated masculine subjects of the Crew of Light, Lecter is the displaced Other to the 'rational' investigators. This works in *Hannibal* by Harris's use of point of view and our access to Lecter's interiority. Although this is used in a much more pervasive way in *Hannibal*, even in *Red Dragon* we are offered Lecter's point of view: 'Lecter felt much better. He thought he might surprise Graham with a call sometime or, if the man couldn't be civil, he might have a supply-house mail Graham a colostomy bag for old time's sake' (Harris 2000: 78). The role played by the reader's, and viewer's, increasing identification with Lecter's point of view is a vital means by which Harris is able to realign Lecter from the position of monstrous Other to Romantic Self.

The final guarantor of the fixity of Lecter's subjectivity is a reversal of the field of the self/other binary, not its dissolution. Lecter is placed in contradistinction to Dollarhyde and Gumb, rather than Starling and the FBI: the fluid or ruptured subjectivities of the serial killers (Gumb is a 'failed' transsexual, Dollarhyde in *Red Dragon* obsessed with his own 'Becoming') throwing into relief the unitary self of Enlightenment rationality and Romantic feeling. The novels had worked, even from *Red Dragon*, to recruit Lecter into the role of investigator rather than investigated. In parallel scenes in the first two novels, Lecter deduces important information about Will Graham and Starling through his sense of smell. He is able to detect, and name the scent that they wear, in something of an echo of Sherlock Holmes, who is another figure of Enlightenment reason destabilised by excessive behaviour and with a taste for disguise. Lecter *is*: his 'evil' is unchanging. Note the echoes of Milton's Satan in

Lecter's self-declared identity (I use this term advisedly) in the following passage:

> Nothing happened to me, Officer Starling. *I* happened. You can't reduce me to a set of influences. You've given up on good and evil for behaviorism, Officer Starling. You've got everyone in moral dignity pants – nothing is ever anyone's fault. Look at me, Officer Starling. Can you stand to say I'm evil? Am I evil, Officer Starling?
>
> (Harris 2000: 409)

This dialogue is absent from the film, where Lecter brushes off the behavioural science questionnaire Starling proffers with the words 'You think you can dissect me with this blunt little tool?' In the novel, Lecter repudiates psychiatric or medical discourse in relation to himself ('Can you stand to say I'm evil?') while using the very same tools of analysis on Starling. Instead he insists upon the 'I': his is the Cartesian, self-identical subject of the Enlightenment, albeit continually ruptured by a transgressive excess of 'passion'. In Lecter's case, the implication of rationality and non-rationality, reason and 'passion', is all too violently manifest.

It is very curious, then, to note what happens towards the end of Harris's *Hannibal*. It is revealed that Lecter once had a sibling: a sister called Mischa. The Lecter children, growing up on the Baltic, suffer the depredations of fleeing German soldiers on the collapse of the Eastern Front in 1944. Just as Clarice had been haunted by the screaming of the lambs, Lecter is haunted by the memory of his lost sister. In an interior scene of recall (denoted by italics), Lecter remembers his own primal scene of trauma:

> *He prayed so hard that he would see Mischa again, the prayer consumed his six-year old mind, but it did not drown out the sound of the axe. His prayer to see her again did not go entirely unanswered – he did see a few milk teeth in the reeking stool pit his captors used between the lodge where they slept and the barn where they held the captive children who were their sustenance in 1944 after the Eastern Front collapsed.*
>
> (Harris 2000: 994; italics in original)

This is a terrible passage in many ways. Its off-hand revelation of Mischa's death through cannibalism is made still more obscene by its association with the 'stool pit': here we find Kristeva's abjection in extreme form. It is also close to blasphemous: although it affirms God's presence through the 'answer' the young Hannibal receives, this only confirms a cruel, malignant, even diabolical Godhead. Lecter's later activities, and his Satanic stylings, are decodable firstly as a rebellion against, yet mirror-image of, the God that rules the revolting world of humankind; and, second, as the manifestation of the very trauma that deforms him, that makes him monstrous. The discourse of religion as recourse for explanation of 'evil' is placed in opposition to a psychological model of trauma and 'acting out'. Throughout the novels, Harris seemingly has an investment in debunking the explanatory power of behavioural science and other rational scientific discourses, when faced with the excessively transgressive acts of the serial killers (Lecter, in *The Silence of the Lambs*, pithily dismisses psychoanalysis, somewhat ironically, as a 'dead religion' (Harris 2000: 546)). In the figure of Mischa, the lost sibling, childhood trauma restores psychiatric discourse (the discourse of reason), evacuating the discourse of the monstrous/ 'evil', making Lecter finally explicable. This is, perhaps, the end point of the process of heroisation and identification I noted above.

Lecter first considers Starling to be Mischa's replacement, or as a vessel ('a place in the world') for the lost Mischa to inhabit if, through his monstrously transgressive acts, Lecter were able to complete his 'real' project: to reverse time. (This is perhaps his most grandly Satanic aspect, and conforms to another incarnation of Mario Praz's Byronic Fatal Man: he 'dreams of perfecting the world by committing crimes' (Praz 1954: 78). In another echo, the Mischa/ Clarice identification seems to suggest a quasi-incestuous relationship, suggesting Byron's reputedly 'incestuous' adultery.) Lecter, at the end of *Hannibal*, stands in his most transgressive guise: the typical Romantic masculine poet/ hero. His insertion into a curious (perhaps grotesque) romantic couple with Clarice Starling comes at some cost, however. Lecter's 'silencing' of Starling's lambs is not merely a healing, but a destruction of the Other. The 'overcoming' of the boundary between self and other here results in the ultimate colonisation: the displacement of Starling's identity. Anne Mellor uses very similar language, of assimilation and cannibalism, in her characterisation of what she calls 'masculine Romanticism':

> In masculine Romanticism, we often see the poet appropriating whatever of the feminine he deems valuable and then consigning the rest either to silence or to the category of evil . . . The male imagination speaks for female nature; the male lover casts the beloved as a female version of himself; the male poet cannibalizes the female emotions of mercy, pity, love.
>
> (Mellor 1993: 26, 27)

It is interesting to note to what extent Mellor's 'masculine Romanticism' seems to recapitulate the process of abjection outlined at the beginning of this chapter. The final recourse of the novel is to fix Lecter in the role of the Self, a self that has seemingly absorbed the Other. The serial killer fiction finally makes manifest the violence of the construction of the Enlightenment/Romantic self, a construction of a masculine subject completed by Lecter's symbolic cannibalisation of Clarice Starling, the destruction of his own (feminine) Other.

All this returns the narrative, rather surprisingly, to rationality: 'evil' is contained within medical discourse. Discourses for understanding the 'mad' return 'madness' (rationality's other) to reason: history, explanation, psychology.

Harris at first insists that 'Madness' (or the 'evil' subjectivity of the serial killer) exceeds the bounds of rational discourse: 'Senator Martin and Hannibal

Lecter considered each other, one extremely bright and the other not measurable by any means known to man' (Harris 2000: 581). He then, however, contains this by reasserting a psychological framework for understanding Lecter not as an incomprehensible 'evil' entity, but a pathological one. The failure to understand madness/the serial killer through reason was outlined in *Red Dragon*:

> Dr Lecter is not crazy, in any common way we think of as being crazy. He did some hideous things because he enjoyed them. But he can function perfectly when he wanted to . . . They say he's a sociopath because they don't know what else to call him . . . He's a monster.

(Harris 2000: 61)

Throughout the novels, Harris refers to Lecter as 'the fiend', 'the monster', yet ultimately cannot resist psychologising his protagonist, just as he had Starling, Graham, Dollarhyde and Gumb. While serial killer fictions indicate the limits of rational discourse, and gesture towards the discourse of religion ('monster', 'evil', 'sin') to signify that which lies outside the explicatory powers of science, medicine or reasoned understanding, Harris's Lecter novels cannot embrace this radical destabilisation, and in fact work hard to reinstate the unitary subject by repressing the polyvalent subjectivities of Dollarhyde and Gumb, returning us finally to the comforts of reason and the unitary subject.

WORKS CITED

Butler, Judith (1990) *Gender Trouble: Feminism and the Subversion of Identity*, London: Routledge.

Clover, Carol J. (1992) *Men, Women and Chainsaws: Gender in the Modern Horror Film*, London: BFI.

Cohan, Steven (1997) *Masked Men: Masculinity and Movies in the Fifties*, Bloomington, IN: Indiana University Press.

Corber, Robert J. (1993) *In the Name of National Security: Hitchcock, Homophobia, and the Political Construction of Gender in Postwar America*, Durham, NC: Duke University Press.

Creed, Barbara (1986) 'Horror and the Monstrous-Feminine: An Imaginary Abjection', *Screen*, 27(1): 44–70.

Day, Aidan (1996) *Romanticism*, London: Routledge.

Demme, Jonathan (dir.) (1991) *The Silence of the Lambs*.

Dollimore, Jonathan (1991) *Sexual Dissidence: Augustine to Wilde, Freud to Foucault*, Oxford: Clarendon Press.

Dyer, Richard (1992) 'Don't Look Now: The Male Pin-Up', in M. Merck (ed.), *The Sexual Subject: A Screen Reader on Sexuality*, London: Routledge.

Foucault, Michel (1980) 'The Eye of Power', in *Power/Knowledge: Selected Interviews and Other Writings, 1972–1977*, ed. Colin Gordon, trans. Colin Gordon *et al.*, Brighton: Harvester.

Gay, Peter (1973) *The Enlightenment: An Interpretation*, in 2 vols: *The Rise of Modern Paganism* and *The Science of Freedom*, London: Wildwood House.

Harris, Thomas (2000), *The Hannibal Lecter Omnibus: Red Dragon, The Silence of the Lambs, Hannibal*, London: BCA.

Hendershot, Cyndy (1998) *The Animal Within: Masculinity and the Gothic*, Ann Arbor, MI: University of Michigan Press.

Hurley, Kelly (1996) *The Gothic Body: Sexuality, Materialism, and Degeneration at the Fin de Siècle*, Cambridge: Cambridge University Press.

Mann, Michael (dir.) (1986) *Manhunter*.

Mellor, Anne (1993) *Romanticism and Gender*, London: Routledge

Miles, Robert (1999) 'The Eye of Power: Ideal Presence and the Gothic Romance', *Gothic Studies*, 1: 10–30.

Neale, Steve (1993) 'Masculinity as Spectacle: Reflections on Men and Mainstream Cinema', in S. Cohan and I. R. Hark (eds), *Screening the Male: Exploring Masculinities in Hollywood Cinema*, London: Routledge.

Praz, Mario (1954), *The Romantic Agony*, trans. Angus Davidson, London: Oxford University Press.

Savran, David (1998) *Taking it like a Man: White Masculinity, Masochism, and Contemporary American Culture*, Princeton, NJ: Princeton University Press.

Sedgwick, Eve Kosofsky (1985) *Between Men. English Literature and Male Homosocial Desire*, New York: Columbia University Press.

Segal, Lynne (1997) *Slow Motion: Changing Masculinities, Changing Men*, London: Virago.

Smith, Andrew (2004) *Victorian Demons: Medicine, Masculinity, and the Gothic at the Fin-de-Siècle*, Manchester: Manchester University Press.

Stevenson, Robert Louis (1999) *Strange Case of Doctor Jekyll and Mr Hyde*, ed. Martin A. Danahay, Peterborough, OH: Broadview.

21

QUEER GOTHIC

ELLIS HANSON

QUEER THEORY, GOTHIC NARRATIVE, TRAUMA ENVY

I find I commiserate with Jane Austen's Catherine Morland (*Northanger Abbey*, 1818) when she fails to become a heroine in a novel by Ann Radcliffe. Although she is a parody of a reader whose imagination is fruitlessly agitated by Gothic fiction, she seems to me also a version of a particularly modern figure of disappointment: the queer reader whose passionate emotional life was met with disdain or incomprehension, not just by her everyday acquaintances but also in the realist fiction that meticulously invoked their point of view. Catherine arrives at Northanger Abbey fully prepared to embrace a passionate destiny she has merely glimpsed in Gothic fiction, only to find herself set up at every turn as the dupe for Jane Austen's ironic jabs at the genre. On a tempestuous or perhaps merely windy night rich in shadowy foreboding and strange fancy, Catherine searches a large and anatomically suggestive chest in a deep recess of her bedroom, and with knees trembling and eyes astonished she lights upon a mysterious manuscript whose secrets she takes to bed with her to hoard for a suspenseful night before she finally gives in to the temptation of a scandalous read: 'Her greedy eye glanced rapidly over a page. She started at its import. Could it be possible, or did not her senses play her false? – An inventory of linen, in coarse and modern characters, seemed all that was before her! If the evidence of sight might be trusted, she held a washing-bill in her hand' (Austen 1988: 172). Shamed by this irony into a reassessment of her fantasy life as mere folly, she hides the evidence of her adventure and, as any Austen heroine would, casts about for a redeeming lesson from her experience: 'She felt humbled to the dust. Could not the adventure of the chest have taught her wisdom?' (173). How envious I am of readers with such a greedy eye, but like Catherine I feel called upon to resign myself to the washing-bill of realism and refinement, not to mention a gently satirical castigation of immoderate sensations, now that it is abundantly clear that I could, for the moment, muster no more harrowing nightmare than to be trapped not in a creaky castle with infernal secrets, but in a novel by Jane Austen.

Furtiveness, passionate over-determination, shame, disappointment – the queer reader instantly recognises Catherine's predicament as she seeks through disreputable fiction to give hasps and hallways to a fantasy life hopelessly irrelevant to the society at hand. Criticism on Gothic fiction does not want for accounts of the genre's uncanny appeal to our unconscious, as it is called – our anxieties, our traumas, our panics, our repressed desires – but Catherine Morland gives us a very different account of cause and effect in the Gothic reader. To psychoanalyse her would be a dry business, since she is woefully untraumatised. She betrays no accomplishments as a hysteric, a paranoid psychotic or a sexual pervert, the three psychic paradigms that Freudian criticism has set down for our understanding of those demonic and obsessive characters who populate Gothic novels. The literature she reads leaves her with no more dire pathology than what we might call 'trauma envy'. It makes her tremble not with the unconscious desires she already has, but with the decidedly self-conscious desires she wishes she could muster. She is capable of investing even a washing-bill with sublime emotional and spiritual meaning, as long as she can fail to read it. I suspect that it is this imaginative capacity, and not merely the wisdom resulting from its usual disappointment, that renders Austen's protagonist endearing. We learn from the opening line of the novel that a certain want of imagination is endemic to her world: 'No one who had ever seen Catherine Morland in her infancy, would have supposed her born to be an heroine' (13).

Paradoxically, critics of the Gothic usually establish our faith in their sophistication by asserting their immunity to the very narrative pleasures they anatomise. Psychoanalytic criticism suffers from the same irony: one can analyse the powerful unconscious appeal of a text only because it is not powerfully unconscious to oneself (and must therefore be a trifle weak and obvious after all). The unconscious is only attributable to other people, a conveniently naïve reader. Such critics are obliged to perform a psychological sophistication that is at odds with the foundational assumption of their own argument. One argues, in other words, that yes, I know, but I act as though I do not know – which is to say I am fully conscious of my unconscious and can avow my disavowals. Such discussions of the unconscious easily degenerate into a bland knowingness. One limits oneself, in other words, to the dubious pleasure of outsmarting one's own enjoyment. Queer theory is arguably most valuable to Gothic criticism, and vice versa, in its resistance to psychoanalytic truisms about the relation of desire to narrative and reading. In its more Foucauldian mode, queer theory might see the Gothic as an occasion not for diagnosing or moralising, but for the creative transfiguration of the self through the readerly pleasures of fear and abjection.

What has queer theory made of the many queer pleasures of the Gothic? From its very inception, and indeed before the term was even coined around 1990, queer theory has had a powerful investment in the Gothic, and its main contribution to criticism in the genre is its close analysis of the often paranoid and shame-addled pleasures of Gothic epistemology and hermeneutics. By queer theory I mean the radical deconstruction of sexual rhetoric as a form of resistance to sexual normalisation. Although it takes as foundational its insights into the instability of language and the historical contingency of sexuality, queer theory is not a unified doctrine or political agenda, but a highly mobile practice of imminent critique that draws its form and content from the shifting rhetoric of sexual politics. It interrogates the oppositions that have traditionally characterised sexual politics, in particular such familiar oppositions as heterosexuality/homosexuality, masculine/feminine, sex/gender, closeted/out, centre/margin, conscious/unconscious, nature/culture and normal/pathological, to name a few. It has also sought to bring sexual politics, in particular anti-homophobic critique, to the fore of intellectual debate. As Eve Kosofsky Sedgwick writes in *Epistemology of the Closet*, 'an understanding of virtually any aspect of modern Western culture must be, not merely incomplete, but damaged in its central substance to the degree that it does not incorporate a critical analysis of modern homo/heterosexual definition', especially from the 'relatively decentered perspective of modern gay and anti-homophobic theory' (Sedgwick 1990: 1).

Some of queer theory's most noted proponents are also innovative commentators on the Gothic, and I will focus here on the work of Sedgwick, George Haggerty, D. A. Miller and James Kincaid. I myself have been writing about queer theory and Gothic literature my entire career, and I would like to consider why that juxtaposition has always seemed appropriate to me. Queer criticism on the Gothic is fraught with ambivalence and contradiction: the Gothic often reproduces the conventional paranoid structure of homophobia and other moral panics over sex, and yet it can also be a raucous site of sexual transgression and excess that undermines its own narrative efforts at erotic containment. However haunted it may be by the spectre of Freud, queer theory's main contribution to criticism on the Gothic has been a historicising, Foucauldian challenge to the pathologising topologies of psychoanalysis. It has also taken the Gothic as a paradigm for modern moral panics about sexuality and a paradigm even for literary criticism itself insofar as it has been preoccupied with a 'hermeneutics of suspicion'. It has further offered a richly historical and political language for valorising those disreputable sexualities that the Gothic has traditionally rendered monstrous, not so much to purge them as to invest them with a sublime narrative energy.

Queer studies of the Gothic have typically shifted registers between the Freudian and the Foucauldian, or, roughly speaking, between psychologising and historicising modes of critique. The most familiar gesture in this sort of criticism is to find the queerness, the deviant sexual pleasure, occluded by its monstrous or villainous representation in a paranoid narrative. George E. Haggerty, for example, in a series of books – *Gothic Fiction/Gothic Form* (1989), *Unnatural Affections* (1998), *Men in Love* (1999) and most recently in *Queer Gothic* (2006) – historicises the sexual rhetoric of the Gothic and discusses dissident sexuality in the life and works of writers such as Horace Walpole, Matthew Lewis, Charles Maturin and Ann Radcliffe; furthermore, he discusses the influence of the Gothic on later sexual movements such as the rise of sexology at the end of the nineteenth century and the lesbian and gay movement at the end the of the twentieth. In his essay 'Queer Gothic', Haggerty reaches for 'a non-teleological reading of Gothic – a queer reading' (Haggerty 2005: 386) – by claiming that 'no matter how tidy, no marriage at the close of a Gothic novel can entirely dispel the thrilling dys-(or different) functionality at the heart of Gothic' (384). In this tradition, queer reading rescues us from homophobic paranoia by reading Gothic narratives against the grain.

A certain immunity to the paranoia of the text is required for this criticism to succeed, but the readerly pleasures of this deviant sophistication are many. In Sedgwick's work we find the paranoid rhetorical patterns of the Gothic closet most exquisitely anatomised. Her residual contempt for the Gothic has always been evident, but so has her fascination with it. She opens *The Coherence of Gothic Conventions* (1980), her first book, with an apology for how bad the novels often are. In *Between Men*, a landmark work of queer theory and criticism with two chapters specifically on the Gothic, she notes that Gothic novels are usually just another reading option 'to pass up at the supermarket' (Sedgwick 1985: 96). Nevertheless, her discussions of sexual secrecy, subjective opacity, panic and triangulated desire are often grounded in canonical Gothic novels, from Hogg's *Confessions of a Justified Sinner* (1824) to Wilde's *The Picture of Dorian Gray* (1891). Sedgwick has done more than any other critic to enliven feminist criticism by putting it in its most productive dialogue to date with gay studies and by defining the parallels between modern homophobia and Gothic narratives. She wisely notes in *Between Men* that the era that gave us homosexuality as a concept might also be defined as the Age of Frankenstein,

> an age philosophically and tropologically marked by the wildly dichotomous play around solipsism and intersubjectivity of a male paranoid plot – one that always ends in the tableau of two men chasing one another across a landscape evacuated of alternative life or interest, toward a climax that tends to condense the amorous with the murderous in a representation of male rape.
>
> (Sedgwick 1985: 163)

She gives a more Foucauldian and deconstructive account of this dynamic, one that eschews references to the Freudian uncanny. She sets psychoanalysis aside with respectful efficiency when she notes that many canonical Gothic plots 'might be mapped point for point onto the case of Dr Schreber' (91) and then pointedly refuses to engage in that critical activity herself. She neatly draws our attention away from biographical speculations about the homosexuality of certain Gothic writers by saying simply, 'Beckford notoriously, Lewis probably, Walpole iffily' (92), and then taking a broader view that seeks to 'read the novels as explorations of social and gender constitution as a whole, rather than of the internal psychology of a few individual men with a "minority" sexual orientation' (115).

At about the same time, Sedgwick was inspiring and drawing inspiration from a related analysis by D. A. Miller in *The Novel and the Police* (1988), which is also a key text for queer theory and an important meditation on the Gothic. Unlike Sedgwick, Miller does not analyse canonical Gothic novels; instead, he offers a Foucauldian reading of social discipline in more or less realist Victorian novels in which the quotidian policing of modern subjectivity takes place for the most part in the absence of an actual police force. The operations of social surveillance in these novels have been dispersed, disembodied and internalised.

Miller is understandably most like Sedgwick when he is reading a sensation novel reminiscent of the Age of Frankenstein, in this case Wilkie Collins's *The Woman in White* (1860). He describes the paranoid tendency of men to 'monitor and master what is fantasised as the "woman inside them"' (Miller 1988: 156), and, by projection, turning homoerotic desire between men into an often violent relationship of men to women. He is also adept at tracing the shift of that paranoia from character to reader, particularly in the Victorian sensation novel which, like the earlier Gothic canon, relies on highly somatic responses of shock and suspense that emphasise the erotics of reading itself. He writes, 'Like the characters who figure him, the reader becomes – what a judge is never supposed to be – paranoid. From trifles and common coincidences, he suspiciously infers a complicated structure of persecution, an elaborately totalising "plot"' (156). The novel 'makes nervousness a metonymy for reading' (151). Miller gives us the reader, indeed the literary critic, not as Schreberian psychotic, but as Foucauldian paranoid, ever suspicious of institutional discipline in whatever form and always trying, however improbably, to outsmart the forces that bring his subjectivity into being. In this way, it is perhaps Miller's reading of Anthony Trollope's decidedly not Gothic novel *Barchester Towers* (1857), that mild-mannered chestnut of Victorian survey courses, that reveals him at his queer Gothic best, and the result dangerously approaches self-parody, as much great Gothic fiction does. He scrutinises the relatively genial, diplomatic, scrupulously moral world of Trollope in search of aggression, monstrosity and sexual deviance. One can never be paranoid enough about even the blandest of Victorian novelists, it seems. Mrs Proudie is a 'castrating woman' (143), while Mr Slope is a 'fascist' whose sexuality is 'buried alive, and its reemergence from the vault is correspondingly violent' (125). Even banality has 'terroristic effects', and such liberal mainstays as pluralism, tolerance and moderation are deemed insidious forms of social discipline. On the final page of the essay, he writes, 'When I read Trollope, it is all I can do not to be bored' (145), and after the fashion of Catherine Morland, he succeeds.

In her 1997 essay, 'Paranoid Reading and Reparative Reading, or, You're so Paranoid, You Probably Think this Essay Is about You' (reprinted in *Touching Feeling*, 2003) Sedgwick sought to challenge the primacy of this paranoid hermeneutics that she saw as central to queer theory and to propose in its place a 'reparative' reading, drawing the term loosely from Melanie Klein. She cites Miller's *The Novel and the Police* in particular, along with Judith Butler's *Gender Trouble* (1990), as typifying a paranoid style of queer critique, by which she means readings that emphasise the anticipatory (the suspenseful preparations against unpleasant surprises), the reflexive and mimetic (it takes one to know one), strong theory (a preference for the totalising gesture), negative affects (the news is always bad), and a faith in exposure (I am in command of this astonishing secret whose mere revelation will change everything). As she points out, paranoid reading does some things very well (suspicion, high moral seriousness, political immediacy), and other things not at all (exploring a range of affects, a range of conceptual accounts, a range of hermeneutical possibilities), and she proposes the 'reparative' as a way of acknowledging the insidiousness of discrimination and violence while developing a style of reading and critique that would seek to repair psychic damage by exploring what makes a threatened life liveable, by exploring, for example, the possibilities in literature for queer pleasure, positive identification, consolation and belonging. Ironically, this essay does not do reparative reading very well and has been criticised as a paranoid reading of paranoid reading; however, the reparative style is certainly evident elsewhere in her work (and in the work of Miller and Butler), especially the essays she anthologised in *Tendencies* (1993).

The work of James Kincaid on child molestation panics is an excellent example of reparative reading from this early period of queer theory. Significantly, he offers a very Foucauldian critique of Foucault that acknowledges that the conceptual linking of sexuality and power does more to incite paranoia than to relieve it, and he invites us to tell a less Gothic story about sexuality and children. With the notable exception of the AIDS panic in the 1980s, the ferocity of Western homophobic paranoia has waned in recent decades, but our paranoia about child sexuality has grown ever stronger since the late 1970s and has now become arguably the definitive sexual panic of our time. Children are queer, their sexual activities, real or imagined, are deemed an occasion for the utmost surveillance and anxiety, and no punishment is considered too severe for any adult who transgresses the rigid standards of propriety in the matter. With considerable wit, Kincaid analyses the highly improbable and often violent stories we tell about childhood innocence and its lurid violation, stories that help us to produce the child as a docile blank, an empty page, for our most convenient and salacious projections. In *Child-Loving* he writes:

> In terms of pedophilia, one can locate these tales everywhere, in the gothic construction of the pedophile, for instance: the lurking stranger with the candy, the mentally retarded village hang-about, the homicidal wanderer. That people who in fact do engage in sexual relationships with children virtually never fit these images does not seem to matter.
>
> (Kincaid 1992: 25)

In *Erotic Innocence* he elaborates on the importance of Gothic narrative in helping us to reassert our moral panic over child sexuality without necessarily working through it:

> Our story of child molesting is a story of nightmare, the literary territory of the Gothic. On the face of it, the Gothic is not a promising form for casting social problems. Instead of offering solutions, such tales tend to paralyze; they do not move forward but circle back to one more hopeless encounter with the demon. Why would we want that?
>
> (10–11)

This rhetorical question has a good answer: his description of Gothic sounds like a description of good sex, which we like to repeat endlessly, hopelessly, enthusiastically, not because it is traumatic or pathological or even particularly imaginative, but because it is exciting. The tales make for dubious social policy, but quite serviceable pornography, albeit perhaps only pornography for puritans. Kincaid calls for stories of child sexuality that are not so Gothic and bruising, and he even valorises Wordsworthian sentimentality as a Romantic antidote to our paranoia: a way of accommodating our erotic relation to children without flying into a panic about it.

Kincaid is offering a reparative reading of contemporary Gothic by criticising our violent overdependence on it in telling those stories about our sexuality that make us most anxious. Might there also be a reparative reading of the Gothic that celebrates its pleasures? In his essay 'The Contemporary Gothic: Why We Need It', the queer theorist Steven Bruhm draws on psychoanalytic trauma studies, particularly the work of Cathy Caruth, to define the contemporary appeal of Gothic as a repetition compulsion (much as Kincaid does), but he speaks of the pleasure of returning to our own worst nightmares to work through them. His approach is ultimately therapeutic and redemptive: we survive by proxy, we experience a guarantee of life even in the face of so much death, we appeal to the imagination as 'a way of healing the perpetual loss in modern existence' (Bruhm 2002: 274). From this perspective, Gothic is good medicine. I am struck, however, by a brief detour in his argument, an even queerer irony, where the psychoanalytic mechanism is oddly set aside in favour of a perspective that is closer to my reading of Catherine Morland: 'Indeed, as an individual reader or reviewer, I may not *be* traumatized at the moment of reading, but I certainly join with the Gothic mode in *feeling like one who is traumatized*' (272). Bruhm does not pursue the implications of this trauma envy, but it poses a challenge to the usual understanding of Gothic as symptomatic of social anxiety. What if Gothic were, on the contrary, motivated by a wish that social life could be more traumatic, more anxious, more paranoid, more sexually transgressive and bizarre, more overwrought: in short, more interesting than it generally is? The insight is eminently Foucauldian: Gothic literature is not so much exploiting our perversity and pathology as helping us to produce it. I am reminded of a poster I once saw in London for Trauma!, 'a polysexual club for the brave and curious': a cartoon woman with tears in her eyes sighs to herself, 'I've been traumatised . . . and I want more.'

Significantly, Sedgwick's essay on reparative reading begins with an anecdote about paranoid concerns that the AIDS epidemic might have been a government plot. Queer theory derived much of its early political impetus not merely from homophobia, which was nothing new, but from the moral panic incited around AIDS in the 1980s. Paranoid reading and reparative reading may be seen as two responses within queer theory to a particular historical crisis: that rather Gothic moment when an illness without a name seemed to appear out of nowhere to wreak destruction in the lives of millions of already stigmatised people, as if social disdain had magically sublated itself into natural or divine vengeance. Fittingly, my own first published work of criticism, an essay with the decidedly Gothic title 'Undead', appeared in about the same year the term 'queer theory' was coined, and it was what Sedgwick would deem a 'paranoid' discussion of the general cultural tendency to think of people with AIDS as vampires of a sort. In 1999, however, in an essay called 'Lesbians Who Bite', I returned to that essay to rethink some of its assumptions about representation and the Gothic, and to discuss certain much maligned representations of queer vampires in the cinema. I took a much more reparative approach, beginning with the question of why I like these films, even though I could cite plenty of queer and feminist critical writing that attacked them. Much of my work in recent years, including essays on such Gothic classics as Henry James's novella *The Turn of the Screw* (1898), William Friedkin's film *The Exorcist* (1973) and Freud's case study of Schreber, considers how we might understand the queer pleasures of paranoia and horror without limiting our response to pathologising, moralising or just giggling. What conceptual, political, psychological work might be performed by our pleasure in fear, anxiety, abjection, shame and alienation? Do we have to transcend it in order to enjoy it? Is there a reparative reading of Gothic that does not seek to redeem us from the genre? A reparative reading of paranoid reading? As many have pointed out, much of the appeal of Gothic literature lies in its transgressive eroticism. After the fashion of the recent queer issue of the journal *Gothic Studies* (2005), one need only glance at the erotics of Goth culture, the inviting ghoulishness of certain trends in queer pornography and s/m fetish culture, or the fandom around the novels of Anne Rice and Stephen King and around the various cinematic permutations of *Frankenstein*, 'Carmilla' and *Dracula*, to see that Gothic style generates pleasures and communal bonds that might repair some of the damage of unjust discrimination (or, for that matter, sexual boredom). Horror so aestheticised, eroticised, even ironised, has always been a hallmark of the Gothic genre, and one more reason why queer readers, like Catherine Morland, might wish to lay claim to it.

WORKS CITED

Austen, Jane (1988) *Northanger Abbey*, in *The Novels of Jane Austen*, vol. 5, Oxford: Oxford University Press.
Bruhm, Steven (2002) 'The Contemporary Gothic: Why We Need It', in Jerrold Hogle (ed.), *The Cambridge Companion to Gothic Fiction*, Cambridge: Cambridge University Press.
Haggerty, George E. (1989) *Gothic Fiction/Gothic Form*, University Park, PA: Penn State University Press.
—— (1998) *Unnatural Affections: Women and Fiction in the Later Eighteenth Century*, Bloomington, IN: Indiana University Press.
—— (1999) *Men in Love: Masculinity and Sexuality in the Eighteenth Century*, New York: Columbia University Press.
—— (2005) 'Queer Gothic', in Paula Backscheider and Catherine Ingrassia (eds),

22

GOTHIC CHILDREN

SUE WALSH

Childhood has a particular and complex relationship to the Gothic, a relationship that a number of critics express in terms of a sense of ambivalence or contradiction. Dani Cavallaro, for instance, writes that in 'Narratives of darkness' children are, on the one hand,

> associated with innocence, simplicity and lack of worldly experience . . . unsullied by the murky deviousness of socialized existence. On the other hand, precisely because children are not yet fully encultured, they are frequently perceived as a threat to the fabric of adult society.
>
> (Cavallaro 2002: 135)

Similarly, for Steven Bruhm, twentieth-century Gothic makes visible a contradiction in contemporary ideas of the child because it is there construed both as 'fully-fledged and developed' and as 'an infinitely malleable, formable being who can turn out right if only the proper strategies are employed' (Bruhm 2006). Though these comments register different constructions of childhood, they also point to a desire to attain a stable answer to an implicit question: 'What is the child really?' For its part, the Gothic is a genre that has been discussed as having a preoccupation with uncovering 'real' horrors behind surface appearances and proprieties (especially evident in fictions such as Robert Louis Stevenson's *The Strange Case of Dr Jekyll and Mr Hyde* (1888) and Oscar Wilde's *The Picture of Dorian Gray* (1891)), or with establishing the reality of the supposedly supernatural (as in the case of Bram Stoker's *Dracula* (1897); see Punter 1996: 48). Thus, when the 'child' enters the fray it is implicated in a structure of critical thinking which focuses on 'the spatial metaphor of depth from among the Gothic conventions, taking that metaphor to represent a model of the human self' (Sedgwick 1986: 11). In such critical models the child is produced as a certain version of the unconscious, the '"irrational" . . . locus of the individual self' concealed and repressed by 'superficial layers of convention and prohibition, called the "rational"' (11). This can be seen in David Punter's discussion of *The Turn of the Screw* (1898), where he reads Henry James as interested in childhood 'first as a time when lies may originate and control future development, and second as a symbol of the locked room of the unconscious' (Punter 1996: 48). Here then, childhood, as a 'symbol' of a spatial metaphor for the unconscious, becomes part of a psychological model in which the 'primal' or 'irrational' is understood by most critics as the truth of the self, which therefore 'could or should pass to the outside' (Sedgwick 1986: 11). As such the unconscious is figured as 'the site of some irrational truth' (Rose 1994: 13–14) and childhood is produced as the talisman of that truth. Therefore, despite Punter's claim that *The Turn of the Screw* calls into question 'the relation between surface and hinterland' (Punter 1996: 48) that the Gothic traditionally relies upon, there seems no real doubt that for him there is after all a 'surface' that is distinguishable from a 'hinterland', and his reading precisely reinstates such a structure, since childhood is still positioned as the point from which 'lies may *originate*' (48).

Sedgwick's fundamental argument with the critical tendency outlined above is that it serves to 'both justify and conceal a premature methodological leap from images of containers and containment . . . to something rather different in the criticism: an eagerness to write about content' (Sedgwick 1986: 140). The thrust of her critique is that this produces untheorised distinctions between 'form' and 'content', 'rhetoric' and 'subject matter' so that the ways in which form *is* content and rhetoric *is* subject matter are not addressed. In other words, what remains to be addressed is the question of perspective – 'the *how* rather than the *what* of what is being said' (Royle 2002: 263; see also Felman 1982: 119) – and so the question becomes not 'What is the child really?' but 'What are the implications of writing the child?'

In this essay then I will be using a piece of children's literature, Lucy Lane Clifford's 'The New Mother' (1882), not with the aim of making speculations about child readers and their responses,[1] but of reading closely the wider implications of the relationship, as I read it there, between 'the child' and the Gothic. A number of critics comment on this story as 'spectacularly terrifying' (Prickett 1979: 93), as strange and 'haunting' (Moss 1988: 53), as 'full of pity and terror' (Darton 1999: 283), and as 'uncanny' (Wood 1996: 302). What these assessments of the text have in common is their sense of it as generating uncertainty. For Naomi Wood, for example, the story 'thematizes knowledge as a battleground in which the interpretative stakes are high . . . [and] the two protagonists grapple with . . . whether to "read" utterances literally or metaphorically' (293). According to my reading, however, the uncertainty generated by the text goes much further than simply suggesting, as Wood has it, that things might not be as they seem, for this implies an acceptance of the premise of the distinction between the literal and the metaphorical which is simply a repositioning of reality, or of what is considered real. Rather, by repeatedly turning around the question of perception and thus foregrounding the importance of perspective, 'The New Mother' raises the very question of whether there *can* be an unproblematic and literal knowledge, or a reality as such.[2] In this tale the narrative perspective is always divided against or alien to itself, but not in any clear topographical sense with a 'surface' and a 'hinterland', which is the notion that Sedgwick critiques, but in a way that threatens its very constitution as a 'self'. Hence this essay will draw on Nicholas Royle's reconsideration of narration[3] in order to suggest that there is a problem with reading Gothic child characters either as 'children', or as 'characters', since these two concepts suggest entities that are somehow separate from the narration that produces them and of which they are constitutive.

From the very opening of the story, the concept of childhood can be read as subject to question:

> The younger [child] had once, *while she was still almost a baby*, cried bitterly because a turkey that lived near to the cottage, and sometimes wandered into the forest, suddenly vanished in the middle of winter; and to console her she had been called by its name.
>
> (Clifford 1993: 120, emphasis added)

Here childhood is on the one hand presented as a distinct and delimited state of being, whilst on the other hand it is produced as a stage between other states of being, a position between a past (baby) and a future (adult). As such, each discrete position (baby, child, adult), because it is at the same time part of a narrative of progression, is already divided within itself, and can be read as bearing the traces of past and future within its present instance (see Culler 1982: 94–5). The point being that this is not only about the incorporation of different perspectives within the narration, but that these 'different' perspectives, being *constitutive* of each other, are not securely distinguishable from each other.

The children, named Blue-Eyes and the Turkey, live with their mother in a cottage on the very edge of the forest and are regularly sent by their mother to the post-office in the village to see if there are any letters from their seafaring father. On the way back to their cottage one day,

> just before they reached the bridge, they noticed, resting against a pile of stones by the wayside, a strange dark figure. At first they thought it was some one asleep, then they thought it was a poor woman ill and hungry, and then they saw that it was a strange wild-looking girl, who seemed very unhappy, and they felt sure that something was the matter. So they went and looked at her.
>
> (Clifford 1993: 122)

Here the narration seems to shift between giving an exterior perspective (that could, however, also be read as its constitution of the children's perspective) and commenting on what it produces as the children's perspective: how they interpret what they see. However, what the children see is what they interpret, that is to say that their vision is a function of their perspective and their interpretations. Indeed the narration produces shifts in the children's perspective: 'At first they thought . . . then they thought . . . and then they saw', but what they notice is nevertheless consistently marked by the narration as 'strange'. This use of 'strange' could well be read as an adoption by the narration of the children's perspective – thus seeming to corroborate what it produces as their view – yet at the same time the narration also potentially undermines this perspective by producing it as contingent, and by distancing itself through its construction of them precisely as 'them'. Alternatively the narration's employment of 'strange' could be read as a predetermined framework within which the children must arrive at their own perspective, but if this is a predetermined framework the children's ownership of this perspective is consequently illusory. This draws attention to the problems of reading the narration as separate from 'them', the children, since 'theirs' is a perspective that is nevertheless produced *by* and *within* the narration.

What is crucially important for my reading here, then, is the disruption to any idea of a unified, coherent and stably singular narrating position, despite the fact that this story apparently employs what might more conventionally be called a third-person narrator – that 'person' here would seem to incorporate *persons*, or at least different perspectives. As Royle argues, there is 'no purity or propriety of a single "point of view", no single perspective' (Royle 2002: 266–67), and what appears to present itself here as a unified and discrete 'speaking' position can never be any such thing.

The attention to how things 'seemed' and 'felt' to the children, although apparently 'sure', undermines the supposed certainty attached to what they finally 'saw', despite the way 'and then they saw' replaces 'at first they thought' and 'then they thought'. Here 'seemed' can be read as indicating a doubled perspective where 'seem', as well as introducing an idea of 'child' perspective, can also be read as a present judgement on past knowledge now configured as erroneous belief. The point here is that both these perspectives are present at the same time and are not extricable from each other, and the traces of past and future within the narration here can be read in relation to the text's construction of childhood as discussed above.

Likewise, as the description of the girl continues, there are what seem to be definite or omniscient statements (statements of what *was* the case) such as 'she was dressed in very ragged clothes' which are then juxtaposed with descriptions that point to an element of uncertainty: 'The girl seemed to be tall', she 'was about fifteen years old' (Clifford 1993: 122). That perspective is at issue here becomes most clear in the 'statement': 'she wore no bonnet'. The apparent neutrality of this is belied by the way 'bonnet' here is produced as an absence in relation to a state ('bonneted') which thus implies something is wanting – this is similarly the case with the girl's 'uncombed and unfastened' hair (122). This idea of what should be the case would seem to be the backdrop against which the narration's judgement that the girl is 'strange' is made. However, where this notion of lack in the girl's appearance comes from remains unclear; indeed it opens up once more the question of the nature of the relationship between the narration and the children that are its productions.

In a later description of the girl she admonishes the children as follows:

> 'You really seem quite excited,' she said in her usual voice. 'You should be calm; calmness gathers in and hides things like a big cloak, or like my shawl does here; for instance'; and she looked down at the ragged covering that hid the peardrum.
>
> (132)

Here the girl analogises calmness as hiding excitement in the way her shawl hides the peardrum. This comment could be read as a warning to the children against transparency or self-revelation, but it can also be read as a revelatory statement in itself since implicitly her own calmness obscures an excitement the children should be wary of. What is more, the shawl, though claimed here as hiding the peardrum, in fact does no such thing, since the girl informs the children that this is what it is doing. The idea of an interiority veiled by an exteriority is in fact put under interrogation here as it is throughout the text which repeatedly calls into question the notion of the hidden, presenting on the one hand the idea that there are things hidden waiting to be unveiled – like the little man and the little woman dancing that the children so crave to see – while at the same time suggesting that everything to be seen is already evident, always already visible, on the surface as it were, except that the notion of 'surface' would reinstate precisely the depth model that I am reading as under challenge here. The 'hidden', waiting to be revealed, is then the production of a certain way of seeing, of reading.[4]

In the initial meeting with the girl, during an exchange about whether tears have been shed, the children respond to her because 'she wiped her eyes just as if she had been crying bitterly'. Again what the children see is already a function of their interpretation, but they are shocked by the girl's rejoinder, which is to redirect their own question ('Are you crying?') back to them, because 'anyone could see that they were not crying' (123). At the same time the narration here seems to present ideas of intent with respect to the girl: 'She sat watching the children approach, *and* did not move or stir *till* they were within a yard of her; *then* she wiped her eyes *just as if* she had been crying bitterly, *and* looked up' (122, emphases added).

The idea of intention appears here through a sequence of connected actions (or narrative), while the 'just as if' is readable as the narration's knowledge or understanding rather than that of the children who, after all, believe the girl to be crying. Furthermore the retrospective nature of the narration – as the perspective of memory *producing* (not simply recording) sequences and connections – means the 'just as if' can be read as the construction of a *present* narrating knowledge which is implicitly an adult knowledge constituting itself as not available *then* to the children, or to the *then* children. The issue here, which has significance for Gothic fiction's fascination with the past and with memory, is the production of the past in and by the present, where childhood is produced as the past, and therefore as the condition of the present – in short, *as* perspective.

The narration proceeds with the girl 'still speaking in a most cheerful voice'. Thus the cheerfulness is attributed to the voice rather than the girl as such. It describes what it constitutes as the children's reaction to this and how the girl looks to them but it cannot comment on the scene from any position that could be claimed as either objective or omniscient, and neither can it do so from a securely interior perspective. The 'perspectives', suggesting not only more than one identity, but also division within 'identities', are not pure, cannot be clearly

187

distinguished from each other, and are indeterminate. It is worth noting here that much Gothic literature either makes use of framed narratives (as is the case with Mary Shelley's *Frankenstein* (1818), Emily Brontë's *Wuthering Heights* (1847) and James's *The Turn of the Screw*) or demonstrates a preoccupation with splintered identities (Stevenson's *Dr Jekyll and Mr Hyde* and James Hogg's *The Private Memoirs and Confessions of a Justified Sinner* (1824)) in such a way that it can be read as a fiction that implicitly (or explicitly) undermines the kind of narratorial 'omniscience' and character 'unity' that Royle takes issue with in critical thinking. My reading here, moreover, opposes those readings that see these frames and splits as discrete demarcations and clear separations.

With respect to the unnamed girl in 'The New Mother', the view of her is always exteriorised. Her words are 'reported', as are the children's reaction to or interpretation of them, but her own understandings or views are not given other than as they appear in her 'dialogue'; there is no 'for . . . ' to explain her utterances or her behaviour and thus her motives are open to question. In comparison to the children who are written as asking 'shyly' or saying 'gently', with respect to the girl it is the voice that she adopts that is attributed certain qualities, rather than herself as such ('speaking in a voice that was almost affectionate' (123); 'said . . . in the voice of one who had heard a pleasant but surprising statement', 'added in a satisfied voice' (124)). Thus an idea of performance – and consequently of pretence or falsehood – is connected to the girl by the narration which, when it 'reports' the girl's response to the children's claim to be good, seems to take the 'children's' part in terms of how it views 'goodness': '"I really could not have believed that you were good", she said reproachfully, as if they had accused themselves of some great crime' (125). The 'reproachfully' employed here may be read alongside other adverbial phrases that are used about the girl. If grouped together and placed in contrast with the various descriptions of voices that she uses, the suggestion is that whereas cheerfulness, satisfaction, decisiveness and unconcern are part of a performance on her part – an *assumption* of certain 'voices' or 'tones' – she is in fact reproachful, scornful, blithe in the face of the children's distress, and finally triumphant.

The children's encounter with the girl leads them by degrees to embark on more and more naughtiness in an effort to win her approval and a glance at the little man and little woman dancing that she claims to keep in a small box attached to the peardrum. Added to this is the enticement of the little woman's secret, which she tells while she dances (128). The revelation of hidden secrets is a major feature of the Gothic, as can be read in the very title of Ann Radcliffe's *The Mysteries of Udolpho* (1794), but, as I have already indicated above, this story, like *The Turn of the Screw*, both plays with the notion that there is something hidden and frustrates it. The children persist in their bad behaviour, which is always deemed insufficient by the girl, despite their mother's threat to leave them and allow her replacement by the eponymous new mother, with her 'glass eyes' that flash and 'wooden tail' that drags along the ground (139). At the end of the story the mother leaves, or is driven away by the children's naughtiness, and is indeed replaced by the new mother from whom the children flee into the forest that encroaches on the cottage at the beginning of the story. Despite everything the children do not get to see the little man and little woman dance, or hear the supposed secret – there is no revelation.

And yet, at the start of the penultimate paragraph a revelation does occur, for the narrative perspective announces an identity for itself as it brings its story into the present with 'They are there still, my children'. As such the narration constitutes itself here, implicitly at any rate, as a mother, and, given the direction the story has taken, a fair question would be: 'What kind of mother is this?' My reading of the girl above, as *adopting* voices or *performing* behaviours, has implied that her nature is essentially other than it appears. This is a reading, however, based again on accepting the narration's figuration of 'parts' of itself as separate from itself. Throughout this essay I have been trying to resist the compulsion to read the narration as *adopting* perspectives which are thus conceived of as not its own, instead drawing attention to these as its productions. However, the identity that is revealed is an identity that is constituted by its relation to 'children' that are not itself and yet are productions of itself. At the same time, the narration has throughout *been* comprised of perspectives that it has also identified as 'children's'. What are the implications of writing the child? The revelation that childhood is by definition produced as a perspective that cannot be its own is what both constitutes its relation to the unconscious and also explains why children are uncanny: the narrating position that names childhood as such constitutes it as both the most familiar (the perspective most fully understood) and yet necessarily as the most distant and alien.

In Freud's 'The Uncanny', he argues that the word

> *[H]eimlich* [homely/canny] . . . belongs to two sets of ideas, which are not mutually contradictory . . . – the one relating to what is familiar and comfortable, the other to what is concealed and kept hidden. *Unheimlich* [unhomely/uncanny] is the antonym of *heimlich* only in the latter's first sense, not in its second.
>
> (Freud 2003: 132)

Since *heimlich* already contains the notion of the hidden ('removed from the eyes of strangers', 133), the hidden-ness that the *unheimlich* refers to is that which is hidden not from others but from ourselves, 'a species of the familiar' (134) because it is (a part of) the self, but repressed – the unconscious – and hence fundamentally unknowable to the self.[5] In her essay on *Villette* (1853), Lucie Armitt explains the uncanny-ness she attributes to the child as a product of a 'splitting of the self . . . a dynamic in part required by the narrative structure', an effect of a 'first-person narrative the voice and persona of which ghosts her own character as played out in the text' (Armitt 2002: 225). My point, however, as Royle has suggested, is that a first-person narration is not necessary for this to happen. For, while the concept of the unconscious enables the articulation of the self as split, it also means, since it is *unconscious*, that neither the constituent 'parts' of the split, nor the 'self', can be securely identified, labelled and delimited (kept in their place). It is in being given the role of securing adult selfhood that the child has its connection with the 'Gothic' since both have been read as embodying the unconscious as something there waiting to be revealed by the critical act.[6] A concept of selfhood erected on narratives of childhood, however, produces this very self as uncanny: the most intimately known to itself and yet the most foreign. Whether that foreignness is named the unconscious, or the child, it is not 'the site of some irrational truth', but 'a constant pull against our seeming identity . . . [and] its truth is merely this repeated slippage' (Rose 1994: 13–14).[7]

NOTES

1 See Lesnik-Oberstein who points out: 'critics disagree amongst themselves with respect to their views on childhood, on writing, and on reading, and this already warns us that they are not basing themselves on a common field of knowledge' (Lesnik-Oberstein 1994: 7). See also Rose (1994: 9).
2 This is perhaps what 'The New Mother' has in common with *The Turn of the Screw*. Yet, as Shoshana Felman has argued, *The Turn of the Screw*'s engagement with the problem of narrative perspective is often not really addressed even in criticism that purports to take it into account. A relevant example is the opening of Steven Bruhm's online *Work in Progress: The Gothic Child* (2006):

   James's nineteenth-century child increases the effects of horror because s/he is presumed innocent of those complex and repressed emotions that constitute the Gothic. Indeed James's story pivots on the discrepancy between how much the narrating governess presumes the children see and what little – at least by way of the supernatural – they do see.

3 Royle argues that 'There is no single, unitary or unified point of view in a work of fiction' and the use of such terms as 'point of view' and 'omniscience' 'continues to leave unquestioned the unity of the one who sees and of the one who speaks: the "function" of seeing can simply be "delegated" by one identity to another, without this apparently having any implications or effects for thinking about the unity of either of these identities as such' (Royle 2002: 263–4).
4 See Sedgwick on veils (1986: 144–6); also Thomson (2003: 275–9); and Felman (1982: 161–71).
5 'It may be that the uncanny is a feeling that happens only to oneself, within oneself, but it is never one's "own": its meaning or significance may have to do, most of all, with what is not oneself, with others, with the word "itself"' (Royle 2002: 2).
6 One of the things contemporary Gothic children's literature may be read as 'revealing' is that childhood is a prison from which children want to grow up. We can find this kind of reading of Roald Dahl's *The Witches* and Lemony Snicket's *The Bad Beginning*. However, such readings (as well as those which by contrast question the 'subversive-ness' of this fiction) tend not to address the narratorial construction of childhood as such.
7 Thanks to Catherine Spooner, Karín Lesnik-Oberstein, Sarah Spooner, Simon Flynn and Andrew Mangham for their invaluable help and advice.

WORKS CITED

Armitt, Lucie (2002) 'Haunted Childhood in Charlotte Brontë's *Villette*', *The Yearbook of English Studies: Children in Literature*, 32: 217–28.

Bruhm, Steven (2006) *Work in Progress: The Gothic Child*, Halifax, Nova Scotia: Mount St Vincent University. Available at: http://faculty.msvu.ca/sbruhm/gothchild.htm (accessed 14 March 2006).

Cavallaro, Dani (2002) *The Gothic Vision: Three Centuries of Horror, Terror and Fear*, London: Continuum.

Clifford, Lucy Lane (1993) 'The New Mother', in A. Lurie (ed.), *The Oxford Book of Modern Fairy Tales*, Oxford: Oxford University Press.

Culler, Jonathan (1982) *On Deconstruction: Theory and Criticism after Structuralism*, Ithaca, NY: Cornell University Press.

Darton, F. J. Harvey (1999) *Children's Books in England: Five Centuries of Social Life*, 3rd edn, revised by B. Alderson, London: British Library and Oak Knoll Press.

Felman, Shoshana (1982) 'Turning the Screw of Interpretation', in S. Felman (ed.), *Literature and Psychoanalysis: The Question of Reading: Otherwise*, Baltimore, MD: Johns Hopkins University Press.

Freud, Sigmund (2003) 'The Uncanny', in A. Phillips (ed.), *The Penguin Freud: The Uncanny*, Harmondsworth: Penguin.

Lesnik-Oberstein, Karín (1994) *Children's Literature Criticism and the Fictional Child*, Oxford: Clarendon Press.

Moss, Anita (1988) 'Mothers, Monsters, and Morals in Victorian Fairy Tales', *The Lion and the Unicorn*, 12(2): 47–60.

Prickett, Stephen (1979) *Victorian Fantasy*, Hassocks, Sussex: Harvester Press.

Punter, David (1996) *The Literature of Terror: A History of Gothic Fictions from 1765 to the Present Day, vol. 2: The Modern Gothic*, London: Longman.

Rose, Jacqueline (1994) *The Case of Peter Pan, or the Impossibility of Children's Fiction*, rev. edn, Basingstoke: Macmillan.

Royle, Nicholas (2002) *The Uncanny*, Manchester: Manchester University Press.

Sedgwick, Eve Kosofsky (1986) *The Coherence of Gothic Conventions*, rev. 2nd edn, New York: Methuen.

Thomson, Stephen (2003) 'The Instance of the Veil: Bourdieu's Flaubert and the Textuality of Social Science', *Comparative Literature*, 55(4): 275–91.

Wood, Naomi J. (1996) '"The New Mother": Domestic Inversions, Terror, and Children's Literature', *Journal of Narrative Technique*, 26(3): 292–309.

Part IV
GOTHIC MEDIA

23

GOTHIC MEDIA

CATHERINE SPOONER

Gothic has never been solely a literary phenomenon. In the eighteenth century, the public appetite for horrid thrills found satisfaction not only in fiction, but also in magic-lantern shows and sensational theatre productions. These spine-tingling spectacles became modulated into the stage melodrama of the nineteenth century, and eventually into the horror cinema of the twentieth. By the end of the twentieth century, Gothic influences were visible within all sorts of media, including television, comics, theme park rides, video games and the world wide web. In Goth subculture, which first emerged in the late 1970s and continues to enjoy huge popularity today, Gothic was transformed into a visual look, a subgenre of popular music and a lifestyle.

Nevertheless, until very recently, the academic study of Gothic was largely restricted to English departments, and non-literary Gothic, with the exception of a few incursions into film, was neglected. Within film and cultural studies departments horror film received plenty of attention, but was often discussed in isolation from the literary tradition, as if an entirely separate phenomenon. Despite recent monographs from Edmundson (1997), Hopkins (2005), Spooner (2006) and Wheatley (2006), as well as several publications on Goth subculture – most prominently Hodkinson (2002), Siegel (2006), Goodlad and Bibby (2007) – substantial academic interest in the TV series *Buffy the Vampire Slayer*, and an ongoing preoccupation with contemporary Gothic culture in the broadsheet press, the proliferation of Gothic media still remains a relatively under-researched area. This section aims to provide an introductory handbook to the subject, indicating some of the possible lines of enquiry for future researchers and students.

'Gothic media' thus explores Gothic from an interdisciplinary perspective, looking in detail at some of the major non-literary cultural forms that Gothic has taken in the late twentieth and early twenty-first century. The opening essay by Fred Botting tackles the idea of 'Gothic culture', an increasingly popular critical term used to refer not only to Goth subcultures but also to incursions of the Gothic into society in general. Botting ranges widely through the ephemera of this culture, but focuses particularly on the contemporary fascination with vampires, from The Birthday Party's early Goth B-side 'Release the Bats' (1981), through Anne Rice's *The Vampire Lestat* (1985) to the so-called West German 'Vampire Killers', Daniel and Manuela Ruda. Botting's concern with the literalisation of the vampiric metaphor of consumption in a world drained of

195

authenticity leads to his framing his essay as disposable object, to be ripped out, the pages reordered at will, and ultimately thrown away.

The following four essays look at developments in dramatic media. Emma McEvoy begins by examining developments in contemporary theatre, focusing among other things on the creation of Gothic spaces in site-specific work. This is followed by two essays on cinema. Kamilla Elliott explores the significance of parody in film adaptations of classic Gothic novels, suggesting that these apparently lightweight, superficial productions can be read as exposing the preoccupations of academic criticism, both by playing on notions of belief and disbelief, and by comic distancing from the expected effects of terror and fear. Benjamin Hervey addresses the thorny problem of how far Gothic and horror can be said to coincide, looking at the use of realism and contemporary settings in horror film from Val Lewton's *Cat People* (1942) to Eli Roth's *Hostel* (2005). Finally, Eddie Robson explains why Gothic is as at home on the small screen as the large in an essay on Gothic television, arguing that conventional assumptions that restrictive broadcasting codes and the demands of a mass audience can only ever produce 'Goth lite' are completely unfounded, with reference to an array of British and American series including *Doctor Who* and *The X Files*.

The concluding three essays address forms that may be thought of as cult interest. Andy W. Smith surveys the use of Gothic in the graphic novel, from *Batman* to *The Sandman*, suggesting that 'millennial graphic novels have obtained a cultural legitimacy sustained by their relationship to the Gothic imagination'. Paul Hodkinson compares some of the different critical approaches that have been taken to Goth subculture, and argues for careful sociological study rather than an over-reliance on literary models, suggesting that textually based study can overlook meanings invested in subcultural practices by the participants themselves. Finally, Jason Whittaker looks at the newest form of contemporary Gothic: its incursion into new media, including computer games, hypertext and, most significantly, the world wide web. He shows that the 'postmodern mix of happy, connected workers, white goods and the occasional absurd mascot' promoted by companies like Intel and Microsoft has 'a doppelgänger of violence, pornography, crime and extremism' in the tabloid media – neither of which accurately reflects the uses to which Gothic is put in emerging media technologies.

What this final section of the book makes evident is that, in the opening decade of the twenty-first century, Gothic remains an incredibly fertile and diverse cultural form. Whether on MySpace or at the multiplex, Gothic continually reinvents itself, and is reinvented, at both the level of the individual producer/consumer and of the multinational corporation. Gothic is both the stuff of big-budget blockbusters, and of underground bands and cult comics. Now more than ever it is impossible to summarise: it is branching out in new directions, spreading into new territories.

WORKS CITED

Edmundson, Mark (1997) *Nightmare on Main Street: Angels, Sadomasochism, and the Culture of Gothic*, Cambridge, MA: Harvard University Press.

Goodlad, Lauren M. E. and Michael Bibby (eds) (2007) *Goth: Undead Subculture*, Durham, NC: Duke University Press.

Hodkinson, Paul (2002) *Goth: Identity, Style and Subculture*, Oxford: Berg.

Hopkins, Lisa (2005) *Screening the Gothic*, Austin, TX: University of Texas Press.

Siegel, Carol (2006) *Goth's Dark Empire*, Indianapolis, IN: Indiana University Press.

Spooner, Catherine (2006) *Contemporary Gothic*, London: Reaktion.

Wheatley, Helen (2006) *Gothic Television*, Manchester: Manchester University Press.

24

GOTHIC CULTURE

FRED BOTTING

PERVASION OF THE BODY SNATCHERS

'Frank N. Stein' was a comic monster who served in the privatisation of national electricity utilities in Britain in the 1990s (Botting 1991). 'Count Duckula' and 'Count Chocula' were, respectively, cartoon characters and breakfast cereal icons, Gothic figures for children in a period full of little monsters and friendly ghosts. Buffy slew vampires with ease but found it harder to lay teenage angst to rest. Hollywood remakes old and new horrors, so many nocturnal returns, dawns of living dead munching and shopping their way through malls and across screens. Clothes, puppets, masks, lifestyles, dolls, sweets, locate Gothic images in a thoroughly commodified context in which horror cedes to familiarity. No longer exceptions, Gothic figures collude with the norms they once negatively defined (Botting 2002).

The phrase 'Gothic culture' is oxymoronic (though one may want to delete the first two syllables). Or just another sign of what, quite recently, used to be called a 'postmodern condition' where anything went in a free play of free market cultural forms and values, of collapsed socio-political institutions and grandly narrated, ideological structures, of a multitude of transversal and inde-terminable meanings and boundary crossings where both terms circulate and conjoin in polymorphous abandon.

In a modern sense, however, 'culture' and 'Gothic' were strictly opposed, the one defined in terms of what the other lacked or negated: Enlightenment values of the eighteenth century (reason, virtue, moderation) emerged on the basis of their difference from Gothic darkness (passion, vice, excess), in a move from feudal savagery and landed property to bourgeois exchange and commerce (Botting 1999). The move imbricated 'Gothic' (as an invented amalgam of pre-Enlightenment forms) in the construction of new aesthetic and cultural hierar-chies: Gothic 'transgressions' and 'excesses' redrew the limits of taste and acceptability; Gothic figures (monsters, vampires, ghosts, sexual deviants, crimi-nals, foreigners) condensed (class, sexual, ethnic, colonial) anxieties and fanta-sies about those others occupying social, political and cultural margins.

Now, Maurice Lévy speculates, 'Gothic has become our surrounding culture' (Lévy 2004: 34). 'Organisational Gothic' (Parker 2005), 'Cybergothic' (Land 1998), 'Frankenfoods'. It pervades media screens, public discourse, everyday life: 'our entire culture is full of this haunting of the separated double' (Baudrillard 1993: 142). Pervasion describes the everyday effects of hyper-reality as it takes its leave from modern oppositional structures: 'no more black magic of the forbidden, alienation and transgression, but the white magic of ecstasy, fascination, transparency' (Baudrillard 1990: 71). Beyond transgression, all the paraphernalia of Gothic modernity change: the uncanny is not where it used to be, nor are ghosts, doubles, monsters and vampires. Nor are the systems which produce them. Spectrality instead describes ordinary operations of new technologies and their hallucinatory, virtual effects (Kittler 1990; Virilio 1995). At the limit of cultural norms, monsters ('monstrous monstrosity') once pointed to a future that was not 'predictable, calculable, and programmable' (Derrida 1992: 386). Domesticated, welcomed, assimilated, 'normal monstrosity' eclipses the possibility of difference and otherness: 'monsters cannot be announced. One cannot say: "Here are our monsters", without immediately turning the monsters into pets' (Derrida 1990: 80). Our monsters, ourselves; our selves, our pets: the arena of indifference leaves only a predictable and programmed – digitally and genetically – future, one, perhaps, already marked out by those fish from Taiwan that glow in the dark – 'Frankenstein pets'.

MAKING LOVE TO A VAMPIRE WITH A MONKEY ON MY KNEE

'Whooah Bite!' (Birthday Party, 'Release the Bats', 4AD Records BAD 307). An impassioned howl fights through a rumbling screech of metal, skins and amplified wire. 'Sex bat horror vampire sex'. A vocalist writhes and flails, tall and skinny in a shiny-dark second-hand suit, head topped with a mess of back-combed black hair. Nineteen-eighties Goth chic sutures punk and metal in dark swathes of leather, dye and eyeshadow. But there are not many Goths on stage: drummer and guitarist have sensible haircuts and the bassist, cropped under a ten-gallon hat, wears a tight bodybuilder's t-shirt! 'Sex vampire, cool machine'. The audience, however, enjoys the dark. 'Bauhaus', with a poised artschool glamourgloom, have already celebrated the undeath of Bela Lugosi. And there is much more yet to crawl from the crypt of sound, style and press release. 'Release the Bats' howls in anticipation: 'Release the Goths', it seems to say, and the machine of popular culture complies.

Sung about a vampire-loving lover, the song's commentary does not look favourably on the emerging world of Goth: 'my baby is a cool machine'. Dolled up as a vampiric femme fatale, she yearns for something more: 'Horror Vampire / How I wish those bats would bite!' A wish, unfulfilled. 'Bite!' she demands. But she does not get it. Like any self-respecting femme fatale, she registers disappointment: 'She says damn that horror bat / Sex vampire, cool machine'. All she wants is a little nibble of the real thing; all she gets is a 'cool machine'. Fabrication, like Gothic always was.

'Release the Bats' is far from a call to unleash the wolverine children of the night. A song of dis-illusion: a scruffy band of Australians arrive in early 1980s London expecting a vibrant and anarchic music scene but find the bright-burning negativities of punk guttering in the made-up face of Goth's plundering of an all-too-familiar cultural wardrobe. A repertoire littered with degradation, sexual horrors and sacred abjection does little to dispel their assimilation as a 'crucial proto-Goth' group (Reynolds 2005: 433). The comedy is not lost on everyone: 'it rocks so rabidly it just can't help being as funny as fuck' (Mulholland 2002: 164). Despite a history of comedy and camp Gothic (from Abbott and Costello to Rocky Horror), indulgently gloomy self-delusion appears impervious.

'Release the Goths'. A song of dark mockery: disappointed in her demand for some serious bloody tooth action (bite me!), her invocation exposes the masquerade in which she and her dark kind cloak themselves. Any call for a release of some primordial energy, some sex-death-horror-joy, or for an expression of some dark truth, is mockery. 'Bite!' The injunction vainly exclaims in Goth's gaping fangless maw. Maybe some fantasised thrill of sex-death-horror-vampire lingers on, repeatedly disappointed. 'Release the Bats' exposes a culture in which the Oedipal imbrications of sex and death, dressed up in familiar figures of horror, have passed beyond their sell-by date. What use is a toothless vampire? What psychic or cultural apparatus can it horrify or support? Except the banal circuits and little thrills of consumer culture. A different kind of release is implied: a release *from* rather than *of* the bats. Just let them go. Put them out of their indulgent misery. Unchain them from the tired cycle of fantasy and vain masquerade.

DISNEYGOTHIC

Reports of turmoil in Transylvania reached the British press in March 2002. UNESCO heritage experts were sent to Sighisoara, Europe's only inhabited citadel and a world heritage site. With the support of 85 per cent of the local population, the Romanian government was preparing to open a Dracula terror park on the basis that the fifteenth-century Count Vlad Tepes (Vlad the Impaler) may have been born there. A ghost castle, Dracula hotels and a 'vampirology' centre had been designed; snack bars serving blood-red candy-floss, plates of brains, garlic-flavoured ice cream and blood pudding were lined up. The exclusive rights to soft drinks sales had already been sold to Coca-Cola (for £330,000) and negotiations with the Austrian beer company, Brau Union, and the hotel chain, Best Western, were well in hand. Before you book your holidays, the row between the government and UNESCO resulted in the plans being shelved. Historical heritage, perhaps only temporarily, won out over the more commercial myth market. Do not be disappointed, however. The Castel Hotel Dracula is open. Located in Bistrita-Nasaud, Romania, at an altitude of 3,600 feet in the Carpathian mountains, it is a mock-Gothic edifice with a turret night-club built between 1983 and 1985. It has been refurbished and re-branded since then. At the time of building no references to Dracula were permitted: it was built for Nicolae Ceauçescu.

Disneygothic, of course, has already happened. The Romanian government were only trying to cash in on a lucrative market long since opened up by Hollywood. The terror park need not have been located in Romania, but a tiny touch of the real always helps heritage marketing: Vlad the Impaler, a possible historical model for Dracula, *may* have been born in Sighisoara, while the Castel Hotel boasts a Carpathian setting. Not that reality really matters when it comes to the Gothic heritage business. Disney, as Baudrillard notes in his account of the end of history, already includes Gothic. As a place 'where all past and present forms meet in playful promiscuity, where all cultures recur in mosaic', Disneyworld presents 'a prefiguration of the real trend of things'. 'Magic Country, Future World, Gothic, Hollywood itself' are sites where 'the whole of the past and the future [are] revisited as living simulation' (Baudrillard 1994: 115). Gothic, curiously, is prominent, a tacit acknowledgement, perhaps, of its role in modern history's fabrication. It is an appropriate inclusion none the less, providing an image of dead simulations living on vampirically, freezing all culture and history in their immortal bite. But simulations have another function: they work differentially and retrospectively in the play of imaginary and real. Disneyland, supposedly imaginary, maintains the illusion that America is real even though it is already given over to the unreal. So too with Gothic: it preserves the illusion of darkness, death and sexuality in a world given over to the omnipresence of virtual light and life on screens. Its trajectory is double, however: Gothic illusions of mortality and the sexed body emphasise bloody corpses, ripped flesh and oozing wounds. Its imagined return to the pulsing reality of the body evokes re-pulsion, a pulsion to the body and of the body, but also away from the body, a repulsion that accelerates the career towards further simulations and idealised bodily forms. Abjection Inc.

GIRLY-GIRLY GOTHIC

Girly-girly Gothic does not – though it could – refer to *Buffy* or *Angel*. It is an adaptation of Mark Twain's term, 'girly-girly romance' for the disease with which Walter Scott infects the Southern character: romance. New Orleans, in Twain's account, oozes with this illness: its architecture, manners and festivals are hooked on Scott's 'medieval business'. Rational and democratic progress, much to Twain's indignation, are stalled by Scott's 'enchantments': he 'sets the world in love with dreams and phantoms', 'with the sillinesses and emptiness, sham grandeurs, sham gauds, sham chivalries of a brainless and worthless long-vanished society' (Twain 1981: 219).

Anne Rice's vampire mythology begins in New Orleans: the chivalric, mannered gentleman turns into the affected vampire; medieval enchantment revived in fantasies of the undead. Exaggeration and exhaustion chart the predictable trajectory of romance. *The Vampire Lestat* (1985) compounds the romantic excesses of *Interview with the Vampire* (1976): in it, Lestat mourns the passing of romance and the great oppositions of good and evil that gave life and death meaning. He attempts to restore the universal binaries of romantic projection but, in the process, takes it in a direction already worn out by popular culture. The 1980s of the novel sees a romantic vampire revived in best-sellers, rock stardom and music videos. Lestat, having become a rock star, is adored by millions:

> 'COME ON, LET ME HEAR YOU! YOU LOVE ME!' . . .
> Everywhere people were stomping . . .
> 'HOW MANY OF YOU WOULD BE VAMPIRES?'
> The roar became a thunder.
>
> (Rice 1995: 584)

Overblown, sillier and emptier than anything Twain could have imagined, the romanticised vampire is just another celebrity image, a figure of identification and adoration receiving fan mail from teenage wannabe victims (Rice 1995: 568).

There are works that mock the pretensions of the celebrity vampire. One graphic novel tells the story of a hitchhiking vampire who arrives in New Orleans to encounter a more familiar creature of his kind: 'Eccarius' is dressed in dark velvet breeches, voluminous white shirt, long boots and shoulder-length hair. In his library with its chandeliers, leather chairs and grand piano, a crystal glass of blood in his hand, he speaks: 'You are like me, a lord of nightfalls, piercing veins and drinking crimson, walking the shadows of the mortal world' (Ennis and Dillon, 1998: 13). The scruffy, unshaven jeans-wearing hero is not impressed, going on to demystify all vampiric affectations, from blood drinking and coffin sleeping, to garlic, crosses, churches and reading matter. The mockery pursues a gathering of want-to-be vampires: 'Les Enfants du Sang' or, 'translated', 'a pack of poncy Gothic rich-kid wannabes' (25). Decidedly unimpressed, the vampire returns to his preferred haunt, a local bar, to drink a few beers. He does not seem so evil – he even has ethics, killing his dressed-up counterpart for feeding unnecessarily on human blood and for being 'too much of a wanker'. The story has a moral, too: 'we've the whole wide world out there waitin' for us, an' we've forever to make the most've it. And that's the thing, mate: enjoyin' life' (36). Enjoying life no longer means consuming it to the point of death but, beyond death, making the most of endless consumption. It could be a slogan for a genetically enhanced American dream or Coke Cola, or both.

HOPELESS MONSTERS

'Never before has a horror film embodied such hope in the conquering power of love beyond death' (Dika 1996: 399). The reading of Francis Ford Coppola's *Bram Stoker's Dracula*, a film notable for its romantic and sentimental treatment of a murderous aristocratic bloodsucker, celebrates 'a work of innovative and affirmative exultation': vampiric undeath becomes a joyful condition, one beyond the familiar contours of Gothic horror with its associations of exclusion, violence and repression. Love your monster.

Anne Rice's vampire-hero, Lestat, 'exemplifies a style of cyborg existence' by evincing the 'pain and complexity' of adapting to a society, lifestyle, language, culture (and species) that is not one's own (Stone 1995: 178). Donna Haraway, 'on the side of vampires', links them to developments in genetic and information science (Haraway 1997: 213). 'High-tech Frankenstein' elides humans and machines as everyone goes online. Minds and bodies are rewired by screens, prosthetics and biotechnology: the tale of terror turns into 'a romance with an alien cyborg, a monster who is already none other than ourselves' (Poster 2002: 29–30). Post-human monsters become the norm.

Since Mary Shelley's monster, a romanticised, suffering, curiously humanised creature has turned against institutional exclusion and relocated monstrosity from those cast out or rendered 'other' to callous and repressive systems of normalisation and injustice that make monsters. Unlike Frankenstein's monster, however, cyborgs do not expect the father-creator to save them or return a shocked and threatened humanity to itself. Where 'monsters have always defined the limits of community in Western imaginations', cyborgs 'define quite different political possibilities' (Haraway 1990: 192, 213). Repulsion flips into identification, fantasies of self-fulfilment and liberation trailing in its wake. Monsters, ghosts and vampires become figures of transitional states repre-senting the positive potential of post-human transformation: they participate in a fantastic flight from a humanised world towards a borderless, inclusive virtual culture. Figures of political change, they are multitude: undermining bourgeois familial structures and hetero-normative reproductive sexuality, vampires – 'still social outsiders' – help us 'to recognize that we are all monsters – high school outcasts, sexual deviants, freaks, survivors of pathological families', and to imagine new social and political forms. 'Frankenstein [the monster?] is now a member of the family'. Love your monster; hate 'the monstrous horrible world that the global political body and capitalist exploitation have made for us [the monsters?]' (Hardt and Negri 2006: 193–6).

Ambivalent, contradictory, banal, the pervasive identification of Gothic figures as harbingers of the new, suggests there is little special about monstrosity in an age of cybernetics and Frankenstein pets (Botting 2003). The future, once so monstrous, has already collapsed on an indifferent present (Botting 2004). Gothic cedes to 'Cybergothic': cloaked in the reassuringly familiar images of vampire–cyborg–zombie–monster, a very different technological system envelops humanity in something resolutely inhuman and truly monstrous: 'v(amp)iro finance' devastates the bodies and systems that once seemed to operate in the service of human production and reproduction; 'reproductive order comes apart into bacterial and intergalactic sex, and libidino-economic interchange machinery goes micro-military' (Land 1998: 80, 86–7). Terminators, replicants and cyborgs camouflage themselves 'in wolf-pelts, and cross into beserk zones of alien effect', virtual spaces of 'voodoo economics, neo-nightmares, death-trips' (Land 1993: 479–82). Their dressing up is a matter of infiltration, usurpation, destruction; they are figures of a thoroughgoing transformation of all the relationships and differences of modernity, a transvaluation in which life is lived beyond human terms.

HORREALISM

A teenager in Anglesey cuts out the heart of an old-age pensioner. His computer reveals extensive interest in vampirism websites. North American students go on high school shooting sprees: horror films, Goth music and violent video-games are cited as their hobbies. 'Scream' killings occur across Europe, the killer wearing a mask popularised by the stalking villain of Wes Craven's movie. In Germany in 2002 a notoriously bloody case unfolded: a Goth couple, Daniel and Manuela Ruda, were sentenced for hammering, stabbing and carving their 33-year-old male victim with a pentagram, drinking his blood. 'Pitch black vampire seeks princess of darkness who hates everything and everyone.' Daniel and Manuela met through small ads placed in a heavy metal magazine. 'Sex bat horror vampire cool machine.' They enjoyed visits to graveyards and ruins; they practised devil worship; at home they slept in silk-lined coffins. He had animal fangs implanted and filed down; she became a vampire during visits to London Goth clubs – clubs where, according to Ruda, one can 'have a perfectly normal chat and drink some blood'.

'How I wish those bats would bite.' Where do simulations begin or end? Does horror or abjection counter their thrust or feed the cool machine with a fleeting bite? 'Real Gothic' horrors seem to defy simulation with bloody, violent and all-too-real acts. Simulations have effects. The world of these killers is, or is presented as, one suffused with Gothic images and myths. The Rudas' lifestyle takes its bearings from fictions: their act interpreted as a 'Gothic horror' (McGowan 2002: 5). Boundaries between fiction and reality have become blurred, one interpenetrating and shaping the other, to dismantle conventional patterns of differentiation. For the Rudas, vampirism entered everyday life, the drinking of blood becoming a banal, routine activity. At the same time, ascriptions of 'Gothic horror' attempt to register repulsion at the enormity of their act: its horror lies beyond reality or hyper-reality even as it is rendered almost palatable in fictional and generic terms. Normal and excessive, routine and repugnant, attributions of horror retroactively confirm the act as both a simulation and irruption of (simulated) reality. Vampires of course have only ever been unreal creatures of nocturnal fantasy: to live as a vampire turns the unreal of conventional horror images into ordinary reality at the point that ordinary reality is itself opened up. In taking its bearing from fiction, in violently realising scenes from page and screen, such a lifestyle simultaneously rejects and returns to a world of simulations: desire and fantasy, coordinated by image, music and text, seek out the horrifying plenitude of a real displayed and deferred in simulation. Hence the paradox (or what in modernity's terms would appear as paradox – or psychosis): to simulate vampirism (to the extent of turning it into an everyday lifestyle) is undertaken with the aim of breaking through sanitised screens of hyper-reality, of finding something of the real in blood and horror. But bloody, violent, horrifying reality – shaped by Gothic figures and fictions – is returned as Gothic horror by the media. Simulation spins on, despite the murderous mimickry of a creature that never was. Artifice, conformism, convention remain at work, despite the efforts to break through their frames in acts of violent realisation, a nostalgia for modernity, perhaps. 'Horror bat. Bite!'

WORKS CITED

Baudrillard, Jean (1990) *Fatal Strategies*, trans. Philip Beitchman and W. G. J. Niesluchowski, London: Pluto Press.

—— (1993) *Symbolic Exchange and Death*, trans Iain Hamilton Grant, London: Sage.

—— (1994) *The Illusion of the End*, trans. Chris Turner, London: Polity.

Botting, Fred (1991) *Making Monstrous*, Manchester: Manchester University Press.

—— (1999) 'In Gothic Darkly: Heterotopia, History, Culture', in David Punter (ed.), *A Companion to the Gothic*, Oxford: Blackwell.

—— (2002) 'Aftergothic', in Jerrold E. Hogle (ed.), *Cambridge Companion to the Gothic*, Cambridge: Cambridge University Press.

—— (2003) 'Metaphors and Monsters', *Journal for Cultural Research*, 7(4): 339–65.

—— (2004) 'Resistance is Futile', *Anglophonia*, 15: 265–93.

Derrida, Jacques (1990) 'Some Statements and Truisms about Neologisms, Newisms, Postisms, Parasitisms, and Other Small Seismisms', in David Carroll (ed.), *The States of 'Theory'*, Stanford, CA: Stanford University Press.

—— (1992) 'Passages – From Traumatism to Promise', in *Points . . . : Interviews, 1974–1994*, trans. Peggy Kamuf *et al.*, ed. Elisabeth Weber, Stanford, CA: Stanford University Press.

Dika, Vera (1996) 'From Dracula – With Love', in Barry Keith Grant (ed.), *The Dread of Difference*, Austin, TX: University of Texas Press.

Ennis, Garth and Steve Dillon (1998) *Preacher: Dixie Fried*, New York: DC Comics.

Haraway, Donna (1990) 'A Manifesto for Cyborgs: Science, Technology and Socialist Feminism in the 1980s', in *Feminism/Postmodernism*, ed. Linda J. Nicholson, New York: Routledge, pp. 190–233.

—— (1997) *Modest_Witness@Second_Millennium*, London: Routledge.

Hardt, Michael and Antonio Negri (2006) *Multitude*, London: Penguin.

Kittler, Friedrich (1990) *Discourse Networks 1800/1900*, trans. M. Metteer with C. Cullens, Stanford, CA: Stanford University Press.

Land, Nick (1993) 'Machinic Desire', *Textual Practice*, 7(3): 471–82.

—— (1998) 'Cybergothic', in Joan Broadhurst Dixon and Eric J. Cassidy (eds), *Virtual Futures*, New York: Routledge.

Lévy, Maurice (2004) 'FAQ: What is Gothic?', *Anglophonia*, 15: 23–37.

McGowan, Patrick (2002) 'We Killed a Man . . . ', *Evening Standard*, 17 January, p. 5.

Mulholland, Garry (2002) *This is Uncool: The 500 Greatest Singles since Punk and Disco*, London: Cassell Illustrated.

Parker, Martin (2005) 'Organisational Gothic', *Culture and Organisation*, 11(3): 153–66.

Poster, Mark (2002) 'High-Tech Frankenstein, or Heidegger meets Stelarc', in Joanna Zylinska (ed.), *The Cyborg Experiments*, London: Continuum.

Reynolds, Simon (2005) *Rip It Up and Start Again: Postpunk 1978–1984*, London: Faber and Faber.

Rice, Anne (1995) *The Vampire Lestat*, New York: Warner Books.

Stone, A. R. (1995) *The War of Desire and Technology at the Close of the Mechanical Age*, Cambridge, MA: MIT Press.

Twain, Mark (1981) *Life on the Mississippi*, New York: Bantam Books.

Virilio, Paul (1995) *The Art of the Motor*, trans. Julie Rose, Minneapolis, MN: University of Minnesota Press.

25

CONTEMPORARY GOTHIC THEATRE

EMMA MCEVOY

Gothic, since its inception, has enjoyed a close relationship with theatre. The early Gothic novel situated itself in relation to theatre and to Shakespearean tragedy in particular as, in itself, a mixed genre. It invoked and mediated drama: Walpole's *Castle of Otranto* (1764) is notable for its use of a very theatrical mode of public display and soliloquy rather than internal cogitation. Theatre also lent other concerns to the Gothic novel – the insistence on space and setting, the concern with surfaces. The figure of the theatre has been frequently an object of Gothic insistence, not only within the novel – Gaston Leroux's *Phantom of the Opera* (1910), Anne Rice's *Interview with the Vampire* (1976), for example – but also, self-referentially, on stage – the many versions of *Phantom of the Opera*, Stephen Mallatratt's adaptation of Susan Hill's novel *The Woman in Black* and Improbable's *Theatre of Blood* (itself adapted from the Hammer film of 1973). The figure of the theatre, as a site where the past can be performed within the present, and the present within the space of the past, has possessed a particular appropriateness for a mode whose defining characteristic has been its twinning of history and place.

Gothic narratives lend themselves to theatrical treatment, and the period from (approximately) 1768 to 1830 saw the dominance of the Gothic drama on the British stage. Jeffrey Cox, in his introduction to an issue of *Gothic Studies* devoted to the Gothic drama of this period, reminds us that technology was central to these productions which 'took full advantage of advances in lighting, machinery, and staging to offer overwhelming sets and supernatural special effects' (Cox 2001: 119). Among these special effects were the vampire trap (a kind of trapdoor which enabled the actor playing a vampire seemingly to disappear) and the manipulation of gas light and a system of mirrors to present ghosts. Other aspects noted by Paul Ranger in his *Terror and Pity Reign in Every Breast* (1991) are the detailed instructions for the use of powerful noise (he informs us that the production of Maturin's *Bertram* (1816) required sound effects for the roar of the sea, a ship's distress signals and the tolling of a monastery bell), and fire scenes with flames up to 18 feet in height.

Gothic drama proper has not dominated the stage for almost two centuries and the history of Gothic on stage since then has not been continuous. Some nineteenth-century melodramas and some of the plays in the Grand Guignol tradition of the first half of the twentieth century may be described as Gothic, but the traditions are not synonymous. There has been recently, however, a renewed interest in putting Gothic on stage and this essay will consider some of the ways contemporary Gothic productions have sought to engage and provoke their audiences.

Gothic on the contemporary stage may be found in world-touring shows like *Shock-Headed Peter* (the dramatisation of the Tiger Lillies' musical rendition of Dr Hoffmann's nineteenth-century children's rhymes), in fringe theatres, which can play effectively on the sense of intimacy and proximity, and, more and more frequently, in the 'found' spaces employed for site-specific performance. Somewhat bizarrely, the main area of contemporary theatre in which Gothic (or Gothic pastiche/spoof usually lacking the element of fear) flourishes is the musical, with examples including *The Phantom of the Opera*, *The Woman in White*, *Little Shop of Horrors, The Dracula Spectacula* and *The Rocky Horror Show*; these, however, are beyond the remit of this chapter.

Theatre and dramatic performance have the potential for introducing potent factors into the Gothic work – real space and real time, and it is the manipulation of real-time experience within a Gothicised space that many contemporary productions have capitalised on. Site-specific performance and installation have proved to be fruitful modes for the Gothic. Cross-over media have also proved to be effective. Theatre can import the locales of the Gothic, literalising the circus, the fairground, the freak show and burlesque with the resultant theatrical spaces becoming liminal Gothic locales in themselves, so, for example, the work of companies like Archaos give us the circus as theatre. The Californian company Antenna in their *Euphorium* explored the undercroft of Camden's Roundhouse, recreating it as Gothic labyrinth as audience members promenaded through a space that was both a physical realisation of the drug-fuelled nightmares of Coleridge and De Quincey and a virtual space created by multimedia technology.

Much Gothic theatre thrives on its incorporation of other media and a sense of generic trespass. Gothic concern with framing and the story-within-a-story is effected by some vertiginous generic crossings. *The Woman in Black* makes reference both to *film noir* and to written narratives. The programme of Season of Terror 2006 was performed as something of a medley, incorporating aspects of cabaret, burlesque, the freak show, Punch and Judy and projection. Forkbeard Fantasy's *Fall of the House of Usherettes* also revels in multi-media; supposedly set in an old cinema, it uses film and mechanical sets, as well of course as referring to the original Poe short story. It is worth pointing out that many examples of the Gothic (as might be expected because of the phenomena of transmission and framing) on the modern stage are adaptations – from novels, short stories or films.

THE WOMAN IN BLACK: MATERIALISING THE PHANTASMAL

The sense of theatre itself as Gothic space is resourcefully exploited in Robin Herford's production of *The Woman in Black* (originally written for the Stephen Joseph Theatre, Scarborough) which has been running in London's West End since 1988 at the Fortune Theatre. The venue has been essential to the success of the play. The Fortune, which opened in 1924, is small by West End standards, seating just over four hundred people. Musty, old-fashioned, slightly pokey, it is the perfect distressed theatre for the play. Stephen Mallatratt's adaptation of *The Woman in Black* is set in a theatre, and the process of becoming an actor is at the outset established as one that is meant to effect an emotional exorcism. Watching *The Woman in Black* the audience is in the theatre it is set in – but because of this self-referentiality the play becomes not so much an exorcism as a summoning up of the ghost. Integral to the effect of *The Woman in Black* is its cunning use of what Irving Wardle (1989) called the 'black magic of theatre'. *The Woman in Black* has proved so successful because of its playing to the uncanny nature of theatricality itself.

One of the specialities of the Gothic novel is its power of rendering the material phantasmal and the phantasmal material.[1] The Gothic novel, being composed of written words, is able to indulge the sense of phantasmal materiality to the extreme; the reader may luxuriate in terror, assailed by her or his imagination. Film, where the spectator is seated before the two-dimensional image, the trick of light, the re-playing of acting that took place in the past, takes the phantasmal aspect even further. Theatre, however, has a temporal and material presence that neither the novel nor the film has: the material is both physically present and the action is unfolding in the same time dimension as the audience. *The Woman in Black* uses some ingenious devices to render problematic its materialisation, effectively using the scrim (the translucent gauze) to present the scenes in the nursery and the graveyard. It suggests the claustrophobic and uncanny atmosphere by literalising the trope of the veil. It also constantly plays with our understanding of the visible/invisible, by the device of having an invisible dog, and a ghost that is sometimes visible and sometimes invisible.

However, there is a further sense in which it could be said that *The Woman in Black* renders the material uncanny, and this is in the way it seems to put noises, persons and things in quotation marks. It does this primarily through its central device of the play within a play. The central character, Mr Kipps, has come to the Actor (who, like the heroine of Du Maurier's *Rebecca* (1938) has no name) in order to be able to tell – and thus exorcise – the story that has been troubling him for years. In order for the story to be conveyed to its audience, the Actor tells Mr Kipps, he must be able to relay it in an interesting way. The play moves from being elocution lesson to acted performance. Each aspect of performance is introduced as such: the Actor comments on the recently invented technique of the sound effect; on the way that an actor may make a wicker basket seem to be a horse-drawn carriage; on the nature of hand-held props. Thus the audience encounters each of these theatrical devices as devices, experiences them both within the central narrative and without it. Because the focus is on the effect and also on the audience's capacity to create a transformation through a Coleridgean 'suspension of disbelief', these objects and techniques start to acquire an uncanny doubleness.

Doubleness is a pervasive aspect of *The Woman in Black*. The main characters become disturbing doubles of each other, in a way that plays to the doubleness of acting itself. In *The Woman in Black*, the audience sees both Mr Kipps and the Actor becoming other characters and is made aware of their increasing skill; it also sees the Actor becoming Mr Kipps. Instead of achieving the hoped-for exorcism, Mr Kipps, through the process of performing his story, is forced to talk about himself in the third person, to see someone else become him, and to become other than his self. The process is extended in the coda of the play where it is revealed that the Actor is to double Mr Kipps in his impending fate.

Why is the Woman in Black herself so terrifying? At each appearance of the ghost there are screams from the audience. One reason is that there is something about her presentation which is cliché personified or convention materialised – the black, late-Victorian costume, the exaggerated make-up, the conniving use of lighting. Faced with this Gothic convention the audience knows the conventional response. Another reason is that, unlike cinema, where the spectator's gaze is already focused by the camera, *The Woman in Black* plays to the relatively undirected gaze of the theatre audience by letting the audience discover the Woman in Black in their own time, and members of the audience react to the ripples of fear and recognition that they sense around them. *The Woman in Black* thrives on the communality of the theatre experience. The audience shrieks, gives solace, and becomes a coherent entity. Audience interaction is allowed to generate fear and suspense – in a way which is not possible with any other medium. The 'here and now' of theatre experience is exploited extremely effectively. Much of the action takes place beyond the proscenium arch. The audience is swathed in smoke, plunged into darkness, subject to blood-curdling screams that issue from speakers set right into the auditorium. The theatre experience, unlike any other, has the ability to put its audience into the haunted house, to let it hear its sounds and become lost in it.

MIXING FRAMES

The Seasons of Terror have been running at the Union Theatre in Southwark, London, annually since 2004 under the artistic direction of Adam Meggido. The Union is an atmospheric venue: a fringe theatre set beneath the arches of a railway line. Playing Gothic theatre in a fringe venue has many advantages. The audience members are very much aware that these are all real bodies before them, that they themselves are not spectators at a remove but an audience in an enclosed space who may be (literally) touched by the action. The actors in Terror 2006 did indeed play beyond the proscenium arch, stage blood did splatter the audience, a 'murdered man' did appear at the back of the audience and the audience at one point was plunged into real darkness.[2]

Terror 2006 took many of its cues from Grand Guignol – its use of an intimate venue, and of the technique of '*la douche ecossaise*, a "hot and cold shower"' (Hand and Wilson 2002: 6), whereby horror and humour were alternated. However, in its use of humour, Terror 2006 distinguished itself from Grand Guignol. Hand and Wilson (2002) stress that the place of humour in Grand Guignol was not within the horror pieces but the comedies which interspersed them. Meggido, however, built in laughter as response to the play, not only to bring down the audience after moments of terror but also to relax it so that it dropped its guard. Terror 2006 showed a canny ability to elicit the laughter of knowingness and irony. At the opening of Daragh Carville's adaptation of M. R. James's *The Disappearance* there were sound effects of constant rain and massive gusts of wind, which were almost parodically conjured up as stock fare of the ghost story. Terror 2006 demanded a complex range of emotional responses and undercutting of those responses; it gave a retrospect on tradition and a double-take on that retrospect, and, most significantly, employed the device of framing at a variety of levels.

Meggido's direction of Terror 2006 very deliberately mixed frames. Actors from one play mingled with those of another. After *The Disappearance*, Kidman and Gallop performed a burlesque sadomasochistic freak show act/self-harm gag. Scott Christie who played the vicar in the second play, *The Rose Garden*, also played the actor, Barry Stevens, who was acting the vicar; he entered while the nephew from *The Disappearance* was clearing up, to perform a 1970s stand-up routine during the business of stage set-up. The effect was that of Gothic contamination, bleeding boundaries and generic transgression. William Stewart's adaptation of *The Rose Garden* effected a positioning of theatre as 1970s sitcom in the style of *George and Mildred* or *Terry and June* but with the subject of an M. R. James story. The framing and ironising of response also characterised the use of sound effects. During the Punch and Judy murders in *The Disappearance* there was a knowingly conventional use of the high sustained string sound beloved of horror films. The sound effects both played on convention and also collapsed the elaborate frames they set up. At the moment of the murder there was canned laughter. During the scene where the Nephew dreams of Punch murdering the baby (where again a frame was breached as the Punch and Judy show came out of its frame and giant puppets walked on settling themselves on the Nephew's bed and within his reality) there was a highly effective moment when the sound effect of a baby crying (which was of a real baby) was replaced by the noise of the actor playing Punch making a baby sound. At this moment the production played with the idea of the realness of theatre itself. Which was the real baby in terms of the stage? Punch's 'real' noise in real time or the real baby noise?

Terror 2006 might be said to have created a theatre in quotation marks, as the set for *The Disappearance* was the nineteenth-century stage itself. At the beginning of the evening, the actors who were to play Kidman and Gallop hoisted the red plush curtains; at this point of the show they were both inside and outside the action, evidently acting (laughing with an unsettling lack of visible motive), they were not yet placed within the show that they were opening. The centre of the playing area was occupied by the mock-up of a stage which was lit from below with modern approximations of nineteenth-century footlights. The plush red curtains and the footlights shining up and lighting the actors' faces from below were both integral to the play and an outside comment on the Gothic nature of nineteenth-century stage practice itself.

A similar concern with framing was achieved by the 1998 production of *Shock-Headed Peter*, designed and directed by Julian Crouch and Phelim McDermott of Improbable. Crouch's set played particularly on the potential for surreal framing provided by the Punch and Judy show. The Tiger Lillies narrating the action through song were for the most part placed outside of or embedded in the set, which perched like a life-size Victorian toy theatre on the stage. Beyond the (already framed) proscenium arch were three further receding frames giving grotesque and amusing opportunities for false perspective, as when characters entered through the furthermost frame and proved to be too large for it. Actors played alongside life-size puppets and the production made the most of the uncanny reversals that ensued; in the 'snip snip' song the actors, masked in stage make-up were the more automaton-like and threatening, while the child puppets wore countenances of confusion and pain.[3] *Shock-Headed Peter* Gothicised stage tradition, creating a play that held itself up as an artefact from the past. Self-referentially the event in the theatre was itself the claustrophobic Gothic event, concerned with surface and populated by a Gothic array of characters – the vampiric master of ceremonies, the cruel parents, the suffering children.

OPEN HOUSE: SITE-SPECIFIC GOTHIC AND GHOSTLY AUDIENCES

On 1 and 2 June 2004, final year dance, drama and music undergraduate students at Bath Spa University under Andy W. Smith performed a piece they had devised – *Post-Mortem: A Site-Specific Installation* – at the Octagon, Milsom Street, Bath. The building itself, as Smith points out, 'has had a long history, being built as a chapel in the 18th century, and used respectively as a poor house, auction house, grain store during the war and eventual home of the Royal Photographic Society'.[4] In *Theatre/Archaeology* Mike Pearson writes that site-specific performances

> rely, for their conception and their interpretation, upon the complex coexistence, superimposition and interpenetration of a number of narratives and architectures, historical and contemporary . . . Performance recontextualises such sites: it is the latest occupation of a location at which other occupations – their material traces and histories – are still apparent . . .
>
> (Pearson and Shanks 2001: 23)

Post-Mortem Gothicised the Octagon: a child dressed in a white dressing-gown could be fleetingly spotted in various parts of the building (in accordance with local rumour that the building is haunted by the ghost of a child); fragmented writings appeared, as yellowed paper inscribed with eighteenth-century sermons dropped from the balcony; sounds issued from deserted rooms. Not only were the 'material traces' of the past still present but the performers and devisers of the piece imprinted other traces, Gothically inscribing their found space: there were chalk scrawls on the wall and child's garments scattered around, actors came out of walls and secret hideaways. For Smith and his students 'spectral presences' were 'embedded inside the geography of space: liminal absence inside a material presence'. Their insistence that 'the architecture was not only the space for performing but the performance itself' was remarkably faithful to the principles of both site-specific performance and the Gothic.

Site-specific performance can bring the audience into the haunted house, materialising the spaces of Gothic. These spaces, however, are liminal in many respects. *Post-Mortem* positioned itself on a boundary between fiction and reality that much Gothic fiction/architecture from *Otranto* onwards has strad-dled. Such found spaces as the Octagon are palimpsestic, summoning up the overlay of pasts that have inhabited the building and evoking other pasts within the present. Other site-specific works fruitfully play on the discrepancy between the spaces they create, the fictions which inhabit them and the spaces in which the performance takes place: in its eerie mismatch of place and performance Punchdrunk's *Faust* (discussed below) capitalised on what Nick Kaye has called the 'ellipses, drifts, and leaks of meaning' in site-specific work 'through which the artwork and its place may be momentarily articulated one in the other' (Kaye 2000: 57).

Sarah V. Chew's 2005 production of Helena Thompson's *Open House* (co-produced by SPID – Specially Produced Independently Directed – theatre company and the Riverside Studios) also brought the audience into the haunted house. *Open House* took place in SPID's base, a series of community rooms in the modernist Kelsall House council estate in north London. The company adapted their biggest room, blocking off the stage at the end by building a fake wall and adapting the space to feel like a decaying council flat pervaded by the smell of damp and overflowing ashtrays. Here a necessarily small audience was invited to look on at the unfolding of a domestic drama presided over by an overbearing father guilty of some unspecified sin while the younger characters are haunted by memories of their dead lover who committed suicide. Audience members promenaded through the flat with the ends of scenes signalled by the actors turning out the lights and moving to another area. They moved from a living-room where, by means of some partially cut-away walls, they were able to eavesdrop on the scene taking place in the bedrooms, to a dining-room where they could peep through the hatch or the door to the scene going on in the kitchen. The partially torn-down walls eerily married materialisation of the Gothic fragment with the function of eavesdropping – and gave a startling new immediacy to the concept of 'fourth-wall' drama.

The experiment of siting Gothic narrative in a space at once 'real' (this, after all, was on a bona fide London council estate) and fake (the flat was a custom-ised theatre space) bore interesting relation to some earlier Gothic theatre spaces – the fake asylums or prisons of Lewis's plays, the liminal spaces whose incomplete transformation becomes an uncanny experience in itself. The audience was not only invited into the acting space but transported into the fiction. Audience members became trespassers, walking within the set of the drama itself, in the actors' space, and, in the process it became ghostly. The characters threw plates at each other in the dining-room as the audience stood in their midst. Actors, seemingly possessed by their performance in the parallel world of the play, moved amongst the audience members without seeming to notice them. Space itself becomes doubled when the actors' space and the audience space become one. Eve Kosofsky Sedgwick emphasises the Gothic predicament of moving from one prison to another (Sedgwick 1986) and this experience has been wrought imaginatively many times and in different ways on the stage.[5] When *Open House* introduced a promenade audience into a site-specific work an interesting change was wrought on the audience who were, very Gothically, placed within the blocked impassable space – unable to break through to the world of the drama, moving parallel to it and ghostly in relation to it.

Punchdrunk's 2006 site-specific production *Faust* (produced under the auspices of the National Theatre) also Gothicised its audience, playing on the sense of trespass endemic to installation pieces. *Faust*, though not a thorough-going Gothic work, harped on the Gothic at many points. Set in a massive, dilapidated warehouse in Wapping, London, *Faust* was a 'physical and visual narrative spread across the entire internal landscape of 21, Wapping Lane'.[6] Punchdrunk's audiences were 'given the freedom to roam entire buildings, to follow any theme, plot line or performer they choose, or simply soak up the atmosphere of magical yet fleeting worlds'.[7] The audience, though it would cluster together at certain points, was also often fragmented and very often was to be found exploring the empty motel rooms or living spaces of houses that had been created within the warehouse. These rooms were constructed with a painstaking realism that belied the sense of location, creating an eerie overlay or palimpsest of place, evoking phantasmal presences and rendering the most simple objects uncanny. In its creations of these rooms Punchdrunk played upon the anonymity and solitariness of the installation spectator rather than the communality of a theatre audience. The audience, walking into a 1930/40s bedroom, examining the dingy decor, picking up the scraps of jewellery, or toys, or staring emotionlessly at a religious statue, was made prurient, invasive. The very act of participating in the show became a kind of corruption – and *Faust* pointed this up by giving the audience diabolic carnival masks to wear.

Gothic on contemporary stages has taken many forms but certain patterns emerge. Many of the productions discussed in this chapter are characterised by their potent materialisation of the Gothic locale and their complicated generic journeyings. Many use elaborate framing devices. Nowadays there is no attempt to use special effects to conjure up apparitions by means of lights and mirrors; however, many productions find other ways to call up ghosts – by experimenting with a sense of physical presence and absence, with our sense of the doubleness of the theatrical experience, and with our sense of the palimpsestic nature of found spaces.

NOTES

1 See Terry Castle's analysis of the uncanny in the eighteenth century, in which she argues (following Freud) that what makes things uncanny 'is precisely the way they subvert the distinction between the real and the phantasmatic' (Castle 1995: 5).
2 In this section I shall be referring to the more Gothic part of the 2006 programme, particularly focusing on the M. R. James adaptations *The Disappearance* and *The Rose Garden*.
3 Recorded excerpts from the show may be seen at: www.shockheadedpeter.com/video.html.
4 Andy W. Smith, email to the author, 6 December 2006. All subsequent quotations about this performance derive from this source.
5 For example, Matthew Lewis's adaptation of *Venoni* (1808) which had the bars of the dungeon wall strikingly placed at the front of the stage and can be seen as an interesting translation of the Gothic device where prison abuts prison.
6 Quotation from the programme for *Faust*. No page numbers.
7 www.punchdrunk.org.uk (accessed 2 April 2007).

WORKS CITED

Castle, Terry (1995) *The Female Thermometer: Eighteenth-Century Culture and the Invention of the Uncanny*, Oxford: Oxford University Press.
Cox, Jeffrey (2001) 'Introduction: Reanimating Gothic Drama', *Gothic Studies* 3(2): 107–16.
Hand, Richard J. and M. Wilson (eds) (2002) *Grand-Guignol: The French Theatre of Horror*, Plymouth: University of Exeter Press.
Kaye, Nick (2000) *Site-Specific Art: Performance, Place and Documentation*, London: Routledge.
Pearson, Mike and Michael Shanks (2001) *Theatre/Archaeology*, London: Routledge.
Ranger, Paul (1991) *'Terror and Pity Reign in Every Breast': Gothic Drama in the London Patent Theatres, 1750–1820*, London: Society for Theatre Research.
Sedgwick, Eve Kosofsky (1986) *The Coherence of Gothic Conventions*, rev. 2nd edn, London: Methuen.
Wardle, Irving, *The Times*, 19th January 1989.

26

GOTHIC – FILM – PARODY

KAMILLA ELLIOTT

This chapter begins with an introduction to and overview of Gothic film parodies. Given the brevity of the chapter and the breadth of the subject, the overview is limited to film parodies of the Gothic triptych: *Frankenstein*, *Dracula* and
The Strange Case of Dr Jekyll and Mr Hyde. Although definitions of and critical
approaches to 'Gothic', 'parody' and 'film' have undergone significant changes
in the past 35 years, the overview considers both traditional formal and recent
theoretical approaches. The chapter ends with a discussion of contemporary
theoretical intersections between Gothic, film and parody and some ways in
which Gothic film parodies inform contemporary critical uses of the Gothic.

Most studies of Gothic film identify James Whale's *Frankenstein* (1931), Tod
Browning's *Dracula* (1931) and Rouben Mamoulian's *Dr Jekyll and Mr Hyde*
(1931) as a foundational triptych, from which they look back to earlier Gothic
films and forward to later ones.[1] The triptych is also a central focus for film parodies from Abbott and Costello films (1948 and 1953) to *The Nutty Professor*
(1963 and 1996), *Young Frankenstein* (1974), *Old Dracula* (1974), *The Rocky
Horror Picture Show* (1975), *Jekyll and Hyde, Together Again* (1982), *Frankenweenie* (1984), *Dr Jekyll and Ms Hyde* (1995), *Dracula, Dead and Loving It* (1995)
and *Frankenthumb* (2002). Animated parodies include *Mighty Mouse Meets
Jekyll and Hyde Cat* (1944), *Dr Jekyll and Mr Mouse* (1947), *Hyde and Hare*
(1955), *Hyde and Go Tweet* (1960), *Mad Monster Party* (1969) and *Alvin and the
Chipmunks Meet Frankenstein* (1999). Pornographic parodies include *Hollow-
my-weenie, Dr Frankenstein* (1969), *Dracula the Dirty Old Man* (1969), *Dr Sexual
and Mr Hyde* (1971), *Dracula Sucks* (1979), *Frankenpenis* (1996), *Mistress
Frankenstein* (2000), *Dr Jekyll and Mistress Hyde* (2003) and *Dracula's Dirty
Daughters* (2003). Parodies like *Dr Jekyll and Mr Hyde, Done to a Frazzle* (1914)
and Laurel and Hardy's *Dr Pyckle and Mr Pryde* (1925)[2] predate the triptych, as
theatrical parodies (such as *Frankenstitch*, Surrey Theatre, 1824; and *Dr Freckle
and Mr Snide*, Dockstader's Minstrel Hall, New York, 1887) predate and inform
the film parodies.

Gothic film parodies play with Gothic conventions, film forms and audiences.
Some stick closely to the triptych's plots, characters, historical periods and cinematic techniques. Others depart from them, modernise them, position themselves as sequels featuring (great)-grandsons of original characters, add
characters and/or change character genders, sexual orientations, nationalities,
religions and species (Frankenweenie is a dog). Gothic film parodies do range
outside the triptych: for example, Roman Polanski's *Dance of the Vampires*

(1967) parodies Hammer films; Mel Brooks' *Dracula, Dead and Loving It* parodies *Nosferatu* (1922), Abbott and Costello parodies, Hammer films, Coppola's *Bram Stoker's Dracula* (1992) and a host of other films and media outside the scope of this essay.

Filmmakers and formal critics are primarily concerned with how Gothic film parodies parody Gothic film forms: sets, costumes, acting, cinematography, editing, special effects, sound and music. Mel Brooks argues that 'The music and the art direction and everything around the comedy has to be utterly real or [the parody] doesn't work.' Consequently *Young Frankenstein* meticulously reproduces the black and white cinematography, expressive lighting, elaborate Gothic sets, ominous music, slow trundles, spins and wipes of Whale's *Frankenstein*. Against these elements, the film sets comic dialogue, 'deliberately artificial' acting, fake accents, 'forced perspectives' and 'dropped frames' that puncture, distance and distort Gothic convention, realist illusion and psychological terror and horror.[3]

Yet in spite of Brooks' invocation of the word 'real', the attention parody draws to film forms heightens awareness of their constructedness and, by extension, the constructedness of the Gothic. The cartoonish gargoyles and oversized door knockers of Mel Brooks' sets, the camp transvestite costumes of *The Rocky Horror Picture Show*, the impossible amounts of blood that spurt from Brooks' staked Lucy (Lysette Anthony), the pimp jewellery bursting through Jekyll's skin along with the conventional hair in the transformation scene of *Jekyll and Hyde, Together Again* and the extra loud creaks of coffin lids in the Abbott and Costello films all operate according to traditional concepts of parody as incongruity, disproportion and exaggeration, dislocating, distancing and puncturing Gothic terror and horror. As Avril Horner and Sue Zlosnik observe, 'it is the Gothic's preoccupation with "surface" [I would add, "form"] that enables it so easily to embrace a comic as well as a tragic perspective' (Horner and Zlosnik 2005: 9).

The casting of the Abbott and Costello parodies further highlights the constructedness of the triptych. Fred Botting observes: 'Stock formulas and themes, when too familiar, are eminently susceptible to parody and self-parody' (Botting 1996: 168). By the late 40s, so many sequels had been made that the triptych was already ripe for parody. *Abbott and Costello Meet Frankenstein* (1948) casts the triptych's Dracula, Bela Lugosi, as its Dracula, simultaneously highlighting the actor-as-character and obscuring it through recycling and typecasting. Joining Lugosi are Lon Cheney, Jr as the Wolf Man, his role in several 1940s Universal sequels (he also played Dracula and the Frankenstein monster), and Glenn Strange as Frankenstein's monster, his role in *House of Dracula* (1945).[4]

Even as such casting reinscribes and recycles roles and types, it fuses and confuses them. All three actors had played Frankenstein's monster in at least one sequel, while Boris Karloff, the triptych's Frankenstein monster, is Abbott's and Costello's Jekyll and Hyde. His Jekyll and Hyde is more than a double role.

Although his Hyde resembles Frederic March's monkey, he climbs a wall like Dracula, and plays a classic Gothic patriarch seeking to coerce a young ward into marriage. These parodies add 'further layers of fakery' to the Gothic 'refaking of fakery'[5] when they surround their Universal actor–monsters with waxwork monsters and costumed party-goers, simultaneously showing how the originals were constructed and claiming they are more real than other more layered constructions. Paradoxically, the 'additional layers of fakery' draw attention to the real costumes, actors, make-up, etc. used to create the original fakes.

Formal parodies, however, are never simply formal affairs: they always undertake parodic commentaries on art, history, culture, politics, ethics, psychology and/or epistemology. Cartoon gargoyles and oversized knockers suggest the regression and infantilism of Gothic fear; impossible amounts of blood parody Gothic science and the fine line between horror and humour; transvestite costumes foreground the construction of sexuality and gender; skin that grows jewellery mocks the cultural construction of what is deemed essentially evil.

If Gothic allows for an 'easy dialectic between the rational and irrational, emotion and intellect, artificiality and authenticity and, above all, horror and laughter' (Horner and Zlosnik 2005: 9), Gothic film parodies go further to challenge one of few remaining polarised oppositions in Gothic criticism: that between left-wing and right-wing politics. In *Rocky Horror*, murder, incest and cannibalism become camp sing-along affairs, politically incorrect from both left and right political stances. Its Dr Frank-N-Furter (Tim Curry), a sexually liberated bisexual transvestite, is also a rapacious, murderous cannibal needing to be overthrown as much as any conservative heterosexual patriarch. Parody here quells outrage with outrageousness, turning horror to laughter.

Gothic film parodies undermine antipathy and resistance to patriarchy, while never ceding its power. Parodied patriarchs are comical, romantic, superannuated, entertaining, fallible, even loveable. *Frankenthumb*'s monster dances amiably in chains. Hyde (Mark Blankfield) is a harmless party 'dude' in *Together Again*. *Dead and Loving It*'s Dracula (Leslie Nielsen) slips on bat droppings and his hypnotic powers miss their targets. But he never entirely cedes his capacity to terrify. *Love at First Bite* sends patriarchy to the rescue after the travesties of the 60s and 70s. Dracula (George Hamilton) is an ageing, romanticised patriarch ousted from his castle and the centre of society in the late 1970s by Soviet gymnasts to wrestle on and with its vilified margins: feminists, sexually liberated women, homosexuals, youth culture, blacks, Hispanics, Jews, Catholics, psychologists, criminals, the police and New York traffic, which oppress and are oppressed by the has-been, would-be-again patriarch. As Vlad the Impaler seeking a former love reincarnate (Susan Saint James), Dracula manifests a historical patriarchal prerogative: he has dominated the woman before and will again, against her aspirations to live as a liberated woman. The battle here is ideological rather than physical: a battle of sound bites rather than neck bites. The heroine agonises discursively rather than erotically: 'Part of me still wants to be independent; part of me wants to be taken care of. Part of me would like to be a wife and mother; part of me thinks I am just like an expensive whore.' In the end, she cedes her will to Dracula's word: 'I just don't know what to do. You have to tell me what to do.' Similarly, when Dracula seizes the wheel from and abuses a working-class driver (Ralph Manza), the driver figures patriarchal usurpation as rescue. Renfield (Arte Johnson) terrorising an assertive professional female with a cobra, insists 'In this case, we are the good guys.' The bad guy is a left-wing, socially tolerant, Jewish psychiatrist, played by Richard Benjamin as a heartless, mindless rogue, whose reluctance to judge according to right-wing values corresponds to a selfish refusal to commit romantically to the heroine. Although Dracula wins the heroine, there is no place for him on the margins of or at the centre of society, so he and the heroine turn to bats and fly from it.

Cartoon parodies never definitively overthrow or cede victory to patriarchs, but endlessly reverse and recycle hierarchies of predator and prey, as when *Hyde and Go Tweet*'s Tweety Pie turns into a bird of prey menacing Sylvester Cat or when Jerry morphs into a giant rodent while Tom shrinks to fly size in *Dr Jekyll and Mr Mouse*.

Other identity politics also blur lines between left and right politics. In *Abbott and Costello Meet Dr Jekyll and Mr Hyde*, suffragettes by day become chorus girls by night, to whom 'equal rights' means returning a kiss. In *Rocky Horror*, the explosion of straitlaced, middle-American teen sweethearts (Susan Sarandon and Barry Bostwick) into rampant, variegated sexualities queries the strength of values deemed human, religious and natural apart from social context. Yet it equally challenges the values of its bisexual, transvestite, social rebel. In *Dr Jekyll and Ms Hyde*, gender is determined by 'the unstable gene', evoking Gothic criticism of unstable gender boundaries. However, the film draws on gender stereotypes to undercut gender boundaries when it represents the change from Dr Jacks (Timothy Daly) to Ms Hyde (Sean Young) as a heterosexual orgasm and constructs femininity as castration and as culturally detachable, as clothing that can be bought, donned and doffed. Jacks repeatedly awakens clad in lingerie, rescued only by a homophobic amnesia regarding his actions as Hyde. In spite of conservative strains, the film maintains a variegated gender ambiguity and highlights the constructedness of gender distinctions. Indeed, it would be as erroneous and reactionary to argue that one ounce of right-wing politics makes a film 'right-wing' as to argue that one drop of black blood makes one definitively black.

This is the preoccupation of *Vampira*, which parodies white obsessions with racial purity. When Dracula's (David Niven's) love (Teresa Graves) dies from anaemia contracted from peasant blood, he resurrects her with a blood transfusion that (con)fuses blood and racial (stereo)types. Although only one of four donors is black, Vampira is, according to the racist tenet that one drop of black blood makes one black, resurrected black. Likened to white laundry stained by a blue sock, she requires further washings with other whites (white blood transfusions) to restore racial purity. But the film mocks such idea(l)s as much as it pursues them.

Gothic film parodies, then, unsettle Gothic, film and critical conventions alike, refusing themselves to settle in any ideological camp. Some parody the theories that govern Gothic criticism didactically, flagrantly outing the sexual subtexts that Gothic critics work so hard to unveil, re-presenting what psychoanalytic critics figure as trans-historical, libidinal realities as constructions and clichés. Late twentieth-century Gothic films typically dramatise beautiful young women awakening to sexuality in didactically sexual encounters with Gothic monsters. The pornographic parodies do so most blatantly across a range of sexualities, from the heterosexual bestiality of the Jackal man (Billy Whitton) in *Dracula the Dirty Old Man* to the lesbian ravishings of *Lust for Frankenstein*, *Mistress Frankenstein* and *Dr Jekyll and Mistress Hyde*. Young men too awaken as sexual prey in the bisexual romps of *Rocky Horror* and the homosexual encounters of *Hollow-my-weenie, Dr Frankenstein*.

Gothic parodies further delight in ludicrously literalising psychoanalytic symbolism. The Dracula of *Dracula Sucks* (Jamie Gillis) bites breasts and penises rather than necks. *Frankenpenis* crassly literalises Freud's castration complex when John Wayne Bobbitt's penis is severed by an undersexed wife (Veronica Brazil, as Lorena Bobbitt), surgically restored and enhanced, only to fail in satisfying the hyper-sexed Bride of Frankenpenis (Nina Cherry). *Dr Jekyll and Ms Hyde* (a mainstream rather than pornographic film) also literalises Freudian theories of castrated males and phallic women when Dr Jacks watches his penis vanish beneath his clothes and alter ego Ms Hyde is dubbed 'a woman with balls' and outdoes him in both professional and domestic spheres.

Freud himself takes a parodic drubbing when Brooks' Van Helsing (Mel Brooks) looks like Freud, speaks gibberish and propounds 'the theory of yes or no'. The film's sedately waltzing Dracula (Nielson) and Mina (Amy Yasbeck) cast 'dirty dancing' shadows on the wall, dubbed 'shadows of the id' in the DVD commentary. *Love at First Bite* parodies both psychoanalysis and left-wing politics when its liberal psychoanalyst, a grandson of Van Helsing, is himself locked up as insane. In *Abbott and Costello Meet Dr Jekyll and Mr Hyde*, pacifists critiqued for curbing natural instincts and policemen turning en masse into Hydes anticipate and anachronistically parody recent socio-political psychoanalytic criticism.

Gothic film parodies further inform contemporary critical uses of the Gothic, as Gothic, film and parody interpenetrate not only in Gothic film parodies, but also in academic discourse. All three are erstwhile devalued aesthetic forms recuperated by late twentieth-century humanities theories, serving in turn as proof texts for these theories in their battles against the high-art humanism, formalism and right-wing politics that dominated prior criticism.

Such interpenetrations have led to the widespread rejection of formalist definitions of 'Gothic', 'parody' and 'film'. 'Gothic' no longer requires maidens imprisoned by tyrannical patriarchs in castle ruins, but becomes increasingly abstract, psychological, metaphorical and ideological – an 'effect' for Chris Baldick (2001: xix), a 'spirit' at odds with its 'trappings' for Lisa Hopkins (Hopkins 2005: 1). Much recent Gothic criticism applies psychoanalytic theories, deemed universal and trans-historical, to local contexts, manifesting as 'cultural anxieties' assessed by leftist politics and deconstructed by poststructuralisms. Gothic is hailed for deconstructing hierarchical binarisms, blurring boundaries and revealing opposed entities as doubles.[6] Gothic films are read as manifesting 'cultural anxieties' about World War I in the 1910s; xenophobia and immigration in the 1920s; American isolationism and the Great Depression in the 1930s; World War II in the 1940s; sexual repression, changing gender roles, communism and the Cold War in the 1950s; gay and women's liberation, civil rights, drugs, nuclear disarmament and the Vietnam War in the 1960s and 70s; new-wave feminism, alternative sexualities, AIDS, incest, sexual harassment and child abuse in the 1980s and 90s; and capitalism, consumerism, science and technology throughout the twentieth century into the twenty-first.[7]

Contemporaneous studies of parody similarly reject 'standard dictionary definitions' (Hutcheon 1985: 5), so that 'parody' no longer necessitates low mockery of serious high art, but manifests as a dialogical, deconstructive, commentative, metafictional, problematising dynamic (Dentith 2000: 15–16; Phiddian 1995: 13–14) that no longer requires 'ridiculing imitation' (Hutcheon 1985: 40). Parody is a subversive, carnivalesque cultural force for Mikhail Bakhtin (1968), a conservative, mainstream one for Roland Barthes (1974) and Dan Harries (2000), holds subversion and conservatism in tension for Linda Hutcheon (Hutcheon 1985: 27), and deconstructs them for Jean Baudrillard: 'parody makes obedience and transgression equivalent and that is the most serious crime, since it cancels out the difference upon which the law is based' (Baudrillard 1983: 40). Historically, the newly defined parody controversially epitomises both modernism (Jameson 1984; Horner and Zlosnik 2005) and postmodernism (Hutcheon 1985).

Intriguingly for this discussion, in the 1980s 'parody' became a catchword for the theoretical turn in film studies from 'textualism' to 'what is considered state-of-the-art in cinema/video studies today . . . an amalgam of Lacanian psychoanalysis, Althusserian Marxism, Barthesian poststructuralism and French feminism' (Starenko 1986). The turn similarly involved a rejection of formal approaches to film, whether semiotic, generic, structuralist or narratological. Starenko explains 'where the various notions and theories of parody fit in': 'The new attention to audience response by film/television theorists has also made them more receptive to the way that film and televisionmakers play with *their* audience.'

In spite of its rejection of formalism, theoretical Gothic criticism draws on formal aspects of the triptych – the metamorphoses of Dracula, the constructedness of Frankenstein and the simultaneously blurred and polarised boundaries of Jekyll and Hyde – to establish its ideologies and, in so doing, fuses and confuses texts and criticism. The moral of Dracula that you are what you eat/

what eats you, popular confusions of Frankenstein and his monster and the always already known surprise that Jekyll is Hyde serve not only to break down the social, philosophical and political boundaries that concern Gothic critics, but also the boundaries between criticism and criticised.

Nowhere is this more prevalent than in critical uses of Gothic (dis)belief. Gothic, parody and film have all been read as pseudo-supernatural forms responding to declining religious belief. For Peter Brooks, Gothic is 'a form for a post-sacred era' (Brooks 1976: viii); for Botting, it is 'an attempt to reconstruct the divine mysteries that [Enlightenment] reason had begun to dismantle' (Botting 1996: 23). The Gothic literary triptych itself parodies religious doctrine: *Frankenstein*, the creation of man; *Jekyll and Hyde*, religious dualism; *Dracula*, Holy Communion and eternal damnation/salvation. For Friedrich Nietzsche in *The Gay Science* (1882–7), parody is the only possible aesthetic response to the death of the gods. Since the gods can no longer rescue or cause tragedy, parody is the only recourse (Gilman 1976: 19–20). Film scholars detail how spectral film technologies gesture to and displace the supernatural (e.g. Castle 1988). Ken Gelder (1994) likens the operations of vampires to cinema. Dialogue celebrating powers 'capable of bestowing animation upon lifeless matter' in *Young Frankenstein* evokes the undead life of the moving image as much as it does the Gothic supernatural.

If the Gothic parodies religion and film technology parodies the Gothic, Gothic film parodies further parody these parodies. A Jewish vampire (Alfie Bass) in *Dance of the Vampires* is impervious to a cross; concomitantly the Dracula of *Dead and Loving It* is immune to a Star of David. This film mocks the Gothic supernatural, filmic special effects and criticism highlighting Gothic boundary crossings when it superimposes Nielson's face on a bat.

Parodies of Gothic (dis)belief inform contemporary critical uses of the Gothic most of all. Supernatural Gothic works generally undertake narratives of belief and disbelief. In novels by authors like Ann Radcliffe and their parodies by Jane Austen and others, characters journey from terrified belief in the Gothic supernatural to rational disbelief. In novels by authors like Matthew Lewis, in the Gothic triptych, its film adaptations and their parodies, characters journey in the opposite direction: from scoffing disbelief to fearful belief. While some Gothic societies believe in the supernatural, others pathologise such belief. *Dracula*'s Renfield and *Love at First Bite*'s Van Helsing are both locked in asylums for believing in Dracula. Lanyon dies from an unbearable rupture between belief and disbelief in Stevenson's *Jekyll and Hyde*. Costello, playing believer to Abbott's unbeliever, turns regressively into infant and mouse. But in the end, pathologised, regressive and even dead believers guide unbelievers to credence in, combat with, and victory over Gothic supernatural monsters.

In both Abbott and Costello parodies, Costello plays lone believer in the midst of a dangerously rational, disbelieving world. The unbelieving Abbott directs aggression against Costello's belief more than the Gothic monsters who threaten him. Made during the Cold War, the films reflect the national obsession with invisible, discursively constructed enemies. (Dis)belief in these films is complicated by the juxtaposition of harmless folk clad in monster costumes and masks and fake waxwork monsters with real ones. Initially Costello sees real monsters, while Abbott encounters only costumes and waxworks. When the real monsters appear, Abbott continues to see them as illusory or constructed. Disbelief here increases danger.

Beyond their immediate historical context, these parodies inform a contemporary critical context that emphasises discursive constructedness over physical reality. They press the Gothic supernatural from pseudo-scientific objectivism towards abstraction and the humanities through word play like, 'You've gone bats', and:

'In half an hour the moon will rise and I'll turn into a wolf.'
'You and 20 million other guys.'

Yet the transubstantiation of Gothic physics to word play does not insubstantiate the physical threat. Indeed, the belief that a physical threat is simply a figure of speech (or a constructed costume or waxwork) increases danger by decreasing fear. Character rescue from danger requires a rescue from disbelief.

Concomitantly, audience investment in Gothic danger requires a willing suspension of disbelief. Supernatural writing for Coleridge requires 'a semblance of truth sufficient to procure for these shadows of imagination that willing suspension of disbelief for the moment, which constitutes poetic faith' (*Biographia Literaria* (1817) in Coleridge 1985: 314). The willing suspension of disbelief is not belief, however; nor is it permanent. By contrast, much recent Gothic criticism marshals unstable Gothic belief and disbelief to advance permanent belief in theoretical ideologies. Academic Gothic criticism is predicated on disbelief in the Gothic supernatural and a belief that it must be representative of something else. It takes something that it does not believe in (the Gothic supernatural) and uses it to press belief in something that it does (psychoanalysis, feminism, left-wing politics, poststructuralism, etc.). Sublime and maddening mysteries constrict to didactic ideologies that resist their own blurring even as they blur other boundaries. The frequency with which Gothic film parodies serve as star, director, writer, character or genre vehicles epitomises and parodies such theoretical uses of Gothic.

Gothic criticism is equally concerned with creating disbelief in the creeds of its ideological enemies. When Horner and Zlosnik aver that 'most critics would probably agree that Gothic writing always concerns itself with boundaries and their instabilities, whether between the quick/the dead, eros/thanatos, pain/pleasure, "real"/"unreal", "natural"/"supernatural", material/transcendent, man/machine, human/vampire, or "masculine"/"feminine"', their inverted commas indicate targets of contemporary ideological disbelief (Horner and Zlosnik 2005: 1).[8] These represent ideological rather than scientific disbeliefs ('vampire' is not encapsulated).

Gothic criticism goes further to channel the fear, loathing and judgement aroused by the Gothic supernatural towards the 'real' dangers of capitalism, the tyranny of patriarchy, the evils of right-wing politics and the perils of consumerism and commodification. Epitomising this dynamic are scenes where Costello re-enacts his terror of monsters before a disbelieving Abbott. Terror in the absence of the original stimulus is comical, while Abbott's scolding bullying serves as a mundane replacement for monster menace.

Gothic film parodies rupture such affiliations by creating distance from the usual emotions and identifications aroused by Gothic works and exploited by ideological criticism. We laugh at rather than share Costello's terror, Abbott's angry didacticism and Elizabeth's (Madeline Kahn's) sudden shift from revulsion to rapturous song as *Young Frankenstein*'s well-endowed monster (Peter Boyle) mounts her. *Love at First Bite* parodies unions of belief and discursive authority when psychiatrist and policeman ally and fail in their attempts to enforce belief and to destroy the object of belief. Dracula, as always, escapes, freed for his next appearance in Gothic criticism, film or film parody.

NOTES

1 See Horner and Zlosnik (2005), Punter and Byron (2004), Kavka (2002), Kaye (2001) and Punter (1996).
2 Hyde's victims here are victims of practical jokes.
3 All citations are from the DVD commentary.
4 Full details of sequels and roles can be found on the Internet Movie Database (www. imdb.com).
5 Horner and Zlosnik (2005: 10) citing and commenting on Hogle.
6 Recent overviews by Hopkins (2005) and Horner and Zlosnik (2005) delineate these trends.
7 See, for example, Punter and Byron (2004), Kavka (2002), Kaye (2001) and Botting (1996).
8 See also Kavka (2002: 210–11).

WORKS CITED

Bakhtin, Mikhail (1968) *Rabelais and His World*, trans. Hélène Iswolsky, Cambridge, MA: MIT Press.
Baldick, Chris (2001) 'Introduction', in *The Oxford Book of Gothic Tales*, Oxford: Oxford University Press.
Barthes, Roland (1974) *S/Z*, trans. Richard Miller, New York: Hill and Wang.
Barton, Charles (dir.) (1948) *Abbott and Costello Meet Dr Jekyll and Mr Hyde*.
Baudrillard, Jean (1983) *Simulations*, trans. Paul Foss, Paul Patton and Philip Beitchman, New York: Semiotexte.
Botting, Fred (1996) *Gothic*, London: Routledge.
Brooks, Mel (dir.) (1974) *Young Frankenstein*.
—— (dir.) (1995) *Dracula, Dead and Loving It*.

Brooks, Peter (1976) *The Melodramatic Imagination: Balzac, Henry James, Melodrama and the Mode of Excess*, New Haven, CT: Yale University Press.

Castle, Terry (1988) 'Phantasmagoria: Spectral Technology and the Metaphorics of Modern Reverie', *Critical Inquiry*, 15(1): 26–61.

Coleridge, Samuel Taylor (1985) *Samuel Taylor Coleridge: The Major Works*, ed. H. J. Jackson, Oxford: Oxford University Press.

Dentith, Simon (2000) *Parody*, London: Routledge.

Dragoti, Stan (dir.) (1979) *Love at First Bite*.

Gelder, Ken (1994) *Reading the Vampire*, London: Routledge.

Gilman, Sander L. (1976) *Nietzschean Parody: An Introduction to Reading Nietzsche*, Bonn: Herbert Grundmann.

Harries, Dan (2000) *Film Parody*, London: British Film Institute.

Hopkins, Lisa (2005) *Screening the Gothic*, Austin, TX: University of Texas Press.

Horner, Avril and Sue Zlosnik (2005) *Gothic and the Comic Turn*, Basingstoke: Palgrave Macmillan.

Hutcheon, Linda (1985) *A Theory of Parody: The Teachings of Twentieth-Century Art Forms*, London: Methuen.

Jameson, Frederic (1984) 'Postmodernism, or the Cultural Logic of Late Capitalism', *New Left Review* 151 (July–August): 59–92.

Kavka, Misha (2002) 'Gothic on Screen', in Jerrold E. Hogle, *The Cambridge Companion to Gothic Fiction*, Cambridge: Cambridge University Press.

Kaye, Heidi (2001) 'Gothic Film', in David Punter, *A Companion to the Gothic*, London: Blackwell.

Lamont, Charles (dir.) (1953) *Abbott and Costello Meet Frankenstein*.

Nietzsche, Friedrich (1974) *The Gay Science*, trans. Walter Kaufmann, New York: Vantage.

Phiddian, Robert (1995) *Swift's Parody*, Cambridge: Cambridge University Press.

Price, David (dir.) (1995) *Dr Jekyll and Ms Hyde*.

Punter, David (1996) *The Literature of Terror: A History of Gothic Fictions from 1765 to the Present Day*, Vol. 2: *The Modern Gothic*, New York: Longman.

—— and Glennis Byron (2004), *The Gothic*, London: Blackwell.

Starenko, Michael (1986) 'Where's the Text? Cinema Studies in the 80s', *Afterimage*, 14(1), at: www2.rpa.net/~vsw/afterimage/starenko.htm (accessed 12 May 2006).

27

CONTEMPORARY HORROR CINEMA

BENJAMIN HERVEY

'I never want to climb out of another fucking coffin again!'
                                                    Barbara Steele

With these words, the most iconic and prolific actress of 1960s horror cinema quit the genre, sick of being typecast in baroque tales of castles, crypts and bygone centuries. But Steele returned to horror with *Shivers* (1975), an aggressively contemporary film about sexually transmitted parasites in a luxury tower block. The director, David Cronenberg, shared her impatience with period settings. He looks back on his early work as 'part of bringing horror into the twentieth century': 'At the time I started to make *Shivers*, there was already *Night of the Living Dead*. But for the most part horror was gothic, distant, not here' (Rodley 1997: 60).

Cronenberg's attitude is understandable. Universal Studios consolidated horror as a popular genre, notably with *Frankenstein* and *Dracula* in 1931, and defined its norms until it wound down in the mid-1940s. Themes and characters from nineteenth-century fiction dominated – and did so again when Hammer, a British company, revived the genre with *Curse of Frankenstein* (1957) and *Dracula* (1958). Universal's films were not set in period (they occasionally show cars and planes) but in an indeterminate Europe, a foggy parallel universe of horse-drawn buggies, gypsy caravans, candle-lit castles and thatched cottages, where scared villagers brandish flaming torches and aristocrats retain obscure feudal powers. Hammer's usual nineteenth-century locale was similarly vague and anachronistic: fans call it 'Hammerland'. The studio's vast successes inspired other film cycles, like Roger Corman's Poe series. Steele worked mostly in Italy, once a primitive setting for quintessential Gothic novelist Ann Radcliffe. Her directors, notably Mario Bava, explored high Gothic motifs: family curses, haunted castles, sadistic inquisitors and dripping torture chambers.

'Gothic', 'distant, 'not here': taken individually, Cronenberg's epithets ring true. These films perpetuated familiar Gothic literary sources and trappings. They depicted a world that was not only 'distant': it had never existed. But is Cronenberg right to imply that such distance is a defining characteristic of Gothic cinema? This chapter will examine key works that rebelled against the Universal–Hammer tradition and pushed horror cinema toward the credible contemporary settings that are now standard: films that bridged that 'distance'. Can they nonetheless be considered Gothic?

First, what is 'Gothic'? Definitions generally focus on literature. Most critics cite a distinctive use of settings. Obscure, perilous and awesome landscapes evoke Edmund Burke's theory of the sublime. Gothic architecture symbolises the fiction's themes: dungeons and labyrinths suggest confinement, the secret and forbidden; castles embody the past's oppressive weight. Probably the most enduring definition of Gothic is that advanced by Baldick and Mighall (2000): that it pits contemporary heroes against archaic villains to celebrate the victory of modernity over the past, rationalism over the irrational. This thematic conflict overlaps with a generic one: an ambivalent tension between realism and fantasy has characterised the Gothic since *The Castle of Otranto*. Walpole described his novel as 'an attempt to blend the two kinds of romance, the ancient and the modern. In the former all was imagination and improbability: in the latter, nature is always intended to be, and sometimes has been, copied with success' (Walpole 1964: 7).

This tension was central to Val Lewton, the first significant filmmaker to break systematically from the Universal mould. When RKO hired him in 1942 to produce a low-budget horror strand he screened numerous 1930s horror films to define 'what he did *not* want to do'. As Kim Newman argues, Lewton's were perhaps the first horror films to strive for credibility. Lewton called his characters 'normal people – engaged in normal occupations'; their clothes came from ordinary shops, not studio wardrobe departments. To avoid horror's traditional histrionics, the actors were directed to speak quietly and minimise gestures (Bansak 1995: 89; Nasr 2005; Newman 1999: 37, 65; Siegel 1972: 26–31; Haberman 2005).

Yet these remain horror movies. Lewton married realistic themes – marital problems, depression – to quintessential Gothic motifs: ancestral curses, atavism, devil-worship. Irena, in *Cat People* (1942), believes that her Serbian ancestors were witches who transformed into savage cats, and fears that she will do the same if she consummates her marriage. In *The 7th Victim* (1943), orphaned Mary finds her missing sister Jacqueline in the clutches of an ancient Satanist cult. Jacqueline, a lifelong suicidal depressive, joined the cult, then changed her mind and betrayed its secrecy by telling her psychiatrist, Dr Judd. The Satanists are respectable professionals, seen politely pouring tea, but this realism makes them more threatening. They imprison her to pressure her into committing suicide; when she escapes they send a killer after her.

Cat People and *The 7th Victim* spurn Universal's pseudo-Europe for modern, recognisable New York City settings: the 14th Street subway station, a YWCA swimming pool, a bus, Central Park. But Lewton's team wring an urban sublime from these humdrum spots, using techniques that again deliberately flout precedent. Universal's style prioritises visual spectacle: stop-motion transformations, monstrous make-up, ghostly superimpositions, lofty sets and *trompe l'œil* backdrops. It is an aptly cinematic approach, but so is Lewton's: his films exploit the darkened theatre's capacity for sensory deprivation; their ambiguous plotting is matched by visual obscurity. In *The 7th Victim*, Mary brings a detective to a beauty salon where the Satanists may have imprisoned her sister. The locked room (a Gothic trope) lies at the end of a darkened corridor, where the shadows converge into inky black. Mary urges the detective on, and he slowly submerges into this great darkness as if into a heavy liquid. Death mysteriously claims him there. Lewton starves our ears too: the music usually stops for these black scenes, and we strain like Ann Radcliffe's heroines for tiny, hinting sounds.

Universal films build to greater spectacles, but Lewton's fade to invisibility. *The 7th Victim* inexorably darkens: early scenes are conventionally, evenly lit; gradually, shadows carve the visual field; by the end, isolated bright patches highlight a predominantly dark screen, as in a Caravaggio painting. The light changes in quality, not just quantity. Traditional film technique balances key lights, which brightly illuminate important areas but cast heavy shadows, with fill lights, which soften the harsh contrasts into subtle shadings. As *The 7th Victim* progresses, these fill lights fade away, to nightmarish effect. Characters are over-shadowed by monstrous distortions of themselves. Black bars cast by blinds, window-frames and banisters cage Jacqueline, visualising her entrapment by the Satanists and her own death wish. Similar shadow-bars surround Irena and the apartment where she pines for sexual freedom. She obsessively visits a caged black panther in the park zoo that reminds her of the animalism locked within her. As in *The 7th Victim*, darkness vanquishes the light. When Irena finally becomes a panther, we see no Wolfman-like transformation: her face was simply darkened frame by frame in post-production, fading to black.

This play of light and darkness symbolically underlines both films' Gothic conflicts between rational and irrational, present and past – which Lewton never simplistically equates with good versus evil. In *Cat People*, Irena's husband hires a psychiatrist (Dr Judd again) to talk her out of her family curse. *The 7th Victim* also concerns an attempt to free a woman from the past's tendrils, a theme that both share with Bram Stoker's *Dracula* (1897). Jacqueline's band of would-be liberators resembles Stoker's 'Crew of Light': psychiatrist, lawyer, detective, artist, sister, husband. Both set-ups seemingly fit Baldick and Mighall's theme: modern heroes and archaic villains. But in Lewton there are no heroes. In each film the servants of modernity and rationalism, distracted by selfish motives, lose interest in saving the woman: they would rather have her out of the way. Jacqueline escapes the Satanists but hangs herself, betrayed and lonely, while her husband makes love to her sister. Irena, *Cat People*'s monster but also its most sympathetic character, almost *does* overcome her dread of sex and the past, but too late. Her frustrated husband has fallen for a colleague, and Dr Judd coolly persuades the new couple to institutionalise the bothersome wife: she will be out of their hair and at his mercy. Finally, the psychiatrist hired to exorcise Irena's inner panther awakens it by forcing himself on her sexually: she becomes a cat and kills him. Trapped by destiny, Irena looses the zoo's panther to devour her. Judd had irresponsibly implanted her suicide method, pointing out the 'temptation' that the zookeeper often leaves behind the key to the panther cage: 'all of us carry within us a desire for death', he elaborates.

This cynical plotting bespeaks a broader scepticism regarding modern scientific rationalism's ability to tame the primordial and irrational. Psychoanalysis became a popular theme in 1940s cinema, generally presented as an ultra-modern miracle cure, the present's tool for uprooting the past's mistakes. Lewton's films make Freudian therapy itself seem sinister and Gothic. Judd tries to supplant Irena's dread of her ancestry with another narrative of the past's grasp: childhood trauma, repression, sublimation. Lewton's psychiatrist is jaded, amoral, decadent, a snide philanderer armed with a swordstick. He snubs requests for help unless the work promises esoteric knowledge and sexual adventure. In *The 7th Victim*, Judd fraternises with the Satanists, entertaining them with magic tricks: 'It's purely a matter of the mind', he explains. Is his psychoanalysis like his hocus-pocus – a feat of manipulation and misdirection? Lewton's films attack the distinctions between science and superstition, enlightenment and barbarism, reality and nightmare.

Critics have demonstrated Lewton's influence on Hitchcock and Michael Powell (Newman 1999: 28–9; Bansak 1995:195, 392). Powell's *Peeping Tom* (1959) and Hitchcock's *Psycho* (1960), made during Hammer's heyday, like Lewton's films emphasise believable contemporary settings and psychological themes. *Psycho*'s success inspired a wave of contemporary psychological horror films, including several from Hammer. Again recalling Lewton, *Psycho* and *Peeping Tom* doubt the power of rationalism, specifically that of psychoanalysis, to conquer the irrational. *Psycho* ends with Norman diagnosed but certainly not cured. *Peeping Tom* goes much further: here the enlightened impulse to systematise the mind's irrational zones *causes* the disorder. The protagonist, Mark Lewis, stalks women with his camera: he films them as he stabs their throats with a bladed tripod leg, forcing them to watch their own reflections as they die. He obsessively reviews the films in his private lab, agonising over their imperfections. Helen, his tenant, befriends him and learns about Mark's past. His late father was a respected psychologist, specialising in fear and child development, and from infancy Mark knew no privacy. His father filmed everything: every hint of sexual awakening, every trauma; he even manufactured traumas to torture Mark. Mark fully recognises his own insanity and even learns the name of his condition (scoptophilia); he wants to be cured and has shelves full of psychoanalytic monographs. But to no avail: like Lewton's doomed heroines, he kills himself.

Contemporary critics reviled *Peeping Tom* for what *The Spectator* called its 'direct emotional realism': 'We have had glossy horrors before . . . but never such insinuating, under-the-skin horrors, and never quite such a bland effort to make it look as if this isn't for nuts but for normal homely filmgoers like you and me.' *Peeping Tom* was far from Hammerland: with its middle-aged prostitutes, sleazy newsagents and prefab housing blocks it felt closer to the milieu of 'new wave' social realism. (On its reception and relationship to realism, and for the *Spectator* review, see Lowenstein 2005: 55–82.) But the Gothic spirit is still felt here and in *Psycho*: they recall *The Monk*, whose protagonist erupts into sexual violence after years of containment and repression. Both films are about past tyrannies overshadowing, dominating the present: Mrs Bates' bullying and Dr Lewis's experiments; both parents are like psychic vampires. In true Gothic style, the grip of the past is figured architecturally, in the looming, archaic Bates house (Hitchcock called it 'California Gothic' (Truffaut 1986: 415–16)), where the dead mother still lurks in secret recesses. Mark too remains in his ancestral home, surrounded by reminders of his father's regime.

The house's hidden heart is Mark's inherited laboratory: once the nerve centre of his father's experiments, now Mark's dark room and the repository of his own crimes. Helen penetrates its mysteries like a Gothic heroine, risking her life to understand her tormented host. Stylistic flourishes enhance the Gothic redolence of catacombs and secret chambers. Shadowed corners make the room's surprising size hard to gauge; photographic chemicals create a sepulchral dripping sound straight out of Universal or Hammer. This hiding place of Mark's past, of his secret desires and crimes, evokes various Gothic archetypes. It was the torture chamber of Dr Lewis's inquisition: like Catholicism in the high Gothic novel, psychoanalysis was for him an orthodoxy, a religion that tortures to interrogate. And it is the laboratory where the mad doctor, Frankenstein-like, made his son into a monster. Again, style underlines the link: Mark's dark room is lit not only with the usual red, but a deathly green. The bold, saturated hues recall Hammer, especially the red and green colour scheme that pervades *Curse of Frankenstein* – whose lab pulses with red light as the creature begins to stir. Finally, Mark's secret chamber is haunted: film provides a modern equivalent for the Gothic novel's ghosts. Mark refuses to film his beloved Helen because his projector shows only the endlessly repeated images of the dead: the father who still controls him from beyond the grave, the corpse of Mark's mother on her death bed, his victims' final breaths. Film and audiotape become séance *mediums*, conjuring the dead, replaying the past. Mark, the only living person to flicker on that screen, is trapped among the ghosts. As in Lewton's films, the past cannot be overcome, and the solution is the same. Mark becomes his own final victim, impaling himself as cameras record everything, trapping his ghost to retrace his last steps.

Realism confronted the Gothic even more starkly in Peter Bogdanovich's *Targets* (1968), with Boris Karloff. As the creature in Universal's *Frankenstein*, Karloff had become horror talkies' first and biggest star, and his career had spanned the genre's history. Here, he essentially plays himself: Byron Orlok, elderly horror icon. *Targets* begins with an ending: in a screening room, Orlok discontentedly watches the finale of his latest film (a real Corman quickie, *The Terror*). All the Gothic clichés are there: secret passageway, crypt and vengeful revenant; the castle's collapse into a storm-lashed sea. But when the titles come up, we realise that what is at stake is not merely *The End* of *a* Gothic film but of *Gothic film*. Orlok announces his retirement, condemning as 'an antique . . . an anachronism' both himself and the 'Victorian' horror cinema that he personifies.

The rest of the film intercuts Orlok and a second protagonist, Bobby. Young, handsome, smiling, American and clean-cut, Bobby is the opposite of Karloff's monsters and gloomy aristocrats. But without any Jekyll-and-Hyde transformation Bobby becomes the film's real horror. He shoots his wife and mother for no specified reason and snipes at motorists from a gas tower. This is all filmed in a clean, antiseptic style antithetical to the Gothic opening: no shadowy corners, no shock cuts, no non-diegetic music. Finally these paths cross: Bobby ducks into a drive-in cinema hosting Orlok's final personal appearance. While *The Terror* shows, he snipes at the audience from behind the screen. The deadpan horror of these random deaths (based on the recent crimes of real-life sniper Charles Whitman) makes the Gothic scares on screen look as obsolete as Orlok predicted.

Targets rings a death knell for period horror, but Gothic themes survive even here. True to Gothic, it sets up a clash between 'anachronism' and modernity: as Orlok bows out, saying that 'The world belongs to the young', we cut to Bobby. But how contemporary would Bobby have seemed in 1968? The psychedelic rock blaring from his car radio only emphasises his *distance* from youth culture. Bobby's boy-scout face is unmoved by, impermeable to, the ear-hurting guitars. His square grey suit, the checked hunting jacket he wears at leisure, feel anachronistic, especially for hippy-filled California. He contrasts strikingly with a floppy-haired, slang-spouting hipster DJ who interviews Orlok. Bobby calls his father 'Sir' and his father calls him 'Bobby-boy', as if trapped in a father-knows-best 1950s sitcom. In the evening the well-groomed family relax around the electronic hearth as if posing in a 1950s advertisement for televisions, watching Joey Bishop, Rat Pack member and 1950s game show regular. Their sterile, pastel, all-mod-cons home, so unlike Karloff's castle, nonetheless feels like a relic of a more recently bygone era, with its mounted antlers, mass-produced paintings and Hawaiian honeymoon photos. The defining scene shows the family around the dinner table, bowing their heads to say grace before Pops, authoritative with his military-looking haircut, carves the roast. Bogdanovich (2003) calls it 'a Norman Rockwell image', invoking the painter whose magazine covers (like *Saying Grace*, 1951) idealised old-fashioned, small-town American life.

Bobby's world echoes the *Leave it to Beaver* idyll created by 50s ads and television: an idyll that the 1960s counter-culture had denounced as a propagandist fantasy, a cloak for an era and a way of life that a new generation considered insular, oppressively patriarchal, blithely consumerist, repressive and repressed (Bloom and Breines 2003: 1–11; Graham 1991). And yet 1960s radicalism had not banished those values: many Americans still lived in 'the fifties', as demonstrated by the 1968 presidential election of Richard Nixon, arch-Cold War scaremonger and vice-president from 1953 to 1961. Moreover, the Commie-fearing 1950s worldview was still killing people in the Vietnam War. A repressive order, pronounced dead and yet clinging onto the present, its blinkered repressions erupting into violence: *Targets* proves the Gothic's adaptability, not its irrelevance.

Targets proved timely. Period horror faded into the margins as the 1960s became the 70s, owing partly to two other iconoclastic 1968 films, Polanski's *Rosemary's Baby* and (as Cronenberg notes) Romero's *Night of the Living Dead*. Both self-consciously manipulated and inverted horror conventions, and insisted on credible, even banal, contemporary characters and settings. Like *Targets*, *Night* exorcises Karloff's Gothic legacy: the zombies' first victim dies after impersonating Karloff. The innovations of 1968 did not kill the Gothic, but liberated it from settings and conventions that had become, in Orlok's words, 'high camp'. Filmmakers in the 1970s brought contemporary approaches to Gothic themes. The rural Gothic strain, begun by *Deliverance* (1972), pitted travellers from the city against backwoods primitives – and continues to do so in *Wrong Turn* (2003) and *Wolf Creek* (2005). This subgenre's sublime landscapes echo the high Gothic; it replaces castles with dilapidated shacks and farmhouses. In *The Texas Chain Saw Massacre* (1974), fashionable youngsters are tormented and dismembered by a cannibalistic family of slaughterhouse workers displaced by mechanisation. Such films, made as the hippy ideals of the 1960s collapsed into cynicism, rarely end by restoring order, and even seem to celebrate their assaults on civilised values. Often they present civilisation as hypocritical, and rural barbarity partly as what it represses or exploits. In *Deliverance*, the inbred yokels' sodomy of a 'city-boy' seems like a metaphor, or retribution, for a power company's 'rape' of their habitat. The backwater primitivism in *Chain Saw* seems to stand partly for truths that the more civilised prefer not to face: 'I like meat', one victim-to-be wails when talk turns to abattoirs, 'Please change the subject!'

Wes Craven's *Last House on the Left* (1972) and *The Hills Have Eyes* (1977) render civilisation and barbarism symmetrical. In each a respectable suburban family confronts a monstrous, murderous one: rapists in *Last House*, inbred cannibals in *Hills*. The veneer of civilisation slips as the 'good' family sadistically avenges its own: in *Last House* a prim mother seduces her daughter's killer and chews off his penis. In *The Wicker Man* (1973), a British variant, a Christian policeman takes on Scottish islanders who have reverted to ancient paganism and human sacrifice. It is unclear, though, who is the anachronism, especially as horror films are usually marketed to the young. The policeman's colleagues mock his old-fashioned primness, while the pagans' values seem closer to the radical youth culture of *Easy Rider*: free love, hedonism, new-age mysticism and communal farming. The casting of Christopher Lee, Hammer's Dracula, as the islanders' charismatic leader compounds the film's fraught relationship to the Gothic.

Halloween (1978), and the ensuing flood of body-counting, materialist 'slasher' films, proved a greater setback to the Gothic tradition, but did not extinguish it – as the most popular horror films of recent years confirm. In *Hostel* (2005), affluent American students are lured to Eastern Europe by the promise of sex-hungry girls, and end up trapped in a subterranean labyrinth where sadists pay to torture captives: Americans fetch the highest price. The cells literally drip with the Gothic atmosphere of Inquisition dungeons. The town (supposedly Bratislava), with its cobbled lanes and half-timbered houses, recalls Universal or Hammerland, though its prostitutes, street urchins and corrupt police perpetuate more recent stereotypes of Eastern European backwardness. Ostensibly this is a traditional Gothic tale of contemporary travellers confronting backwoods barbarism. But the categories of modernity and anachronism become blurred: the Americans also confront a reflection of themselves and their country. The torture trade is heavy-handedly likened to the backpackers' own sex tourism; moreover these images of bondage and cruelty inevitably invoke recent photographs of US soldiers abusing Iraqis at Abu Ghraib.[1] Three torturers have speaking roles: two come from Japan and Germany, the countries most notorious for brutalising prisoners-of-war in the past; the last and most prominent is a macho American. The barbarism of former times is brought home and up to date, linked to the realpolitik that props up enlightened civilisation's living standards: the Gothic novel's feudal tyrannies on an international scale.

The Exorcism of Emily Rose (2005) is a hybrid of courtroom drama and horror movie, in which a Catholic priest is tried for causing a sick girl's death by keeping her from medical treatment. Disregarding a diagnosis of psychotic epilepsy, the priest encouraged Emily's belief that demonic possession caused her seizures and visions, and that only exorcism could help. He was supported in this by her family: stern, devout, bovine types who disapprove of dancing, and whose battered, isolated Southern Gothic house contains no ornaments but crucifixes and devotional statuettes. The violent exorcism failed (because of the epilepsy drugs, the defence claims) and Emily died of injuries and malnutrition. The theme is quintessentially Gothic: a confrontation between a Catholic who favours 'irrational and archaic superstition', as the Methodist prosecutor calls it, and the massed forces of the Enlightenment (medicine, psychiatry, Protestantism, the legal system), with a virgin's tortured body as battleground. But the film, though nominally even-handed, systematically favours the priest. A pro-Catholic, pro-yokel horror tale: it is a remarkably direct inversion of the high Gothic novel.

So should the films discussed here be called Gothic? Their contemporary settings are no obstacle. Stoker's England is strikingly up-to-date, and if Gothic fiction's present can move, surely its past can too. To a society in such rapid flux as late-1960s America, even the last decade's lingering values can seem Gothic. Arguably *Targets* was truer to Gothic themes than the declining period films it quoted, in which the past increasingly seemed to menace only the past. These films, though, rarely sit well with what Baldick and Mighall consider the Gothic message: contemporary heroes and anachronistic villains; modernity's victory. Most show the victory of the past, of barbarism and irrationality; some relish assaulting the civilised present and exposing its hypocrisy. Lewton carefully invokes contemporary reality the better to undermine it. But this is how genres thrive. Any genre's classics include examples that radically interrogate its values and conventions: *The Wild Bunch* and *Little Big Man* re-imagine the Western from the perspectives of outlaws and Indians; *Chinatown* and *The Godfather* reversed fundamental expectations of the detective and gangster genres. The way to stifle a genre is to ignore it: by attacking, transforming or even inverting it, one proves its adaptability and continued relevance. Films like *The 7th Victim*, *The Exorcism of Emily Rose* and even *Targets* show that Gothic themes remain meaningful to audiences, even if looked at askew or upside-down.

NOTE

1 *Hostel*'s director, Eli Roth, has announced a remake of the anti-Vietnam War zombie film *Deathdream*, updated to Iraq.

WORKS CITED

Baldick, Chris, and Robert Mighall (2000) 'Gothic Criticism', in David Punter (ed.), *A Companion to the Gothic*, Oxford: Blackwell.

Bansak, Edmund G. (1995) *Fearing the Dark: The Val Lewton Career*, Jefferson, NC: McFarland.

Bloom, Alexander and Wini Breines (eds) (2003) *'Takin' it to the Streets': A Sixties Reader*, Oxford: Oxford University Press.

Bogdanovich, Peter (2003) *Targets*, DVD audio commentary, Paramount Pictures.

Graham, Alison (1991) 'Journey to the Center of the Fifties: The Cult of Banality', in J. P. Telotte (ed.), *The Cult Film Experience: Beyond All Reason*, Austin, TX: University of Texas Press.

Haberman, Steven (2005) *The 7th Victim*, DVD audio commentary, Warner Video.

Lowenstein, Adam (2005) *Shocking Representation: Historical Trauma, National Cinema, and the Modern Horror Film*, New York: Columbia University Press.

Nasr, Contantine (producer) (2005), *Shadows in the Dark: The Val Lewton Legacy*, Warner Video.

Newman, Kim (1999) *Cat People*, London: BFI Publishing.

Rodley, Chris (ed.) (1997) *Cronenberg on Cronenberg*, rev. edn, London: Faber and Faber.

Siegel, Joel E. (1972) *Val Lewton: The Reality of Terror*, London: Secker and Warburg in association with the British Film Institute.

Truffaut, François (1986) *Hitchcock by Truffaut*, rev. edn, London: Paladin.

Walpole, Horace (1964) *The Castle of Otranto*, London: Oxford University Press.

28

GOTHIC TELEVISION

EDDIE ROBSON

In his book *Goth Chic*, Gavin Baddeley surveys Gothic television and wonders 'whether TV could ever prove a suitable medium for Gothic drama' (Baddeley 2002: 106). His answer is firmly in the negative, particularly in relation to American television. He asserts that the concerns of Gothic are not shared by the television audience at large, and that a medium he describes as 'ruthlessly bland' cannot support shows that are 'dark or offbeat' (Baddeley 2002: 106). If one is of the opinion that Gothic is essentially a minority interest, dealing in dark and unpleasant subject matter, which must therefore be watered down in order to appeal to a mass audience, it would seem that American television – with the largest mass audience in the world – must be an inhospitable environment for Gothic. However, if one takes the view that Gothic is a 'safe' way of indulging and excising our fears – as Fred Botting writes, 'transgression, by crossing the social and aesthetic limits, serves to reinforce or underline their value and necessity, restoring or defining limits' – then television is a space as well suited to Gothic as any other. Botting also points out that 'In popular culture . . . Gothic writing thrived' (Botting 1996: 7, 15) during the eighteenth and nineteenth centuries, in which case television might well be the first place one would look for contemporary Gothic. Helen Wheatley, in her recent study of *Gothic Television*, argues that the link is quite natural, referring to these texts as 'the most domestic of genres on the most domestic of media' (Wheatley 2006: 25). Furthermore, an examination of Gothic material on television suggests that it is more deeply embedded in the American televisual language than it is in Britain.

Baddeley frames his overall argument with Stephen King's (overwhelmingly negative) thoughts on television: '[it] has really asked the impossible of its handful of horror programs – to terrify without really terrifying, to horrify without really horrifying'. Later he tells us that 'at heart *The X Files* [1993–2002] is a horror show' (Baddeley 2002: 90, 103), as an attempt to classify it more as Gothic than science fiction or crime. Yet such a move simplistically equates 'Gothic' with 'horror'. It is true that horror in the modern cinematic sense is not well suited to mainstream television due to broadcasting restrictions, but *The X Files'* tendency to leave its threats wholly or partly unknown – not fully seen or properly explained – was not just a way of contending with censorship and a modest budget. The notion that limitations of production resources can be a spur to creativity is a cliché repeated so often as to be banal, but it is less often recognised that limitations of censorship can, when approached intelligently, force creators to approach subject matter from unusual angles and generate fascinating ambiguities. The horror B-movies created by Val Lewton at RKO in the 1940s provide a fine example: produced under the strictures of the notoriously stringent Production Code, their horror was psychological and their supernatural elements were left ambiguous. If they are Gothic – and they have been repeatedly identified as such – then there is no reason why the censorship restrictions of modern television would preclude the production of Gothic material. Indeed, the ambiguity present in *The X Files* came to define the show, as it developed a sprawling, complex conspiracy back-story which even its creators struggled to pin down. In this sense (and in others), a series like *The X Files* is more Gothic than numerous horror films which aim to shock.

SOAP AND THE NATURE OF 'REALITY' IN AMERICAN TELEVISION

The discussion regarding the generic classification of *The X Files* highlights Gothic's genre flexibility. A good example of this flexibility is one of *The X Files'* key precursors, *Twin Peaks* (1990–1), which styles itself as a soap opera and has been identified by Wheatley as 'originating ... the Gothic trend in North American television drama in the 1990s and into the twenty-first century' (Wheatley 2006: 161). Yet *Twin Peaks* did not Gothicise the soap opera, but merely continued a tradition of Gothic elements in American soap.

Admittedly it is dangerous to overstate the extent to which British soaps are 'realistic' compared to their American counterparts. As Daniel Chandler notes,

> Viewers differ in the extent to which they judge soaps as 'reflections of reality'. Whilst American soaps such as *Dallas* and *Dynasty* are seen (at least by British viewers) as largely in the realms of fantasy, British soaps are more often framed by viewers in terms of 'realism'. However, it is misleading to regard even 'realist soaps' as simply 'representing real life'. The representation of 'reality' is not unproblematic: television is not a 'window' on an objective and unmediated world.
>
> (Chandler 1994)

Yet we can think of realism as an aesthetic, a strategy to give a piece of fiction the appearance of greater reality, and British soaps do make use of this. 'We don't make life, we reflect it' (cited in Geraghty 1991: 16) declared Julia Smith, co-creator of *EastEnders* (1985–present). This has long been seen as the role of the soap opera in Britain: to reflect its audience, which is seen as largely working-class. As Smith said, 'I expect the audience to consist of working people who watch television around tea-time before going to the bingo or the pub' (cited in Buckingham 1987: 577). There is evidence that much of the audience does not treat soap opera as being as realistic as creators and critics often assume – 'Viewers familiar with the characters and conventions of a particular soap may often judge the programme largely in its own terms (or perhaps in terms of the genre) rather than with reference to some external "reality"' (Chandler 1994) – but the aim of the creators certainly seems to be for realism, and the unobtrusive, conventional visual style of British soap supports this reading.

The priorities of the American soap opera are markedly different: Tania Modleski identifies that, whilst the commercials that run during American daytime soap operas reflect the everyday lives of the audience,

> The saggy diapers, yellow wax build-up and carpet smells making up the world of daytime television ads are rejected by soap operas in favour of 'Another World', as the very title of one soap opera announces, a world in which characters only deal with the 'large' problems of human existence: crime, love, death and dying.
>
> (Modleski 1984: 588)

Not only do American soaps frequently revolve around wealthy and glamorous characters who could not possibly reflect the lifestyles of the majority of their audience, but also the American soap's willingness to embrace melodrama has, at times, extended into outright fantasy and the supernatural. *Dark Shadows* (1966–71) included vampires and werewolves among its central characters; one of the characters in *Passions* (1999–2007) was a 300-year-old witch; whilst *Desperate Housewives* (2004–present), which restored the traditional soap to primetime, is narrated by a dead woman. Even those soaps with no supernatural elements can have a Gothic quality: hokey plot devices, such as amnesia, long-lost twins and the return of characters thought dead, raise Gothic themes such as fear of the past and the uncanny presence of the doppelgänger. Noting these and other aspects of the American soap, Richard Davenport-Hines concludes that 'television soap opera provides the twentieth-century equivalent of Gothic novels' (Davenport-Hines 1998: 144). (One could even argue that the cost-cutting measure of filming many daytime soaps entirely indoors gives them a claustrophobic quality – in contrast to British soaps, which make extensive use of backlots crafted to look like real streets.) *Twin Peaks* did not invent Gothic tropes within the soap opera – it merely recognised them and replayed them in a more overtly Gothic manner. Notably, when British television tried to do a 'fantasy' soap – *Springhill* (1996–7), about a Liverpool family unwittingly manipulated by celestial forces – it enjoyed a cult following but did not become a mainstream success.

The soap opera is an extreme example of American television's tendency to deal in heightened reality more than British television does: directly reflecting the audience's world appears less of a priority for American programme-makers. This perhaps explains why contemporary-set American drama has proved more amenable to non-realist themes than its British counterpart (though this is not to deny that British examples exist). The best example is the long-established tradition of the 'fantasy' comedy, such as *Bewitched* (1964–72), *Mork and Mindy* (1978–82) and *Third Rock From the Sun* (1996–2001). This tradition has easily encompassed Gothic tropes, as in *The Addams Family* (1964–6) and *The Munsters* (1964–6) – albeit usually to subvert them for comic effect.

244

In an environment such as American TV where genres are very clearly defined, generic hybrids are easier to create and this suits Gothic well. *Buffy the Vampire Slayer* (1997–2003) is an obvious example, dismissed by Baddeley as 'At best . . . Goth-lite' because 'Most of the Gothic elements that draw connoisseurs to the genre – decadence, deviance, death – are mere window-dressing for the show's primetime themes of teen trauma and adolescent angst, if they're there at all' (Baddeley 2002: 104). This view fails to consider how the teen drama and supernatural thriller aspects of *Buffy* are integrally linked. The fact that the characters in *Buffy* really do deal with matters of life and death, and possess knowledge of a darker side to the world which separates them from their blissfully ignorant peers, communicates how important teenage problems can feel to teenagers: as Rhonda Wilcox succinctly puts it, 'In *Buffy*'s world, the problems teenagers face become literal monsters . . . From the earliest episodes, it was apparent to attentive viewers that *Buffy* operated on a symbolic level' (Wilcox 2005: 18). The addition of Gothic stylings to *Buffy* is far from superficial. It is one of many recent American series to which notions of the afterlife are central, such as *Dead Like Me* (2003–4), *Medium* (2004–present) and *Six Feet Under* (2000–5): in the last of these, the 'ghosts' are not used to drive the storylines, but as a means by which the characters work through their issues (and it is never clear whether the 'ghosts' are real or imaginary). In *Six Feet Under* the dead are a part of everyday life.

The fact that British society is more secular perhaps accounts for its more cautious approach to similar subject matter. It is notable that the recent rise in British Gothic television demonstrates clear American influences, and has followed the rise of Gothic television in America: *Sea of Souls* (2004–7), *Afterlife* (2005–6) and *Torchwood* (2006–present) all show the lasting influence of *The X Files*,[1] whilst *Strange* (2002–3) and *Hex* (2004–5) followed in the wake of *Buffy*.[2] It is also notable that much British Gothic television has sought to 'explain' the supernatural: *The Stone Tape* (1972) reveals ghosts as psychic impressions embedded in stone, whilst *The Nightmare Man* (1981) is a horror narrative with a sci-fi premise. *Doctor Who* (1963–89, 1996, 2005–present) balances Gothic tendencies with a strongly rationalist and secular attitude. In the *Doctor Who* serial 'The Dæmons' (1971), a dormant devil-like figure is revealed to be an amoral alien scientist, and black magic is one of the remnants of his race's advanced science; another alien scientist in 'Ghost Light' (1989) discovers the futility of opposing progress, and is defeated by Enlightenment itself. 'The Face of Evil' (1977) concerns a religious war on a planet where the 'God' followed by the warring factions is discovered to be a schizophrenic computer with the Doctor's personality.

Head writer Russell T. Davies openly applies an atheist view to the twenty-first-century revival of *Doctor Who*: 'I'm deeply atheist. If they haven't reached that point by the Year Five Billion, then I give up! . . . That's what I believe, so that's what you're going to get' (Cook 2005: 18). The 2006 episodes 'The Impossible Planet' and 'The Satan Pit' depict a creature claiming to be the mythical devil, eventually revealed to be a creature originating from before the birth of our universe; its presence influences the mythology of countless cultures. The creature's provenance runs counter to the Doctor's own experience, as he admits:

> It's funny, isn't it? The things you make up, the rules. If that thing had said it came from beyond the universe, I'd believe it. But before the universe? Impossible. Doesn't fit my rule. Still, that's why I keep travelling. To be proved wrong.
>
> (*Doctor Who* 2006)

The Doctor's approach to such matters is scientific in spirit, even if the science of the series is usually totally invented. In a sense this is just semantic: giving an alien provenance to Satan or black magic does not alter the fact that they are beyond what we can understand. However, through the figure of the Doctor – whose knowledge is far in advance of ours – we are given the promise that they can be understood. By comparison, the rationalist figure in *The X Files* is, more often than not, shown to be incorrect.

THE X FILES: ONGOING NARRATIVE AS GOTHIC TRAP

The fact that the 'monsters' of *The Addams Family* and *The Munsters* are not unsettling, but merely incongruous, in the 'normal' world of the sitcom is characteristic of American TV of the 1960s and 1970s. Television of this era tended to produce self-contained episodes, where what transpired one week had no bearing on the next. This limits the potential for Gothic because the world these programmes take place in is essentially stable: the continued existence of the Munsters and the Addamses in their environment is never seriously threatened. It is notable that many of British TV's best-known examples of Gothic horror were not formatted as ongoing series, instead taking the form of one-offs such as *The Stone Tape*, serials like *The Nightmare Man* or anthology series like *Hammer House of Horror* (1980). Similarly, the most overt American Gothic television series prior to the 1980s were anthology series like *The Twilight Zone* (1959–64, 1985–9, 2002–3), which had no requirement to maintain the status quo for the following episode.

This tendency towards self-contained narratives might suggest that Gothic is not well suited to the ongoing series format. However, by embracing the notion that events in one episode could have permanent ramifications, *The X Files* demonstrates that this is not the case. It is useful to compare the show with one of its major influences, *Kolchak: The Night Stalker* (1974–5), which follows a reporter for a Chicago news service who encounters aliens and supernatural beings. Its fantastical elements aside, the style of *Kolchak* is akin to any number of 1970s detective series; however, as *X Files* writer Frank Spotnitz noted, applying these stories to this self-contained format caused problems. 'One of the things I struggled with', he said when promoting his 2005 remake of *Kolchak*, was how could it be that Carl Kolchak was a reporter for a newspaper and, first of all, managed to come across these things every week, and second, comes across them, and it doesn't change the world based upon his reporting.

(Anon. 2006b)

The fact that the mysteries were totally unconnected created a sense of absurd coincidence, and although Kolchak would be left in no doubt that supernatural forces were at work, he would lack concrete evidence or his story would seem implausible – often leaving the plot less than fully resolved. As Spotnitz noted, the set-up had been more effective in the two TV movies from which the series was a spin-off – *The Night Stalker* (1972) and *The Night Strangler* (1973) – which suggests that the series did not take advantage of the specific properties of television as a medium.

The creative team behind *The X Files* determined to learn from *Kolchak*. The criminal element of each *X Files* story is often resolved – if it is a murder mystery, for example, the murderer is often identified and caught, or dies – but significant questions are left unanswered. The investigators have done their jobs (unlike Kolchak, who never seemed to get any stories in print), but Mulder is eager to locate the supernatural explanation and is frustrated by the presentation of plausible, rational alternative solutions. Although the viewer generally gets heavy hints towards the truth, most cases end with an element of ambiguity. This approach, which allows *The X Files* to exist in a space between two sets of generic requirements, works because it is an ongoing narrative, inspired by the movements of 1980s series such as *Magnum, P.I.* (1980–8): '*The X Files*, like *Magnum*, walks an intermediate path between the episodic series and the open-ended serial, one that is for the most part episodic but in which certain ongoing plotlines carry across episodes and even seasons' (Reeves, Rodgers and Epstein 1996: 33). Previously the ongoing narrative had largely been the province of the soap opera: as Wheatley notes, 'the open-ended soap-style narrative lends itself very well to the Gothic, as a genre of uncertainty' (Wheatley 2006: 148) and it is this which *The X Files* exploits for its Gothic qualities. Even though an episode of *The X Files* might not reach any conclusions on its own, it still makes a contribution towards the viewer's understanding of the central characters (who are often changed by their experiences, Scully's remarkably resilient scepticism notwithstanding) and expands the world in which the series takes place. Its resistance to closure therefore becomes one of its most appealing factors for its audience.

As *The X Files* told more stories about its world, it developed an ongoing back-story which was appropriate to the theme of conspiracy: the conspiracy theorist sees potential links between everything, and so *X Files* viewers were encouraged to seek links between episodes. The conspiracy is what makes *The X Files* truly Gothic. In his introduction to *Gothic Tales*, Chris Baldick notes that:

typically a Gothic tale will invoke the tyranny of the past (a family curse, the survival of archaic forms of despotism and of superstition) with such weight as to

> stifle the hopes of the present (the liberty of the heroine or hero) within the dead-end of physical incarceration.
>
> (Baldick 1992: xix)

In *The X Files*, the 'tyranny of the past' is that of the political and economic elite of the 1950s, 1960s and 1970s, most obviously the legacy of Watergate but also that of the generation who profited from America's post-war renaissance. In the series these forces take the form of the 'Syndicate', a group formed after WWII to enact government cover-ups by the use of diversionary tactics such as faked UFO sightings, illustrating Catherine Spooner's comment that the 'construction of fake histories is integral to Gothic texts' (Spooner 2006: 38). The syndicate acquired so much influence and autonomy that they were able to manipulate events in their own interest. Most significantly they encountered an alien plot to colonise the earth, which they cooperated with. The effect this has on their descendants reflects the issues faced by members of the post-baby-boom 'Generation X', confirming the notion of them as overshadowed, disenfranchised and with a lingering impression that they are being left to deal with the fallout from their parents' golden age. In this context, the title of *The X Files* is remarkably apt: it takes the conviction of many Generation X-ers that their parents had effectively mortgaged their future for short-term gain and turns it into a specific threat.[3] (*The X Files* then complicates the issue by revealing that the Syndicate has also been stalling the colonisation in the hope of sabotaging it, but the younger generation's sense that their future is not in their own hands remains.)

Through the domination of this regime, the hopes of the present are stifled and although the hero, Fox Mulder, is not physically imprisoned, his sense of freedom is curtailed because he lacks certain truths that are important to him (chiefly, the fate of his abducted sister). In a sense he is also imprisoned within the institution of the FBI: he pursues his investigations by making use of the FBI's apparatus, but his own employers – the US government – are responsible for the conspiracy, and he is within their control. Mulder is himself revealed to be another of their diversionary tactics, weakening the credibility of believers in extraterrestrial life by the force of his unfounded conviction. The conspiracy's use of fake sightings, artefacts and abductions to deflect attention from the truth about extraterrestrials reflects how 'the Gothic . . . is continuously based on ghostings of the already spectral or at least resymbolisations of what is already symbolic and thus more fake than real' (Hogle 2001a: 295). The fakes are, paradoxically, evidence of the real, because they would not have been produced if there was no genuine extraterrestrial life to conceal.

The entire series can therefore be seen as a labyrinth in which Mulder is trapped by the oppressive relics of an earlier regime, pursuing cases which may or may not be significant to the bigger picture, and never able to locate the definitive truth: a rendition of the Gothic narrative which is specific to television, and specifically post-1980s television. Susan Sontag criticises this model of narrative when comparing television to literature:

The so-called stories that we are told on television . . . implicitly affirm the idea that all information is potentially relevant (or 'interesting'), that all stories are endless – or if they do stop, it is not because they have come to an end but, rather, because they have been upstaged by a fresher or more lurid or eccentric story.

(Sontag 2007: 6)

This is a reductive view of television's narrative possibilities, as the medium has frequently been used to tell self-contained 'novelistic' stories: it also suggests that television narratives strive to create the impression that they do not make choices and instead display unmediated reality, a mode of story-telling which Sontag regards as encouraging moral detachment, because it does not suggest judgements as to what is better or more important. It is difficult to reconcile this view of how television works with the heightened reality of much American television, especially a stylised series like *The X Files* which is concerned with seeking hidden truths. Furthermore, television is more apt to make use of parallel narratives, offering closure in one thread whilst another begins (*Twin Peaks* does this, as do all soaps), rather than merely 'upstaging' the old story and forgetting about it. *The X Files* is an example of a show which genuinely does 'upstage' its own stories, but it draws attention to this process by not merely dropping them but actively debunking them. This is key to the way that *The X Files* achieves its effects, creating its atmosphere of uncertainty. Jerrold E. Hogle notes that:

Any level of 'truth' beyond illusion is deferred indefinitely, particularly since we cannot now be sure if the latest revelations are but simulations designed by hidden manipulators (like those at Fox-TV) to steer the responses of the interpreters in the story and the viewers of the series.

(Hogle 2001b: 170)

Not only does television offer a suitable home for Gothic, it is also a unique site, offering narrative possibilities unavailable elsewhere and the potential for a distinctive kind of Gothic. A recent increase in the production of such texts, initiated by American television and followed by its British counterpart, means that interest in Gothic on television is on the increase – *Buffy* in particular has inspired a wealth of scholarship – and this has led to greater recognition of the substantial common ground between the aesthetic and the medium, and acknowledgement that television fits into Gothic's heritage as a part of popular culture. Far from being sidelined as a watered-down form of the genre, television Gothic merits recognition as the means by which the aesthetic is arguably most widely disseminated today.

NOTES

1 *Torchwood* was described by its creator Russell T. Davies as '*The X Files* meets *This Life*' (cited in Anon. 2005) in its first BBC press release, whilst *Afterlife* creator Stephen Volk originally conceived the show in the mid-1990s when 'ITV was fleetingly

interested in producing a homegrown supernatural series because of *The X Files'* success over here' (O'Brien 2005: 16).

2 *Hex* executive producer Dean Hargrove acknowledged that the series was aimed at *Buffy* fans, but said that '*Buffy* was a send-up of the genre. *Hex* takes itself seriously' (cited in Anon. 2006a). This comment arguably indicates a basic misconception at the heart of *Hex*: certainly the series performed very poorly compared with *Buffy*, which originally aired in the UK on the same network, Sky One.

3 Douglas Coupland, author of *Generation X* (1991), later wrote *Girlfriend in a Coma* (1998), in which some central characters work on a science fiction series produced in Vancouver. The series is unnamed, but is clearly *The X Files*.

WORKS CITED

Anon (2005) 'Captain Jack to Get his own Series in New Russell T. Davies Drama for BBC THREE', www.bbc.co.uk/pressoffice/pressreleases/stories/2005/10_october/17/torch.shtml (accessed 2 April 2007).

—— (2006a) 'Summer TV: June 2006', www.ew.com/ew/article/0,1200094_2,00.html (accessed 2 April 2007).

—— (2006b) 'X Marks the Night Stalker', www.scifi.com/sfw/issue441/news.html (accessed 28 March 2007).

Baddeley, Gavin (2002) *Goth Chic*, London: Plexus.

Baldick, Chris (1992) 'Introduction', *The Oxford Book of Gothic Tales*, Oxford: Oxford University Press.

Botting, Fred (1996) *Gothic*, London: Routledge.

Buckingham, David (1987) 'EastEnders: Creating the Audience', in Paul Marris and Sue Thornham (eds), *Media Studies: A Reader*, Edinburgh: Edinburgh University Press.

Chandler, Daniel (1994) 'The TV Soap Opera Genre and its Viewers', www.aber.ac.uk/media/Modules/TF33120/soaps.html (accessed 16 March 2007).

Cook, Benjamin (2005) 'Tooth and Claw – The Russell T. Davies Interview (Part Two)', *Doctor Who Magazine*, 360, 18 August.

Davenport-Hines, Richard (1998) *Gothic: 400 Years of Excess, Horror, Evil and Ruin*, London: Fourth Estate.

Doctor Who, 'The Satan Pit' (2006) scr. Matthew Jones, dir. James Strong, Cardiff: BBC Wales, 10 June.

Geraghty, Christine (1991) *Women and Soap Opera: A Study of Prime-Time Soaps*, Cambridge: Polity Press.

Hogle, Jerrold E. (2001a) 'The Gothic Ghost of the Counterfeit and the Progress of Abjection', in David Punter (ed.), *A Companion to the Gothic*, Oxford: Blackwell.

—— (2001b) 'The Gothic at our Turn of the Century: The Culture of Simulation and the Return of the Body', in Fred Botting (ed.), *The Gothic*, Cambridge: D. S. Brewer.

O'Brien, Steve (2005) 'Ghost Watching', *SFX*, 128: 16.

Reeves, Jimmie L., Mark C. Rodgers and Michael Epstein (1996) 'Rewriting Popularity', in David Lavery, Angela Hague and Marla Cartwright (eds), *Deny All Knowledge: Reading the X-Files*, London: Faber and Faber.

Sontag, Susan (2007) 'Pay Attention to the World', *Guardian* Review, 17 March, pp. 4–6.

Spooner, Catherine (2006) *Contemporary Gothic*, London: Reaktion Books.

Wheatley, Helen (2006) *Gothic Television*, Manchester: Manchester University Press.

Wilcox, Rhonda (2005) *Why Buffy Matters*, London: I. B. Tauris.

29

GOTHIC AND THE GRAPHIC NOVEL

ANDY W. SMITH

INTRODUCTION

The history of comic art has seen the medium draw upon a range of generic influences that have established the critical ground from which to assess its impact upon contemporary culture. From the early science-fiction fantasy of Depression-era America, through to the horror of the 1950s *Tales from the Crypt* (EC), the comic form has adapted and assimilated different genres, culminating in the populist superhero subgenre. Similarly, Gothic fiction has also adopted and assimilated different textual and thematic materials, diversifying into theatre, cinema and new media. It is precisely in these areas of generic hybridity that comics and the Gothic find a shared textual *and* contextual space. As Fred Botting notes about the historical status of the Gothic:

> Existing in relation to other forms of writing, Gothic texts have generally been marginalized, excluded from the sphere of acceptable literature ... however, in the realm of popular culture, Gothic writing thrived and exerted an influence on more properly literary forms.
>
> (Botting 1996: 15)

This chapter will argue for ways in which the thematic, structural and historical conventions and tropes of the Gothic have been appropriated within the field of comic art. At the same time, it will assess the impact comics have had upon the Gothic, suggesting a mutual generic convergence. Whilst acknowledging the range and importance of comic art that originates from Europe, Asia, Australia and South America, the argument will focus primarily on British and American writers and artists who have influenced the way 'graphic novels' have explored the motifs, themes and visual signifiers of Gothic literature and cinema.

THE ART OF COMICS

This ability of comic art to create a series of visual effects with prose allows the medium to conflate image with text in a way that neither cinema nor literature can imitate. The aesthetics of comics is defined by the unique use of montage, graphic matching, juxtaposed framing and the colour coding of speech and action. The comic book format allows for different-sized panels, spoken dialogue, narrative prose and characters' interior monologues to create multifaceted meanings for a reader. The use of capitals as script is a tradition in comic book lettering, with emphasis on certain words usually conveyed by bold or italics. David Ian Rabey has written: 'The simultaneous presentation of image and text permits a narrative speed and focus comparable only to film, but the permanence of these allows for reverberate juxtaposition and studied recall, narrative second by second' (Rabey 1989: 74). Quite often the placement of a particular image within a panel is designed to affect the reader's experience of the word/image correlation, as the comics writer Alan Moore notes:

> The reader can focus upon one panel for as long as it takes to absorb all of the information that is there, and then move on to the next. If they want to see whether there's some correlation between a bit of dialogue and something that happened a couple of scenes ago, they can, in a matter of seconds, flip back.
>
> (Moore 2003)

A comic book can be read in a variety of ways by the reader, where the image is placed in conjunction with narrative strategies that move through different spatial frames and can take place in a range of temporal moments – the past, present and future. The emphasis on excess, bricolage and juxtaposition that can be found in comics is also a feature of the development of Gothic literature, signifying fantasy, horror and the uncanny as outside of realist forms of representation.

The 'studied recall' of image/text becomes one way in which Gothic forms are appropriated by the comic book format. Julia Round has written that 'Structural multiplicity is a defining feature of the gothic tradition' which can also be found in the way comic art uses 'visual strategies' to allow 'the narrative to sustain contradictions and interruptions' (Round 2005: 359, 361). One way in which the Gothic can be re-evaluated through the medium of graphic novels is through exploring various narrative and visual strategies that comic art uses to retell old stories in new ways, as Round notes:

> The many narrative elements that the comic book medium has at its disposal would seem to testify to the supplementary nature of its use of colour and framing techniques – and so perhaps their inclusion serves another purpose: sustaining the gothic tradition.
>
> (Round 2005: 362)

The collaborative nature of the medium includes pencillers, inkers, letterers and colourists, and whilst the work of visual artists is fundamental to the art form, it is the authorship of writers such as Alan Moore, Frank Miller, Neil Gaiman and Garth Ennis that has contributed to the development of graphic novels as a branch of Gothic literature.

GOTHIC APPROPRIATION

The comic superhero subgenre underwent a radical makeover in the mid-1980s, primarily through the work of the American Frank Miller and the English writer

Alan Moore. Miller's prescient *The Dark Knight Returns* (1986, DC Comics) is a re-working of the Batman character, a figure already replete with Gothic meaning. Miller changes the established perception of Batman's environment by placing the action in a future which is also paradoxically the present, where an ageing, embittered Bruce Wayne is tempted out of retirement by a Gotham City ruled by a lawless gang culture. The fictional world of the book is situated in a Cold War America controlled by a right-wing Reagan administration, whose soporific population is fed an endless diet of television talk shows and lifestyle programmes. Batman's traditional nemesis the Joker, having undergone psychiatric rehabilitation, is awakened out of his catatonic state by seeing the Bat symbol on a late-night television talk show, where social commentators debate the resurrection of the vigilante: 'THE ONLY THING HE SIGNIFIES IS AN ABERRANT PSYCHOTIC FORCE, MORALLY BANKRUPT, POLITICALLY HAZARDOUS, REACTIONARY, PARANOID – A DANGER TO EVERY CITIZEN IN GOTHAM!' (Miller 1986: 33)

Batman's return to vigilantism is in direct conflict with the government edict banning all superheroes apart from Superman, who works covertly for American Intelligence against the Soviet threat. Miller reinvents Batman as a 'political liability' in a society where moral certainties are constantly in question, facing off in one last fight against an Establishment Superman who, in the words of Batman, has become 'a joke'. In this final climatic battle Batman fakes his own death and the conclusion of the graphic novel sees Bruce Wayne training a covert underground guerrilla force, preparing his students for a war against a world without heroes.

One of the major elements that comics have borrowed from the Gothic is that of the doppelgänger or double identity. Miller reinterprets the ambivalence of the established Batman universe as a series of sublimated psycho-sexual doppelgängers: the Joker can only co-exist in Batman's presence, as he exclaims when coming out of his catatonia: 'DARLING!' Despite undergoing extensive therapy, Harvey Dent can only control his criminal personality 'Two-Face' through the flipping of a scarred coin. The figure of Batman's sidekick Robin is recast by Miller as a girl, thus referencing and critiquing the homoerotic subtext that has haunted that relationship since the 1950s. Most importantly, there seems to be a final reconciliation of the Bruce Wayne/Batman secret identity schematic that is a staple of the superhero genre – the end of the graphic novel sees the 'death' of Batman and the regeneration of Bruce Wayne, thus bringing to an end the 'doubleness' that characterises the genre.

The moral consciousness, transgressive energy and political cynicism of *The Dark Knight Returns* mark it out as one of the most important comic book publishing events of the last 30 years. Originally published as four 46-page comic books, the assembling of *The Dark Knight Returns* into one volume popularised the term 'graphic novel', a commercial function as well as giving the comic industry legitimacy as a serious form of literature. Miller's further reinvention of the superhero genre with *Elektra: Assassin* (1988, DC) and his retelling of Batman's origins in *Year One* (1987, DC) were symptomatic of a wider movement in the late 1980s that sought to introduce transparent political and ideological themes and ideas into the world of comics. Alan Moore's *Swamp Thing* (1983–7, DC), *V for Vendetta* (1982–5, 1988–9 drawn by David Lloyd, Titan) and *Watchmen* (1986–7, drawn by Dave Gibbons, DC) were also part of this output in the 1980s. Recognised within the comics industry as a key figure in the development of the graphic novel, Alan Moore has been working at the very margins of conceptual comic art during the course of his career.

GOTHIC HYBRIDITY

Swamp Thing began as a horror-influenced comic from DC in the 1970s. Created by Len Wein and Berni Wrightson, Swamp Thing is the mutated form of scientist Alex Holland, who, whilst working on a new 'bio-restorative formula' to develop plant life, is blown up by rivals and deposited into the swamps of Louisiana. Emerging from this primordial matter, Holland is transformed into a 'walking, thinking bog monster' (Moore, Bissette and Totleben 1987). In Moore's hands what was a fairly predictable horror/fantasy comic is taken into the realms of Gothic excess; not only does the figure of the Swamp Thing reference archetypal myths such as the golem and classic Gothic conflicts between science and the supernatural, it also becomes a sublime evocation of environmental awareness and political action, exemplified by Moore's invocation of the creature as a 'plant elemental' connected to all living plant organisms on earth. As Moore himself noted, 'Swamp Thing isn't a typical horror story, nor is it a superhero book. It's a mutant. A hybrid' (Moore *et al.* 1987).

Moore has further explored the referencing of Gothic conventions in *From Hell* (illustrated by Eddie Campbell, 1989–96) and *The League of Extraordinary Gentlemen* (illustrated by Kevin O'Neill, America's Best Comics, 1999–2006). The latter is a secret society composed of classic figures from Victorian Gothic fiction. This group comprises Miss Mina Murray from *Dracula*, Mr Edward Hyde (and his alter ego Dr Henry Jekyll), 'The Invisible Man' Hawley Griffin, Allan Quatermain and Captain Nemo. This band of retroactive anti-heroes are there to 'defend the Empire', with Moore drawing upon nostalgic visions of Albion to create a comic that interrogates the ideology of Victorian England through an absorption and rewriting of Gothic forms.

In volume II of *League of Extraordinary Gentlemen* (2003), England is under attack from Martian aliens. Moore's graphic novel obviously invokes H. G. Wells' *War of the Worlds* (1898), as well as characters from Wells' *The Island of Dr Moreau* (1896). Miss Murray and Allan Quatermain are sent on a mission to obtain a secret weapon to defeat the Martian invasion force. The 'secret weapon' turns out to be one of the hybrid animal experiments of Dr Moreau, who has created horrific versions of Rupert the Bear and Toad of Toad Hall in a typical Moore referencing of cultural tropes taken from English children's stories. Moore's deployment of Gothic signifiers is reflexive, humorous and inventive: in volume I, the Invisible Man is first discovered causing havoc in an all-girls school; in volume II, Edward Hyde brutally rapes and murders Griffin on discovering Griffin's betrayal to the Martian invaders. Murray and Quatermain engage in an intense sexual relationship, their bodies marked by their Gothic inscription. Murray's neck bears a tattoo of vampire bites, 'not quite the two discreet puncture-marks of legend' (Moore 2003). Quatermain is a recovering opium junkie whose frail and withered body is in direct contrast to portrayals of the character as the embodiment of virile Imperial masculinity.

In *From Hell*, Moore presents a series of 16 chapters that explore the stories and myths that have surrounded the Jack the Ripper murders from a number of different perspectives. Subtitled 'A Melodrama in Sixteen Parts', *From Hell* investigates classic Ripper tropes involving Masonic ritual, conspiracy theories involving the Royal Family and the resultant Establishment cover-up. Moore uses various Ripper apocrypha to create a graphic novel that exposes the Ripper murders not as some titillating Victorian Grand Guignol (as has been so often portrayed in cinema) but as a series of dreadful atrocities committed by a deranged and psychotic sadist, culminating in the extraordinary ritual mutilation of Mary Kelly. Moore notes that:

> What I wanted to do was to actually make this a genuine horror book, if you like, in that I wouldn't allow the readers that escape. If they wanted to see what it was like to cut up women, then I wanted to show them the plain and awful truth of it, unadorned. Particularly in the Mary Kelly chapter, where we spend almost the entire 40-page episode in a room with him cutting up the final victim.
>
> (Moore 2003)

In dedicating the book to the victims – 'You and your demise: of these things alone are we certain. Goodnight, ladies' – Moore offers a fictionalised account of their lives that places them as individuals within the social context of the period. In freeing the victims from being objects of violence to subjects of memory, Moore represents their horrific murders not as a vicarious pleasure but as a tangible, awful and pathetic reality.

In Chapter 14 entitled 'Gull, ascending', the perpetrator of the murders, Dr William Gull, has a vision of moving through space and time whilst locked in an asylum cell as his nurse and doctor engage in an act of intercourse. In a meticulously researched chapter Moore connects, amongst other images, the nightmares of Robert Louis Stevenson, the visions of William Blake, the Moors Murderers Ian Brady and Myra Hindley and the 'Yorkshire Ripper' Ian Sutcliffe. In doing so Moore and Campbell employ the architecture of Ripper mythology as a way of prefiguring the rise of the twentieth-century serial killer, a horror that no Gothic fiction can sensationalise.

GOTHIC VERTIGO

Both Moore and Miller were the forerunners of a new generation of artists and writers who were to transform the cultural context of comic art, resulting in major institutional changes to the production, reception and marketing of comics for 'mature readers'. One of the most important elements in the development of graphic novels as a Gothic art form was the establishment of independent comic publishing houses such as Dark Horse Books (founded 1986), and the realisation within the management of DC that a separate arm of their publishing empire was needed to cater for a host of writers and artists whose work explored 'adult' themes and scenarios. The imprint Vertigo was created by DC to specifically cater for a mature, adult readership that was outside the comic book demographic of teenage readers.

Vertigo's remit was to attract writers and artists who would create continuing stories for a mature audience within the traditional structure of the 24-page monthly comic book. This attempt to maintain the structural format of the comic allows writers to build in story arcs and character development in the best tradition of serial story-telling: the most popular Vertigo imprint, Neil Gaiman's *The Sandman*, ran for 75 issues between 1987 and 1996. *The Sandman* resulted in ten volumes of graphic novels, each containing a series of interlocking stories about Morpheus, also known as Dream, and his 'family of anthropomorphic personifications' (Bender, 1999: xii) known as 'the Endless'. Made up of Destiny, Desire, Despair, Delirium, the missing brother Destruction and Death, they exist in 'realms' that personify specific human traits and emotions. The character of Death, Dream's 'big sister', is costumed all in black with an Egyptian ankh as her 'sigil' and ornate eye make-up. Death is here configured as a subcultural 'Goth', whose sunny disposition and cheerful optimism are in stark contrast to her melancholic and obsessive brother. It is the metonymic function of the characters, as well as the thematic and structural formats of the work, that links Gaiman's *Sandman* series to Gothic fantasy and horror.

The Sandman excavated unfamiliar, arcane and well-known myths, stories and beliefs. One of the major mythic figures that Gaiman reinvents is that of Lucifer. Gaiman's Lucifer was first seen in the collected volume *Season of Mists* (1992, DC/Vertigo), where Dream travels to Hell to face the 'Lightbringer' but instead finds the Lord of Hell quitting his realm and handing the keys over to Dream. Lucifer has his wings sliced off and ends the story sitting on a beach in Australia, admiring the sunset. The unity of vision that Gaiman had for all 75 issues established the integrity of its fictional universe, often looping themes and characters in a playful ontological commentary on dreams and stories. As Hy Bender writes:

> Over the course of the series, we meet mythic figures such as Lucifer, Kali, and Orpheus; historical figures such as Augustus Caesar, Marco Polo, Geoffrey Chaucer, and an ageing John Belushi; bizarre figures such as a librarian who preserves books that were dreamt of but never written, a woman who keeps house with the ghost of a man who impregnated her, and a nightmare who uses his teeth-filled eye sockets to munch on the eyeballs of his victims.
>
> (Bender, 1999: xii)

Gaiman's narrative work on *The Sandman* was accompanied by artists who helped shape the design of the comic, none more so then Dave McKean, whose vivid cover images, composed of tableaux that utilised different materials and textures, were an important part of defining the specific visual composition and *mise en scène* of the dreamlike scenarios conceived by Gaiman. Mikal Gilmore's introduction to the last collected volume *The Wake*, places the series within Gothic metafiction's penchant for layered narratives:

> the inventive way that Neil [Gaiman] told stories about the real world and fantastic realms, so that both the narratives and their provinces circled around and within one another, each changing the other's fates and setting off events and probabilities that would reverberate years later at unexpected junctures in the overall tale.
> (Gilmore, introduction to Gaiman, Zulli, Muth and Vess 1997)

In the ninth volume, *World's End* (1995), Gaiman places the action inside a 'reality storm' where travellers from different worlds gather in an inn to share stories whilst waiting for the storm to subside. Their telling of tales utilises different genres and archetypes, sometimes combining stories within stories, all connected by a shared urge to divulge and confess. It is within this layered structure of storytelling that Gaiman's work responds to Gothic antecedents, equally beguiling and horrifying in its referencing of the uncanny and grotesque.

GOTHIC PASTICHE

The work of writer Garth Ennis and artist Steve Dillon on *Preacher* and *Hellblazer* (DC/Vertigo) parodied its own sense of Gothic verisimilitude. John Constantine from *Hellblazer* is a chain-smoking Liverpudlian Magus who traverses the world in search of supernatural phenomena. Although Ennis is just one of a number of writers who have worked on *Hellblazer*, his cultural and literary references in both that comic and *Preacher* disrupts *and* inscribes previous examples of comic and Gothic history. Julia Round refers to the self-enabling commentary of contemporary comic culture: 'The gothic's absorption of other genres is also echoed by the development of the American comic book industry through what I call "superscription" – the overwriting and adaptation of previously existing characters' (Round 2006: 359).

The character of Cassidy from *Preacher* is a 100-year-old Irish vampire who is described by the eponymous Jesse Custer as 'SORTA LIKE IF BRENDAN BEHAN FUCKED BRAM STOKER AN' THEY LET THE BABY DO CRACK ALL THE TIME' (Ennis and Dillon 1998: 80). Cassidy is aware of the myths that surround vampirism and is keen to disprove them at every opportunity, drawing upon the cultural references of cinema and literature to conceive his own unique place in the Gothic framework. *Preacher* references vampire fiction, Grail mythology and the iconography of Westerns and, like the 'neo-noir' Vertigo title *100 Bullets*, reveals how fluid and responsive comics can be to shifting patterns of representation, constantly borrowing from different genres to good effect.

Gothic superscription can work on a number of different levels, as evidenced by the graphic novel *Bite Club* (written by Howard Chaykin and David Tischman, illustrated by David Hann, 2005). That the comic is about a vampire mafia family who run Miami's crime scene is just one aspect of its superscription. The assimilation of vampires into the world of *Bite Club* as 'ethnic minorities' displaces the usual generic conventions that the Gothic operates by. The reader is made aware of the historical tradition that the text draws on whilst also collaborating in the re-working of generic conventions: in *Bite Club*, Leto, one of the vampire scions, is America's first ordained vampiric priest: 'IT'S TOUGH ENOUGH BEING A CATHOLIC VAMPIRE – BUT A CATHOLIC PRIEST, TOO?' (Chaykin, Tischman and Hann 2005: 31).

This superscription overwrites previously held assumptions about the conflict between Catholicism and the supernatural that can be found in early examples of Gothic fiction. At the same time it also references the importance of Catholicism to the gangster genre, as the conclusion of Coppola's *The Godfather* (1972) testifies. The narrative prose that accompanies the opening four pages of *Bite Club* acts as a cinematic voice-over in the style of *film noir*, positioning the text in relation to a series of generic references that draws upon vampire and gangster traditions in order to refract their meaning in new ways.

CONCLUSION: GRAPHIC GOTHIC

The continuing popularity of *The Sandman* can be seen in the spin-off Vertigo monthly comics that use the same characters and scenarios created by Gaiman, namely *The Dreaming* and Mike Carey's *Lucifer*. The importance of Vertigo is reflected in the context of a wider cultural phenomenon that has developed around the paraphernalia of comics. Many publishers acknowledge the importance of a core fan base that sustains the creative life of the product; comic book stores like Forbidden Planet (UK) sell a range of comic-related material that in the case of *The Sandman* (as a popular example) also includes statuettes, dolls, posters, Dave McKean's cover art and trading cards. The symbiotic relationship between comic art and a 'Goth subculture' creates a fan base through the fantasy world of cult titles like *The Sandman*, *Preacher* and Mike Mignola's *Hellboy* (Dark Horse Comics).

Certain comic writers and artists resist generic formulas whilst also employing visual styles that are very different from traditional 'superhero' comic art. Charles Burns' *Black Hole* (2005), drawn in stark black and white, is about a group of teenagers in the North American Pacific North-West who are infected by a virus that mutates their bodies. Drawing upon the generational angst of writers like Douglas Coupland, Burns projects a world where the teenage mutation is both a metaphor for adolescence and also a violent transformation of the liminal body. The visual style and emotional texture of *Black Hole* denies any obvious generic identification with science-fiction/horror; rather, its layered narrative builds up a series of relationships between the teenagers where the mutations are seen, like sex and drug taking, as a rite of passage into adulthood. It *is* horrific, but only through the psychological and emotional traumas the kids undergo, with an ending as bleakly pessimistic as any found in modern fiction.

Audrey Niffenegger's *The Three Incestuous Sisters* (2005) is a hand-printed art work with prose on opposite pages. Out of all the works discussed it is the 'purest' Gothic text, not appropriating or overwriting generic codes but through a combination of graphics and story offering a tale of suicide, incest, circus-flying angels and reconciled ghosts. Like Alan Moore's *From Hell*, it offers a way forward for comic art outside the nexus of cult fantasy that at times verges on parody. The pioneering comics of Moore, Gaiman, Miller and Ennis have led to a slew of imitators, often without the cultural-political relevance that informs much of their work. From being a niche market 15 years ago, the 'adult comic' has grown into a marketing event, as evidenced by DC Comics' take-over of the independent publisher Wildstorm in 1998, acquiring a raft of new radical titles like *Planetary*, *DV8* and *The Authority*. Through the continuing work of writers and artists like Grant Morrison, Charles Burns, Mike Mignola and Warren Ellis, millennial graphic novels have obtained a cultural legitimacy sustained by their relationship to the Gothic imagination.

WORKS CITED

Bender, Hy (1999) *The Sandman Companion*, London: Titan Books.

Botting, Fred (1996) *Gothic*, London: Routledge.

Burns, Charles (2005) *Black Hole*, London: Jonathan Cape.

Chaykin, Howard, David Tischman and David Hann (2005) *Bite Club*, New York: DC Comics.

Ennis, Garth, and Steve Dillon (1998) *Preacher: Dixie Fried*, New York: DC Comics.

Gaiman, Neil, Michael Zulli, Jon J. Muth and Charles Vess (1997) *The Wake*, introduction by Mikal Gilmore, New York: DC Comics.

Miller, Frank (1986) *The Dark Knight Returns*, London: Titan Books Limited.

Moore, Alan (2003) Interview with *The Onion*, www.theonionavclub.com.

Moore, Alan, and Eddie Campbell (1999) *From Hell*, Paddington: Eddie Campbell Comics.

Moore, Alan, and Kevin O'Neill (2003) *The League of Extraordinary Gentlemen,* vol. II, La Jolle, CA: America's Best Comics.

Moore, Alan, Steve Bissette and John Totleben (1987) *Swamp Thing*, London: Titan Books Limited.

Niffenegger, Audrey (2005) *The Three Incestuous Sisters*, London: Jonathan Cape.

Rabey, D. I. (1989) 'Watching the Watchmen', *Planet*, 73, Feb–March: 74–81.

Round, Julia (2005) 'Fragmented Identity: The Superhero Condition', *International Journal of Comic Art*, 7(2): 358–69.

30

GOTHIC MUSIC AND SUBCULTURE

PAUL HODKINSON

The significance of the contemporary Goth music subculture has been the subject of some debate among academics, critics and participants themselves. For some, the Goth scene constitutes merely the latest manifestation of the ongoing broader tradition of Gothic literature, art and culture. Meanwhile, some attempts to understand contemporary Goth by means of textual analysis have concluded that the subculture embodies specific forms of cultural transgression rooted in the history of Gothic. This chapter provides an introduction to a music- and style-based subculture which, I argue, draws selectively upon elements of Gothic literature, art and film, but which – like various other youth music cultures – is centred for the majority of its participants upon the consumption of music and fashion, the enjoyment of a strong sense of shared identity and of socialising with one another at events such as gigs and night clubs. I briefly outline key elements of the style and its history here before considering some of the different ways in which we might make sense of Goth subculture. Specifically, I suggest that it may be mistaken to assume all the details and explanations about the motivations, behaviours and identities of Goths can be found beneath the surface of Goth or indeed Gothic cultural texts.[1]

A BRIEF HISTORY

Among the various bands who have been credited with 'founding' Goth music, former Punk band Siouxsie and the Banshees were of particularly direct importance, having adopted a darker, more sinister style towards the beginning of the 1980s. And if the distinctive dark make-up, backcombed hair and black clothing of vocalist Siouxsie Sioux provided key ingredients for the female Goth look, then a similar early impact on male Goth fashion was exerted by Bauhaus, whose somewhat tongue-in-cheek emphasis upon the macabre was epitomised in the whitened faces and dark eye make-up of members of the band as well as in the tone, tempo and lyrics of their music. As fans began to imitate such imagery, the British music press began to report on and reinforce the new genre. Particular attention was focused upon a London club called the Batcave, which acted as a melting pot for emerging bands and fans who had been influenced by the likes of Bauhaus and Siouxsie and the Banshees and also by pioneering Los Angeles band, Christian Death. By the mid-1980s, the deep vocals, jangling guitars and sombre bass lines of The Sisters of Mercy – alongside black clothes, long coats, dark shades and pointed boots – had established them as the archetypal 'Goth rock' band (see Mercer 1988). A period of chart success for the 'Sisters', alongside other bands including The Mission, Fields of the Nephilim, The Cure and others, would ensure that by the late 1980s Goth music and fashion enjoyed international exposure and a substantial youth following.

Such exposure had waned by the early 1990s, however, and for much of that decade the subculture became more reliant upon small-scale specialist record labels, retailers and venues – as well as DIY subcultural media such as fanzines and, eventually, websites (Hodkinson 2002). During the same period, sounds and images associated with more electronic, dance-oriented genres became incorporated into the Goth style. In addition to specialist Industrial bands such as Front 242, Skinny Puppy and Front Line Assembly, such influences included higher-profile cross-over acts, including the massively successful United States-based Nine Inch Nails, as well as the unique blend of dance and industrial developed by former ravers the Prodigy, and the increasingly dark sounds and lyrics of the long-established Depeche Mode. Such influences resulted in the development of what some referred to as 'Cybergoth' – an electronic, dance-oriented version of the Goth sound whose principal exponents included Scandinavians Covenant and Apoptygma Berzerk. Yet this new variation was not universally accepted and those who continued to prefer earlier, guitar-based sounds became known as 'trad-Goths'. Meanwhile, the rise to fame and notoriety of Marilyn Manson prompted the return of Goth to the media spotlight, as well as the development of a harder, more metal-oriented version of Goth, which also included the likes of Type O Negative, Lacuna Coil and Cradle of Filth. Also disliked by many 'trad-Goths', this more metal-oriented version of the style was particularly influential upon new generations of teenagers who regarded themselves as Goths during the first few years of the twenty-first century.

GOTH STYLE – CORE THEMES

In spite of its elements of internal diversity and change, the Goth style has retained considerable internal consistency and external distinctiveness. For Gavin Baddeley (2002), such consistency can be explained through reference to a coherent history of Gothic culture, from the original fourth-century Goths, to eighteenth- and nineteenth-century art, poetry and literature, to twentieth-century horror cinema and television. And Goth music and style have indeed drawn upon at least some elements of this tradition. An overall emphasis on dark horror imagery pervades the style, whether through gloomy or sinister musical tones and lyrics, in the trademark black hair and clothing of participants, or their ghostly white foundation offset by thick dark eyeliner and lipstick. Indeed, many Goths have incorporated into their appearances tell-tale signifiers from the horror tradition, from crosses to bats, and even horror-style make-up. Such imagery can also be found in the lyrics of some Goth songs, not least Bauhaus's playful references to Bela Lugosi, star of Tod Browning's 1931 version of *Dracula* in the song 'Bela Lugosi's Dead'. Meanwhile, although not an

especially prominent theme in the 1980s 'Gothic rock' era, the Victorian fashions associated with classic horror fiction – and Hollywood adaptions of it –
undoubtedly encouraged an embrace among some Goths of what Spooner
(2004) calls the 'decadent aristocracy' associated with such fiction, including
corsets, lacy or velvet dresses, top hats and morning coats.[2]

Yet there have been other equally important influences on Goths which
ought not to be reduced to the traditions of Gothic culture. The dark mix of
emotion, angst and energy often associated with Goth music, for example, may
be linked by some to elements of Gothic literature, but has at least as much to
do with the influence of longstanding themes from within contemporary popular
music. Key influences include The Velvet Underground, David Bowie, Iggy Pop
and Joy Division, as well as a range of 1980s Indie bands, including Echo and
the Bunnymen, The Smiths and so-called 'shoe-gazers' such as My Bloody
Valentine, Lush and Curve. Meanwhile the androgynous style and synth-pop
music associated with early 1980s bands, including Soft Cell, Orchestral
Manoeuvres in the Dark, Gary Numan and Adam and the Ants, also acted as an
ongoing influence and such music continues to fill dance-floors in some Goth
clubs today. And the influence of dance culture and techno during the course of
the 1990s included not only the incorporation of mechanical beats and electronic sequences into otherwise gloom-ridden, sinister forms of music, but also
the appropriation into Goth fashion of reflective or ultra-violet-sensitive
clothing, fluorescent make-up, glow sticks and hair extensions.

From a fashion point of view, an even more important influence has been the
fetish scene. PVC and rubber skirts, tops, corsets and collars, for example, have
all been among the most popular styles of clothing for Goths of both genders for
many years. Although themes of sexual transgression have been identified as an
important feature of the history of Gothic culture, the particulars of the contemporary fetish scene and the ways in which it has been drawn upon by Goths ought
not to be reduced to this history (Spooner 2004: 17). The initial appropriation of
fetish fashion by some early Goth bands reflected the direct influence of the
Punk scene, which had pioneered the taking of such items of clothing onto the
street. Yet it was in the early 1990s that overt fetish-oriented clothing and
imagery became a standard element of Goth style. And an additional mediating
factor here was the influence at that time of bands such as Nine Inch Nails,
whose lyrics and image brought together various themes of contemporary Goth
style with an overt embrace of sadomasochistic imagery.

There are also a variety of other general links between Goth style and that of
Punk and alternative rock music culture. These include the consistent importance of piercings, tattoos, coloured hair, combat trousers, black jeans and large
black boots to Goth musicians and participants. Meanwhile, it is perhaps easy to
forget that the most frequently worn item of clothing among Goths throughout
the course of their subculture's existence, has been the humble band T-shirt,
something distinctive to the Goth scene in the specific artist name and design,
but otherwise comparable with various genres of rock and metal.

Crucially, then, rather than being a simple transposition of Gothic culture into the present, Goth should be regarded, like many other subcultural styles, as a fairly complex amalgam. It is most immediately identifiable by its dark and/or macabre themes, but has drawn selectively upon a variety of distinct styles and influences, many of which relate to the recent history of popular music and youth culture. That such an amalgam has remained externally distinctive and internally consistent, then, ought not to prompt easy reductionist conclusions with respect to stylistic origins. In the second part of this chapter, I want to argue that the reductionist urge ought also to be resisted when it comes to the crucial question of how to interpret the significance and meaning of contemporary Goth style – and of those living breathing human beings with whom its consumption is associated.

MEANINGS AND USES

Studies of youth subcultural styles in the past have often focused upon trying to understand such groups via analysis of the cultural artefacts with which they were associated. Theorists associated with Birmingham University's Centre for Contemporary Cultural Studies (CCCS) produced detailed analyses of the stylistic and textual properties of the clothing and music enjoyed by Mods, Skins, Bikers, Punks and others. Analysis of such cultural objects ultimately prompted the conclusion that the subcultural groups with whom they were associated embodied a form of symbolic resistance on the part of working-class youth, a political response to their disadvantaged and contradictory social position within post-war Britain (J. Clarke *et al*. 1976). Hebdige, for example, asserts that the creative combination of scooters, smart clothes, narcotics and rock 'n' roll music which characterised the Mod subculture represented an eloquent form of 'guerrilla warfare', which parodied and subverted Establishment values (1976, 1979).

My own approach to researching the Goth scene towards the turn of the millennium largely avoided the 'interpretation' of cultural objects associated with Goths in favour of a sociological, participant-centred approach, characterised by over three years of in-depth interviews and observations focused on the practices and identities of Goths themselves.[3] Influenced by a tradition of ethnographic studies of youth cultural groupings dating back to the Chicago School, I resisted suggestions from some that I should seek to explain the apparent sociopolitical and/or psychological significance of so dramatic and distinctive a subcultural style through textual analysis. In so doing, I adopted an approach which contrasted not only with much of the CCCS's work, but also with the literary tradition of Gothic criticism, which has since the 1930s regularly been focused upon the identification through textual analysis of either psychological or transgressive meanings (Baldick and Mighall 2001). In the latter respect, my methodology can also be set apart from that of critics of the contemporary Goth scene such as Baddeley (2002) and, in particular, Carol Siegel (2006), who seek to identify the essential meanings of the culture primarily through the examination of texts.

Consistent with the CCCS and various literary scholars of the Gothic, Siegel's analysis of Goth texts prompts confident claims about the transgressive, resistant significance of the subculture. Employing the theoretical perspective of poststructuralists Deleuze and Guattari, she interprets the Goth subculture as a dark, twisted subversion of prevailing conservative cultural values (Siegel 2006). Such transgression is illustrated through a range of literary, musical and cinematic examples, from the overt embrace of dark, sadomasochistic imagery and lyrics in Nine Inch Nails, to the exploration of the trappings of conventional masculinity in The Cure, to the gender fluidity and masochistic bisexual Goth heroes in the work of Poppy Z. Brite, to examples of female sadism and power such as Angela Carter's 'Lady Purple'. In the context of a dominant US culture of abstinence campaigns and passive consumption, the Goth scene is summed up as 'a perversely eroticized embrace of death' (Siegel 2006: 7), a resistant culture centred upon hedonistic unbounded sexuality and desire focused upon sadomasochism, gender fluidity and an emphasis upon 'the terrible beauty of the grotesque' (2006: 166).

Siegel's account is a compelling contribution to the growing body of academic discourse on the Goth scene. Yet, for me, there is reason for caution about the unqualified reading of such political resistance into the activities and identities of Goths and about the largely textual approach on which such conclusions often seem to be based. Spooner (2004) rightly reminds us that the identification of transgressive meanings within Gothic texts can sometimes tell us as much about the theoretical and cultural agenda of the critic as about the texts themselves, less still the broader culture they are purported to represent (also see Baldick and Mighall 2001). All too often, she argues, academics have fallen into 'a kind of idealisation of Gothic as a genre, privileging it as a site for whatever transgressive purposes the critic particularly subscribes to' (Spooner 2004: 162). And, interestingly, the same criticism has regularly been levelled at scholars such as Hebdige, who read a neo-Marxist form of resistance into the activities of Punks, Mods and others (G. Clarke 1981; Redhead 1990; Muggleton 2000).

My concern here is less with the plausibility of individual textual interpretations, though, than with the suitability of textual analysis itself in those cases where it is used as the primary means of understanding the meaning and significance of a living, breathing youth culture. My decision to steer clear of such an approach reflected a belief that it is fundamentally mistaken to assume that academic analysis of the content of a particular set of songs, books, films or assemblages of clothing can somehow tell us all or most of what we need to know about a group of consumers with whom they happen to be associated. At the outset, it is unclear on what basis the particular textual examples selected by the critic should be deemed representative of or important to the culture which they are being employed to explain. Arguably it is impossible to come up with an appropriate selection in the case of Goths, not least because of the diverse range of influences from which their style has drawn and the variation between individual Goths in respect of which elements are valued.

More substantially, the use of textual analysis as an approach to subcultural research privileges the particular interpretation of the (usually theoretically driven) critic and presents this as representative of the lifestyles and identities of subcultural participants. This prompts Steve Miles to lament the failure of CCCS theorists to focus on 'the actual meanings that young consumers have for the goods that they consume' (Miles 1995: 35). Miles's comment is pertinent since for the subcultural theorist to place such emphasis on their own interpretations entails an assumption either that such interpretations are shared by all or most subcultural members or that the subjective meanings of such participants are unimportant to an understanding of their activities. Hebdige (1979), in accepting that Punks may not have recognised themselves in his account, clearly opted for the latter assumption. In contrast, Siegel (2006) regards her 'Deleuzoguattarian' readings as consistent with the views of members of the subculture – a bold claim which is justified through some rather unspecific references at the beginning of her book to having observed and spoken to Goths and also to having received favourable comments on her book from Goth acquaintances.[4]

Crucially, however, as well as having a distinct and well-documented tendency to be at least a little mystified by elements of the interpretations of academic critics, subcultural consumers – Goths included – tend significantly to differ among themselves in respect of their interpretations and uses of cultural artefacts. My own detailed and open-ended interviews with Goths demonstrated numerous examples of this. For example, while vampire fiction was consumed by many Goths, disagreements over its significance were extensive. Most notably, for every participant who read into such films transgressive undercurrents and who regarded the latter as central to their own subcultural participation, there were several others who enjoyed consuming the occasional film or novel, but tended to regard such narratives as relatively marginal to their overall identity. Such differential interpretations even led to a degree of animosity in some cases, as in the comment below, which reflected an uneasiness among some about those deemed to take vampire fiction too seriously:

> David: The vampires – you know the ones that play masquerade [vampire role-playing game] . . . and they dress up as goths and they have really bad horrendous makeup and so on and it invariably involves fake blood running down their faces . . . they turn up at goth clubs and they fail to fit in completely, because they've completely missed the point.

Another example. For some Goths, the consumption of music and imagery with textual connotations of fetishism or androgyny was connected with an active embrace of bisexuality and/or sadomasochism. And for such individuals the Goth scene as a whole certainly tended to offer a more tolerant, open-minded atmosphere than various other youth cultures (Hodkinson 2002). Nevertheless, for most Goths, involvement in fetishism and/or non-heterosexual activities extended no further than a degree of awareness and theoretical open-minded-ness. In practice, sexual interest, contact and relationships among Goths were overwhelmingly heterosexual, something which included many of the most femi-nine-looking male Goths (also see Brill 2007).[5] As was the case with the Punk scene of the 1970s, for many, the wearing of fetish-oriented or androgynous clothing was primarily about looking good and asserting subcultural distinctive-ness rather than about being a serious fetishist or sadomasochist. Meanwhile, among a minority, I even came across a hint of reticence about the connotations of such clothes:

> Susie: I don't know if they get the impression that you're dodgy – that you have to be dodgy to wear it [PVC and other clothing purchased from sex stalls or shops].

> Tanya: That annoys me – sometimes you have to go to these places [sex stalls, shops] and get the stuff that you want.

None of this is to deny that there is much to be said about the significance of the Goth scene with respect to gender and sexuality. In addition to the work of Siegel this has been explored usefully by the recent sociological work of Dunja Brill (2007). What I have hoped to show here, however, is that, like the use of vampire texts, uses of and meanings for apparently sexually transgressive cultural artefacts are far from uniform, even within a close-knit subcultural group. However 'subversive' a particular artefact or text may look or feel from the point of view of the academic critic, then, we should be cautious about the blanket attribution of 'transgression' to those who consume it. As Spooner has put it: 'To enjoy a discourse of transgression . . . is not necessarily the same thing as being transgressive' (Spooner 2004: 165). Indeed, the essential status of Goths – like most other youth cultural participants – as avid consumers of commercially produced and subculturally marketed music, clothing and films of whatever content – is arguably reason in itself for at least a degree of caution as to the extent of their subversion of bourgeois or dominant values. Although the Goth scene has in recent years had various run-ins with hostile news media,[6] we should remember that its initial emergence owed a considerable debt to posi-tive promotion from music magazines and the recording industry, both of which – alongside newer outlets such as specialist television and radio channels – continue consciously to promote elements of it – and its supposed 'transgression' – as a means to sell cultural products to young people.

As well as providing evidence of considerable diversity among Goths with respect to their uses and interpretations of the cultural texts, the adoption of a participant-centred research approach revealed elements of their activities, identities and motivations which are largely absent from the content of the arte-facts which they consumed. In spite of their undoubted passion for Goth music and fashion, what was most important for many Goths was not the particular meanings – transgressive or otherwise – of such texts, but the social relationships and shared cultural identity for which they acted as focal point. In other words, to some extent, Goth artefacts acted as a means to an end rather than merely an end in themselves. For example, when I invited interviewees to reflect in detail upon how and why they had come to become involved in the Goth scene, extensive emphasis tended to be placed on the gaining of friendships and a feeling of being accepted and of acquiring social status, sometimes for the first time:

> Ken: First of all you liked the music, and also you were embraced by a lot of people. People came and talked to you and stuff . . . It was being part of a community . . .

> Ruth: I expect that was why I wanted to get into it really because I wanted friends as well . . . because it seems like quite a close-knit community where everyone stuck together . . . I have got an awful lot of friends through this which is really good for me . . . The goth scene has given me an awful lot of confidence . . . I just basically like the scene a lot because I've found a lot of friends through it – a lot of people accepted me, which is something I've never had before.

By way of further illustration, as part of a small-scale survey carried out during my project, I invited respondents to rank the importance of a list of activities and features to their participation in the Goth scene. The most popular item on the list, by a considerable margin, was not music, fashion, books or films, but 'socialising' (see Hodkinson 2002: 201).

My reason for briefly drawing attention to the importance of apparently obvious social factors such as friendships and belonging to Goths is not to imply that the distinctive content of Goth style is of no importance or that there is no value in analysing it. Rather my hope is to illustrate that we cannot learn from such content everything we need to know about those who consume it. Indeed, what was revealed by research focused upon Goths themselves was that, while they often differed amongst themselves in the meanings they attached to the content of their music, clothes and fiction, what united them was that their style acted as both symbol and focal point for participation in a strong, like-minded community – a community characterised by dressing up, going out, watching bands, dancing, drinking, spending time with friends and enjoying a strong and exclusive sense of belonging and identity. As one of my survey respondents succinctly put it: 'It's about dressing up in your best stuff – socialising and making new friends and listening to great music.'

What is illustrated by the importance of such features to participation in the Goth scene, is that – in spite of its undoubted stylistic distinctiveness, and the importance of this to its members, in some respects the Goth scene may be regarded as comparable to a variety of other music-related youth groupings or subcultures. And it is this crucial point that brings the different strands of this chapter together. The reduction of Goth music and style to a current manifestation of the long tradition of Gothic culture, and the attribution of transgression to Goths on the basis of textual readings, are not coterminous positions of course, even if there tends to be a significant overlap between those who adopt them. However, they share a tendency to overestimate the distinctiveness and separation of Goth culture from the broader world of popular music and youth culture within which it has always been thoroughly embedded. Those who focus on the history of Gothic culture as the only significant precursor to or influence on Goth usually do so to the exclusion of any analysis of the influence of a range of musical and youth styles in the past and present. Similarly those who reduce the subculture to the texts and artefacts which render it distinctive underestimate the similarities between the everyday practices, priorities and meanings of its participants and those of Punks, Metallers, Skaters, rock 'n' roll fans and the members of various other groups, however different from Goths they may look or sound.

NOTES

1 My thanks to several long-term participants of the Goth scene whom I consulted about the argument of this article – and in particular to Gwilym Games for his detailed comments on an earlier draft.

2 Such Hollywood adaptations include *Bram Stoker's Dracula* (Francis Ford Coppola 1992) and *Interview with the Vampire* (Neil Jordan 1994).

3 The research centred up extensive participant observation of Goth clubs, pubs, gigs, websites and online discussion groups over three years, in addition to in-depth open-ended interviews (typically lasting up to two hours) with over 70 individuals from across and beyond the UK, including general participants as well as DJs, promoters, bands and producers of fanzines. An 'insider researcher', I had been involved in the subculture myself for several years prior to the project. While this position probably entailed some advantages (see Hodkinson 2005), the research approach was based, in part, on the achievement of a degree of critical distance in order to outline, explain and account for the activities of Goths through rigorous cross-comparison of the range of accounts I received from Goths with my own extensive observations.

4 The primacy of textual analysis as the basis for Siegel's conclusions, though, is clear from the extensive and impressive textual detail provided throughout the chapters of her book. In contrast, the words of the Goths with whom she spoke are almost entirely absent from the account; likewise any real detail on her observations of their activities.

5 Dunja Brill has recently cautioned against exaggeration of the sexual transgression represented by the adoption of feminine clothing by male Goths. Brill argues that typically such males are heterosexual in a fairly traditional sense, justify their stylistic transgression through reference to traditional masculine traits such as 'guts' and courage, and expect traditionally feminine features and characteristics in women (2007).

6 As I write this, the subculture is again being linked with violence by media reporting of a college shooting in Montreal. The perpetrator's presence on a Goth website has prompted negative publicity for the subculture, comparable to that which followed the Columbine school shootings in 1999.

WORKS CITED

Baddeley, Gavin (2002) *Goth Chic: A Connoisseur's Guide to Dark Culture*, London: Plexus.

Baldick, Chris and Robert Mighall (2001) 'Gothic Criticism', in David Punter (ed.), *A Companion to the Gothic*, Oxford: Blackwell.

Brill, Dunja (2007), 'Gender, Status and Subcultural Capital in Gothic Style', in Hodkinson, P. and W. Deicke (eds), *Youth Cultures: Scenes, Subcultures and Tribes*, New York: Routledge.

Clarke, G. (1981) 'Defending Ski-Jumpers: A Critique of Theories of Youth Subcultures', in Simon Frith and Andrew Goodwin (eds) (1990) *On Record: Rock, Pop and the Written Word*, London: Routledge.

Clarke, J., S. Hall, T. Jefferson and B. Roberts (1976) 'Subcultures, Cultures and Class: A Theoretical Overview', in S. Hall and T. Jefferson (eds) *Resistance Through Rituals: Youth Subcultures in Post War Britain*, London: Hutchinson.

Hebdige, Dick (1976) 'The Meaning of Mod', in S. Hall and T. Jefferson (eds), *Resistance Through Rituals: Youth Subcultures in Post War Britain*, London: Hutchinson.

—— (1979) *Subculture. The Meaning of Style*, London: Routledge.

Hodkinson, Paul (2002) *Goth: Identity, Style and Subculture*, Oxford: Berg.

Mercer, Mick (1988) *Gothic Rock Black Book*, London: Omnibus Press.

Miles, S. (1995) 'Towards an Understanding of the Relationship between Youth Identities and Consumer Culture', *Youth and Policy*, 51: 35–45.

—— (2000) *Youth Lifestyles in a Changing World*, Buckingham: Open University Press.

Muggleton, David (2000) *Inside Subculture: The Postmodern Meaning of Style*, Oxford: Berg.

Redhead, Steve (1990) *The End of Century Party: Youth and Pop Towards 2000*, Manchester: Manchester University Press.

Siegel, Carol (2006) *Goth's Dark Empire*, Indianapolis, IN: Indiana University Press.

Spooner, Catherine (2004) *Fashioning Gothic Bodies*, Manchester: Manchester University Press.

31

GOTHIC AND NEW MEDIA

JASON WHITTAKER

The appeal of information and communication technologies has often appeared to be in direct opposition to notions of the Gothic. In advertising and commerce, companies such as Intel, Google and Microsoft promise a postmodern mix of happy, connected workers, white goods and the occasional absurd mascot (to show that the technological behemoths of the twenty-first century possess something that could be misconstrued for a sense of humour). Theorists and critical commentators are often more concerned with the experiences of social networking in a global village, where shared electronic experiences can contribute to a potentially liberatory public sphere – though one, as Papacharissi (2002) observes, compromised by inequities of access, fragmented political discourses and the demands of international capital. Despite such disadvantages, the characteristics of such a virtual sphere tend to cluster around open communication and democratic participation. Cyberspace, however, has its own Gil-Martin, a doppelgänger of violence, pornography, crime and extremism that is often fixated upon by a sensationalist media as evidence of what Sardar called the 'psychotic inner reality' of rootless individuals 'hoping that the next page on the Web will take them to nirvana' (Sardar 1996: 25).

The impact of the internet on an open society or as a transgressive force tends towards grand gestures, which often distract from the more immediate ways in which new media have changed our practices and perceptions. The influence of such technologies on the role of Gothic has often been clearest in terms of online communities and subcultures, but can also affect the formation of texts themselves. At its simplest, as Landow points out, hypertextuality makes any traditionally non-linear series of texts potentially contiguous in a fashion that is both 'inevitably open-ended' and 'inevitably incomplete' (Landow 1997: 255). Such rhizomatic intertextuality is often appealed to by web theorists as the (equally 'inevitably') empowering nature of hypertext as 'a mode of textuality that encourages writerly, active reading rather than passive consumption' (Gaggi 1997: 104). Yet as Gaggi goes on to point out, such 'empowerment may be specious' (105), the result of disorientation rather than any meaningful freedom – random links followed (and determined) by the interaction of contemporary late capitalism more than purposeful activity on the part of the reader. Nevertheless, new media have had a powerful impact on ways of configuring reading, most notably in the wake of Espen Aarseth's (1997) notion of the cybertext, whereby feedback during the act of reading radically transforms the narrative. The cybertext is object-orientated rather than linear and has existed since antiquity (for example in the form of the *I Ching*, whereby after casting sticks the reader consults the text to determine the meaning of various shapes). At its most radical, a cybertext precludes from the outset the possibility of ever returning to the same narrative, and for Aarseth and subsequent critics such as Eskelinen (2001) and Gee (2003), cybertextuality is a *perspective* on literature rather than a particular genre or medium. The most obvious cybertexts we encounter tend to be computer games, but Aarseth also points out that many electronic texts are designed for purely passive or linear consumption. This is not to deny, however, that cybertexts and electronic media have made a contribution to Gothic texts: the most notable example – and, indeed, a classic of the potential for a new textuality – has been Shelley Jackson's *Patchwork Girl* (1995). Starting from the proposition that Mary Shelley created the monster, throughout her text the 'Frankenstein' reader stitches together the limbs and patches of her digital collage, the scars of the creature's body (according to Seidel (1996)) offering an analogy for hypertextuality itself, the body of the text cut and seamed together in an appealingly monstrous reconfiguration. (Interestingly, one of Jackson's more recent projects was SKIN, a story tattooed on the body of 2095 volunteers, one word at a time.) The medium in which *Patchwork Girl* was created, Storyspace, never had the same appeal (outside schools and colleges) as alternatives such as Flash and HTML, but despite the limitations of the format, it remains one of the best examples of how Gothic as a fractured and dismembered genre can capture the disjunctive readings foregrounded by new media.

A rather more mundane use of the internet is as a distribution medium for Gothic texts. As well as the transfer of classic books and stories into electronic format, with a useful range of links and e-texts to be found at the Literary Gothic (www.litgothic.com) and Fred Frank's the Sickly Taper (thesicklytaper. pagedepot.com), a number of authors have made use of the net to publish their own works, for example at Gothic.net, the Eternal Night (www.eternalnight.co. uk) and the Shining Darkness (shiningdarkness.freecyberzone.com). As with any venue for self-publishing, the quality of work available is variable, from the atrocious to the almost sublime via large quantities of the ridiculous. Eternal Night functions as a fairly interesting example of fanzine literature, with blog entries and reviews providing materials that used only to be available via a rather restricted magazine, *Pirate Writings*. Gothic.net, in its own words the site of 'bone chilling literary culture', is one of the more stylishly presented sites; while most of the stories do not necessarily fulfil this visual promise it does demonstrate the vicarious pleasures of online fandom. As Marianne Cantwell observes, 'fan "activity" around knowledge and the extra textual informs the fan reading of the textual, and . . . this is invoked and/or rejected as "intense knowledge"' (Cantwell 2004: 1) As such, message boards, postings and interaction with a Gothic community – the opportunity for feedback into an evolving Gothic cybertext – is as important as the stories and articles themselves.

One important format where Gothic has often played a much more profound role is that of video and computer games. Particularly since the gaming revolution of the 1990s, titles have been released with increasingly adult themes that have appropriated some of the elements of other media, particularly those staples of Gothic film: supernatural horror and gore. One of the first games to be released on the new medium of CD-ROM in 1992 was *The 7th Guest* by Trilobyte: incorporating live-action footage to depict a house haunted by ghosts and demons, this may have been clichéd fare for movies but was innovative enough at the time to inspire a considerable fan-base. The impact of Trilobyte's game, however, was nothing compared to that of id Software's *Doom* (1993), the influential first-person shooter, and its successor *Quake* (1996). Inspired by H. P. Lovecraft and the *Alien* movies, the creators John Romero and John Carmack created a series of games that were responsible for significant transformations in popular culture (Kushner 2003). While *Doom* and *Quake* were vital in the extension of that often elusive component of computer titles, gameplay, many subsequent Gothic-influenced titles were content simply to repeat truisms from older media. Thus German developer Piranha Bytes' *Gothic* (2001) was generally a fairly standard fantasy role-playing game (RPG), while the *Silent Hill* (1999–2006) and *Resident Evil* (1996–2006) franchises have generally been less innovative in terms of expanding the genre of 'survival horror' (established by Infogrames's *Alone in the Dark*, released in 1992) than in improving graphics. This is not to deny, however, the success of such titles in creating or even exceeding the horrific ambience of the movies that originally inspired them, and Gothic influences do occasionally throw up a true original, such as Black Isle Studios' *Planescape: Torment* (1999). This was an RPG that explored themes of guilt, regret, redemption and perceptions of reality in a bizarre and evocative 'City of Doors' similar to the labyrinthine creations of Clive Barker: although too complex in many ways to match the appeal of Capcom's *Resident Evil* (selling 400,000 copies against *Resident Evil*'s 30 million), it quickly became a cult classic and has frequently topped gaming charts, such as those at Gamespot (www.gamespot.com) and Gamespy (www.gamespy.com).

As well as developments in new media such as games and texts, perhaps the most significant impact of the internet is its contribution to the popular resurgence of a Goth subculture in recent years. When considering what have become known as Net.Goths, the most important developments come from the opportunity to form online communities. This, of course, is something that is far from peculiar to Net.Goths, applying as it does to a huge variety and range of subcultures, and the significance of online communities has attracted considerable critical attention from a number of web theorists in the past decade. As Paul Hodkinson points out with reference to this particular group, new media technologies are particularly important to the formation of subcultural identities because they have been especially fertile in opening up spaces where users can invent, or reinvent, themselves (Hodkinson 2003: 286). Thus identity is less a product of such things as economic activity in the twenty-first century or, more simply, image is all. From such a starting point, as Burnett and Marshall point out, the web is particularly fruitful as an active site for the construction of identities and 'online self presentation provides a level of information control that is not normal in real life interaction' (Burnett and Marshall 2003: 68).

'Information control' is, in one sense, merely a new way of looking at a phenomenon that has affected Goths and other subcultural groups for decades. Subcultural capital in the form of such things as music, taste and fashion is all about offering and engaging with information flows: it is perhaps because subcultures spend so much time crafting the presentation of data so self-consciously that they often feel they are not engaged in 'normal' levels of real-life interaction, and so ascribe a particular significance to identity formation. What the internet has added to this mix is the ability to form a sense of mutually dependent groupings that can ignore physical and geographical prescriptions at an unprecedented level. At its simplest, sites such as Dark Side of the Net (www. darklinks.com) and Gothic.Startheaven.com offer links and resources to shops, groups, music and fashion around the world, while others such as SFGoth.com and Darknation.pl provide social sites (in this case for Goths in the San Francisco area or Poland). A more interesting phenomenon is the Cybergothic scene, itself a subcategory of the cyberpunk and cyberculture styles: emerging out of rave and clubbing scenes, Cybergoths tend to combine an interest in new technologies with electronic music – although (in a rarefied example of one-upmanship) so-called 'Rivetheads' who prefer hardcore Industrial music tend to mock Cybergoths for being too populist.

The endless fragmentation of these groups indicates why calling them communities, as is increasingly common, can be very problematic: at one end is the utopian vision of commentators beginning with Rheingold (1994), which posited an almost ideal, frictionless public sphere of communication in which there is no conflict of interests. Alternatively, sceptics such as Ostwald (1997) and Wilbur (1997) simply refute the possibility of their existence: 'virtual community is the illusion of a community where there are no real people and real communication' (Wilbur 1997: 10). It is worth, however, remarking on how theories of online communities have informed and been shaped by the perceptions and desires of various participants. As David Bell (2003) observes, the idealised notion that was prevalent in the early days of web theory (and which can still be encountered as a kind of technological sublime in many online communities) draws on the nostalgic *Gemeinschaft* of an English village or American small-town life (as opposed to wider civil society or *Gesellschaft*). Online communities draw upon factors that were common in at least some groups that pre-existed the internet, but give special privilege to the communication of shared interests. One common outlet for online communities exists in the form of fandom. In some cases, these consist of individual websites dedicated to the work of a particular group or writer, such as the Poppy Z. Brite fan pages at www.geocities.com/BourbonStreet/Bayou/1088/, or the *Buffy* blogs hosted at schala.net/buffy. Yet the demands of online fandom can bring it into conflict with those textual sources that give rise to it in the first place. Simone

Murray points out that many fan sites have become increasingly important to primary providers such as television and film studios or publishers as a 'driver for content streaming', but that this often creates a range of problems for those providers:

> Corporations have thus manoeuvred themselves into the paradoxical position of seeking to generate maximum emotional investment by consumers in a given content brand, but of needing to corral such emotional attachment into purely consumptive – as opposed to creative – channels.
>
> (Murray 2004: 10)

While the internet is often filled with the garbage of democratic discourse, one of its great pleasures is that it frequently does provide a creative opportunity for fertile discussion: Cantwell, for example, notes that while online piracy provides plenty of opportunity for 'wild feeds' of a programme such as *Buffy the Vampire Slayer*, fan communities often include spoiler sections that are not simply there to offer this forbidden knowledge, but also to protect the wider community that does not wish to ruin forthcoming pleasures. Such sections, where 'spoilt knowledge' can be articulated in diverse ways, creates what Cantwell calls 'communities-within-communities' – in this case, of a close-knit group of 'Spoiler Whores' (Cantwell 2004: 6).

The importance of postings as a discursive framework is particularly significant, because it is potentially the most democratic. At root, the basic format was established by newsgroups, although the past five years or so have seen a movement away from Usenet to web-based sites or social forums. The growth of blogging, particularly in conjunction with social networks such as MySpace and LiveJournal, has provided a fruitful new forum for Net.Goths. Thus, for example, Goths (www.myspace.com/gothics) is a place to meet and discuss the subculture, while the related discussion group (groups.myspace.com/goths) is more concerned with music and clubbing. The virtue of these social sites is that they provide access to what MySpace calls an extended network, where users can subscribe as 'friends': thus visitors who have an interest in Goth music, fashion or culture can quickly connect to a whole range of personal MySpace pages and communicate via comments, forums, email or instant messaging. Similarly, at the time of writing a list of over 2000 relevant Yahoo! groups can be found at dir.groups.yahoo.com/dir/Cultures_ Community/Groups/Gothic, with the most active groups ranging from the salacious (Lady Carol's Dungeon) to the more esoteric (industrial-gothic music from the Ukraine), while LiveJournal has attracted a large number of blogs dedicated to Goth-related themes. Like so much activity on the internet, the whole blogging and social network phenomenon represents a fragmentation of online involvement away from what now appears to be the relative coherence of Usenet (once considered the epitome of unregulated net participation) to a much more interesting and media-rich fractal constellation of text, graphics and video grabs.

Online communities enable individuals to draw on what Bell describes as 'disembedded' experience, no longer restricted to one place, a deterritorialisation that allows them to participate in global flows. This, in turn, probably does reflect a way in which Net.Goths, like many other internet users, present themselves. As Wilbur observes, 'many computer users seem to experience the movement "into" cyberspace as an unshackling from real-life constraints – transcendence rather than prosthesis' (Wilbur 1997: 11). Certainly reading the various postings on Net.Goth forums such as alt.gothic and alt.gothic.music gives the reader a sense that for many Goths it is online that they feel truly able to be themselves. As one of many youth subcultures that self-consciously define themselves through alienation, disembedded participation online enables connection to like-minded individuals in a world of information overload. In a relatively early commentary, Sherry Turkle provided a definition of what has become a commonplace view of online identity, as 'fluid, emergent, decentralized, multiplicitous, flexible and ever in progress' (Turkle 1996: 263–4), a definition that was clearly intended to be ambivalent: ironically, the actual practice of participation in online communities is precisely the one place where Net.Goths often feel they fulfil their identities and share a sense of belonging. Yet do new media forms offer a particularly Gothic space? The tendency when discussing the sites of online communities is often to concentrate on openness and transparency of communication, and yet the subcultural formations of Goth create a much more subversive space: as Amy Wilkins (2004) has pointed out, women often use this particular subcultural scene – on- and offline – to resist notions of mainstream sexuality precisely because it is hidden from the outsider view. This is not specific to this subculture, of course, but Net.Goths often prefer to communicate their fascination with macabre and morbid topics via decentralised sites that more closely resemble the maze-like prisons of Piranesi rather than a glossy hyper-reality.

Another important contribution of new media technologies to the Net.Goth phenomenon (as elsewhere) is via music distribution and file sharing. Along with style, music is the most important defining factor in Goth subcultural formation: in Hodkinson (2002) the music scene is identified repeatedly as a primary means of defining this particular group. Likewise, Joshua Gunn, writing before file sharing and legitimate downloading had become part of everyday consumption, remarked on the ways in which the 'metonymic logic' of a classification such as Gothic provides the core of a genre, 'so that future musical acts with similar sounds may expand generic boundaries with the legitimate value of difference' (Gunn 1998: 42). For Hodkinson and Gunn, writing at the turn of the twenty-first century, the logic of musical subcultural style still depended very much on the physical presence of CDs, cassettes and, occasionally, vinyl. The difficulty of distributing such music before mass participation in the internet was an important factor in the development of subcultural capital. Even in the brief space since the publication of Hodkinson's book and Gunn's paper, the transformation of online music and the ubiquity of the iPod (in its original, pristine white version an anti-Goth device if ever there was one) have offered a new lease of life to this group as to many others, while also potentially blurring some of the boundaries of the subculture. Will Straw (1993) made the telling observation that the reason why heavy metal music was so lacking in such capital was that it was simply too easily available, dominated as it was by megabands working for major labels with a controlling share of large retail outlets.

While digital distribution may blur some of the once clear-cut boundaries of subcultural identities, these have not disappeared but have often been reformulated in new ways. Work undertaken by Adar and Huberman (2000), Cooper and Harrison (2001) and Ebare (2004) concentrated on the ways in which file sharing often operates according to a series of implicit rules, often geared towards 'gift economies', where participants who contributed files and information could be classified as 'power users' or 'citizens', while those who simply took what they required without reciprocation would be identified as 'leeches'. File sharing still remains a significant activity of course, but with the success of iTunes as well as the (ironically) relaunched legitimate Napster, previously the bête noire of the music companies, it is of course increasingly likely that visitors to the digital frontier will find the bars of the Wild West converted into family-friendly condos.

In terms of music distribution, most Goth bands use the net in a predictable manner. Pages for artists such as HIM (www.heartagram.com), Diamanda Galas (www.mutelibtech.com/diamandagalas/index.html) and Bauhaus (www.bauhausmusik.com) offer links to biographies, tour dates, discographies and merchandise with little more in the way of innovative content – even if, as in the case of the Bauhaus site, it is dressed up with charmingly meaningless Flash animations. Where official sites become more interesting is in terms of community forums: the site for The Cure (www.thecure.com), for example, has an extremely active set of bulletin boards, and one that encourages members to post on whatever topic takes their fancy – from rumours of American tours to Robert Smith's favourite football team. (As a sign of the changing times, it is also noteworthy that their last EP release, 4Play, is only available as a download from iTunes.) What becomes clear from any number of groups is that the internet provides a great many opportunities to share and promote artists whose access to more conventional media is severely limited, even if these opportunities bring with them the associated problems of piracy and illegal file sharing. One very active thread on gothic.net (www.gothic.net/boards/archive/index.php/t-1731.html) throughout February 2006 concerning suggestions for new music diverted into a heated discussion on the pros and cons of file sharing.

And yet the medium continues to mutate. One interesting recent phenomenon that demonstrates how new technologies can affect subcultural practice is the rise of so-called 'guerrilla bands'. Commenting on the (admittedly non-Goth) band The Others, Amy Spencer (2005) discusses how technology plays an integral part in enabling such groups to connect with their audience: cryptic messages on websites as well as text messages allow plenty of contemporary groups to build their own fan-base, and guerrilla-gig networks are one way of providing communities, with the ideal of forming nomadic tribes that will delight in deterritorialisations. The real opportunities for new media can extend much further than simply sampling or even sharing online communities. The Situationist stomp rock group Laibach (part of the NSK, or Neue Slowenische Kunst), who combined elements of Goth and industrial music in albums such as *Nova Akropola* (1986) and *Sympathy for the Devil* (1990), have taken the possibilities offered by the internet to promote their state without boundaries online. The electronic embassy of the NSK (http://www.nskstate.com/index.php) provides links to a range of documents, including the Internal Book of Laws and official NSK artefacts (such as stamps and passports), while Laibach's official site (www.laibach.nsk.si) is a platform for a totalitarian ideology based on 'the organizational system of industrial production'. As Alexei Monroe (2005) remarks, following Slavoj Žižek, this totalitarianism is intended to make visible the 'hidden underside' of systems and regimes:

> If current political and cultural trends continue, total transparency might be achieved on the surface, but (with luck) it will never be possible entirely to monitor the most esoteric, recessed and deepest aspects of culture and thought. Cultural mystery, secrecy and ambiguity have to be preserved, since freedom and spontaneity reside in such shadowy, nondetermined spaces . . . A key slogan of hackers and anarchists is 'encrypt and survive', and this is equally valid for culture. Encryption, the reproduction of obscurity, is a means of preserving autonomy.
>
> (Monroe 2005: 269)

The extreme industrial manifestations of Laibach and the NSK appear to offer a rigidly reified example of everything opposed by the rhizomatic networks. And yet the motif of encryption (the title, incidentally, of a 2002 album by Electrogoth band Pro-jekt) indicates that this is, in fact, a radical *détournement* of established hierarchies and organisations, the obfuscation via duplicity that, as Harriet Hustis (1999) observes in relation to Poe's hoaxes, trickery and use of ciphers, has long been part of the Gothic experience of reading. Online, where so much that once was hidden is visible, once abstruse but now immediately available, cultural encryption becomes the primary means by which subcultures such as Net.Goths form their communities (or even anti-communities) and preserve something of their own autonomy.

In a different context, particularly with reference to biotechnologies such as cloning, Botting discusses how the techno-science of code provides 'a complete technology combining an organizing framework or form of language and the technical capacity to materialize or realize itself, thereby changing things in the world' (Botting 2003: 358). By concentrating on new media technologies of encryption and pirated distribution, a particular, Cybergothic vision emerges which finally reflects back on the nature of certain dark corners and webs of the internet itself. One model for this can be found in Rapatzikou's discussion of the worlds of William Gibson's cyberpunk fictions as Gothic mindscapes, each one combining the 'general atmosphere of transience evoked by virtual reality' with the threat of corporate secrets that threaten the individual and can only be countered by other secret knowledges' (Rapatzikou 2004: 212). Hacking as a 'reproduction of obscurity' offers precisely the ambiguous spaces in which alternative cultural formations can flourish but also functions as one of Botting's metaphors for technology itself. The new media of electronic communications may be seen by the Wintel monopolies of this world as the bringing together of business, government and community in a seamless and gleaming network; nevertheless, alienation, paranoia, perversion and secrecy are interwoven into its nodes, the conditions for a Foucauldian heterotopia, entry to which is not available to all, but guarded by ritual practice and secret codes.

WORKS CITED

Aarseth, Epsen (1997) *Cybertexts: Perspectives on Ergodic Literature*, Baltimore, MD: Johns Hopkins University Press.

Adar, Eyton, and Bernardo Huberman (2000) 'Free Riding on Gnutella', *First Monday*, 5.10, www.firstmonday.org/issues/issue5_10/adar.

Bell, David (2003) *An Introduction to Cybercultures*. London: Routledge.

Botting, Fred (2003) 'Metaphors and Monsters', *Journal for Cultural Research*, 7(4): 339–65.

Burnett, Robert, and P. David Marshall (2003) *Web Theory: An Introduction*. London: Routledge.

Cantwell, Margaret (2004) 'Collapsing the Extra/Textual: Passions and Intensities of Knowledge in *Buffy the Slayer* Online Fan Communities', *Refractory: a Journal of Entertainment Media*, 5, http://www.refractory.unimelb.edu.au/journalissues/vol5/cantwell.html.

Cooper, Jon, and Daniel Harrison (2001) 'The Social Organisation of Audio Piracy on the Internet', *Media Culture and Society*, 23: 71–89.

Ebare, Sean (2004) 'Digital Music and Subculture: Sharing Files, Sharing Styles', *First Monday*, 9.2, www.firstmonday.org/issues/issue9_2/ebare.

Eskelinen, Markku (2001) 'The Gaming Situation'. *Game Studies*, 1(1), www.gamestudies.org/0101/eskelinen.

Gaggi, Silvio (1997) *From Text to Hypertext*, Philadelphia, PA: University of Pennsylvania Press.

Gee, J. Paul (2003) *What Video Games Have to Teach Us About Learning and Literacy*. New York: Palgrave Macmillan.

Gunn, Joshua (1998) 'Gothic Music and the Inevitability of Genre', *Popular Music and Society*, 23(1): 31–50.

Hodkinson, Paul (2002) *Goth: Identity, Style and Subculture*, Oxford: Berg.

—— (2003) '"Net.Goth": Internet Communication and (Sub)Cultural Boundaries', in David Muggleton and Rupert Weinzierl (eds), *The Post-Subcultures Reader*, Oxford: Berg, pp. 285–98.

Hustis, Harriet (1999) '"Reading Encrypted but Persistent": The Gothic of Reading and Poe's "The Fall of the House of Usher"', *Studies in American Fiction*, 27: 3–20.

Jackson, Shelley (1995) *Patchwork Girl*, CD, Watertown, MA: Eastgate Systems Ltd.

Kushner, David (2003) *Masters of Doom: How Two Guys Created an Empire and Transformed Pop Culture*, London: Random House.

Landow, George (1997) *Hypertext 2.0: The Convergence of Contemporary Critical Theory and Technology*. 2nd edn, Baltimore, MD: Johns Hopkins University Press.

Monroe, Alexei (2005) *Interrogation Machine: Laibach and NSK*, Cambridge, MA: MIT Press.

Murray, Simone (2004) '"Celebrating the Story the Way it Is": Cultural Studies, Corporate Media and the Contested Utility of Fandom', *Continuum: Journal of Media and Cultural Studies*, 18(1): 7–25.

Ostwald, Michael J. (1997) 'Virtual Urban Futures: Identity and Community in Cyberspace', in David Holmes (ed.), *Cyberspace*, London: Sage.

Papacharissi, Zizi (2002) 'The Virtual Sphere: The Internet as Public Sphere', *New Media and Society*, 4(1): 9–27.

Rapatzikou, Tatiana G. (2004) *Gothic Motifs in the Fiction of William Gibson*, Amsterdam: Rodopi.

Rheingold, Howard (1994) *The Virtual Community*, London: Secker and Warburg.

Sardar, Ziauddin (1996) 'alt.faq.civilizations: Cyberspace as the Darker Side of the West', in Ziauddin Sardar and Jerome Ravetz, *Cyberfutures: Culture and Politics on the Information Superhighway*, New York: New York University Press.

Seidel, Erica (1996) 'Patchwork Girl: The Hypertextuality of Scars . . .', www.thecore. nus.edu.sg/cpace/ht/pg/espatch.html.

Spencer, Amy (2005) *DIY: The Rise of Lo-Fi Culture*, London: Marion Boyars.

Straw, Will (1993) 'Characterizing Rock Music Culture: The Case of Heavy Metal', in Simon During (ed.), *The Cultural Studies Reader*. London: Routledge.

Turkle, Sherry (1996) *Life on the Screen: Identity in the Age of the Internet*, London: Weidenfeld and Nicolson.

Wilbur, Shawn P. (1997) 'An Archaeology of Cyberspaces: Virtuality, Community, Identity', in D. Porter (ed.), *Internet Culture*, London: Routledge, pp. 5–22.

Wilkins, Amy (2004) '"So full of Myself as a Chick": Goth Women, Sexual Independence, and Gender Egalitarianism', *Gender and Society*, 18(3): 328–49.

Index